CONFIDENCE IN LIFE

T&T Clark Enquiries in Theological Ethics

Series editors
Brian Brock
Susan F. Parsons

CONFIDENCE IN LIFE

A Barthian Account of Procreation

Matthew Lee Anderson

LONDON • NEW YORK • OXFORD • NEW DELHI • SYDNEY

T&T CLARK
Bloomsbury Publishing Plc, 50 Bedford Square, London, WC1B 3DP, UK
Bloomsbury Publishing Inc, 1385 Broadway, New York, NY 10018, USA
Bloomsbury Publishing Ireland, 29 Earlsfort Terrace, Dublin 2, D02 AY28, Ireland

BLOOMSBURY, T&T CLARK and the T&T Clark logo are
trademarks of Bloomsbury Publishing Plc

First published in Great Britain 2024
Paperback edition published 2025

Copyright © Matthew Lee Anderson, 2024

Matthew Lee Anderson has asserted his right under the Copyright,
Designs and Patents Act, 1988, to be identified as Author of this work.

For legal purposes the Acknowledgments on pp. ix–x constitute an
extension of this copyright page.

All rights reserved. No part of this publication may be: i) reproduced or transmitted in
any form, electronic or mechanical, including photocopying, recording or by means of
any information storage or retrieval system without prior permission in writing from the
publishers; or ii) used or reproduced in any way for the training, development or operation
of artificial intelligence (AI) technologies, including generative AI technologies. The rights
holders expressly reserve this publication from the text and data mining exception as per
Article 4(3) of the Digital Single Market Directive (EU) 2019/790.

Bloomsbury Publishing Plc does not have any control over, or responsibility for,
any third-party websites referred to or in this book. All internet addresses given
in this book were correct at the time of going to press. The author and publisher
regret any inconvenience caused if addresses have changed or sites have ceased
to exist, but can accept no responsibility for any such changes.

A catalogue record for this book is available from the British Library.

A catalog record for this book is available from the Library of Congress.

Library of Congress Cataloging-in-Publication Data
Names: Anderson, Matthew Lee, author.
Title: Confidence in life : a Barthian account of procreation / Matthew Lee
Anderson, Assistant Research Professor of Theology and Ethics, Institute
for Studies of Religion, Baylor University.
Description: New York : T&T Clark, 2024. | Series: T&T Clark enquiries in
theological ethics | Includes bibliographical references and index.
Identifiers: LCCN 2023025204 (print) | LCCN 2023025205 (ebook) |
ISBN 9780567710635 (hardback) | ISBN 9780567710680 (paperback) |
ISBN 9780567710642 (pdf) | ISBN 9780567710673 (epub)
Subjects: LCSH: Human reproduction–Religious aspects–Christianity. |
Life–Religious aspects–Christianity. | Barth, Karl, 1886–1968. | Theology, Doctrinal. |
Christianity and culture.
Classification: LCC BT696 .A53 2024 (print) | LCC BT696 (ebook) |
DDC 113/.8–dc23/eng/20231030
LC record available at https://lccn.loc.gov/2023025204
LC ebook record available at https://lccn.loc.gov/2023025205

ISBN: HB: 978-0-5677-1063-5
PB: 978-0-5677-1068-0
ePDF: 978-0-5677-1064-2
eBook: 978-0-5677-1067-3

Series: T&T Clark Enquiries in Theological Ethics

Typeset by Integra Software Services Pvt. Ltd.

For product safety related questions contact productsafety@bloomsbury.com.

To find out more about our authors and books visit www.bloomsbury.com
and sign up for our newsletters.

"One does *not* have a baby to please the vicar's wife."
Overheard at a coffee shop

"Unless one is the vicar."
A wit on Twitter

CONTENTS

Acknowledgments	ix
INTRODUCTION	1
Protestant Moral Theology on Having Children	3
Procreative Fideism and the Confidence in Life	10
Chapter 1	
(PROCREATIVE) NEUTRALITY IS NOT ENOUGH	17
David Heyd and Procreative Latitude	19
David Benatar's Categorical Anti-natalism	22
Jeff McMahan on The Asymmetry	25
Procreative Neutrality or Procreative Skepticism?	29
Conclusion	32
Chapter 2	
PARENTHOOD AND PROCREATIVE BONDS	35
Relational Reasons to Procreate	36
The Dilemma of Procreative Bonds	40
Kolodny, Moschella, Velleman, and Ferracioli on Biology and Personal Identity	42
Parenthood, Procreation, and Adoption: Equality or Identity?	49
Conclusion	51
Chapter 3	
THE "GIFT OF LIFE": LUCK, THE INVOLUNTARY, AND PROCREATIVE AGENCY	53
Leon Kass on the Giftedness of Life	54
Alex Pruss and the Involuntariness of Natural Reproduction	60
Michael Sandel and Jürgen Habermas on the Value of Our Limits	65
Embryo Death and the Gift of Human Life	70
The Limits of Optimism	73
Chapter 4	
NEITHER OPTIMISM NOR PESSIMISM: KARL BARTH AMONG THE MORAL PHILOSOPHERS	77
The Trinitarian Ground of Creation	83
The Doctrine of Creation against Pessimism and Optimism	95
Barth's Doctrine of Creation among the Analytic Moral Philosophers	102

Chapter 5
BIRTH BETWEEN THE TIMES: PROCREATION IN BARTH'S DOCTRINE OF CREATION — 107
- Procreation in the Doctrine of Creation (III/1) — 108
- Procreation in Barth's Anthropology (III/2) — 116
- Procreation and Providence — 122
- The Relativization of Procreation (III/4) — 124
- Procreation in Barth (So Far): Appreciation and Critique — 132

Chapter 6
RESPECT FOR LIFE AS A REASON TO CREATE — 137
- Theological Anthropology and the Human Constitution — 138
- Human Life as Life in Time — 147
- Respect for Life as Reason to Create — 151
- The Prospects and Limits of Barth's Account of Life — 156

Chapter 7
MARY AND THE ESCHATOLOGICAL CONFIRMATION OF PROCREATIVE BONDS — 161
- The Primacy of Christology for Mariology — 163
- The Virgin Birth as a Sign — 166
- The Ecclesiastical Whence and Natural Parenthood — 173
- The Weight and Dignity of Biological Parenthood — 178
- Conclusion: First Steps toward a Protestant, Barthian Mariology — 185

Chapter 8
HONOUR, AGENCY, AND REASONS TO PROCREATE — 199
- The Honour of Human Life and Agency — 200
- The Honour of Procreative Parenthood — 217
- Mary and the Reasons to Procreate, Revisited — 223
- Conclusion — 230

CONCLUSION — 233
- Barth among the Moral Philosophers, Revisited — 238
- The Honour and Joy of Procreating — 241

Bibliography — 243
Index — 253

ACKNOWLEDGMENTS

If the "acknowledgments" to a book function as an intellectual biography of the project, then it seems fitting to begin these by expressing my gratitude to my parents for the "confidence in life" they showed in being ready to bring me into the world. Their patient support of my vocation has been instrumental to whatever success I have enjoyed. I hope my life and this work bestow honour upon them; I know it is an honour to be their son.

More immediately, I owe a considerable debt to a number of scholars for their encouragement and critiques. Professor Nigel Biggar has dispensed praise and censure as the hour demanded and has served as an exemplar of someone who models generous but critical engagement with moral philosophy (not to mention other disciplines). Professor Stanley Hauerwas' enthusiasm for this topic buoyed my confidence at a moment when it was flagging. I am especially grateful for a rollicking argument about its themes with David Albert Jones and Gerald McKenny. Though I think I left them both variously unpersuaded, I benefited immensely from their feedback. Mike Austin, Ben Rhodes, and Elizabeth Gatewood generously read portions of the manuscript and offered their counsel. I am especially in Elizabeth's debt, whose criticisms significantly improved the final version (even while they continue to haunt me for not doing enough to ameliorate them).

I have been grateful to participate in communities at both Oxford and Baylor that have managed the delicate task of balancing rigor with collegiality and warmth. I am thankful for the friendship of Joshua Hordern, John Perry, and James Orr, all of whom enlivened my time at Oxford and offered counsel and encouragement in realms well beyond ideas. I am grateful to Brian Williams, Emily Gum, Jim van Dyke, and Edward David for lively conversations about this subject and much else besides. The Institute for Studies of Religion at Baylor has been a dream job; I am especially indebted to Byron John and Sung Joon Jang for their friendship and kind support of my work. More broadly at Baylor, I am grateful to the philosophy department for allowing me to work with students on some of these questions and to my colleagues at Baylor in Washington for carrying more of my workload than they should have while I finished this project.

I am grateful to the opportunities I have been given to receive feedback on aspects of this project. The Texas Consortium of Christian Ethics heard a badly underdeveloped version of a paper on Barth's view of honour and was overly generous in their critical feedback. I am especially grateful to Sr. Elinor Gardner, Steve Long, Robin Lovin, Charles Mathews, Jonathan Tran, Paul Martens, Matthew Kaemingk, and to others there for their critical comments. I suspect the final version is no more persuasive, but at least it is more polished. I am similarly grateful to the Southwest Region of AAR for giving me an occasion to think about themes adjacent to this work and to the Brazos Fellows for their generosity in hosting me for a talk. *Christian Bioethics* and *The Journal of Medicine and Philosophy* kindly gave me permission to publish portions of work published there. I have noted those points in the manuscript as appropriate. Materially, I am grateful to Biola University's Gratitude to God project (and vicariously to the Templeton Foundation) for allowing me to expand my thinking this subject in ways I did not anticipate. I am also indebted to financial support from the University of Oxford and the Intercollegiate Studies Institute. And I am thankful to Anna Turton, the team at Bloomsbury T&T Clark, and especially Brian Brock and Susan Parsons for stewarding this project to completion.

I have been unusually lucky in having friends become interlocutors who variously challenge and reshape my thinking. While they are too many to list, I am especially grateful to Frank Beckwith, Paul Billingham, Kate Greasley, Brad East, and Tyler Wittman for helping me sort through some of the philosophical and theological issues at stake here. Natalie Bruce supplied invaluable editorial assistance, without which this book would have been much worse. My colleagues Elisabeth Kincaid and Dallas Gingles have regularly told me how wrong I am with a kindness that I just cannot quit. More broadly, I am indebted to the ongoing intellectual friendship of Jake Meador and Paul Gutacker. My siblings have to a person exemplified the honour we owe to our parents far better than I; I hope to live up to your example someday. My deepest thanks, though, belong to Tom and Katie and the whole Ward family—who have embodied the thesis of this book in ways they never expected, but in ways that have been a tremendous blessing. Tom, thanks for what feels like two lifetimes of friendship.

But no one, of all those mentioned, so deserves gratitude as my wife. In the middle of hard days, she instilled me with confidence that this effort would not be in vain. Without her steady encouragement and her glad assumption of many extra duties, I would yet be toiling away without hope of ever seeing the end. It is very good to be married to one whose joy and love abound so. There is no one to whom I would rather be in debt, nor anyone with whom I would rather face the future.

Sic transit gloria mundi. Soli Deo Gloria.

INTRODUCTION

In her vituperative essay "Why Have Children," Elizabeth Anscombe laments that the "very title tells of the times we live in."[1] What follows is more elegy than argument. The question of whether human beings should have children "simply didn't arise" in previous generations, Anscombe contends, except for those who "were wicked enough to *not* want them and think of ways of preventing them from ever being conceived, or destroying them if they were." By situating the inquiry alongside that of "why we should digest food?", Anscombe attempts to demonstrate what a "weird distorted question" it is.[2] That we can and do ask whether we should have children is simply a sign of our decadence.[3]

Uncertainty about why people should procreate has only become more pervasive since Anscombe issued her jeremiad back in 1989. Most prominently, the Duke and Duchess of Sussex announced in 2019 that they plan to have a "maximum" of two children because of the stresses contemporary population growth has put on the environment.[4] Such sentiments made their way to the periphery of America's

---

1. G. E. M. Anscombe, "Why Have Children?," *Proceedings of the American Catholic Philosophical Association* 63 (1989): 48.

2. Ibid., 52.

3. Theologians have sometimes sounded a similar note. In her unpublished dissertation, Anna Louise Poulson suggests that the question "is indicative of the fact we no longer understand having children to be constitutive of the human good." Anna Louise Poulson, *An Examination of the Ethics of Contraception with Reference to Recent Protestant and Roman Catholic Thought* (PhD diss., King's College, 2006), 196. Poulson argues the question has benefits, and develops her own answer around the 'common good' of the couple. See pages 217–45. While her positive account has merits, her description of the *good* draws most of its power from the contrast Poulson draws with a liberal individualism. In an early essay, Stanley Hauerwas suggests that in procreating we are "carried along by the sheer vitality of life in a manner that makes the question of 'why' seem almost obscene." Stanley Hauerwas, *A Community of Character* (Notre Dame: University of Notre Dame Press, 1981), 208.

4. "From the Archive: When the Duke of Sussex Interviewed the Dr. Jane Goodall about the Future of Sustainability," available online at: https://www.vogue.co.uk/article/prince-harry-jane-goodall-september-2019-issue. Accessed February 1, 2022.

political landscape when popular New York Congresswoman Alexandria Ocasio-Cortez said that young people are being confronted by the "legitimate question" about whether it is permissible to have children.[5] The discussion about procreation in popular culture is following developments in academic moral philosophy, where the question of whether to have children has become especially prominent. For instance, Sarah Conly and Travis Rieder have both argued that procreation should be limited because of climate considerations while David Benatar has notoriously revived Schopenhauer for our time by arguing that procreation is categorically wrong.[6]

While it might be tempting to reject out of hand the question of why we should have children, it is better to see how fundamental it is to our understanding of ourselves and the world. For Anscombe, the question takes philosophy to its very limits: to those who offer "hostility or mere indifference" toward the ongoing existence of the human race, Anscombe proposes that it may take "prophetical revelation or a blind belief in the care of God" to know "our dreadful race is not better all damned … or all abolished."[7] Stanley Hauerwas adopts a similar stance, regarding the question of whether we should have children as a litmus test for the viability of non-Christian outlooks. As he writes, the waning of Christianity presents a "greater challenge for people who think themselves as secular" than it does for Christians. Such individuals must simultaneously disavow any cultural reliance upon Christianity while telling us why "it would make sense to make promises that last a lifetime or to bring children into a world that you think is without purpose."[8] Though his rhetorical register differs from Anscombe's, his point is the same: articulating why we have children raises fundamental questions that may not be answerable outside of revelation.

There is no escaping the question of whether we should have children: the only way forward is by considering seriously, perhaps for the first time in history, the reasons humanity has to perpetuate itself. Though humanity will likely carry on

---

5. Umair Irfan, "We Need to Talk about the Ethics of Having Children in a Warming World," *Vox*, available online at: https://www.vox.com/2019/3/11/18256166/climate-change-having-kids. Accessed February 1, 2022.

6. Travis N. Rieder, *Toward a Small Family Ethic: How Overpopulation and Climate Change Are Affecting the Morality of Procreation*, 1st edn. 2016, SpringerBriefs in Public Health Ethics (Cham: Springer International Publishing; Imprint: Springer, 2016). Sarah Conly, *One Child: Do We Have a Right to More?* (New York: Oxford University Press, 2016). While climate change has put practical shape to the question, it is important to note that the field of population ethics has expanded over the past decades, largely because of Derek Parfit's considerable influence. David Benatar, *Better Never to Have Been: The Harm of Coming into Existence* (Oxford: Oxford University Press, 2009). Benatar does not have many philosophical disciples, but has been profiled by the *New Yorker*. See "The Case for Not Being Born," *New Yorker*, November 27, 2017, available online at: https://www.newyorker.com/culture/persons-of-interest/the-case-for-not-being-born. Accessed February 1, 2022.

7. Anscombe, "Why," 50.

8. Stanley Hauerwas, *The Work of Theology* (Grand Rapids: Eerdmans, 2015), 5.

regardless of what theologians have to say about the matter, widespread skepticism about procreation's value will have moral and political significance and contribute to stigmas on large families.[9] Whether there is a right to procreate, and how stable that right is, might very well depend on what sort of interest in procreating we have. Moreover, any plausible answer to the question of "why procreate" entangles us in judgments about related practices like artificial reproductive technologies or adoption. Understanding why human beings generate new life through an act of sexual intercourse requires a description about what they are doing and how they are doing it. We have known for a long time that it is possible to form families through non-procreative means. Whether we should procreate when those other means are available brings ethics in close contact with the significance of our corporeal origins for our self-understanding. Finally, how the church theorizes infertility and childlessness, and what resources she provides to those couples who face them, are directly correlated with her account of the value of procreation.

Still, important questions remain about the type of therapeutic we need to articulate a compelling, positive answer to the procreative pessimism that increasingly pervades the developed, English-speaking world. In recent years, Protestant moral theologians have rarely addressed the question directly—and when they have, their remedies have either been aimed at different problems or failed to satisfy. Anscombe might be right that "blind belief in God" is necessary to justify carrying on the species. But the task of specifying how such a belief underwrites procreation is more difficult than she assumes.

Protestant Moral Theology on Having Children

Much of Protestant moral theology's writing on procreation has been animated by its opposition to the various pathologies in the culture of reproduction and to analytic moral philosophy's efforts to articulate appropriate norms of reproduction. For instance, Michael Banner's recent *Ethics of Everyday Life* argues that moral theology's captivity to "hard cases" has left it with "very little to say" about kinship, a deficit that can be remedied through closer interaction with social anthropology.[10] Two interrelated themes about infertility emerge from that discipline: the "desperation of childlessness" and the interest in a "child of one's own." For Banner, moral theology should utter an unequivocal "no" to both. Moral theology will "deny the existence of (and repudiate the desire) for

---

9. Though the political questions of procreation are outside the remit of this work, I have addressed the question of 'modest' one-child policies and social stigmas on multiple children elsewhere. See Matthew Lee Anderson, "What the State Owes 'Bastards': A Modest Critique of Modest One-Child Policies," *Journal of Applied Philosophy* 37, no. 3 (July 2020): 393–407.

10. Michael Banner, *The Ethics of Everyday Life* (Oxford: Oxford University Press, 2014), 9, 37.

the child of one's own of supposed contemporary longing, but will also deny the tragedy of childlessness which that child is intended to relieve."[11] Christianity "preferred kinship that is made over kinship that is given."[12] Though they come to opposite practical conclusions about artificial reproductive technologies (ARTs), the Vatican's *Donum Vitae* is in the same moral register as the UK's *Warnock Report*: both presume procreative kinship is the only legitimate form.[13] *Donum Vitae* places couples in a "double bind": they are denied the use of ARTs, and their desire for children is "left solemnly in place on its contemporary pedestal."[14] Against this, Banner is unsparing in his contention that natural kinship has no theological significance. The Church is a "community in which there are no biological ties."[15] While this unqualified rejection of the salience of biological parenthood might entail rejecting procreation, Banner resists such an extension. While Christianity is incompatible with "certain 'pronatalisms ...,'" he writes, "it doesn't follow that it will fall into step with antinatalism."[16] Children "belong to the happiness of paradise and are a blessing even outside of its boundaries." Banner revisits the ritual of the "churching of women," which he thinks incorporates procreation into the church without reducing it to an interest in a "child of one's own." In addition to its denials, then, Christianity asks us "to imagine and to enact ... a kinship beyond biology, in which the child is received as gift."[17]

While Banner's final assertion is attractive, it is also discordant with his unqualified repudiation of the tragedy of childlessness. If a child is a gift, why must the childless couple renounce their desire for one by denying any sense of loss? There is no sense in Banner's work that the Gospel might reframe and reinterpret the tragedy of childlessness by giving childless couples appropriate language to articulate their laments. The absence, I suspect, stems from Banner's decision to let social anthropology frame the experience of infertility, rather than a theological source like the Old Testament. Having discovered people can have idolatrous interests in biological children, he proposes there is no such interest at all. If procreated children are a "gift" as he asserts, though, why are Christians not free to desire them? Banner describes his approach as "radically, therapeutically, and evangelically" responding to social norms. It is radical, to be sure, but hardly therapeutic or evangelical.[18] Banner's "treatment" for the idolatry of the blood tie is to cut it off altogether. And he prefers a broadsword for the work to a scalpel.

The antithesis Banner draws between contemporary attitudes and the notion that children are a gift pervades much of Protestant moral theology. Both Gilbert

11. Ibid.
12. Ibid., 38.
13. Ibid., 57.
14. Ibid.
15. Ibid., 33.
16. Ibid., 61.
17. Ibid., 81.
18. Ibid., 37.

Meilaender and Brent Waters, for instance, have sought to mystify the act of generation.[19] Meilaender's early work responds to John Robertson's philosophical doctrine of "procreative liberty," which presents reproduction as an individual interest that treats persons as "largely isolated wills."[20] Against this, Meilaender proposes an account of bodiliness in which the child becomes the "natural fruition of [the couple's] shared love, not a chosen project." The child on this view is always a "gift," and even "a mystery."[21] Beneath this view lies a reconfiguration of the agency at work in procreation, and of the relationship of the person to their bodies. Our humanity is expressed not only in what we *accomplish*, but what we *do*. The body is the "locus of personal presence," which enables us to "discern the equal worth of the child who springs from the embrace of our bodies."[22] The bond that emerges through such an act is significant precisely because parents did *not* choose it: its involuntary dimension "mirrors a still greater mystery: that anything should exist at all." Procreation is not reproduction, because as an "act of love [it] is not governed simply by the rational will, but a passion that comes over us."[23] Lose this dimension, as John Robertson does, and the child "begins to resemble a product of our wills rather than the offspring of our passion."[24]

This emphasis on the passionate basis of procreation transposes the question of having children beyond one of reasons into the realm of significance and meaning. In an exploration of how fertility interrelates with transience, Meilaender directly addresses why we have children. Rather than follow Plato's solution of immortality, he prefers Aristotle, whose answer "focuses on the imperatives of our animal nature" and may even be a philosophical apprehension of the "divine blessing enunciated in Genesis 1." Yet the spontaneous overflow of animal impulses is not the only plane on which Meilaender thinks procreation operates. Acknowledging that Genesis 1 is a command as well as blessing, he suggests that there is a "meaning and significance" in the sequence of generations, which means we can "set aside a search for what motivates human beings to reproduce themselves" to ask instead what "deeper purposes in human life" procreating serves.[25] The question of why we procreate is unnecessary (or unintelligible) from the standpoint of the couple: they procreate out of their animal impulses. But from a third-person perspective, their generative act serves their character: the "generative life, the relation between the generations, is a school of virtue in which we learn grateful faithfulness to the

---

19. Behind them stand two Protestant moral theologians whose views they variously adopt and adapt, namely Oliver O'Donovan and Paul Ramsey. I leave them aside for space considerations.

20. Gilbert Meilaender, *Body, Soul and Bioethics* (Notre Dame: Notre Dame University Press, 1995), 76.

21. Ibid., 80.

22. Ibid., 84.

23. Gilbert Meilaender, *Bioethics* (Grand Rapids: Eerdmans, 1996), 13.

24. Ibid., 15.

25. Gilbert Meilaender, *Should We Live Forever?* (Grand Rapids: Eerdmans, 2013), 69.

gift of life we have received, generous hopefulness for those to whom we hand on the gift, and the love that freely gives what it has freely received."[26]

Meilaender's theological mystification of procreation is shared by Brent Waters. As Waters puts it, the advent of ARTs means "reproductive mystery is giving way to … reproductive management," in which procreation becomes a "series of discrete tasks."[27] Against this reductionism, Waters advances a "larger moral vision."[28] Waters also regards Robertson's procreative liberty as the "manifesto of [the] emerging pattern of procreation and child-rearing."[29] Such a liberal approach to procreative questions treats gametes and embryos as raw materials, while reducing parenthood to an "assertion of the will."[30] Much of Waters' focus, then, is on articulating and defending a normative framework of marital and family relationships that is distinct from the liberal framework of "individual interests and rights."[31]

As with Meilaender, the framework Waters develops offers an alternative account of the nature of bodily life. Following Oliver O'Donovan, Waters affirms a Christologically ordered natural ethic, in which the cooperative powers of male and female are directed in conformity to God's commands and intentions.[32] He contends that the "orderly transmission of life requires procreative stewardship," but discriminates between pro-*natalist* and pro-*creative* attitudes.[33] The latter approach seeks to procreate on God's behalf: "If humans come to prefer sterility over fertility, they are no longer discharging the duties entrusted to them by God, because they will have rejected the life-giving end for which creation was called into being."[34] Procreation is to be firmly embedded in the family, a "place of mutual and timely belonging," a sphere of "expanding, unfolding and enfolding love."[35] Its operative category is the covenant, which binds parents and children together in a way that "transcends natural instinct" and avoids reducing children to "satisfactory outcomes of parental will, thereby negating any inherent bond between parents and offspring."[36] The family is the whole greater than the sum of all of its parts, and decisions to enter parenthood (or not) are only intelligible through grasping its teleological, providential, and eschatological ordering. Procreation is thus a

---

26. Ibid., 73.
27. Brent Waters, *Reproductive Technology* (Cleveland: Pilgrim Press, 2001), 15.
28. Ibid., 18.
29. Ibid., 19.
30. Ibid., 27.
31. Ibid., 19.
32. Ibid., 34.
33. Ibid., 36.
34. Brent Waters, *The Family in Christian Social and Political Thought* (Oxford: Oxford University Press, 2007), 173.
35. Waters, *Reproductive Technology*, 47.
36. Waters, *Family*, 176.

subordinate category, the (moral) nature of which is only discernible on those terms: "A birth does not in itself connote any providential significance, for a birth does not automatically establish a place of mutual and timely belonging for the one born."[37] Every family presupposes a birth, and biology remains the "substructure" for which moral theology must account.[38] But children are procreated through the "fully shared being of their parents," rather than their wills *per se*.[39]

Waters' expansive alternative to liberal individualism has much to commend it. Yet his account of why we procreate is wanting. Despite explicitly turning toward the question, he instead emphasizes procreation's relativization by Christ, rather than its establishment. The birth of Christ means that the purpose of preparing for "the time when the Word would be made flesh" has been "eliminated."[40] Unlike Meilaender, Waters affirms *in vitro fertilization* on the grounds that it does not diminish the bodily character of procreation. Yet despite acknowledging there is a question about why we have children, he says nothing positive in response.

The problem stems, I suspect, from the dichotomy between *being* and *will* that underlies Meilaender and Waters' approaches, which is animated by their antithesis between Christian accounts of the family and the "procreative liberty" that Waters argues introduces a "fundamental alienation and unfamiliarity" into the parent–child relationship by founding it on choice.[41] Their therapeutic expunging of deracinated accounts of procreation is valuable. Yet as couples can choose between procreating and adopting, they need reasons to procreate. The elusiveness of Meilaender and Waters' account of the value of procreating is both their strength and weakness. The bifurcation between being and will, and between choice and gift, underscores analytic philosophy's voluntaristic character. Yet it also untethers procreation from the reasons agents might have to prefer it when other forms of parenthood are possible. In that way, mystification efforts exacerbate the very bifurcation in agency they are resisting. The mysticism of covenantal, bodily life cannot overcome the voluntarism of liberal, analytic philosophy: it can only contradict it.

The acute difficulty of articulating a positive reason for procreating without reifying procreative bonds is perhaps no more clear than in the work of Stanley Hauerwas, who has addressed the question of why we procreate more consistently than any other contemporary moral theologian. The question appears in essays on disability, on the family, on abortion, on *in vitro fertilization*, and on marriage and singleness. Many of the themes Hauerwas raises in response comport with the accounts offered above. As noted, Hauerwas does not rule out in principle the possibility of secular answers to the question, but highlights the fact that

---

37. Waters, *Reproductive Technology*, 25.
38. Waters, *Family*, 194.
39. Ibid., 183.
40. Waters, *Reproductive Technology*, 57.
41. Waters, *Family*, 184.

it is a puzzle for non-theological views. In a lament about moral philosophy's adherence to rights, he suggests that we "lack a moral account of why we commit ourselves to having children."[42] The problem is endemic to liberal individualism, which reduces parents and children to "friendly strangers." The notion of autonomy that accompanies such a view renders the special relations of involuntary family bonds "ethically anomalous" and makes the family itself "morally irrational."[43] The reasons to have a child are thus either immoral or unintelligible; they either instrumentalize a child for the parents' self-satisfaction or treat the child as a "threat to my autonomy."[44] But Hauerwas is equally clear that the romanticized idealization of the family is equally unable to sustain the reasons to procreate: "familial kinship," he argues, cannot be "sustained on solely interpersonal and psychological grounds." There must instead be a set of "traditions and practices" that are passed on.[45] The "need for future generations" is too important to rest "on anything as fragile as the emotion of love."[46]

Positively, Hauerwas suggests that the question must be "placed in the context of some very substantive claims about the nature of the world and God's relation to it."[47] Hauerwas (unsurprisingly) locates the affirmative stance toward children primarily within the church. A "community's willingness to encourage children is a sign of its confidence in itself and its people."[48] Children are "symbols of our hope"—but *not* the object of hope, which would be "blasphemy."[49] On this basis, Hauerwas speaks of having children in terms of obligations and duties. The early Christians "were called to marriage and to having children as their obligation," as children were "their pledge to be a community formed by the conviction that … God rules this world."[50] Such an obligation binds the Church to time: our "commitment, indeed obligation, to have children is our pledge that our salvation is not ahistorical but takes place through the contingencies of history."[51]

While the church is our primary community in Hauerwas' thought, the family is a historical institution that mediates traditions, rather than a biologically grounded institution. Some thirty years before Banner, Hauerwas objected to IVF's presumption that "biology has some extremely important role to

---

42. Hauerwas, *Community*, 157.

43. Ibid., 165, 172.

44. Ibid., 172.

45. Stanley Hauerwas, *The Hauerwas Reader*, ed. John Berkman and Michael Cartwright (Durham: Duke University Press, 2001), 510.

46. Hauerwas, *Community*, 164.

47. Stanley Hauerwas, *Suffering Presence* (Notre Dame: University of Notre Dame Press, 1986), 147.

48. Hauerwas, *Community*, 209.

49. Hauerwas, *Suffering Presence*, 147.

50. Hauerwas, *Community*, 210.

51. Hauerwas, *Suffering Presence*, 148.

play in parenting."⁵² The claim that biology "makes children 'ours'" is a "pagan assumption."⁵³ While biology might "help us learn to be parents," we must also "be guided by a moral portrayal of parenting that cannot be biologically derived."⁵⁴ God has "not willed the church to be reproduced through biology but through witness and conversion."⁵⁵ Parenting itself is an "office of a community, rather than a description of a biological process."⁵⁶ While intimacy and care are important, "equally important is the initiation of children into moral beliefs and institutions we value."⁵⁷ Against liberal individualism, the language of choice for children should be "qualified and controlled by the more fundamental metaphor of gift."⁵⁸

Hauerwas has answered why Christians should have children, in his own way. As with the interlocutors above, there is something worthwhile about his deconstructive critique of liberalism and corresponding inflation of the Christian alternative. His dichotomy offers a helpful purgative, which clarifies certain elements of the Christian family and provides an intelligibility to certain practices. But by rendering parenthood as an office of the church and undertaking

---

52. Ibid., 145.
53. Hauerwas, *Reader*, 515.
54. Hauerwas, *Suffering Presence*, 152.
55. Hauerwas, *Reader*, 512.
56. Hauerwas, *Suffering Presence*, 149.
57. Hauerwas, *Community*, 173.
58. Stanley Hauerwas, Richard Bondi, and David B. Burrell, *Truthfulness and Tragedy* (Notre Dame: University of Notre Dame Press, 1977), 150. Meilaender has argued that Hauerwas' view of marriage and children represents a "de-mystification" of the bond, which cuts him off from the language of human love to explain God's love. Hauerwas "seldom emphasizes the natural affinities in which the bond of parents and children is grounded." He has "thinned out" the meaning of the unitive good of marriage. Such an approach ostensibly demonstrates the marks of Hauerwas' (infamous) ecclesiastically centered, over-realized eschatology, which does not do justice to creation. In a remark that illuminates his approach as much as Hauerwas', Meilaender objects that Hauerwas does not "bring a sacramental imagination into thinking about the sexual relationship." While it is true Christians "understand the presence of the child as God's gift," this does "not mean that mother and father receive that child as they would a stranger." See Gilbert Meilaender, "Time for Love: The Place of Marriage and Children in the Thought of Stanley Hauerwas," *Journal of Religious Ethics* 40, no. 2 (2012): 255, 259. Whether Hauerwas is inattentive to natural affinities or not, I suspect the Hauerwasian rejoinder would be something like: what "nature," and which "grounds" for parenthood? Meilaender's reading seems like a misreading. If Hauerwas downplays the interrelation of the unitive and procreative dimensions of the sexual act, he nowhere reduces the 'gifted' quality of the child to a relationship of strangers. It is just such an effect from liberal individualism that Hauerwas' account of the family everywhere rejects. That parenthood can be fulfilled by anyone in the church does not reduce its content or quality to the Christian's relationship to strangers, so much as provide the grounds for the Christian community to treat that established relation as parental.

a forceful polemic against biology, he undermines the force of his own argument for why Christians should procreate. The combination of those two competing movements seems to make it *harder* for Christians to justify having children, rather than obligating them to do so. This is especially the case if parenthood can be entered into through adoption, and the church holds forth such an option (as it should) in forming Christians' understanding of the office of parenthood. Moreover, Hauerwas' ecclesiastically centered understanding of the family risks leaving prospective parents without reasons to procreate that are tethered to their well-being. While children might be symbols of hope, such a description seems detached from the types of reasons Christians have for seeking to expand their family through procreating. Hauerwas' approach contains a whiff of procreating for the sake of the kingdom of God, leaving underdeveloped what distinct or unique goods procreative parenthood might supply for the parents.[59] Hauerwas' failure to integrate procreation into the office of parenthood paradoxically untethers children from the rational agency of the parents, reducing the gift of life to a mysterious irruption—a sign of hope that makes the parents glad, to be sure, but which leaves the reasons to procreate indeterminate.

Procreative Fideism and the Confidence in Life

Karl Barth is not an ordinary pro-natalist. Indeed, his contention that the obligation to procreate has been dissolved by the birth of Christ lies at the source of many Protestant efforts to trouble procreative ties, rather than defend them. As he wrote, *post Christum natum* "the propagation of the race ('Be fruitful, and multiply,' Gen. 1:28) has ceased to be an unconditional command."[60] Such a deflationary stance toward procreation is an eminently reasonable position to take for someone writing in the shadow of the Nazis' racialized nationalism and its strident pro-natalism.[61]

Yet Barth was aware of other forces emerging in Europe in the shadow of the Second World War—forces that made him alive to the potential need for something like a Christian pro-natalism. In *Church Dogmatics* III/2, Barth observes that the "signature of modern man" is neither peace nor rebellion, but rather "utter weariness and boredom." The "last and fateful question for Europe is whether it will succeed in shaking off this lethargy."[62] Two volumes in the *Dogmatics* later, Barth writes that there "may even be times in which it will be the duty of the

---

59. The worry is close to, but distinct from Meilaender's above. See n.58.
60. Karl Barth, *Church Dogmatics*, vol. III/4, ed. Geoffrey W. Bromiley and Thomas F. Torrance, trans. Geoffrey W. Bromiley (Peabody, MA: Hendrickson Publishers, 2010), 268.
61. See Maria Sophia Quine, *Population Politics in Twentieth-Century Europe* (London: Routledge, 1996); and Richard Togman, *Nationalizing Sex: Fertility, Fear, and Power* (Oxford: Oxford University Press, 2019).
62. Barth, *CD* III/2, 117.

Christian community to awaken either a people or section of a people which has grown tired of life and despairs of the future, to the conscientious realisation that to avoid arbitrary decay they should make use of this merciful divine permission and seriously try to maintain the race"—an admission that comes only a few sentences after Barth underscores the dissolution of any obligation to procreate.[63] Against such exhaustion and weariness, Barth proposes that those who decide to procreate should do so out of a "homely and courageous confidence in life."[64]

This "confidence in life" is not grounds for reifying an absolute obligation to procreate. Yet it opens up the possibility of a theologically animated therapeutic to the waning interest in procreation that currently besets the developed, English-speaking world. While Anscombe proposed that "blind belief in God" might be necessary for an answer as to why humans should keep the species going, in what follows I attempt instead to develop the theological and anthropological background for this confidence. "Procreative fideism," as I dub the position, is not immune from the need for discursive elaboration and defense. Still, the range of considerations that are necessary to articulate the theological backdrop to our confidence in life is indicative of how pervasive and central procreation's importance is to any account of the world. What follows shall at various points touch on the doctrine of creation, the value of organic human life, the meaning of life's limits, the relationship between grace and nature, ecclesiology, the presuppositions of Christ's birth, and so on. Such considerations weave together to explain both the theological significance of procreation and provide reasons why giving birth is a form of God's blessing that married Christians may—and perhaps should—desire.

Developing this account through close dialogue with Karl Barth's theology is, admittedly, an odd choice given his emphasis on the dissolution of the obligation to procreate after the birth of Christ. It is probably too Pickwickian to simply invert the terms and propose that what appears as vice for my project is actually a virtue. But that is my path. Barth's work is valuable precisely *because* the grain of his thought runs against the obligation to have children. Whereas other theological approaches might take an affirmative stance toward procreating for granted, Barth's broader theological commitments mean it can be a *question*. At the same time, those currents entail that any account of procreative fideism might have to leave behind Barth's thought and become only—though perhaps not *merely*—Barthian.

---

63. Barth, *CD* III/4, 268–9.
64. Ibid., 272. In his 1946 essay "The Christian Message in Europe Today," Barth reiterated the importance of this confidence in the face of the European malaise: "Shall we be able, while always looking to Jesus Christ … to live in spite of everything somewhat more positively than negatively, somewhat more joyfully than sadly, patiently than impatiently, and, in spite of all the decline in Europe, to live with thankful rather than sorrowful hearts, and in confidence rather than in despair?" See Karl Barth, "The Christian Message in Europe Today," in *Against the Stream: Shorter Post-War Writings 1946–52*, ed. Ronald Smith (London: SCM Press, 1952), 179.

For that reason, the argument of this book mines Barth's thought even while finally reading him against himself. Such an approach is perhaps especially important on matters pertaining to sex and the household, given Barth's notorious malfeasance in those arenas. As is well-known, Barth's theological work was deeply dependent upon Charlotte von Kirschbaum's labor.[65] While Christiane Tietz has argued that Barth did not attempt to justify his irregular relationship to von Kirschbaum theologically, Barth acknowledges that the relationship affected his moral theology: "In a very concrete manner," he writes, "I have been forbidden from becoming the legalist that under other circumstances I could have become."[66] Whether Barth sought to theologically justify his conduct or not, his theology in this arena cannot be quarantined from the relational context that enabled him to write it. What should we make of Barth's contention that, even if a couple vows fidelity to each other before God in a church, it might "be that [God] has not called a specific couple to marriage, that the divine basis and constitution are lacking from the very outset, that in the judgment of God and according to His will and command, it has never become a married couple and lived as such"? Is it too "moralistic" to wonder whether this account of marriage, which seems to divide the form of God's action from its substance, might have been self-serving? Barth goes on to suggest that no one can know whether God has really joined them, but that it can "only be suspected, discovered and accepted on the ground of certain terrible indications." He recognizes that such indications might be fallacious and might conceal the fact that God really did join a couple together.[67] So there is no easy escape from an ecclesiastically mediated marriage on his view. Yet it is easy to see how the gap between such performances and divine action Barth introduces might license attitudes and actions that would erode a marriage from within. If we can read Barth on sex and procreation at all, we can only read him critically.[68]

---

65. While there is no doubt that von Kirschbaum supplied much of the research and notes for Barth's work, Christiane Tietz points out that the handwritten excurses available in his archives are in Barth's pen. See Christiane Tietz, *Karl Barth: A Life in Conflict* (New York: Oxford University Press, 2021), 221.

66. Ibid., 409; Barth is quoted on 223.

67. Barth, *CD* III/4, 209.

68. Tietz has cautioned against both moralism and voyeurism in interpreting Barth's relationship. While I concur with the unseemliness of voyeurism, I wonder: is moralism in such matters so bad? See Christianne Tietz, "Karl Barth and Charlotte von Kirschbaum," *Theology Today* 74, no. 2 (2017): 86–111. Rachel Muers' critical analysis of how the Barth–von Kirschbaum relationship has been (mis)construed is challenging. As she observes, eclipsing the political context in which Barth develops his theology leads to questions about moralism and uncritically reproduces a split between public and private. As she notes, "If we ignore the societal, political and economic context that framed the relationships, all we have to talk about is what went on in the bedroom" (200). I am willing to embrace the "moralistic" horn of the dilemma Muers lays down, while acknowledging that this work pays

Yet my hope is that such a posture serves the aim of constructively developing theological resources to undergird the "confidence in life" that Barth astutely named as the source of humanity's willingness to procreate.

As my primary interest is the normative philosophical and doctrinal landscape in which an affirmative decision to procreate can be made, rather than Barth's ethics *per se*, I have not taken up genealogical or other considerations except where they seem determinative for a reading of Barth. Most notably, this means von Kirschbaum's own work on the subject makes only a minimal appearance, as it offers a similar account of procreation *per se*.[69] Similarly, I have not sought to be comprehensive in interacting with Barth himself or with the voluminous secondary literature on his theology and ethics. My effort to elucidate his views is primarily focused on the *Church Dogmatics*, and especially his doctrine of creation in Volume III. I also primarily engage critically or constructively with (English-speaking) secondary literature and have reserved such readings to the footnotes for those who are interested. Readers should bear these limitations in mind. While I have sought to accurately expound Barth's theological commitments, I concur with the Barthian principle that what comes first in presentation is second in priority: my fundamental interest is not Barth's theology and ethics *per se*, but the normative presuppositions that must be in place in order to articulate why the church might occasionally exhort people to have children.

Even so, this procreative fideism is "Barthian" to the extent that I reconstruct his account of procreation using ancillary resources from his thought. Specifically, an account of procreation that takes the primacy of Jesus Christ seriously must tell a story about Christ's birth and therefore about the place of the Virgin Mary in theological anthropology. It is indeed striking how little Protestant moral theologians have had to say about Mary and Joseph in the context of procreative ethics, given their widespread resolution to be forthrightly theological (and Christological) in addressing such questions. Oliver O'Donovan once deployed the Christological formula "begotten, not made" in response to the emerging reproductive technologies.[70] Such a description brought contemporary moral debates into close contact with Christology. Yet the One who was begotten from His Father before all worlds was also born in time from the Virgin Mary. Christ's birth is inextricably linked to His resurrection: if He sets the paradigm in which

---

insufficient attention to the political conditions both inside and outside Barth's household. See Rachel Muers, "The Personal Is the (Academic) Political: Why Care about the Love Lives of Theologians?," *Scottish Journal of Theology* 73, no. 3 (August 2020): 191–202.

69. See Charlotte von Kirschbaum, *The Question of Woman: The Collected Writings of Charlotte von Kirschbaum* (Grand Rapids: W.B. Eerdmans Pub. Co, 1996). Suzanne Selinger's careful examination of where and how von Kirschbaum and Barth's respective theologies come together and apart is still the definitive treatment of the matter. Suzanne Selinger, *Charlotte von Kirschbaum and Karl Barth: A Study in Biography and the History of Theology* (University Park: Pennsylvania State University Press, 1998).

70. Oliver O'Donovan, *Begotten or Made?* (Oxford: Oxford University Press, 1984).

Christians have children, then it seems His being born has something to do with our giving birth. Protestant aversion to considering the Holy Family in such a context is understandable, as it seems like using the obscure and miraculous in order to explain the ordinary and natural. Yet is there a better model to help Protestant theologians attain their aim of destabilizing biological bonds without undermining the value of procreation? Jesus is simultaneously adopted and born, and His parents are a progenitor and steward. If the above theologians are right that the value of procreation is discernible only in the prior context of the family or parenthood as an office of the church, then assessing the significance of Christ's life for ethics requires locating it within the familial and ecclesiastical conditions that stand before and beneath it. Both of those meet in Mary. As such, the final chapters of this work attempt to reconfigure Barth's Mariology in ways that would lend additional theological support to an affirmation of procreation's value. They do so by backfilling Barth's account of procreation with his treatment of honour, which Barth invokes at the conclusion of his doctrine of creation. Despite the theme's centrality to the whole of Barth's ethics, few English-speaking commenters have given it its due. It is possible this reconstruction bends Barth's theology beyond its breaking point. I leave the question to better students of his thought.

However, prior to developing Barth's account I evaluate the philosophical literature surrounding the ethics of procreation. My aim in attending to philosophy is not to expose the discipline (again!) for its insufficient starting points. Critiques of analytic philosophy's de-narrativized method and pervasive individualism have long carried the day in moral theology. Despite Banner's polemic against reducing theology to "hard cases," Protestant moral theology's captivity to analytic philosophy ended with Hauerwas' critiques of its reductionism. The divorce has not necessarily been a happy one, as moral theologians have sometimes been left bereft of the analytic skills that casuistry depends upon. Other forms of moral philosophy might be more amenable to theological concerns than that which dominates Anglo-American philosophical circles. But the literature on procreation in analytic moral philosophy captures and clarifies intuitions that are increasingly shared by a wide range of people and poses serious challenges to those who would attempt to offer an unreflective assertion of procreation's value to the world. The questions analytic philosophy has wrestled with for the past thirty years are formidable: anti-natalist concerns evoke the specter of theodicy problems; the non-existence of the next generation demands an account of why we should generate new sources of obligation when we have existing ones; the reality of adoption challenges whether procreative parenthood has legitimate value; and so on. If moral theology is to offer an account of "confidence in life" stable and forceful enough to offer a meaningful therapeutic to our time, such questions must be accounted for.

Though Barth's (in)famous aversion to natural theology has sometimes been conflated with a hostility to philosophy, this is a mistake. As Gerald McKenny has recently argued, Barth insists that theological ethics articulates "the norm to which both it and moral philosophy are accountable." Yet as philosophical ethics is implicitly oriented toward the same norm, "theological ethics is permitted and indeed obligated to avail itself of the assistance moral philosophy offers it in its explicit articulation of the norm."[71] Such an obligation is especially acute, it seems, in developing an ethics that is formed by the doctrine of creation: Barth frequently engages in close, immanent readings of philosophical interlocutors throughout volume III of the *Dogmatics*, which further his own constructive work and make clear to philosophy the standard to which it must rise in order to be fully persuasive. (There is further discussion of this point in Chapter 4 of this book.) The witness of Christianity need not justify itself at the bar of philosophy. Yet as the revelation of Christ puts to an end any anxiety about Christianity's truth claims, theology is also freed for dialogue with other disciplines.

I suspect this approach will leave no one satisfied: moral theologians may wonder why I bothered with moral philosophy at all, while moral philosophers will blanch at entering the radically different moral universe Karl Barth represents. My aim is not necessarily to persuade moral philosophers to leave their discipline behind and affirm the value of revelation in order to save their intuitions, or their souls—though were that to happen I would certainly not object. But the argument is not an apologetic in that sense. It is in the first place an inquiry, an investigation into the conditions and presuppositions—theological or otherwise—that must be in place to make sense of a practice as basic and fundamental to the human species as procreating.

The church's awakening of a people who are tired of life to its value demands listening attentively to the sources of exhaustion. Once the question of whether we should have children has been asked, it cannot be unasked: once the possibility that the species could come to an end is raised, it can only be reasoned about. Theology has its own questions, its own starting points. But Karl Barth's theological framework converges with analytic moral philosophy at this precise juncture, namely, in feeling the force of whether Christians or anyone else should create new human life in this world. The only real path Christian moral theology can take lies through this question into its own inner logic in order to understand why God cares about procreating in the first place. In following that path, the church can understand why procreating has unique theological significance and reasons and give an account to the world for her glad confidence in welcoming new individuals through childbirth into God's good and fallen world.

---

71. Gerald McKenny, *Karl Barth's Moral Thought*, 1st ed. Oxford Studies in Theological Ethics (Oxford: Oxford University Press, 2021).

Chapter 1

(PROCREATIVE) NEUTRALITY IS NOT ENOUGH

Procreation raises peculiar moral questions, as the person created by the parents' decision does not exist, yet their parents' choice will be among the most consequential of their lives. Every child at the dinner table has at some point marveled at what might have happened had their parents' chosen otherwise. Most moral decisions are about how to treat existing people. But if nobody is born, nobody is harmed or benefited—unless, that is, we conclude that parents can be harmed or benefited by not procreating.[1] Still, it is common to think that the child's prospects in life should have *some* role in parents' deliberations about whether to create. If we expect the child's life to go badly, then we think there is a reason to not create them. If the child's life is likely to go well, then we *at least* think there is no objection to creating them. Yet it is hard to think we have a moral reason to create them, much less an obligation. These intuitions have been codified by philosophers into an asymmetry—The Asymmetry—which distills the basic weirdness about deciding whether to procreate. On the one side of The Asymmetry, we have a moral reason *to not* create a child that we reasonably expect to have a miserable life.[2] On the other side, the reasonable expectation that the child would lead a very happy life gives us *no* moral reason to create.[3]

The Asymmetry effectively localizes theodicy problems into the realm of procreative decision-making: however forceful objections to God's goodness on the basis of suffering might be, they are analogous to questions about whether we should procreate in the face of knowing (or reasonably expecting) that our child will have a life full of pain. Yet these worries about the value of procreating run up against humanity's ongoing practical commitment to peopling the world. As Jason Marsh observes, we are "notably more pessimistic about the basic goodness of

---

1. David Benatar and David Wasserman, *Debating Procreation* (Oxford: Oxford University Press, 2015), 135.

2. Discussions in moral philosophy about The Asymmetry and about generating human life more broadly rarely specify the nature of the agency involved in bringing human beings into the world. As such, I here adopt their custom of using "create," deferring questions about the nature of procreative agency until later in this work.

3. I regard the category of "miserable lives" as controversial.

the world when reasoning about the problem of evil than we are when reasoning about human procreation."[4]

If we take The Asymmetry at face value, it seems plausible to conclude that there is a default or presumptive skepticism toward procreating. The first half of The Asymmetry indicates that the expected harms in a life give prospective parents moral reasons to not create. The second half of the asymmetry enjoins neutrality toward the expected benefits in that life. As every person will experience at least some suffering, it seems that The Asymmetry gives us a presumptive moral reason to not create anyone. The procreative neutrality embedded in the second half is not enough to offset the procreative skepticism enjoined by the first.

In this chapter, I want to argue that defending the presumptive permissibility of procreating means giving up the procreative neutrality expressed by the second half of The Asymmetry. I do so by evaluating responses to The Asymmetry from Anglophone moral philosophy. Sorting out the puzzles surrounding The Asymmetry involves carefully attending to the nature of procreative reasons, which turns on a number of axes. For one, procreative reasons clearly entangle us in complicated judgments about the nature of harms and benefits and whether those categories even apply in procreative decisions. They also raise questions about whether reasons are person-affecting or impersonal: do moral reasons only arise in response to the interests of a particular individual, or does the individual affected supply no part of the act's explanation?[5] And if procreative reasons are person-affecting, whose interests count—the parents, the child, possible people, or all of the above?[6]

In proceeding, I carve a path through the extremely tangled thicket of the philosophical literature by considering views at the extreme edges of procreative permissibility before turning to views that are more modest in their approaches. On the one side, I take up David Heyd's person-affecting *symmetry*. Heyd accepts the neutrality in The Asymmetry's second clause, but denies that the expected misery of a life supplies a moral reason to not create—which means prospective parents can procreate regardless of how much suffering the child would experience. If Heyd's procreative latitude sets one edge of the spectrum of permissibility, David

---

4. Jason Marsh, "Procreative Ethics and the Problem of Evil," in *Permissible Progeny?*, ed. Sarah Hannan, Samantha Brennan, and Richard Vernon (New York: Oxford University Press, 2015), 71.

5. Reasons grounded in the well-being of putative individuals are impersonal, since they apply to anyone, regardless of their individual interests or concerns. See Jeff McMahan, "Asymmetries in the Morality of Causing People to Exist," in *Harming Future Persons: Ethics, Genetics and the Nonidentity Problem*, ed. Melinda A. Roberts and David T. Wasserman, vol. 35 (Dordrecht: Springer, 2009), 49–68.

6. Space considerations do not allow me to undertake a full discussion of the nature of harms and benefits. For an overview, see Fiona Woollard and Frances Howard-Snyder, "Doing vs. Allowing Harm," in *The Stanford Encyclopedia of Philosophy*, ed. Edward N. Zalta (Winter 2016), https://plato.stanford.edu/archives/win2016/entries/doing-allowing/.

Benatar's categorical anti-natalism sets the other. As with Heyd, Benatar adopts a person-affecting approach. Yet he argues that the asymmetry of harm and benefits The Asymmetry presupposes entails that it is *always* wrong to procreate. To this he adds an unmitigated, Schopenhauerian pessimism about human well-being and happiness, which leads him to the conclusion that procreation is both categorically wrong and seriously harmful to those created.

After rejecting both extremes, I then consider Jeff McMahan's attempt to rescue The Asymmetry from its anti-natalist implications by adopting impersonal reasons to procreate. McMahan ends his argument in aporia, as he is unwilling to accept the (putatively) bad implications he sees arising from such a view. His discussion is valuable, though, for identifying the potential costs of affirming that there are moral reasons to create and for clarifying puzzles around how our obligations to benefit existing people intersect with our reasons to create new people. I seize on this final thread to consider more localized and modest objections to procreating than Benatar lays out, which are frequently invoked as a way of establishing a *presumptive* anti-natalism. While the force of many such objections is contingent upon empirical realities, I suggest that we are left floundering on the shoals between a skeptical procreative pessimism and an optimism that animates procreative permissibility. Neutrality about the value of creating a happy life is not sufficient to avoid a *de facto* anti-natalism.

David Heyd and Procreative Latitude

If procreative reasons are person-affecting, in that they arise on the basis of the harms or benefits that particular individuals receive, then we need some answer to *which persons* count. For David Heyd, the answer is: *actual* people, that is, those individuals who will exist regardless of what anyone decides. The existence—future or present—of a morally actual person is a "given fact" for an agent.[7] This means the interests of the prospective child do *not* matter to prospective parents, as until the decision is made the child's existence is only possible.

At the same time, though, Heyd does not think existence *per se* matters for moral reasoning. Value is "always *for* human beings; it has to do with what they—in the broad sense—want or need."[8] Human beings are the measure of value, but are not valuable as such.[9] On his view, "existence is not a moral predicate." An individual is "only of value if it satisfies the volitions of someone."[10] It is only because others exist *as* valuing individuals that they matter to us. Even so, the possible existence of "valuing creatures" (like humans) does not give someone a

---

7. David Heyd, *Genethics* (Berkeley: University of California Press, 1992), 103.
8. Ibid., 84.
9. Ibid., 85.
10. Ibid., 117.

reason to create them. Only those valuing creatures who are morally actual—who will exist regardless of anyone's decision—count for our moral deliberations.

On what basis, then, are decisions to procreate made? Heyd's answer is a thoroughgoingly egoistic one: decisions to create "can and should be guided exclusively by reference to the interests, welfare, ideals, rights and duties of those making the choice."[11] Heyd's egoism is not solipsism: while procreative choices are theoretically unbounded, they are also constrained by empirical realities. We make creative choices in contexts where we have obligations to other "actual" people whose existence is not contingent upon our choice.[12] These empirical realities explain why we have children: it is a "universal cultural fact" that "human beings desire to have children and that they raise them more or less 'in their own image.'"[13]

Yet there are also no reasons behind these empirical constraints on our procreative conduct, which limits their normative force. Any attempt to defend procreation's intrinsic worth illegitimately seeks to "transcend the strict limits of ethics by a metaphysical shift."[14] While this might minimize procreation's significance, it leads Heyd to argue that procreating is a form of "self-transcendence." In making future generations, humanity does not respond to or add value to the world, but rather makes "the world a place in which value is at all applicable."[15] Continuing the species "transcend[s] the senselessness of the valuing activity by making it last beyond their own existence."[16] The game of life has meaning only through its indefinite perpetuation. Despite such lofty rhetoric, though, nothing about this self-transcendence could *reasonably* justify optimism against the radical pessimism of embracing species-cide. The most we can rationally justify is neutrality between affirming humanity's goodness and welcoming its demise. If we look for a non-evaluative ground for value that would tip the balance in favor of the species, we might discover (with Kant) a "metaphysical perspective through which man is elevated to the sublime status of the final end of creation," or our effort might "*equally* give rise to the image of human life as no more than 'a tale told by an idiot, full of sound and fury, signifying nothing.'"[17] In principle, then, Heyd's actualism moves the decision to procreate outside the sphere of moral reasoning: procreative choices "resist any kind of ethical treatment" and "lie beyond the borders of ethics." The practical result of this is startling: no principle can "rule out the willful conception of a defective child," or prohibit the "total extinction of the human race by a voluntary act of collective suicide."[18]

---

11. Ibid., 96.

12. This class of people includes future people whose existence is independent of our choice, not only those who are already real.

13. Ibid., 199.

14. Ibid., 211.

15. Ibid., 213.

16. Ibid., 216.

17. Ibid., 228.

18. Ibid., 193.

Most philosophers view the impossibility of moral wrongdoing in creating as a *reductio* against Heyd's view.[19] Yet there are other reasons to question Heyd's approach. For one, Heyd's view that only "actual" people count entails the implausible conclusion that the *more* control we have over procreation, the *less* responsibility we bear for our choices. As Jeff McMahan argues, a state that introduces policies governing reproduction regards future children as merely potential, which releases the state from any duty to them.[20] That is a bizarre consequence: the contingency of future generations upon our choices should not free us from responsibility for those choices. Additionally, we might draw the opposite conclusion from Heyd's (undefended) claim that value is secured by indefinite extension and argue that games are only valuable because they end.[21] Indefinite perpetuation seems no more meaningful than momentary enjoyment. Furthermore, Heyd's egoism does not explain why humans have an interest in *their* perpetuation, rather than the perpetuation of some other valuing species. He posits that transhuman replication "does not preserve the minimal conditions of identity which make the outcome a continuant of the origin."[22] Yet Heyd's opposition to grounding value metaphysically undercuts such a rejoinder: if valuing survives without human valuers, on what basis can we object to post-human projects? Heyd's appeal to the "minimal conditions of identity" for the indefinite perpetuation of valuing slips in a non-evaluative basis for valuing, a move his approach to ethics disallows.

We should be wary of Heyd's neutrality about humanity's existence. His refusal to assess the value of being human from an independent, external point of view is honest. But removing procreation from the realm of reason leaves us bereft of a plausible explanation for why we should carry on rather than quit the (often burdensome!) "game of life." Heyd's theoretical stance is a serious departure from our obvious practical commitment to perpetuating the species. While Heyd regards such empirical realities as qualifiers on what is normatively permissible, we might instead go the other direction and adopt a normative presumption in favor of procreating on grounds that humanity has long seemed practically disposed to do it, even when conditions are unwelcome. Otherwise, there is little in Heyd's theoretical neutrality about procreating to keep it from becoming a *de facto* anti-natalism.

---

19. McMahan's judgment of Heyd's account is representative: "A view that implies that there is no moral reason not to cause an individual to exist whose life would be filled with intrinsically bad states, uncompensated for by intrinsically good states, cannot be true." See McMahan, "Asymmetries," 60.

20. Heyd, *Genethics,* 217.

21. My point is not to defend the value of death; rather, it is to suggest that Heyd has failed to demonstrate what I take to be a central contention for his view.

22. Ibid., 217.

David Benatar's Categorical Anti-natalism

If Heyd's account stands at one end of the spectrum of procreative permissibility, David Benatar's categorical anti-natalism stands at the other. On his view, to be born is to suffer harms—which makes it categorically wrong to create human life. He arrives at this conclusion through two routes: first, he defends a (complicated) axiological asymmetry between harming and benefiting, in which harms of life count for moral deliberation while the benefits do not. Second, Benatar attacks our optimism about the world and our well-being (the "Pollyanna Principle"), which stands beneath our pro-natalist outlook. If we saw life as it *really* is, we would discover that it is (much) worse than it seems. Benatar contends these two arguments are independent paths to the same anti-natalist conclusion.[23] But, as we shall see, they share similar properties.

Benatar's first argument is complex, but also worth evaluating for the way in which he attempts to explain The Asymmetry by appealing to intuitions. For Benatar, the *existence* of harms and benefits is morally symmetrical: (1) the presence of a harm is bad, and (2) the presence of a benefit is good. However, the *nonexistence* of harms and benefits is asymmetrical: (3) the absence of a harm is a good, even if no one exists for whom it is good, but (4) the absence of a benefit is not bad, unless someone is deprived of it.[24] The moral significance of the absence of harms is thus untethered from whether anyone exists: no harm is good, regardless of whether anyone exists. The moral significance of the absence of benefits, though, is tied to existence: benefits are good *if* one exists, but if no one exists, then the absence of benefits is not bad. Such an account of harm might seem impersonal, since no one exists for whom the absence of harms is good. But Benatar insists he means it in person-affecting terms.[25] We do not know the merely possible person in their "not bad" non-existence, but we are still able to judge the reasons to create "in terms of his or her potential interests."[26] The upshot of this is it is good for an individual not to exist, a sense of "good for" that is "obviously loose."[27]

Benatar's next move is even more complex. He argues that in procreating we weigh the expected goods and bads of existence against the person's non-existence, rather than against each other. In other words, we do not aggregate harms and benefits in a potential life and then create that life if the benefits outweigh the

---

23. Benatar, *Better Never to Have Been*. See also Benatar's responses to his (many) critics in "Still Better Never to Have Been," *Journal of Ethics* 17, no. 1–2 (2013): 121–51, and "Every Conceivable Harm," *South African Journal of Philosophy* 31, no. 1 (2012): 128–64.

24. Benatar uses pleasures and pains, but only as instances of harms and losses. See Benatar, *Better*, 30 ff.

25. Benatar, "Still Better," 125.

26. Benatar, *Better*, 31.

27. Benatar's notion of harm is comparative. 'Good for' is equivalent to 'better for', where the relevant comparison is a counterfactual. The badness of absent harms is not an "intrinsic badness," nor is the absence of benefits an "intrinsic 'not-badness'—neutrality." Ibid., 42.

harms: rather, we compare the harms they would suffer with the non-existence of those harms (1 with 3, above), and the goods they would enjoy with the non-existence of those goods (2 with 4, above). On the first, it is clearly better to have the good of non-existent harms (3) than the bad of existing ones (1). Benatar thinks the second comparison, though, is neutral. Existing benefits in a life (2) are not better than the non-existence of those benefits (4), as their non-existence is "not bad." The non-existence of benefits is *only* bad if there is an actual individual whose life is deprived by not having them. Because the non-existence of benefits is "not worse" than their existence, the existence of benefits is "not an advantage over absent pleasures that do not deprive."[28] To put it differently, the comparison of harms makes the individual's non-existence preferable. And the comparison of benefits is neutral between the existence and non-existence of the individual. The combination of these two comparative judgments renders the non-existence of the individual preferable, and makes being brought into existence always a harm—*even if the expected benefits of a life significantly exceed its harms.*

Benatar defends this counterintuitive conclusion by arguing his axiological asymmetry explains a variety of "common sense" asymmetries, including The Asymmetry. Yet he does not specify why we should accept his radically counterintuitive anti-natalism rather than give up the (allegedly) common sense asymmetries. One such asymmetry Benatar thinks his view explains involves regret: we cannot regret absent benefits for the sake of non-existent individuals, but we can regret present harms for the sake of existing people. Similarly, we regret the suffering of distant existing individuals, but do not regret the "absent [benefits] of those who could have existed."[29] Unless we adopt his axiological asymmetry, these "common moral judgments" go away, and we would be required to view the absent benefits to non-existent people as bad rather than not good.[30] This does not seem like a hard bullet to bite, though—or, at least, it is no harder a bullet to bite than those Benatar's view requires us to chew through. If we can say in an "obviously loose" sense that the non-existence of miserable individuals is better for them, as Benatar does, then it is special pleading to reject regret for non-existent happy people.[31] Moreover, we might untether regret from moral reasoning, and accept that we can have the reactive attitude of regret for absent goods without being required to do anything about it.[32] By contrast, Benatar's categorical anti-natalism

---

28. Ibid., 35n.

29. Ibid.

30. If the absence of benefits is *bad*, rather than *not good*, we should "have to regret, for X's sake, that X did not come into existence. But it is not regrettable." Ibid., 39. But then neither should we be glad at the good of absent harms to non-existent people, as Benatar's view seems to entail.

31. See Christine Overall, *Why Have Children?* (Cambridge, MA: MIT Press, 2012), 98 ff.

32. This is the view of regret that Jay Wallace defends. See Jay R. Wallace, *The View from Here: On Affirmation, Attachment, and the Limits of Regret* (New York: Oxford University Press, 2013).

requires giving up intuitions like: procreation is generally permissible, individuals with extremely happy lives are not harmed by them, and humanity's extinction would be bad. Benatar (rightly) contends that moral theory should not bottom out in intuitions, but he offers no non-arbitrary way of deciding which intuitions to keep.[33] Given the intuitions Benatar's view undermines, accepting that we can regret the non-existence of happy individuals seems like a very low cost to a pro-natalist outlook.

Benatar's second argument for his categorical anti-natalism takes an empirical turn, yet rests upon similar intuitions as his first. Our self-assessments of well-being, Benatar argues, are infected by a "tendency toward optimism" known as the "Pollyanna Principle." The idea life is generally worth living is unreliable, though.[34] Rather than squarely facing our misery, we adapt our preferences to preserve our happiness. Benatar carries out this debunking argument against objective list theories of well-being, which critically assess well-being relative to a species-norm. Benatar grants that many individuals have happy lives relative to other people, but he shifts the comparison class in order to show that their happiness is unwarranted: *sub specie aeternitatis,* human life is much worse than it *could* be. We should compare the objective well-being of humanity against a supra-human context, in which "pain and frustration," death, and other limitations are absent. Any unwillingness to make this comparison is simply a "failure of imagination."[35] Benatar buttresses his unmitigated pessimism by developing a catalogue of human misery. While a very lucky few might escape some of the worst human suffering, no one escapes it all. Because "those (relatively) high-quality lives are exceedingly uncommon," procreation is presumptively bad.[36] This pessimistic outlook means the "optimist surely bears the burden of justifying this procreational Russian roulette." Benatar raises this standard even higher by combining this pessimism with his first argument, which claims there are "no real advantages over never existing for those who are brought into existence." The two together reveal that those who procreate "play Russian roulette with a *fully* loaded gun—aimed, of course, not at their own heads, but at those of their future offspring."[37]

While Benatar's two routes to anti-natalism might seem independent, they both supply an unyielding perfectionism about well-being—a standard that demands sacrificing fairly deep intuitions about the world. Benatar's first argument means that a life with a single harm should not be created regardless of how many benefits it might contain. The Asymmetry's standard of procreative neutrality entails that the benefits of a life do not have reason-giving weight for procreators. But as Jeff McMahan points out, Benatar's approach means benefits do not even have

---

33. Benatar, *Better,* 202 ff.
34. Ibid., 64 ff.
35. Ibid., 84.
36. Ibid., 92.
37. Ibid.

canceling weight against harms: because we do not weigh the *whole* of a life against its non-existence in deciding whether to create on his view, its expected benefits do not cancel out any of the expected harms in our reasoning.[38] That means, though, that a single harm outweighs infinite benefits, even if the harm is as minor as a pinprick. The debunking strategy of Benatar's second, pessimistic argument works similarly. His criticism of the "Pollyanna principle" allows the harms of existence to count for assessments of well-being, but places the benefits beneath skeptical scrutiny. Moreover, Benatar's suggestion that objective well-being must be measured *sub specie aeternitatis,* and his corresponding rejection of a species-norm, raises the threshold of acceptable well-being so high that only an endlessly happy deity can attain it. (How Benatar can reliably assess the world from this standpoint is its own methodological problem. Are we sure his imagination is trustworthy?) Both arguments fail to address whether we should be perfectionists like Benatar: our life might be better without any harms, but it can still be good enough with them.[39]

Jeff McMahan on The Asymmetry

The two person-affecting responses to The Asymmetry considered so far are both unpersuasive: categorical permissibility about procreating seems no more attractive than categorical impermissibility. Heyd adopts a person-affecting symmetry, in that he thinks neither the harms nor benefits of a life count. Benatar defends a person-affecting asymmetry, in which the harms count but the benefits do not even cancel out the harms. Both generate odd conclusions. Yet we might wonder about The Asymmetry itself, and specifically the procreative neutrality that its second condition presumes. While nearly everyone thinks that the benefits in a life should at least cancel out its expected harms, it is reasonable to also think that those benefits supply *some* reason to create—even if that reason is not as weighty or significant as that which the harms of a life might supply us.

In his search for normative reasons beneath The Asymmetry, Jeff McMahan considers the possibility that the benefits of a life give us a moral reason to create it. Yet he argues that troubling implications follow if benefits do have reason-giving weight, leading him into an aporia that threatens moral realism.[40] If we weigh benefits and harms equally (an "impersonal symmetry"), then we have as much reason to create happy people as to bestow equivalent benefits on existing people. Additionally, if actively preventing a good life is worse than failing to create one, early abortion would be worse than failing to create a

---

38. See McMahan, "Asymmetries in the Morality of Causing People to Exist," 49–68.

39. Robert Adams defends an imperfectionist standard for creating in "Must God Create the Best?," *Philosophical Review* 81, no. 3 (1972): 317–32.

40. See McMahan, "Asymmetries," 49.

happy person—even if the embryo is not a person.[41] Even if benefits have *some* reason-giving weight, but harms have *more* (which McMahan calls the "weak asymmetry"), difficulties still emerge. Specifically, (a) cases arise in which there is reason to create new happy people rather than bestow lesser or equivalent benefits on existing people, (b) abortion is presumptively bad if it prevents the existence of a happy person, and (c) there is some number of happy people that makes it more reasonable to create them than save the life of an existing person. For McMahan, these claims are "not impossible to accept," but are "very difficult to believe."[42] Whatever we make of the implications for abortion, it would indeed be difficult if granting that there are (moral) reasons to create means we should procreate *rather than* fulfill obligations to existing individuals. Yet without further specification of how such reasons interact, such an implication seems possible.

Because of this, McMahan makes a second attempt to explain The Asymmetry by locating the moral weight of reasons in the *types of benefits* we bestow, rather than grounding it in an asymmetry between benefits and harms. On this construal, we discount "existential benefits," which are bestowed through causing a person to exist, against the "ordinary benefits" we bestow upon existing individuals. In other words, we think it is better to bestow benefits on an existing person than by creating a new one. However, McMahan suggests this *ad hoc* attempt to save The Asymmetry fails to explain why ordinary benefits count more than existential benefits. One possible reason is that our coexistence in time with other existing people gives us a special reason for concern, which we do not have with possible people.[43] McMahan rejects this, though, as it stretches "the notion of a *special relation* to the point of vacuity." On his view, proximity in space and time does not make a moral difference.[44]

This failure leads to one final attempt to explain The Asymmetry, by arguing that the asymmetry is between benefits with a comparative dimension and those without—regardless of whether they are existential or ordinary.[45] A choice between a happy sixty-year life and happy eighty-year life bestows an existential benefit. But that benefit has a comparative dimension: the person's "getting the 60-year life is *worse for* him than getting the 80-year life would have been."[46] Benefits where the default state of affairs, absent our action, is the individual's nonexistence are

---

41. McMahan lists other implications. However, he suggests that some of them can be mitigated by distinctions between doing and not doing. Ibid., 66.

42. Ibid., 67.

43. McMahan, "Causing People," 5–35, 14–15.

44. While McMahan allows that our intuitions are in part determined by the gap between existing and future people, we are "reluctant to endorse the view that existing people matter more than future people." Ibid., 15.

45. Ibid., 15.

46. Ibid.

non-comparative, as in choices between bestowing existential benefits and not creating. This will be the case for most procreative decisions.⁴⁷ As any choice to benefit existing individuals is comparative, weighing comparative benefits more heavily than non-comparative benefits would explain why it is better to benefit existing individuals rather than create new ones.⁴⁸

McMahan argues that this formulation leads to dilemmas on every side, though. For one, he argues that non-comparative benefits seem to have reason-giving weight—and do so in a wide range of situations. It is clearly better to create an eighty-year happy life than a sixty-year life, even if neither would exist otherwise. Yet our concurrence with that judgment seems to tacitly grant that the benefit of an eighty-year life gives us a reason to create it. If that reason *only* arises when we are choosing *between* creating either of two possible persons, then the weight their happiness supplies is conditional upon our prior, potentially arbitrary decision to create a person at all. It is odd, he argues, to think "a decision made simply on a whim" can "create a *reason* that did not exist antecedently." If noncomparative benefits only matter when we have previously decided to "confer *some* benefit," then the choice to create or not seems like it stands outside moral assessment—a strange congruence with Heyd's account. Additionally, this approach gets the order of reasons backward. If "one had *no* reason to pick apples, one would have no reason to pick better rather than worse apples."⁴⁹ It is because we have a reason to create a happy person in the first place that we can engage in comparative assessments about how happy a person we should create. Noncomparative benefits, then, seem to have at least some weight in every procreative context, and not only in choices between happier and less-happy lives: one has a reason to create an individual when the default would be their non-existence. Such an approach also has the advantage of justifying our intuitions about the badness of human extinction.⁵⁰

However, giving non-comparative benefits reason-giving weight throws us back on the problems it was supposed to solve, as situations can still arise when it is "better to cause a person to exist" than benefit an existing one.⁵¹ If we can add two years to a life or create a person who will live to eighty, we should do the latter. And it entails there "must also be a significant reason to save the life of a fetus" and an "even more significant reason not to kill a fetus via abortion."⁵² Moreover, the stance seems to imply Derek Parfit's "Repugnant Conclusion," in which we have

---

47. Embryo selection is one instance of an "existential benefit with a comparative dimension," as it is a choice between embryos based on their respective qualities. Most choices, though, will be between the individual's existence and non-existence.
48. Ibid., 17.
49. Ibid., 25.
50. Ibid., 26.
51. Ibid., 31.
52. Ibid., 33.

reason to create more individuals whose lives are barely worth living.[53] As such, the "implications of the claim that noncomparative benefits have reason-giving weight in choices between some and none include some that virtually everyone will find counterintuitive."[54] This judgment prompts McMahan's suggestion that problems in the ethics of creation "seem to me to pose the greatest challenge to realism in ethics."[55]

McMahan's discussion does not so much as supply us with moral reasons to procreate as clarify the possible costs of thinking there are any. Some of the implications McMahan finds troubling we might readily welcome, and so be less moved by his dilemma. Yet we can also put a question about the role of intuitions in McMahan's analysis similar to that which we raised against Benatar's view. McMahan's test-cases bring one set of intuitions to the surface, only to set their implications against other intuitive judgments. While Benatar fails to offer a non-arbitrary way of deciding which intuitions to preserve, McMahan's argument raises the specter that consistency in intuitions is impossible. One possibility is that we should simply accept The Asymmetry as a basic postulate of procreative ethics that has no deeper, normative justification. This would be surprising, especially since the intuitions beneath it seem to be contingent upon social circumstances. McMahan contends the neutrality clause of The Asymmetry, which claims there is no moral reason to create a happy person, is "deeply intuitive and probably impossible to dislodge."[56] It seems plausible, though, that such intuitions are recent and localized phenomena, and that previous generations would think the possibility of a very happy life does supply a strong reason to create it.

Despite ending in aporia, McMahan's discussion reveals a fundamental conflict between the reasons to *create* and the reasons to *care* for existing individuals. The puzzle is this: overcoming the presumption of anti-natalism in The Asymmetry requires granting benefits canceling weight against harms and, to be consistent, reason-giving weight. Yet if benefits have reason-giving weight then conflicts between the reasons to benefit existing individuals and to create new ones arise. We might give up The Asymmetry to overcome a presumptive anti-natalism, but we are thrown into an intractable conflict between obligations to existing people and reasons to create new ones.

One way to preserve the primacy of caring for existing people while still granting reason-giving weight to lives we could create would be to accept

---

53. As Derek Parfit put it, "For any possible population of at least ten billion people, all with a very high quality of life, there must be some much larger imaginable population whose existence, if other things are equal, would be better even though its members have lives that are barely worth living." Derek Parfit, *Reasons and Persons* (Oxford: Oxford University Press, 1992), 388.

54. McMahan, "Causing People," 34.

55. Ibid., 34.

56. Jeff McMahan, *The Ethics of Killing* (New York: Oxford University Press, 2003), 300.

coexistence as a special relation. While McMahan allows that is intuitive to think that the generations immediately following ours matter more than distant ones, he does not think differences in space and time are morally salient. When the matter is framed so abstractly, it is hard to disagree. Yet when space and time are indexed by our *agency*, then the moral landscape seems to shift. For instance, we "cause" the existence of our great-great grandchildren only by the mediation of other people's acts. There is no chain of necessity that stands between us and them: each subsequent generation might have acted otherwise, after all. McMahan allows that the nature of one's agency "affects the morality of the action."[57] Yet he tends to frame procreative agency through the sterile descriptions of "causing existence" or bestowing "benefits and harms," which flattens out what happens when we bring life into the world and allows the thought experiments that perplex McMahan to arise.[58] An account of procreative rationality that avoids the reduction of action to cause and effect might also clarify why nearness in space and time matters morally—a stance that seems at least as intuitive as The Asymmetry.

Procreative Neutrality or Procreative Skepticism?

The above responses to The Asymmetry turn on whether the potential good of a life supplies some reason to bring it into existence. The Asymmetry enjoins neutrality toward happy lives: the benefits of a life do not supply someone a (moral) reason to create. Instead, those reasons must come from elsewhere (perhaps the parents' interests) or be a non-moral type of reason that aims at happiness or pleasure. In Heyd's hands, the fact that reasons only arise in response to existing individuals means procreating is outside the realm of moral deliberation, and is only constrained by third-party concerns. For Benatar, harms count while benefits do not—which means that procreating is categorically wrong. For McMahan, the neutrality expressed by The Asymmetry is so intuitive that we must accept it, and the puzzles generated by attempting to avoid it are bad enough to threaten moral realism.

Even if we rescued procreative neutrality at the normative level, though, skeptical challenges based on empirical conditions still lurk. While few philosophers have opted for Benatar's categorical pessimism, many others have raised similar concerns about procreation's presumptive licitness, which would indicate that theoretical neutrality about procreating generates a practical anti-natalism. Debunking arguments broadly fall into three classes: epistemic arguments, arguments grounded in pessimistic judgments, and arguments from third-party considerations. The general features of such arguments merit our consideration.

57. Ibid., 16.
58. Ibid., 7.

In the first place, worries about the unreliability and uncertainty of our ability to assess well-being animate some skeptical approaches to procreative reasons.[59] For instance, David DeGrazia argues procreation is *pro tanto* impermissible and can be justified only if there is "good reason to expect that the individual to be created will come to appreciate and enjoy her life, feeling glad to be alive, without her judgment being deluded."[60] Yet happiness can be opaque. As Jason Marsh argues, many individuals will have a quality of life that is "either highly inscrutable or highly mediocre," which means it is nearly impossible to determine whether procreation is permissible.[61] Because the stakes in procreating are high, the threshold for justifiably doing so is also high—which means uncertainty about a person's future happiness generates a modest anti-natalism.[62]

Second, while Benatar's full-throated pessimism about human happiness might be too extreme, more modest versions are on offer. As noted above, Jason Marsh contends that procreative rationality tracks theodicy problems—except that we are "notably more pessimistic about the basic goodness of the world when reasoning about the problem of evil than we are when reasoning about human procreation."[63] If evil poses a problem for theists, then a *pro tanto* anti-natalism is warranted. Optimistic assessments about human well-being might mitigate this "theodicy" problem: we might respond to Benatar's litany of suffering with a complementary list of ways in which humanity has flourished. However, The Asymmetry is situated in a deliberative context: it rejects a simple aggregation of harms and benefits as the criterion for whether to create or not, as it weighs the badness of imposing harms more than the benefits of bringing about goods. If this is true, though, then in a deliberative context optimistic assessments would have less weight than pessimistic assessments—and so a modest procreative skepticism would be warranted.[64]

Third, a number of philosophers argue duties to adopt trump any putative interest in procreation. Tina Rulli contends there is a *pro tanto* duty to adopt, which is grounded in the magnitude of the orphan crisis. While this duty is generally not defeated by the interest in having a biological child, she makes one exception for a woman "who strongly desires the pregnancy experience."[65] Similarly, Daniel Friedrich argues we have a moral duty to assist those in need when we can with very

---

59. These are distinct concerns: well-being assessments can be reliable, yet still face ambiguities which render judgments appropriately uncertain.

60. David DeGrazia, *Creation Ethics* (Oxford: Oxford University Press, 2012), 160.

61. Jason Marsh, "Quality of Life Assessments, Cognitive Reliability, and Procreative Responsibility," *Philosophy and Phenomenological Research* 89, no. 2 (2014): 452 ff.

62. Ibid., 459.

63. Marsh, "Procreative Ethics and the Problem of Evil," 71.

64. See Ibid., 73 ff.

65. Tina Rulli, "Preferring a Genetically-Related Child," *Journal of Moral Philosophy* 13 (2014): 28. See also "The Ethics of Procreation and Adoption," *Philosophy Compass* 11, no. 6 (2016): 305–15.

little cost to ourselves.[66] Because beginning a relationship through alleviating need "does not rule out forming a relationship rich in affection and mutual concern," an interest in intimacy does not make parents immune to this duty.[67] Travis Rieder adopts the opposite conclusion, contending that the "radical intimacy involved in forming a family" blocks a *pro tanto* duty to adopt. But he then contends that most procreation is still blameworthy, as most people lack the reasons necessary to trump the duty to adopt. His conclusion is that "morality … judges us harshly for our pro-natal bias."[68]

These debunking arguments on the basis of third-party considerations reinforce the idea that even if optimistic and pessimistic stances about procreating are on a par, procreative skepticism and a *de facto* anti-natalism are warranted.[69] Comparing our moral duties to rescue those in need with prudential desires for a parent–child relationship tips the scale against procreating. The discussion of the relative weight of procreation *vis a vis* a duty to adopt thus moves the dilemma that emerged in the discussion of McMahan into a practical context: our reasons to care for existing individuals trump reasons to create. Even if we could defend the moral neutrality of procreation in principle, in practice pre-existing moral obligations would justify procreative skepticism. This suggests procreative neutrality is a *de facto* anti-natalism.

However, the force of such debunking arguments is not necessarily additive, given that they require conflicting judgments about the reliability of our assessments of well-being. Marsh's first debunking argument uses the ambiguities of well-being and the unreliability of our judgments to animate procreative skepticism. However, debunking arguments based on pessimistic judgments or on existing duties to adopt require reliable assessments of both individual and aggregated well-being (both of which are complicated). It seems like one can appeal to either epistemic arguments or pessimistic and third-party concerns, but not both. Against this problem the debunker might add an epistemic asymmetry between harms and benefits, to match the axiological asymmetry that seems to be widely accepted. Such a move would have to show that we have grounds for stronger confidence in assessments of bads or harms than we do about goods or benefits. In other words, just as harms count more than benefits, so they are more epistemically transparent than benefits. Such a view seems to stand beneath procreative debunking arguments and has some intuitive force.

---

66. Daniel Friedrich, "A Duty to Adopt?," *Journal of Applied Philosophy* 30, no. 1 (2013): 25–39.

67. Ibid., 27.

68. Travis N. Rieder, "Procreation, Adoption and the Contours of Obligation," *Journal of Applied Philosophy* 32, no. 3 (2015): 309.

69. Procreative skepticism names the heightened epistemic threshold pro-natalist accounts must overcome. Anti-natalism expresses a normative judgment that most or all procreation is morally bad.

I suspect the conflict between duties to existing individuals and procreative interests is intractable. Procreating inherently creates new burdens on existing individuals (parents) by giving them a new dependent. As such, it invariably comes with an opportunity cost: the new obligations procreation imposes upon us inevitably conflict with our existing obligations. Procreative skepticism forces us to explain why we are justified in adding more obligations when it seems like we are already failing to fulfill those already upon us. To overcome these worries, one must either argue our existing obligations are fewer than the argument presumes, articulate the distinctive value of procreating, or (preferably) both. However, as long as harms count and benefits do not, or as long as benefits count less, optimistic pro-natalist accounts will struggle to reach the justificatory threshold. Though I have not considered the internal claims of each argument, it is doubtful that procreative optimism can do anything more than fight pessimism to a draw. And if that is the best that can be done, the stakes seem to entail skepticism and *de facto* anti-natalism are warranted.

Conclusion

Several crucial questions emerged in the preceding discussion, which set the conditions for a successful defense of pro-natalism. First, the preceding discussion demonstrated the limits of neutrality. On David Heyd's account, it is just as reasonable to prefer the extinction of the species as its indefinite prolongation. Optimism and pessimism are on an equal theoretical plane. Heyd's inability to unequivocally endorse human existence is wrapped up with his unwillingness to step outside humanity's evaluative dimension and affirm the intrinsic goodness of human beings themselves. Yet while his neutrality is shocking, the same problem emerged elsewhere. The discussion of McMahan indicated that affirming procreative neutrality leads to a *de facto* anti-natalism, as giving noncomparative reasons canceling weight seemed to require also giving them reason-giving weight. The final discussion of procreative skepticism indicated that adopting a (highly intuitive) axiological asymmetry, in which there is stronger reason to not harm than to benefit, means that a pro-natalist approach cannot be neutral between optimism and pessimism about the world. If harms count more, then pessimistic concerns count more—and anti-natalism is presumptively warranted. Whatever way we turn, procreative neutrality seems to entail a *de facto* anti-natalism.

The strength of contemporary moral philosophy is that it highlights the deep conflicts in our intuitions and the oddities that emerge when we think about the way reasons for action intersect with people whose existence is contingent upon our choices. However, it is reasonable to wonder whether moral philosophy is equipped to identify stable, normative answers to the questions it poses. Jeff McMahan thinks the conflicts between our judgments that emerge when trying to normatively ground The Asymmetry are enough to threaten moral realism—which would be an extraordinary cost. Heyd recognizes the difficulty of attaining some sort of neutral, non-evaluative standpoint from which we might ground our reasons to procreate and concludes that there is no theoretical difference between procreating and allowing the species to die out. Benatar thinks we should accept the wrongness of procreation because it explains some intuitions—but also thinks that imaginatively surveying the whole scope of humanity should prompt us to give up our intuitions that procreating is permissible. Using one set of intuitions to clarify how we are thinking about others is a helpful exercise. But the discussion indicates that even if an optimistic account of procreating were to succeed, it would need some metaphysical grounding to strengthen it against skeptical critiques.

At the same time, the above responses to the question of procreating are predominately concerned with the well-being of the individuals created. This is understandable: if their well-being does not count, then there may never be a case where procreation would be irresponsible, not to mention illicit (as Heyd's view accepts). This is a high cost to pay. Yet making questions of well-being primary for understanding the ethics of procreation also has costs. For one, such considerations are divorced from the reasons that prospective parents typically have for generating new human life, which often extend beyond "making a happy person" (even if this is included). Those reasons are often elusive or inarticulate. Yet if every prospective parent hopes for a child whose agency will not be impaired by illness or other sources of suffering, such considerations are often secondary or embedded within a cluster of reasons that involve their own aspirations to be parents, with all the responsibilities and joys involved. As noted in evaluating McMahan's account, framing the morality of procreation (exclusively) around the question of suffering and well-being gives the practice a bureaucratic character, in which our distribution of benefits is not differentiated by the various types of relationships we have and by the form of agency extending such "benefits" requires. An account of procreative reasons that takes seriously the uniqueness of the agency involved in bringing persons into the world would both come nearer to how prospective parents actually deliberate about procreating, without necessarily undermining considerations of well-being.

The next chapter considers whether parenthood, or the parent–child relationship, supplies a reason to procreate—and how that reason might intersect with our obligations to existing people. As the value of biological ties has received ample consideration in moral philosophy, I will consider what sort of benefit such bonds might be and what kind of weight they might supply for the interest in procreating *vis a vis* adoption. While parenthood and procreating are clearly connected, the reality of non-procreative parenthood calls into question whether parenthood *per se* can function as a reason to procreate in the face of skeptical or debunking challenges. Procreating might generate parental bonds—but its value might need to exceed or be distinct from the bonds of parenthood for it to be justified.

Chapter 2

PARENTHOOD AND PROCREATIVE BONDS

If the puzzles surrounding procreation arise because the person created does not yet exist, then perhaps they can be solved by adopting a wider understanding of the reasons or goods at stake in bringing someone into the world. Perhaps matters are more simple than The Asymmetry makes them, and that *becoming parents* provides a sufficiently weighty reason to procreate. Every parent is deeply invested in their child's health and happiness. Yet their child's well-being is intertwined with the irreplaceable, partial bonds of the parent–child relationship. Though it is a mistake to say that the child's flourishing is secondary to these bonds of partiality, it is difficult for parents to detach concerns for their child's happiness from this relational context. Nor should we want them to. The partial bonds of parenthood matter for parents and children alike: even if redistributing babies in a manner similar to Plato's *Republic* proved more optimal to a child's flourishing, most people think there would be something amiss in doing so.

However, appealing to parenthood as a reason to procreate faces a number of challenges—the most pressing of which is that adoption renders parenthood conceptually distinct from whatever happens in procreating. Even if we fill out the goods of parenthood in such a way that we successfully defend becoming parents despite our other obligations, we might need to do additional work to show why one should become a parent through creating new human life.[1] Yet the attempt to articulate the value of procreative bonds *vis a vis* adoption thrusts us into a dilemma. On the one side, if the goods of procreative relationships are thin or trivial, then they might not supply a reason to procreate rather than adopt. On the

---

1. It is true that procreating is the most efficient means of becoming parents. Yet its potentially unique burdens and opportunities should prompt us to seek deeper reasons for becoming parents through procreation than such pragmatic considerations. Harry Brighouse and Adam Swift's account of parenthood offers "no principled objection to the redistribution of babies at birth," even while they object to doing so on pragmatic grounds. See Harry Brighouse and Adam Swift, *Family Values* (Princeton: Princeton University Press, 2014). If baby redistribution sounds absurd, Anca Gheaus argues that in some conditions of social injustice such redistribution may be warranted. See Anca Gheaus, "The Right to Parent One's Biological Baby," *Journal of Political Philosophy* 20, no. 4 (2012): 432–55.

other side, if the goods of procreative bonds are thick enough to supply a reason to procreate, then they might also supply reasons for privileging or extending special partiality toward procreated children in families that have also adopted children. Most people find this latter outcome unacceptable. As Tina Rulli writes, the notion that procreative parents have special reasons for partiality toward their procreated children that they would lack toward adopted children is "both unintuitive and reprehensible."[2] Prospective parents need a non-trivial reason to procreate that avoids establishing inequalities or invidious disparities between adopted and procreated children.

In the first place, then, I consider constructivist explanations for why procreating is generally licit, which do not attach reasons to the existence of a particular individual who might be harmed or benefited. Such accounts are attractive, as they satisfy a number of puzzles related to The Asymmetry and closely track the real reasons that people often have in procreating (namely, becoming parents). At the same time, I suggest that they fail to offer sufficiently thick explanations for why people might prefer to become parents through procreation rather than adoption. To address this limitation, I consider a number of explanations for the unique value of procreative or genetic bonds. Though these accounts are illuminating, they also often lower the epistemic threshold for defending their views—which places the interest in procreating *vis a vis* adoption on rather weak footing, leaving the account either insufficiently weighty to overcome our obligations to third parties or susceptible to pessimistic debunking objections. Alternately, they effectively cede the value of such bonds in order to avoid invidious disparities between adoption and procreation. I conclude by considering some of the conditions that might need to be in place to explain the unique value of procreative parenthood, such that it would supply reasons to procreate rather than adopt.

Relational Reasons to Procreate

For Rivka Weinberg and David Wasserman, permissible reasons for action are constrained by what the individual affected has reason to reject.[3] As Wasserman suggests, while we cannot create a child for his own sake, "we can create him for reasons that include his own good."[4] Though any child who is created might be similarly affected by our decision, the individual's good is still at stake—and

---

2. Ibid., 24.

3. For Weinberg's view, see: Rivka Weinberg, *The Risk of a Lifetime* (New York: Oxford University Press, 2016). For Wasserman's, see Benatar and Wasserman, *Debating Procreation*.

4. David T. Wasserman, "The Nonidentity Problem, Disability, and the Role Morality of Prospective Parents," *Ethics* 116, no. 1 (October 2005): 147.

nobody else's. Such views are perhaps best described, then, as person-regarding, rather than person-affecting.[5] Their question is whether the reasons, intentions, and actions of procreators are sufficiently respectful to the individuals created.[6] While that must include attention to the harms and benefits the person created receives, it is not reducible to considerations of well-being.

Weinberg and Wasserman defend the (deceptively) simple claim that we have children to become parents. As Weinberg argues, family life supplies a "mutually beneficial and respectful" reason that affords "unique and valuable" goods to *both* parent and child.[7] In Thomas Scanlon's parlance, the parent–child relationship is a "nonderivative source of reasons."[8] It is the stopping point for explaining why we bring human life into the world. Well-being is still relevant, though, even if "mainly in an indirect way."[9] Weinberg and Wasserman both grant the presumptive force of anti-natalist skeptical concerns, before articulating constraints on the parent–child relationship that would overcome such worries. For both, the risks of procreation mean procreators *must* have reasons to create. As Wasserman puts it, the child is "entitled to a respectful reason for having been brought into a world where she is exposed to the harms and risks so vividly described by the anti-natalists."[10] In other words, because of the risks of harm, procreation is *prima facie* unjustified and parents need exculpating reasons to do it.[11]

---

5. While these accounts might seem impersonal, the individual still plays some part of the explanation of the wrong—even if any individual similarly situated would be affected similarly. Another possibility is to call such accounts 'wide person-affecting' views.

6. For Wasserman, reasons are justified within the relationship of accountability between parents and children. For Weinberg, justification is more explicitly Rawlsian, in that one considers what one could reasonably accept as conditions for one's own birth, and universalizes accordingly. Mianna Lotz's "reasons-relevance thesis" is a closely related view. She differs from them by grounding the constraints on such reasons in collectivist terms. Parents must do what they can to assuage the concerns of their community about the 'message' they might send in procreating. See Mianna Lotz, "Procreative Reasons-Relevance," *Bioethics* 23, no. 5 (2009): 293.

7. Weinberg, *Risk*, 37. Wasserman follows Christine Overall, who writes: "The best reason to have a child is simply the creation of the mutually enriching, mutually enhancing love that is the parent–child relationship." See Overall, *Why*, 217.

8. Thomas Scanlon, *Moral Dimensions* (Cambridge, MA: Belknap, 2010), 92.

9. Benatar and Wasserman, *Debating Procreation*, 248.

10. Benatar and Wasserman, *Debating Procreation*, 200. See also Wasserman, "Nonidentity Problem," 136. On Wasserman's view, if procreators have a sufficiently respectful reason to choose a child with a lower quality of life, such a choice is justified, provided that child's life is above a certain threshold of well-being. See Benatar and Wasserman, *Debating Procreation*, 246.

11. Both Weinberg and Wasserman think that norms of respect require parents to expect their child to have a quality of life significantly above the threshold of a minimally decent life.

The reasons to procreate, however, are prudential rather than moral. As Wasserman writes, prospective parents "have no moral reason to form such relationships rather than forming other kinds of relationships or conferring other kinds of goods."[12] Moral reasons only arise after agents procreate. However, people should not become parents for any reason, as the reasons one has at the beginning of a relationship determine its quality. If a person enters a romantic relationship to win a bet, they disrespect the other person.[13] Similarly for procreation. If people become parents so they can harvest the infant's organs for a sibling, they illegitimately instrumentalize their relationship and the child. The internal content of the parent–child relationship sets the criterion for respectful reasons to enter such a relationship. In that way, it functions as a non-derivative source of (licit) reasons to procreate.

One advantage of constructivist accounts is that they side-step profoundly difficult questions about the role existence plays in procreative ethics. On their view, existence is not morally special, which means that tricky comparisons to non-existence like those David Benatar makes are off the table and that non-identity problems do not emerge.[14] Additionally, these views offer a plausible explanation for The Asymmetry. On the one side, any "sufficiently respectful" reason will have some threshold of well-being that it must cross, which means there is a moral reason to not create a life "worth not living." On the other side, because the reasons prospective parents have to procreate are not moral, the expected well-being of an individual supplies no moral reason to create.[15]

While these constructivist accounts are attractive, they also have little to say about why people might reasonably become parents through procreating rather than by adopting. Weinberg critiques adoption as "not ideal" because of its cost-prohibitive nature, and affirms that there are "biological joys and [a] biological connection … that is often an aspect of biological procreativity."[16] However, she never specifies these "biological joys" or explains why they supply a weighty enough reason to procreate, leaving the impression that they are little more than an *ad hoc* assertion. For his part, Wasserman explicitly acknowledges that the reasons to enter a parent–child relationship "could equally motivate prospective adoptive parents."[17]

---

12. Benatar and Wasserman, *Debating Procreation*, 198.

13. Ibid., 204.

14. Weinberg, *Risk*, 86. The non-identity problem arises when changing the conditions in which a person comes into existence creates a *different* person than would have existed otherwise. A thirteen-year-old girl who waits until she is eighteen to have a child will have a different child than the child she is deliberating having at age thirteen. See Parfit, *Reasons*, 363.

15. For the full argument to this effect, see Johann Frick, "Making People Happy, Not Making Happy People" (PhD diss., Harvard University, 2014).

16. Weinberg, *Risk*, 43.

17. Benatar and Wasserman, *Debating Procreation*, 187.

The weak justification for procreative parenthood makes such views vulnerable to objections based on the morality of risk imposition. If life's risks are so serious that one can only procreate permissibly with sufficient reasons, then it seems presumptively wrong to impose those risks if one can be a parent through other means.[18] Even if procreation and adoption are equally morally hazardous, the fact that the latter satisfies an obligation to benefit an existing person cancels out its hazards in a way that creating a new person does not. Additionally, if existence is not morally special, then the asymmetrical gratitude of adoptive and procreative children may supply a further reason to adopt. As Wasserman argues, adopted children are likely to be "extremely grateful for their rescue," but biological children "are unlikely to be grateful to anyone for having been rescued from the limbo of nonexistence."[19] In this light, it is not surprising that Wasserman acknowledges that parity between adoption and procreation means there may be strong reasons to prioritize adoption instead.[20]

I suspect Weinberg and Wasserman's failure to specify the distinctive significance of procreative bonds is tied to their thin account of procreative agency. While they are right to think the reasons and intentions of procreators are relevant to the assessment of procreation, their approach otherwise seems to reduce procreators to those who "cause existence." For Weinberg, particularly, procreation might be "biologically fascinating," but metaphysically speaking, we "create persons much as we create paintings."[21] Such an account seems false on its face. We do not gestate paintings inside human bodies. Neither do we need another person to create them. Nor does the painting necessarily bear marks that resemble its creators' bodies. If parenthood is to supply reasons to procreate, we might need a similarly relational account of creating life to specify the "biological joys" of doing so.[22]

Weinberg and Wasserman's constructivist accounts have the advantages of rescuing certain intuitions, including those that make up The Asymmetry. They

---

18. It might be preferable to say we "expose" one to risks by creating them, instead of "imposing" risks on them. Yet it is hard to see what sort of moral difference this might make.
19. Ibid., 195.
20. Ibid., 289.
21. Weinberg, *Risk*, 31.
22. One other worry: neither account addresses whether the possible extinction of humanity could transform procreation into a duty. Moreover, the fact that such accounts frame their pro-natalist arguments by assuming procreative skepticism entails that the bar for permissible procreation *goes up* as the population *declines* below a certain threshold. The badness of human extinction is often justified on grounds that it would be burdensome on the final generations. If a population enters a death spiral, the likelihood of well-being for future generations goes down—and the threshold for exculpatory reasons to procreate goes up. This problem will activate sooner for accounts that set the threshold for permissible procreation well above a "minimally decent life." The Last Adam and Eve would *not* have a duty to procreate, and would very likely have a duty to *not* procreate, given the expected unhappiness of their isolated child(ren).

offer an elegant, attractive explanation for why we procreate, namely, to enter into the joy of parenthood. Yet such an explanation may not be weighty enough to justify procreation in the face of skeptical, anti-natalist presumptions. The weakness of their case for prioritizing procreative over adoptive relationships means their approaches are vulnerable to anti-natalist presumptions on the basis of the need for adoption. In order to escape this problem, we should consider whether other views can offer more robust accounts of the "biological joys" that procreative parenthood establishes.

The Dilemma of Procreative Bonds

If constructivist accounts of parenthood do not offer strong reasons to procreate rather than adopt, that is partially because the appeal to parenthood to justify procreating faces a potentially insolvable dilemma. On the one side, if the goods of procreative parenthood are sufficiently thick as to supply a reason to procreate and not adopt, then they might supply reasons for partiality toward procreated children in mixed families. On the other side, if those goods are thin or trivial, then they will not supply a sufficiently strong reason to procreate in the face of debunking considerations. Parents need non-trivial reasons to procreate, but those reasons also might supply grounds to treat adopted and procreated children differently.

A quick survey of defenses of procreative bonds shows the fundamental problem. Rosalind Hursthouse weakly concludes her defense of parenthood by suggesting that it "is, and would be, odd, to want to *have a child* (i.e. be a parent) as an end itself ... without at all wanting *to have one's own child* (in the biological sense)."[23] After defending procreation as the comprehensive creation of the child, Edgar Page concedes that it "cannot be formally demonstrated that the biological relation is an essential or important element of parenthood."[24] Instead, Page defends "a framework of thought" that holds begetting and rearing together as parts of a single process—a significantly lower epistemic threshold that offers nothing to those who would question that framework. Michael Austin's causal

---

23. Rosalind Hursthouse, *Beginning Lives* (Oxford: B. Blackwell, 1987), 310. Hursthouse also defends the intrinsic value of childbearing. However, as these aspects of her view seem to undermine the parity between males and females with respect to the interest in biological bonds, I set them aside.

24. Edgar Page, "Parental Rights," *Journal of Applied Philosophy* 1, no. 2 (1984): 197. Such a weakness stems from Page's decision to bracket various aspects of procreation from parenthood's value—the efficiency of delivering well-being to a child, affections, the 'contingent' biological facts of reproduction—because they are not its core. Once such benefits to procreative parenthood are removed, it becomes significantly more challenging to articulate why biological bonds matter.

account of procreative parenthood asserts that biological ties are important, yet only beneath sharp qualifications that effectively reduce their value to a tautology: "The biological or genetic connections *may be important* to us because they constitute an *important part of* begetting or rearing a child, but the most important components of parenthood are its social, moral, and relational aspects" (emphasis mine).[25] Bernard Prusak argues that procreative bonds make possible a special sort of unconditional love, a "love that attaches to a child's being, the sheer fact of his or her existence."[26] Yet Prusak is unwilling to bite the disparity bullet: because adoptive relationships can be counted on "*as* given" and are often just as involuntary as procreative bonds, how a child comes to be in a family "appears not at all important." As with Page, his concern is "with the ethics of the family as we know it," and in our world, kinship structures built on biology are a "matter of course."[27]

Similar objections arise against symbolic accounts of procreative parenthood. Despite having no principled objection to infant redistribution, Harry Brighouse and Adam Swift grant that the "child is a living symbol, as well as a product" of a sexual union, a feature which can be an "enriching experience" to parents.[28] Similarly, Tina Rulli allows that a "child is a natural product of [the couple's] love, the literal product of their coming together." Children are a "powerful symbol of their romantic relationship and commitment to one another, physically manifesting the new life they have made together."[29] Despite this lofty rhetoric, critics contend that there is no disparity between adoptive and procreative relationships in this respect. Levy and Lotz contend *any* child can be the embodiment of the love of two people: there is "no reason why an adopted child cannot be considered the physical expression of a couple's love for one another."[30] Echoing Page's account, they propose it is "not biology that underlies our personal ties, but (at best) our beliefs about biology."[31] Similarly, Rulli argues that it is "uncharitable" to think that the symbolic account requires a physical union. The shared values of the family have nothing to do with biological connectedness. The child, instead, "embodies their union because she is some body who is the beneficiary of this surfeit of romantic love," even if her body does not "literally come from them."[32] Adopted

---

25. Michael W. Austin, *Conceptions of Parenthood: Ethics and the Family*, Ashgate Studies in Applied Ethics (Aldershot, England; Burlington, VT: Ashgate, 2007), 17.
26. Bernard G. Prusak, *Parental Obligations and Bioethics* (New York: Routledge, 2013), 16. Ibid., 1.
27. Ibid., 21.
28. Brighouse and Swift, *Family Values*, 106.
29. Rulli, "Preferring," 19.
30. Neil Levy and Mianna Lotz, "Reproductive Cloning and a (Kind Of) Genetic Fallacy," Bioethics, 19-3 (2005), 245.
31. Ibid. In this respect, they are similar to Page, who sought to ground the tie in the "world of thought" that accompanies genetic ties, rather than the ties themselves.
32. Rulli, "Preferring," 20.

children are thus "no less inclined" than biological ones to assume their parents' values and belief.[33]

The difficulties of specifying the value of procreative bonds are thus acute, even if there are reasons to think we should not be too quick to flatten the differences between procreative and adoptive bonds (as I will discuss below). Once the value of genetic similarity or procreative ties is called into question, it can only be answered by pointing to some *other* feature of the world that explains why it is valuable (unless we conclude that the value of such ties is basic in some way). Yet when we attempt to explain genetic bonds by appealing to the benefits they support or contribute to, questions arise as to whether we could not just as well enjoy those goods from other means, and the threat of dissolving biological bonds into convention re-emerges. If the defense of procreative parenthood is not going to be a brute assertion of biology's salience, we need some account of how the biological and causal relationship that procreation establishes is linked to other goods and values that we care about.

Kolodny, Moschella, Velleman, and Ferracioli on Biology and Personal Identity

Niko Kolodny's account of genetic "resonance" does not escape the above dilemma—but it does offer an intriguing account of why partiality on the basis of genetic relationships is licit. On his view, resonance occurs when "one has reason to respond to a decision by which someone expresses an intention ... that a person or thing fare a certain way." Such a response is a "reactive attitude" that incorporates a general concern for well-being, but also "reflects the distinctive importance of how others regard whom or what one cares about."[34] This partiality might arise from a "shared history of encounter," or from having "common personal histories and situations"—even if both parties have not met.[35] Parents have a reason for partiality toward their children because of their history of fulfilling the general responsibility to support their child's well-being.[36] This history predominately explains parent–child partiality, rather than any type of genetic bond. Genetic children have reasons for partiality only if genetic parents fulfill their obligations.

---

33. Ibid., 21.

34. Niko Kolodny, "Which Relationships Justify Partiality?," *Philosophy and Public Affairs* 38, no. 1 (2010): 44–5.

35. Ibid., 51.

36. Ibid., 60. This relationship of partiality is both reciprocal and conditional. So, the "child has reason for filial partiality to any adult who has had a history of *responsibility* for it." The child reciprocates partiality only in response to the parent. And the history of the parent–child relationship is conditional upon the parents' fulfillment of their responsibilities. Children have no reason for partiality toward abusive parents, who do not satisfy this condition.

Otherwise, the reasons "a genetic relationship provides are simply redundant" when there is already a history of responsibility.[37]

Despite this admission, Kolodny still argues that genetic resonance is a unique, non-reductive form of resonance that occurs when two people share a sufficient amount of genetic material. Genetic partiality stems from "the fact that the child's creation was, and its biological life has been, later stages of a continuous biological process (i) that began as an episode in the biological life of the parent and (ii) that has been governed throughout, in part, by the parent's genetic code: or, less clinically, by the parent's principle of organization, or specific Aristotelian Form."[38] This view requires adopting two principles about egoistic concern. First, egoistic concern extends to one's own organic and genetic material. Second, egoistic concern extends to organisms that have sufficient continuity with one's own organism (including one's future organism). If one has reason to be partial to one's own genetic material, then there is reason "for a kind of partiality to my genetic children that nevertheless reflects the fact that this latter relationship is to a separate and independent person."[39] We do not live on through genetic children. But because both individuals consist of a "continuous biological process, governed by the same genetic code, ... there is a natural way to see them as counterparts." As Kolodny observes, even if this defense of genetic partiality fails, it makes clear that the "significance, if any, of biological relationships lies in the significance, if any, of biology to personal identity."[40]

Kolodny's creative account flounders on the horns of the "procreative dilemma" we saw previously. As Tina Rulli argues, either genetic resonance supplies unique reasons for parents to prefer genetically related children, or it is trivial.[41] Kolodny's concession that biological partiality is "redundant" when a history of relationship exists between parents and children makes it clear he prefers the latter horn. But then we are left wondering why biological resonance matters and what prevents it from collapsing into the history that progenitors have with their offspring. Kolodny has almost no answer for this, as is clear from his struggle to say how the history of responsibility that grounds parenthood begins. Kolodny does not think parenthood should be purely contingent upon the history of parents' responses to children. Parenthood is "response-independent." Otherwise, an individual who never responds partially to their genetic child would not be a parent, an implication Kolodny is keen to avoid.[42] Yet Kolodny brackets a genetic explanation for the response-independent basis of parenthood, because adoptive parents are equally parents. How, then, does parenthood begin, if not genetically? "If Nature or convention so conspires," Kolodny writes, "an adult may come to share a history of

37. Ibid., 68.
38. Ibid., 70.
39. Ibid., 71.
40. Ibid., 73.
41. Rulli, "Preferring," 23–4.
42. Kolodny, "Which Relationships," 58.

[collective responsibility] encounters with a specific child."[43] Such a history is what makes them a parent—which functionally reduces the origins of the relationship to happenstance. Notice as well that this history of parenting means being merely the most proximate deliverer of the benefits society collectively owes children for their well-being. Such a history of caretaking is insufficiently parental, even if it supplies grounds for being sufficiently partial. It functionally reduces parenthood to a history of encounters by the most proximate and efficient deliverer of care to the child. Yet reducing the unique parent–child bond to such a relationship risks, once again, bureaucratizing it.

David Velleman's attempt to explain the moral salience of genetic relationships appeals not to partiality or resonance, but to the self-knowledge such bonds supply for children. Our biology forms the "objective reality of the creature who I am," which must be integrated into our "egocentric perspective."[44] The task of subjective identity-formation works on "raw materials that are not infinitely plastic."[45] Our genetic inheritance sets the contours of our personal identity, even if it does not rigidly determine its content. But incorporating one's "genetic endowment" into our personal identity makes us retrospectively concerned about the persons whose genetic material combined to create the objective (biological) reality of our life. A child benefits from their genetic parents through seeing both halves of their genetic endowment incorporated into their parents' personal identity.[46] Knowing our biological lineage puts us in touch with "the objective order" through allowing us to locate ourselves "in the web of causality."[47] Through enfolding the causal antecedents of our bodies—our biological origins—into our "egocentric perspective," our causal origins thus become our personal origins.

While such self-knowledge seems intrinsically valuable, Velleman's construal of "life" makes it essential for well-being. Velleman rejects the idea that life is a "gift," and instead proposes that parents throw their biological children "into a predicament" and confront them "with a challenge in which the stakes are high, both for good and for ill."[48] The nature of our predicament is specified by the objective conditions of our genetic endowment, which transforms the imperative to know one's genetic relatives into a "personal need."[49] Personal knowledge of how individuals with the same genetic stock navigated their predicament helps the child successfully negotiate their own.[50]

While Velleman draws the strong conclusion that those who are deprived of knowing their biological kin "must be like wandering in a world without reflective

---

43. Ibid., 59.
44. Velleman, "Gift," 262.
45. Ibid., 257.
46. Ibid., 258–9.
47. Ibid., 262.
48. Ibid., 251.
49. Ibid., 246.
50. See Velleman, "Family," 370.

surfaces, permanently self-blind," he also builds in structural vagueness to his account and lowers the epistemic bar that he is attempting to clear.[51] He contends that family resemblances can give us "paradigms or images but no specific definition," such that the contents of this self-knowledge "cannot be articulated."[52] At the same time, Velleman (like Page) lets himself off the hook by adopting a lower epistemic standard than many of his critics would want: he "cannot prove" that biological relatedness is "part of the minimally adequate provision for a child," but can only "make plausible the venerable and worldwide conviction to that effect."[53] The argument thus leans on something like pre-existing intuitions or the deliverances of literature for its normative force, making it more vulnerable to critique.

Many of Velleman's critics miss his proviso and so offer arguments aimed at showing why biological relatedness is not necessary for self-knowledge.[54] For instance, Charlotte Witt argues Velleman conflates *kinship* and *similarity*, which are not mutually entailing. On her account, family is about kinship rather than resemblance, which means there is no "conceptual connection tying biological ancestry relations to resemblances as the metaphor of family resemblances might suggest."[55] Sally Haslanger argues in a closely related vein that what constitutes similarities are contextual, such that a particular social framework may make similarity in certain attributes important while downplaying similarities in other attributes (like temperament). Even if the similarities Velleman cares about were important, they do not sufficiently ground the need for a relationship between parents and child. As she puts it, when adoptees see their biological parents, "How much more than a glimpse is needed?"[56]

The strongest critique, though, is that Velleman's account effectively bottoms out (again!) in a defense of conventional norms, which is an insufficient basis for defending the moral salience of genetic ties. Velleman's "bionormative" argument,

---

51. Ibid., 368.

52. Ibid., 366.

53. Velleman, "Gift," 257.

54. Charlotte Witt, "A Critique of the Bionormative Concept of the Family," in *Family-Making*, ed. Francoise Baylis and Carolyn McLeod (New York: Oxford University Press, 2014), 49–64; Sally Haslanger, "Family, Ancestry and Self," *Adoption and Culture* 2, no. 1 (2009): 12; Rulli, "Ethics." Witt makes two empirical claims as counter-examples to the argument that those who do not know their biological parents are 'rootless'. First, she observes that many of us lack ties to extended family, yet do not lack in self-understanding. Second, she suggests some fathers might unwittingly be raising a non-biological child. Velleman cannot say it makes "no difference whether the father is the biological parent of the child or no." But if neither party knows the mistake, it is "very implausible to think that the fact that the child's father is not biologically related to her would make a difference in the child's psychological development." Witt, 54.

55. Ibid., 55.

56. Haslanger, "Family," 18.

Haslanger argues, is "locally self-affirming." Adopted children who grow up in contexts that value biological ties are "more likely to have identity problems and search for their biological relatives"—which means that their sense of rootlessness cannot be used to defend the existing paradigm.[57] Even if keeping biological parents and children together is practiced universally, the "'naturalness' or ubiquity of a practice" does not render it moral.[58] The bond between biological mother and child is pervasive, but only because it arose "simply from the fact that from the very earliest twilight of human society every infant was found to be in a state of needing a lactating woman, the nearest being its biological mother."[59] As Tina Rulli clarifies, Velleman's use of family resemblances to justify genetic relationships begs the question.[60]

While such critiques have force, Velleman's argument would not supply reasons to enter procreative parenthood *vis a vis* adoption even if it were successful. Insofar as his argument focuses on the way such bonds help us successfully navigate the predicament of life, it is limited to our retrospective efforts to enfold the biological presuppositions of our lives into our egocentric perspective. His defense of the importance of such bonds focuses on the child's perspective, but overlooks their value to parents or others. Such an approach has the benefit of satisfying intuitions that genetic bonds matter less as they become more distant, both in proximity and in time: it is easier to care about the fate of one's grandchildren than it is one's great-great grandchildren. The salience of our genetic origins matters less, it would seem, to those who have spent a lifetime navigating the "predicament" of their lives than those who are just setting out. Yet it also leaves open why, in a deliberative context, we should seek to add new genetic ties—or why we should do so by procreating rather than, say, by cloning.

In her attempt to describe the basis for parental obligations, Melissa Moschella reaches behind convention and defends the relative importance of biology itself for our personal identity. Yet even her substantive, metaphysically grounded defense of procreative bonds faces the same difficulties as those above. On her view, there is a unique good to "knowing oneself to be loved *by one's biological parents*, by those out of whose bodies and bodily union one came into existence."[61] The basis for this is that biological progenitors are the irreplaceable cause of a genetically similar individual. This relationship "calls for" an interpersonal relationship between parent and child and makes the general obligations created by the child's dependency non-transferable. As Moschella writes, it is "because biological parents stand in a permanent, unique and intimate relationship to their children *as the cause* of those children's existence and identity, that they are irreplaceable to their

---

57. Ibid., 17.
58. Ibid., 26–7.
59. Ibid., 28.
60. Rulli, "Preferring," 14.
61. Ibid., 41.

children in this way," namely, as sources of love and affection.[62] Still, biological bonds are only the "starting point" for the more comprehensive psychological and affective bonds that we typically associate with such relationships. As adoptive parents are true parents, parenthood means "engendering a new human being not only biologically, but also psychologically, morally and intellectually."[63] This concession places the bulk of the reason-giving weight and value of parenthood on its non-biological dimensions. Biological causality generates parental obligations. But it is not clear that it can explain why prospective parents might prefer to procreate rather than adopt.[64]

Luara Ferracioli picks up the thread of the permanence and irreplaceability of biological bonds in her own forceful defense of their salience. On her view, the value of parenthood lies in the depth and robustness of the loving bond between parents and children, and that "the *mere* fact of intentional procreation for purposes of parenting provides a *weighty* pro tanto reason for parenting of this kind."[65] The *pro tanto* reason that the "mere fact" of *intentional* procreation supplies is important because, in a sense, it precedes the child's development of lovable qualities and endures if those qualities would be lost. "The core idea here," she writes, "is that the procreative aspect of procreative-parenting justifies love in the most difficult of circumstances, and in so doing, it is the closest we get to unconditional love"—a claim similar to Prusak's.[66] Ferracioli seems to pin the value of such bonds on their durability and permanence. As she notes, the relational fact of *being one's progeny* "obtains prior to the establishment of a parent–child relationship and cannot be lost by the child nor possessed in greater degree by anyone else."[67] Conversely, the "mere fact" of adoption offers no *pro tanto* reason to love: someone whose adoption fails because the social workers decide a different family is a better fit has no *pro tanto* reason to love the child. Unlike procreation, adoptive love is "justified by an appeal to the facts about the child, facts about the relationship, or (most plausibly) a combination of both."[68]

Ferracioli nominally rejects the notion that procreative parenthood is superior to adoptive parenthood because of this disparity, but it is hard to see how her view avoids it. For one, she argues that the reasons for love that procreation offers

---

62. Ibid., 41. Emphasis mine.

63. Ibid., 45.

64. Moschella acknowledges that her view rests on the metaphysical principle that the body is an "intrinsic and essential aspect of personal identity." But that does not clarify what is lost, morally, if such an aspect is ignored in *this* context. Moschella references Patrick Lee and Robert P. George, *Body-Self Dualism in Contemporary Ethics and Politics* (Cambridge, UK: Cambridge University Press, 2008).

65. Luara Ferracioli, "Procreative-Parenting, Love's Reasons and the Demands of Morality," *Philosophical Quarterly* 68, no. 270 (2018): 78.

66. Ibid., 88.

67. Ibid.

68. Ibid., 89.

parents are outweighed by the demands of justice, so that parents of mixed families should distribute benefits and burdens to their children equally. This is doubtlessly true—but it would be troubling if parents distributed benefits to half their children out of procreative partiality and to the other half out of a sense of justice. We want parity in the reasons parents have for acting toward their children, not just of treatment. This concern is especially acute for Ferracioli, since she seems to grant that the relational fact of procreation does real work *within* the parent-child relationship by giving parents a *pro tanto* reason to love even when the child becomes "extremely difficult." Without such a fact, or a *pro tanto* reason, adoptive love seems conditional on the behavior of the child and on the child maintaining the traits that prompted the parents to choose the child to begin with. Such an account would potentially set a lower threshold for failed adoptions than we might want, as it is precisely when adopted children are most difficult that they are in most need of the security of knowing they are loved by their adoptive parents.

Additionally, Ferracioli's account suffers from an ambiguity around what work the procreative bonds are doing in supplying a reason for near-unconditional parental love. While she stresses that the "mere fact" of procreation offers a *pro tanto* reason for love, she also suggests that only those who *intentionally* procreate have such a reason in order to avoid giving anonymous gamete donors a *pro tanto* reason to love the child whose existence they contributed to. Yet this is a problem: if the mere fact of such a relationship is a reason for something like unconditional love, then it seems arbitrary or *ad hoc* to exclude anonymous gamete donors from having that reason when they stand in the same factual position as those who procreate with the intention to parent. But if the reason arises from the *intention* to parent, then adoptive parents and procreative parents would seem like they have an equivalent reason to unconditionally love their children. While Ferracioli's account is promising, then, her aversion to embracing a genetic or biological reductionism reintroduces the very problem she sets out to solve.

Such accounts underscore some of the challenges of escaping "the procreative dilemma" by appealing to the value of biological bonds. One difficulty is specifying why or how biological bonds matter to us—what role they should play in our set of egoistic concerns—and why that value is not finally reducible to the very conventions that skeptics would call into question. While Velleman comes near to doing that, his argument is limited by its retrospective focus: the value of such bonds predominately matters for learning to navigate the predicament of life, which diminishes their salience for adults and those who are contemplating entering parenthood through generating such bonds. There are reasons, then, for thinking that parenthood and procreation might come apart, such that the reasons the former supplies are not necessarily equivalent to the reasons the latter supplies. As long as parenthood remains undifferentiated between adoption and procreation, then it precludes attending to the differences in how parenthood begins. Adoption and procreation do not generate parenthood in the same way—and, as such, parenthood might not be the right place to turn for reasons to procreate. The constructivists' thin understanding of the value of procreative bonds and their inattentiveness to the agency required to bring them about may go hand in hand. Perhaps the dilemma might be solved not by distinguishing the unique value of procreative bonds, but by separating reasons to procreate from reasons to parent, and by arguing that the latter apply equally to procreative and adoptive forms of parenthood. The final section of this chapter sketches how such a view might go.

Parenthood, Procreation, and Adoption: Equality or Identity?

Is there a meaningful way out of the triviality problem? One path through it might be to reject the assumption that disparities between adoptive and procreative parenthood entail an invidious inequality. While admitting distinctions between them might problematically subordinate adoptive parenthood, denying their differences might impose its own subtle costs on adopted children. Reflecting on her own upbringing as an adopted child, philosopher Kimberly Leighton observes that while she was treated equally, she "also felt an unspoken imperative" to "*be the same as*" her biological kin. Her desire to know her biological origins was a source of danger to the family, even while they assured her that being adopted was "not something [she] should be ashamed of."[69] The worry, as Leighton articulates it, is that the "adoptive family is reproduced as 'natural' through the denial of bodily details and traces in the family, who 'passes' as if it were not produced by law."[70] This expectation rendered Leighton "silent about [her] body," so that it could be "considered as part of the body of her family."[71] Leighton thinks the solution is *more* destabilization of the natural, not less: she does not think we should model adoptive relationships on biological ones. But her account is also an ironic caution against a view of "equality" that flattens or denies the differences between *being born from* and *being adopted by* one's parents. It opens up the possibility that the equality of adoptive and procreative bonds requires seeing them as different in crucial respects.

The differences between adoptive and procreative bonds are valuable, as both together shed light on the moral features of parenthood that make it an admirable vocation to enter. Sacrifice is a feature of parenthood (of any kind): even minimal levels of care for children require parents to set aside some ambitions and pursuits they might otherwise undertake. Yet while adoptive parenthood is often modeled on procreative parenthood, we can also invert them and regard adoptive bonds as paradigmatic for procreative parenting.[72] As a form of rescue, the other-regarding

---

69. Kimberly Leighton, "Being Adopted and Being a Philosopher," in *Adoption Matters*, ed. Sally Haslanger and Charlotte Witt (Ithaca, NY: Cornell University Press, 2005), 151. This danger seems particularly acute for *closed* adoptions.

70. Ibid., 153.

71. Ibid., 152.

72. Framing the goods of parenthood through the lens of sacrifice might seem too self-abnegating. However, the joys and benefits such sacrifices generate are not exclusively the child's alone: parents usually find the opportunity to sacrifice for one they love personally rewarding, even if difficult.

aspects of parental sacrifice are often more transparent and potentially more demanding in adoption than procreation. Adoptive parents love and care for a child who is effectively a stranger at the beginning of the relationship. The adopted child often has a history that the parents do not know, yet adopted parents welcome children as *their* children and undertake the responsibilities that come with such a status. The asymmetrical relationship between them is not a reason to love adopted children more than biological children. Rather, it seems plausible to think that parents have the same *pro tanto* reason to love their children, namely, that they are *their children*.[73]

Such an analysis rests on distinguishing between the reasons that the good of procreating supplies from those that the good of parenthood offers. The idea that procreation has a distinct set of reasons is commensurate with the claim that people procreate in order to become parents—but it would entail that they have additional reasons for creating human life that are not necessarily reducible to benefiting the child by bringing them into existence.

What might those reasons be? As procreation is a question of bringing a person into existence, it seems plausible to think that the reasons to do so are uniquely self-reflexive or self-regarding (since the new person does not yet exist). Describing procreative reasons as self-reflexive or self-regarding is odd, considering that it takes two individuals to create a child.[74] Yet it is just such a dynamic that keeps reasons for procreating from being viciously egocentric: the person who generates a child is necessarily incomplete for the task. One might frame the difference between adopted and biological children in terms of the direction in which they come into the parents' circle of concern: adopted children are brought into the parents' circle of concern, while procreated children arise out of it. Where adoption might be undertaken out of altruistic considerations, as a work of charity for the child, it seems difficult to see how procreation could be undertaken in the same manner.

At the same time, the reasons to procreate are intertwined with the nature of the agency at work in bringing life into the world. We might take cues from the above accounts of the value of procreative bonds, which brought to the surface the relative importance of our biology to our personal identity. While it is possible to overstate the significance of biological genealogy for setting the course for a life,

---

73. The cases that Ferracioli uses to demonstrate that adoptive parents lack a *pro tanto* reason to love their child involve failed adoptions. Yet the analogue to ordinary procreation might be the experience of miscarriages. It seems reasonable to think that the "mere fact" of adoption offers an equivalent *pro tanto* reason for unconditional love that the "mere fact" of procreation does, as both signal the entry of the child into the family. Tina Rulli's defense of the unique value of adoption argues that the partial reasons of parenthood can arise from the impartial grounds of rescue, and similarly argues that the relationship of rescue dissolves over time. See Rulli, "The Unique Value of Adoption," 123.

74. In Ephesians 5:29, Saint Paul writes that "no one hates his own flesh, but nourishes it and cherishes it," before describing the union of husband and wife as "one flesh."

our genetic inheritance frames the opportunities we can pursue (at a minimum).[75] Beyond health considerations, though, our interest in our genetic forebearers depends on the significance we give to the relationship between agents' reasons and actions, and the biological relationships they produce. Genetic kinship as such might give us reason for partiality, but it also indicates shared origins and a common history. The significance of that origin depends upon the reasons progenitors had in bringing life into the world. What is true retrospectively about our origins seems similarly true about our reasons to procreate, though, which seem intertwined with the form in which we bring new human life into the world: the self-regarding or self-reflexive reasons that one has to procreate are intertwined with the egoistic concern that one has for both one's own body and the body of one's spouse. Reasons must be conditioned, at some level, by the form of action that one is choosing.

Conclusion

To succeed, a defense of the moral salience of procreative bonds needs to squeeze into an extraordinarily small box. The procreative dilemma is serious: if we attempt to find normative grounds for the convention of valuing procreative bonds, we risk establishing invidious disparities between adoptive and procreative parenthood. If we affirm that both forms of parenthood are equal, we risk trivializing procreative ties. As I have suggested, the difficulty of establishing their salience might be endemic to the question. Appealing to parenthood to explain procreation can only be non-circular if the argument invokes values or reasons outside of parenthood itself.

This chapter has proposed distinguishing between the reasons to procreate and the reasons to parent. While they overlap, the forms through which children come into a family generate different reasons for each: while adoption might disclose a uniquely other-regarding form of love and sacrifice, procreation is animated by distinctively self-regarding reasons. Such an account does not generate invidious disparities between adoptive and procreative bonds in mixed families, because parents have the same reasons to love each of their children—namely, that they are their children. Moreover, such reasons are intertwined with the nature of the act that generates children: while there is a self-regarding dimension, it is inextricable from the place one's own body and the body of one's own spouse have in one's egoistic concern.

Such an account is only a sketch, and awaits further development. Yet it is important to note the challenges that it faces: while we have not assessed the arguments for a positive duty to adopt, the account of reasons and agency must

---

75. The modesty of Rulli's judgment seems wise: genetics, she allows, should "increase the probability of parent–child psychological similarity over adoption, on the whole." Rulli, "Preferring," 15.

be weighty enough to at least explain why we should generate new obligations when we might not be fulfilling the ones we are currently under (as even we do not have obligations to adopt, procreating carries opportunity costs to benefit others). Additionally, the threshold we set for such arguments matters. As noted above, many prominent defenders of the moral salience of genetic bonds lower the epistemic standard for their arguments. While such a methodology might satisfy certain sorts of conventional practices, it also remains vulnerable to skeptical counterarguments aimed at calling those conventions into question altogether.

Chapter 3

THE "GIFT OF LIFE": LUCK, THE INVOLUNTARY, AND PROCREATIVE AGENCY

Perhaps the notion that life is "a gift" that parents extend to the next generation could ground reasons to procreate if parenthood *per se* cannot. As we have seen, finding reasons to procreate that are strong enough to overcome procreative neutrality is difficult. It seems plausible that the value of procreating is intertwined with our (non-viciously) egoistic, self-regarding concerns and with the form of action required to bring life into the world. Enter the "gift analogy" for human life, which could offer a way of explaining why parenthood *per se* is insufficient for generating procreative reasons. The idea that life is a gift has some broad, intuitive appeal: it is a favorite slogan of Instagram influencers, and has been used effectively to encourage organ donation. At the same time, moral philosophers rarely give the analogy more than a drive-by critique. Rivka Weinberg's summary dismissal is typical: recipients do not exist prior to the gift, life is "often literally one hell of a gift," and existence often seems more like a job.[1] Life is "an odd sort of gift," on David Velleman's view. At most, it is a "benefit that prospective parents toss into the void in the hope that someone will turn out to have snagged it, to his own surprise as much as anyone's." Yet the stakes are too high to regard this "so-called gift" as anything other than equivocal.[2] Catherine Mills argues that "gift" implies a giver, and thus is either theologically grounded or an empty metaphor.[3]

Still, hasty philosophical critiques of the gift analogy miss the nuances its defenders give it. When the analogy has been invoked in theological contexts, it has often been used to signal a strong distinction between "being" and "will" in generating human life. Gilbert Meilaender employs the "gift analogy" to argue that children are both a gift and a mystery because they are fruit of their parents' loving union, rather than a chosen product of their wills.[4] In other hands, the analogy has named the reflexive appreciation for one's own life. While the analogy is

---

1. Weinberg, *Risk*, 17–18.
2. J. David Velleman, "II. The Gift of Life," *Philosophy and Public Affairs* 36, no. 3 (2008): 245, 250.
3. Catherine Mills, *Futures of Reproduction* (Dordrecht: Springer, 2011), 88.
4. Meilaender, *Body, Soul, and Bioethics*, 76.

dependent upon an optimistic construal of life, it especially underscores the limits on human agency in procreating. While life *might* be a gift strictly in the sense that its overall benefits outweigh its harms, the "gift analogy" has more flexible uses in reproductive ethics.

Even when the gift analogy is invoked, though, it is often underspecified. Its proponents often abstract away from the conditions of procreative agency that make the analogy interesting or fail to establish how weighty the analogy is relative to skeptical concerns. Because of these failures, this chapter reconsiders the analogy's plausibility and force through evaluating a variety of construals that emphasize both the bodily character of human life and the limits on our agency in creating other human beings. Any account of procreative agency must be attentive to the different ways that humans can now create human life. As such, assessing whether the gift analogy supplies a reason to procreate will require comparing generative intercourse with homologous *in vitro* fertilization. I first turn to Leon Kass' defense of the gift analogy, which situates procreative norms in a teleological metaphysical biology—that is, within "nature." While some such appeal might be necessary to overcome skeptical objections, Kass' division between the means and results of the gift generates problems for his view. To consider more closely the limits of our agency in procreating, I engage in a critical dialogue with Alex Pruss' work before turning to Michael Sandel and Jurgen Häbermas' respective attempts to articulate the virtues of involuntariness in generating life. However, even if such defenses of the gift analogy manage to make it plausible, objections emerge from features internal to the process of procreating—namely, miscarriages. Responding to John Harris' anti-natalist objection on the basis of spontaneous abortions will help clarify the moral significance of involuntary dimensions of procreative agency and the salience of optimistic or pessimistic construals of nature for our account of the permissibility of procreating. I conclude by evaluating whether the gift analogy provides sufficient resources to overcome skeptical debunking challenges to procreating.

Leon Kass on the Giftedness of Life

Leon Kass' invocation of the gift of life structures his arguments surrounding *in vitro* fertilization and variously names both altruistic and egocentrically oriented benefits. In Kass' early work, the gift of life is a "benefit to a child-to-be."[5] Kass argues that when IVF is framed altruistically in this way, the goods of a child's life justifies IVF, so long as the risks of harm are equivalent to ordinary procreation. Similarly, the deaths of embryos as a result of IVF are analogous to the loss of embryos in normal "*in vivo* attempts to generate a child."[6] Kass argues that in ordinary

---

5. Leon R. Kass, *Toward a More Natural Science* (New York: Free Press, 1988), 55.
6. Leon R. Kass, *Life, Liberty, and the Defense of Dignity* (San Francisco: Encounter Books, 2002), 92.

reproductive activity, over 50 percent of fertilized eggs either fail to implant or naturally abort in other ways. Any couple trying to conceive "tacitly accepts the sad fact of such embryonic wastage as the perfectly tolerable price to be paid for the birth of a (usually) healthy child."[7] Kass' view is not a brute consequentialism. While it might be reasonable to think that the proportionality of risks and benefits to the child should stand on its own as a framework for assessing IVF, Kass argues that motivations make a difference. When parents procreate for their own sake, the risks of harms to the prospective child are more morally weighty than if the parents were altruistically focusing on benefiting the child. Because life is a benefit to the child, IVF satisfies the altruistic constraint and so can be licit.

Kass' later work argues that IVF is theoretically permissible even when parents are animated by egocentric concerns, though. The interest in having a child of one's own, Kass contends, is "a couple's desire to embody, out of the conjugal union of their separate bodies, a child who is flesh of their separate flesh made one." Procreation in marriage means parents have a new branch of their family tree and the child has "solid and unambiguous roots." These "natural ties" supply reasons against creating children for the sake of relinquishing them for adoption—but they do not supply an objection to IVF. Like any other would-be parents, married couples who pursue IVF "celebrate ... their self-identification with their own bodies" and "acknowledge the meaning of the living human body by following its pointings to its own perpetuation." They affirm "the gift of their embodied life" and "show their gratitude by passing on that gift to their children."[8] Whether through IVF or ordinary means, the procreating couple strikes "a blow for the enduring goodness of the life in which they participate,"[9] and affirms "the importance of lineage and connectedness."[10]

Kass thus contextualizes the gift of life within claims about both generational continuity and bodily integration. First, he argues that our self-understanding can only be understood generationally. The "perception of one's place in the line of generations" is "crucial to the development of genuine sociability and culture." In being born we inherit a civilization, and so are indebted to those who came before. "We can pay this debt, if at all, only by our transmission of life and teachings to those who come after."[11] In this way, the gift of life is rendered intelligible by the gratitude that parents have for their own lives. Second, this reception and fulfillment of our debts are inscribed upon the body itself, and so constrained by our mortality. "In the navel," Kass writes, "are one's forebears, in the genitalia our descendants." The human body thus sits within the dual horizons of perishability and perpetuation: it both dies and bears the "leanings toward, and capacities for

---

7. Ibid.
8. Ibid., 99–100.
9. Ibid., 100.
10. Ibid., 97.
11. Kass, *Toward*, 293.

procreation."[12] These two dimensions of our bodiliness are mutually explanatory. In procreation we are "saying yes to our own mortality, making of our perishable bodies the instruments of ever-renewable human life and possibility." Mortality thus becomes a benefit, a limit that establishes a "lifespan" that animates the pursuit of children. Kass' dual commitment to the virtues of mortality and to the interest in perpetuating ourselves means the transcendence we aim at comes through reproduction, rather than the indefinite prolongation of our own lives.[13] Kass repudiates transhumanist aspirations in part because they generate an antinatalism: any coveting of an endless life is "in principle hostile to children, because children, those who come after, are those who will take one's place."[14] The gift of life that the child receives is bounded by the mortality of both recipients and by their respective willingness to be replaced by the next generation. "To reproduce means voting with your feet for your own demise," Kass writes.[15] The egoism that animates our interest in our own indefinite perpetuation is in an irreconcilable tension with the "urge to reproduce."[16]

Kass buttresses this understanding of the gift of life by developing a metaphysical biology that provides independent reasons why we should follow the body's "pointings" toward its own reproduction. Kass' renegade biology contends that organisms are inherently purposeful, that they have an "inner 'striving' toward a goal, both in their coming to be and in many of their activities." Kass owns his vitalism: any of the higher forms of life, like human beings, "must have been 'present' potentially in reanimate matter." Matter "has character; matter has possibility; matter is prefiguratively alive."[17] A Darwinian account of evolution entails that the immanent purposes of organisms cannot be globalized. We cannot say nature as a whole has a purpose. But the absence of a global purpose for nature does not undermine the immanent teleology of organisms: once faculties and powers emerge for the sake of living, they seem to "continue to flourish for the sake of living well."[18]

Even at this stage of his work, however, Kass does not straightforwardly derive moral norms from nature. He argues that the natural provides some guidance by revealing the "beautiful or the noble" and by demonstrating the "natural sociality" which is given "articulate regulation by the 'rational animal, political animal.'"[19] Kass situates his account of what nature supplies for ethics between those who suggest that the natural way is "best, because natural," and those who think "that

---

12. Kass, *Life*, 271.
13. Ibid.
14. Ibid.
15. Ibid., 297.
16. Ibid.
17. Kass, *Toward*, 275.
18. Ibid., 274.
19. Ibid., 347.

the natural has no moral force."[20] Nature matters for ethics, even if it is insufficient: metaphysical biology establishes the boundaries in which the good that grounds norms is discerned. It is thus a necessary presupposition to ethical reasoning, such that if its contents are altered, the norms are altered as well. Yet norms are not simply derived from nature. As Kass argues in a later essay, the given can only serve as a norm if there is "something precious" in it "beyond the mere fact of its giftedness." It is the *good* that supplies norms for action, rather than the content of "human nature."[21]

Despite his unwillingness to straightforwardly derive norms from nature, Kass does invoke human nature to cast suspicion on *in vitro* fertilization—but predominately, it seems, for IVF that is used for non-therapeutic reasons. IVF is a "depersonalized" or "dehumanized" way of creating human beings, which transforms the "natural process of generating" into the "artificial process of making." This loss of the distinction between begetting and making reshapes, "at its very root, the nature of man himself."[22] Such a framework poses a threat to the family and, with it, to society.[23] IVF also distorts the meaning of the body, at least for non-infertile couples. Sexuality allows us a means of "transcending [bodily] separateness through the children born of sexual union." Our identity as male and female derives its "deepest meaning" in the "gender-mated prospects for generation through union." IVF obscures this inner relationship of the couple by obscuring their "bodily natures as male and female, as both gendered and engendering." Yet Kass also seems to exempt infertile couples from his worry here, as IVF for them affirms the goodness of their own bodily strivings. In those cases, the instrumentalization of life comes from third parties: "life in the laboratory also allows *other people*" to treat the body as a "mere tool, ideally an instrument of the conscious will, the sole repository of human dignity."[24] Kass offers no definitive arguments that IVF undermines the gendered identity of sex or its significance of empowering us to overcome our separateness. Instead, he hesitantly wonders whether these gendered aspects of our bodily natures can "be fulfilled through the rationalized techniques of laboratory sexuality and fertilization?" "Does not," Kass goes on, the "scientist-partner produce a triangle that somehow subverts the [conjugal] meaning of 'two'?" Here too we risk "paying in coin of our humanity" by generating sexlessly. His tentativeness is notable.[25]

---

20. Kass, *Life*, 93.
21. Leon R. Kass, "Ageless Bodies, Happy Souls," *The New Atlantis* 1 (2003): 9–28.
22. Kass, *Toward*, 73.
23. Ibid., 74.
24. Kass, *Life*, 100. Emphasis mine. The referent of "other people" presumably includes lab workers, but Kass also expands it to anyone who would either contribute to the blurring of generational lines (like sperm donors and surrogates), or who simply think that creating human life in the lab would be optimal.
25. Ibid., 101.

Kass' argument against IVF creates a division between the means and ends of human generation, a division that seems incompatible with his claim that the norm must be grounded in a benefit and not in the givenness of (a) nature. For Kass, IVF can secure the gift of life for a child, which places it on a par with natural procreation. Additionally, the practice fulfills at least one "aspect of [a married couple's] separate sexual natures and of their married life together."[26] Though Kass contends IVF also leads to a "self-degradation and dehumanization," he does not specify what natural reproduction's irreplaceable benefits or goods might be. Granting that both the child-centric and parent-centric benefits of the gift of life can be satisfied through IVF leaves Kass with few resources to oppose the practice—except those he gains from appealing to the "given" of our sexual natures, the very sort of appeal his methodology ostensibly precludes.

Other problems emerge from Kass' division between the means of generating the gift of human life and the transmission of the gift itself. Specifically, Kass' suggestion that IVF satisfies the procreative aspiration works against his emphasis on generational continuity. Kass thinks IVF fulfills the continuity between parents and children. At the same time, if the nature of the male and female is disrupted by externalizing the means of reproduction, this continuity seems precarious. If the parents' internal relationship does not qualify the significance of the life the child receives, then life seems to be a brute biological reality, which would render assessing the benefits of the gifts of life superfluous. Moreover, such a construal introduces a tacit individualism into his account of generational continuity, a bias that Gerald McKenny also sees when Kass "treats interdependence with others as a feature of human necessity rather than dignity."[27] Construing the gift of life independently from the form of life's creation and the role parents play in it introduces a subtle division between the generations. Kass' only criterion for the gift of life is whether generational continuity is preserved, which means the form of the newborn's dependence upon mother and father is up for grabs. To put the worry in McKenny's terms, Kass' concession to IVF indicates that ordinary procreation is a necessity of our nature—but not a part of our dignity.

Paradoxically, in human generation, Kass' individualism leads to the displacement of the individual by the species. Because there is no immortal soul to ground the individual's perdurance, "immortality" is constituted by our replacement by future generations. Mortality thus makes procreation intelligible, and those who generate life must be willing to be replaced by subsequent generations. This view risks reducing relations between the generations to a zero-sum game: there is no way to affirm the immortality of one generation while permitting the procreation of the next. If children are "truly to flower, we must go to seed; we must wither and give ground."[28] While Kass allows that "immortality

---

26. Ibid., 97.

27. Gerald P. McKenny, *To Relieve the Human Condition* (Albany: State University of New York Press, 1997), 142.

28. Ibid.

for oneself through children may be a delusion ... participating in the natural and eternal renewal of human possibility through children is not—not even in today's world."[29] The illusion of immortality that children provide thus is a "noble lie": the individual perishes into nothingness, while one's society is renewed.

Kass' account of procreation, then, splits into two directions. On the one hand, it affirms an individualistic conception of the gift of life, which introduces a rupture in the generational continuity he otherwise affirms. On the other hand, he suggests that the individual should be willing to accept their own self-negation for the sake of passing on their gift to the next generation. By bifurcating the internal relation of man and woman and the meaning of the gift of life, Kass unintentionally seems to dissolve the very conditions on which the distinctive logic of the family might be based, thus rendering it a problem.

Finally, Kass' requirement that procreation's risks be proportionate to its benefits has intuitive force, but raises questions about what sort of scale of harms and benefits he is deploying. Kass suggests that the "gift of life can be held to be morally at least the equal of therapy," in that it offsets or compensates for whatever harms or suffering a child might experience. The idea that benefits might "outweigh" adversities is pervasive in bioethics.[30] Yet this form of calculating the value of life requires a prior judgment about what kind of standard might be used to "weigh up" such reasons, and how much life "weighs" on its own. It is not clear in Kass' work precisely what "price" is unreasonable to pay for the gift of life. A 50 percent rate of embryo loss seems reasonable if we think the embryo does not have equal moral status to adults.[31] However, if embryos have full moral status, then the value of the gift of life must be extraordinarily weighty to compensate for such losses. And if embryos do have full moral status, presumably *some* number of embryo deaths would render procreation dubious. Kass has little to say about such a threshold, which suggests that how valuable the gift of life might be is left to our intuitions.

Kass' account of the gift of life, then, suffers from a number of limitations. For one, it requires that we take at least some guidance from the givenness of human nature, even though Kass objects to deriving norms from nature. And second, it attempts to bracket the meaning of that nature from the means of generation, such that at least certain aspects of it can be satisfied regardless of whether people procreate in the ordinary way or through IVF—only to turn around and then argue that altering the means might reconfigure the relationship between male and female and deny their nature. Such confusions stem, I suspect, from Kass'

---

29. Ibid., 273.

30. Nigel Biggar seems to adopt a similar stance when he suggests that we can be grateful for our existence "if the substantial benefits that the gift continues to confer are not outweighed by the attendant adversities." See *Aiming to Kill: The Ethics of Suicide and Euthanasia* (Cleveland: Pilgrim Press, 2004), 26.

31. See Ibid., 90. We "do not treat even the fetus as fully one of us," because we do not mourn it.

attenuated description of the begetting that human beings undertake, relative to the making that he associates IVF with. Closer attention to the internal limits of the procreative act thus might help clarify precisely what constitutes the gift of life.

Alex Pruss and the Involuntariness of Natural Reproduction

Alex Pruss' evaluation of the intuitions beneath the gift analogy emphasizes the involuntariness that structures ordinary procreation. Pruss names three aspects of ordinary procreation that make the gift analogy plausible.[32] First, the "connection between intercourse and the child is mediated by many causal steps that occur outside our direct control, and the chance of successful conception appears not to exceed about one half on the most fertile of days." This involuntariness *within* the process seems to give the results a peculiar character: new life is closer to a flower than a painting. Additionally, the beginning of the process can be undertaken for its own sake, not just to have a child. Finally, echoing Kass, Pruss observes the process itself is given: we did not choose to generate new human life in this way. As there is involuntariness *within* procreating, so there is an involuntariness *of* procreation. These three intuitions support the idea that the child is a gift.

Yet these intuitions are not obviously reliable. Pruss argues that while IVF does make it easier to think of a child as a "product", the differences between it and ordinary procreation are less pronounced than it might seem. With respect to involuntariness *within* reproduction, IVF still fails at a relatively high rate and includes processes outside our control. Additionally, we would not object if a couple gained minute control over their reproductive systems. While natural procreation has an element of chance, we might randomize our selection of embryos in IVF and so preserve the lottery element. As such, Pruss thus suggests that there is no "innate difference" in the internal involuntariness of IVF and ordinary procreation, even if we tend to judge IVF's success in terms of efficiency. Regarding the second intuition, Pruss suggests someone might undertake IVF for reasons independent of procreation, such as tax incentives or asceticism, which demonstrates the practice has intrinsic value. (At the same time, such reasons would have to justify a serious invasion of the body, which seems unlikely.) Pruss thinks the third intuition is sound, putting him in the ballpark of Kass: when we engage in a process "that is designed by nature or someone else, it is easier to accept the outcome of that process as a gift."[33]

However, Pruss' concessions to IVF seem too hasty. There are important differences between it and ordinary procreation. Consider the location of conception.[34] As we saw in the discussion of Kass' view, generating "beyond

---

32. Alexander R. Pruss, *One Body* (Notre Dame: University of Notre Dame Press, 2013), 412.

33. Ibid.

34. For an account that treats location as morally determinative, see Helen Watt's *The Ethics of Pregnancy, Abortion and Childbirth* (New York: Routledge, 2016).

[the body's] confines" bifurcates the personal agency required to provide an environment for conception from the material reality of fertilization.[35] As others have noted, Such a division breaks procreation into a series of efficient causes, of which the delivery of sperm and an ovum is only one.[36] As Anscombe writes, though, begetting "is a personal act involving actual union of man and woman. It is not the provision of sperm which is then conveyed to an ovum, even if there should then be conception as a result."[37]

In other words, collapsing the involuntariness of procreating into the generalized description of having "many causal steps that occur outside our direct control" obscures the personal significance of involuntariness within ordinary procreation. Consider the experience of shame at being infertile, which is a widespread response.[38] The fact that more people are involved in IVF makes shame less plausible than when reproduction is wholly internal to the couple. This is not to endorse shame as an appropriate response to involuntary childlessness; rather, such shame is an epistemic indicator of the peculiarly personal stakes of procreating. Additionally, the couple's independence in originating the child's life allows them to unambiguously affirm that the child is "ours" or "of us." As the number of agents in the generative process multiplies, so do the number of individuals against whom prospective parents or their children might have a complaint.[39]

Additionally, Pruss' argument that randomizing embryo selection in IVF would create parity with ordinary procreation presupposes that the moral significance of luck is equivalent regardless of whether it is chosen or not. As noted above, the involuntariness *within* the procreative process exists partly because of the involuntariness *of* the procreative process. Yet what an agent does seems different between environments where the luck is inherent and environments where (some)one has intentionally randomized the process.[40] Intentionally choosing to

---

35. Kass, *Life*, 100.

36. Jeff Bishop's argument that contemporary "metaphysics of medicine casts life in terms of efficient causation and matter in motion" applies to procreative ethics as well. Bishop contends that such an account reduces what constitutes an intention to a choice to begin (or not) the series of efficient causes. See Jeffrey Bishop, *The Anticipatory Corpse* (Notre Dame: University of Notre Dame Press, 2011), 128–30.

37. G. E. M. Anscombe, "On Humanae Vitae," in *Faith in a Hard Ground: Essays on Religion, Philosophy, and Ethics*, ed. Mary Geach and Luke Gormally (Exeter: Imprint Academic, 2008), 197. Such an argument is similar to that advanced by Meilaender and Waters, as noted in the introduction.

38. See Linda M. Whiteford and Lois Gonzalez, "Stigma," *Social Science and Medicine* 40, no. 1 (1995): 27–36.

39. Sarah Zhang, "IVF Mix-Ups Have Broken the Definition of Parenthood," *The Atlantic*, July 11, 2019, available online at https://www.theatlantic.com/science/archive/2019/07/ivf-embryo-mix-up-parenthood/593725/.

40. One can choose to randomize embryo selection for a variety of reasons or with different intentions. While both choice and intentions are morally significant, the moral significance of an act is partially conditional on the options one chooses between for

randomize requires a reason, putting a burden on agents for an explanation of their action that they do not have in other contexts. Pruss' concession that not choosing a process makes it easier to think of its results as a gift seems to depend upon this claim: the significance of the involuntariness *of* the process seems to be diminished if the involuntariness *within* the process is actively chosen by an agent. Pruss notes that the randomization of IVF is in tension with the efficiency-criterion that we generally apply to it. But the efficiency-criterion seems to be inherent in the practice, which is ordered toward overcoming the involuntariness *within* ordinary procreation for those who have lost the genetic or reproductive lottery. Both the involuntariness *of* and the involuntariness *within* ordinary procreation are required to make the gift analogy plausible.

In fact, the luck inherent within ordinary procreation calls into question whether the success of the process can be intended by those who begin it. The belief that one can intend to conceive is practically universal. Yet the conjunction of intentions, probabilities, and biological processes in procreating raises serious questions about the limits of intentions, which have not been adequately considered by moral philosophers (or theologians). My suggestion here is subsequently both speculative and tentative: my aim is to point (inconclusively) toward a plausible explanation for why the luck within procreative processes is essential to the gift analogy. I suspect some people resonate with the gift analogy because they think procreating is, in some sense, an outcome unavailable to an individual's intentions. At most, one can intend to unite bodily in an act that hopefully begins the reproductive process.[41]

First, such a formulation depends upon an intention being an action-predicate, rather than a psychological state or predicate.[42] What one intends is inextricable from both the end that one aims at and the form of action one undertakes. More importantly, however, such an approach treats intentions as instances and

fulfilling an end. An intention in an environment where the options are *unchosen* (because there are no alternatives) is less morally loaded than an act where the options are themselves a matter of choice. As such, Pruss' equivocation between the randomization of IVF and ordinary procreation seems dubious.

41. I have previously published a truncated version of this argument, which borrows some of its paragraphs verbatim, in Matthew Lee Anderson, "Anti-Abortionist Action Theory and the Asymmetry between Spontaneous and Induced Abortions," *The Journal of Medicine and Philosophy: A Forum for Bioethics and Philosophy of Medicine* 48, no. 3 (May 16, 2023): 209–24.

42. My explorations on the nature of intention are influenced by Elizabeth Anscombe and some of her interlocutors. See G. E. M. Anscombe, *Intention* (Cambridge, MA: Harvard University Press, 2000). See also Roger Teichmann, "The Voluntary and the Involuntary," *ACPQ* 88, no. 3 (2014): 465–86. Teichmann suggests that for Anscombe, voluntary acts accept the question 'Why?' as relevant, but do not have an answer. On his view, involuntary acts are determined neither by their physiological dimensions nor by the passivity of the agent. One can voluntarily undertake an end in which one is physiologically restricted,

exemplifications of practical knowledge.⁴³ There is a skill-based component to an intention: one cannot intend what one lacks the skills to perform. No one picking up a bow for the first time can intend to hit the bullseye with an arrow from 100 yards away, nor can one intend to play a Mozart sonata when they first sit down at a piano. Both individuals can try, and *intend* to try. If they somehow succeeded without the relevant skill, we would say they performed the act *intentionally* (it was a "lucky shot"). The intention to try is transparent, in that way, such that its moral significance is indistinguishable from intending an end. But the two intentions are not equivalent, and come apart in contexts where one lacks the practical know-how to bring about an end.⁴⁴

If practical knowledge is a prerequisite for having an intention, then it is important to consider what constitutes it. Here I consider two conditions, both of which must obtain: a probabilistic condition and a modal condition. Probabilistically, it seems like there is some (almost certainly vague) threshold of success below which one cannot claim practical knowledge of the task. A 30 percent free-throw shooter does not have the relevant skill to intend to make the shot, but a 70 percent free-throw shooter might.⁴⁵ Similarly, one cannot intend

---

or the accomplishment of which requires passivity. However, it is not the voluntariness or involuntariness of actions in which I am interested here, but the involuntarily (i.e., unchosen or acted upon in any way) biological preconditions of action. To clarify, consider Helen Watt's description of pregnancy as "a goal-directed activity, not a passive state." Such a locution rightfully ascribes agency to the woman who is gestating. However, it is odd to think of other biological processes as falling under an intention, and so being voluntary in the same way. One might intentionally breathe air—but one cannot intend one's heart to distribute blood, at least if 'intend' is a predicate that orders us toward one's action. Instead, one's heart beating is a precondition for action. That is the sense of involuntariness that interests me here. See Helen Watt, "Intending Reproduction as One's Primary Aim," *Roczniki Filozoficzne* 63, no. 3 (2015): 145–6.

43. I follow Rachel Wiseman's account of practical knowledge here, available in her unpublished exposition of Anscombe, "Practical Knowledge and Knowledge of Facts."

44. What constitutes the difference between a skill and luck may be inherently vague. For more on this account of intention, see Alfred Mele and Steven Sverdlik, "Intention, Intentional Action, and Moral Responsibility," *Philosophical Studies* 82, no. 3 (1996): 265–87. Alfred R. Mele, "Intention, Belief, and Intentional Action," *American Philosophical Quarterly* 26, no. 1 (1989): 19–30. Alfred R. Mele and Paul K. Moser, "Intentional Action," *Noûs* 28, no. 1 (1994): 39–68.

45. These probabilistic constraints may be indexed to the kind of activity one undertakes, and whether other agents are involved. A batter's 30 percent success rate in professional baseball would plausibly make a player an all-star, despite the pervasiveness of their failure. On the other side, a 30 percent success rate would mean a pitcher would be regarded as an abysmal failure. This discrepancy has much to do, I think, with the oppositional nature of baseball, which pits two players against each other (unlike, say, shooting free throws).

to win the lottery: the odds of success are too low, even if one has the relevant know-how to put oneself in a position to win. The modal condition is this: one has the relevant practical knowledge if one *would have* successfully accomplished the project, but was prevented by an intrusion of an unexpected event from outside the process or a mistake within it. A free-throw shooter *would have* made the shot, had his arm not unexpectedly buckled from his opponent hitting it or had his hand not suddenly gone numb. In that sense, having practical knowledge seems compatible with the failure of performances, depending on the reasons for their occurrence. Not every dimension of a performance is equally vulnerable to failure, though: some vulnerabilities are structural conditions of an act, while others are extrinsic to it. If a process is ordered such that failure is extremely likely, like the lottery, then it is the kind of process that brings about an end that is unavailable to one's intentions.

If such constraints are plausible, then "conceiving a child" seems like the sort of end that lies beyond the reach of an intention—even though someone who conceives a child does so intentionally.[46] Consider the various success conditions at which an act of sexual intercourse might aim. Helen Watt argues that in ordinary procreation intercourse is "biologically successful beyond the success of the immediate act."[47] While Watt is right biological process is "goal directed," its successful completion is unavailable to those who undertake it. While couples might intentionally seek to improve their odds by taking supplements, improving their health, and so on, there is nothing a man or woman *can* do in the act itself to make the process "biologically successful" (as many infertile couples will attest).[48] The embryo's formation and development are beyond their grasp, and interventions into the process are inherently mediated by the woman's body. Moreover, the probability of failure seems to be intrinsic to the process. In any particular reproductive cycle, the fecundity rate "rarely exceeds 35%," and even under "ideal conditions, the greatest probability of achieving a clinical pregnancy is 30–40%."[49] Those odds clearly improve as couples try to conceive. Indeed, the likely reproductive failure of a single reproductive act makes its repetition almost necessary for a couple to seriously aim at procreating. This suggests that the most one can do in any particular instance of intercourse is *try* to procreate, rather than

---

46. One possible feature of this view is that there is no such thing as an 'unintentional' child, as there can be no such thing as an intended child. Framing children as a side-effect of an intention does not remove it from moral scrutiny, any more than the side-effects of civilian death are irrelevant to the moral analysis of bombing. Everything one brings about 'intentionally,' ends and side-effects, matters for moral reasoning—even if they do not matter equivalently.

47. Watt, "Intending," 145–6.

48. One difference between procreation and other biological processes is that procreation requires two agents.

49. Giuseppe Benagiano, Manuela Farris, and Gedis Grudzinskas, "Fate of Fertilized Human Oocytes," *Reproductive BioMedicine Online* 21, no. 6 (2010): 733.

intend to procreate. Additionally, the correlation of the act's frequency with trying to procreate means the knowledge that a particular act was successful is *inversely* related to one's intentional attempts at procreating. A couple who increases their reproductive odds through frequent attempts in the right conditions makes it harder to know which act was reproductively successful—unlike if they "unintentionally" became pregnant from a single act.[50] In order to improve the probability of procreation, couples must dilute their own agency to the point that (unlike in IVF) they may not be able to name the place or time that a child was conceived. These oddities indicate that the practical knowledge of procreating stands beneath the "social practice of sexual reproduction" or the repeated attempts to generate life within the conditions necessary for its emergence.[51] But procreation is unavailable to the couple as a discrete end in any particular act itself.

There are reasons, then, to think that the intrinsic vulnerabilities and luck within ordinary procreation are structurally necessary for understanding its "biological success" as a gift. Those who adopt the gift analogy to object to IVF emphasize the unavailability of procreating to the couple who engages in sexual intercourse, even if they do not develop the account of agency as extensively as I have here. Roman Catholic theologian William May, for instance, argues every act of intercourse must be "intended to be *open to* the gift of life," which is a cumbersome locution.[52] How can one intend what one cannot bring about, namely receiving (or bestowing) a gift? But if we adopt the above description of the limits of practical knowledge in procreating, May's formulation becomes intelligible. The only discrete end agents can intend in intercourse is a communicative act of love, affection, delight, and pleasure in one's spouse while remaining open to parenthood. What happens after is not up to them.

Michael Sandel and Jürgen Habermas on the Value of Our Limits

If the gift analogy resonates with intuitions about procreating and explains the oddities that seem to be inherent to procreative agency, that is certainly a point in its favor. Yet it is one thing to explain how procreative agency is transformed when we diminish its vulnerability to failure by mitigating its luck-based dimensions; it is another to specify why those features are good. We should heed Kass' caution

---

50. One upshot of this view is that there is no such thing as an unintentional pregnancy. Every couple has *some* intention that causes them to engage in intercourse. However, there are *unintended* and *unwanted* pregnancies, where the couple has (perhaps) taken steps to avoid conception.

51. The phrase comes from John Harris' "Sexual Reproduction Is a Survival Lottery," *Cambridge Quarterly of Healthcare Ethics* 13, no. 1 (2004): 75–90.

52. Emphasis mine. William May, *Catholic Bioethics and the Gift of Human Life*, 3rd Edition (Huntington: Our Sunday Visitor, 2013), 133.

that the given can only serve as a norm if there is "something precious" in it "beyond the mere fact of its giftedness."[53] Michael Sandel and Jürgen Habermas both attempt to explain the value of the limits on our procreative agency. I begin with Sandel.

Sandel construes the gift quality of human life a number of ways. First, he suggests that giftedness is a recognition that our "talents and powers are not wholly of our own doing, nor even fully ours, despite the efforts we expend to develop and exercise them."[54] While this sense of gift is partially "a religious sensibility," it has a "resonance [that] reaches beyond religion."[55] Second, he deploys the terminology of gift to describe how parents ought to relate to their children. Following William May's suggestion that the gifted character of procreation requires an "openness to the unbidden," Sandel argues a gift ethic requires "accepting [children] as they come, not as objects of our design, or products of our will, or instruments of our ambition."[56] Parents can over-determine a child's life through genetic enhancement or hyperactive parenting, which "represents an anxious excess of mastery and dominion that misses the sense of life as a gift."[57]

In Sandel's hands, the gift analogy allows him to draw a sharp contrast between an "ethic of willfulness" and the "claims of giftedness," which enables him to stay above the metaphysical fray by arguing that an ethic of gift supports crucial virtues. Specifically, the ethic of willfulness reshapes "three key features of our moral landscape—humility, responsibility, and solidarity." Humility is constituted by the refusal to engage in mastery over life through retaining an "openness to the unbidden."[58] Moreover, increased mastery would mean our talents are not "gifts for which we are indebted," but "achievements for which we are responsible."[59] Enhancement would thus mean "the explosion, not the erosion, of responsibility." It is one of the benefits of being "creatures of nature, God, or fortune" that we "are not wholly responsible for the way we are."[60] As areas of life "once governed by fate" are transformed into "arena[s] of choice," parents of disabled children will bear a greater (social) responsibility than when genetic screening was not an option.[61]

---

53. Kass, "Ageless Bodies, Happy Souls," 9–28.

54. Michael J. Sandel, *The Case against Perfection* (Cambridge, MA: Belknap Press of Harvard University Press, 2007), 27.

55. Ibid.

56. Ibid., 45.

57. Ibid., 62.

58. ESCR is permissible on his view, since it is not paternalistically mastering the course of another person's life. Ibid., 101 ff.

59. Ibid., 87.

60. Ibid.

61. Sandel's suggestion that access to a particular power increases the responsibility on *everyone,* regardless of whether they use it, is a concession to John Harris' critiques of an earlier version of his argument. See John Harris, *Enhancing Evolution* (Princeton: Princeton University Press, 2007), 109 ff.

Such an explosion of responsibility also threatens our solidarity with those less advantaged than ourselves. If our talents are gifts of "good fortune," then it is a mistake to believe that we "are entitled to the full measure of the bounty [those talents] reap in a market economy." The sense that our talents are "given" animates an interest in sharing them with those who, "through no fault of their own, lack comparable gifts."[62]

Sandel's virtue-oriented account deliberately prescinds from broader theodicy questions or commitments about whether we could reasonably expect the unbidden to be good, for us or anyone else. Though economical, such broader concerns matter for the view's persuasiveness. As John Harris observes, "Now, illnesses are unbidden, as are accidents, invasions by parasites and viruses and for that matter terrorists and foreign forces. I cannot see any obvious, or even subtle, merit in openness to the unbidden."[63] Pessimists might regard the costs to our virtues of controlling fertility as a reasonable trade-off for the option of not creating (putatively) miserable individuals. And if we have pessimistic expectations about the world, then such a trade-off seems even more attractive. Sandel's view thus seems to have limited persuasive reach.

Jürgen Habermas's defense of limiting procreative agency also attempts to avoid metaphysical commitments. Yet rather than orienting his argument around virtues, Habermas argues (eugenic) genetic interventions impinge the freedom and autonomy of children and so disrupt the equality of generations. Following Hannah Arendt's concept of natality, Habermas argues that freedom requires a beginning that "eludes human disposal." Humanity must have a reference point outside one's "socialization fate," or the "lines of tradition and the contexts of interaction which constitute the process of formation through which personal identity is molded in the course of a life history."[64] Birth is a "natural fact" that meets the "conceptual requirement of constituting a beginning we can not control." In other words, birth functions as a given, which establishes a neutral reference point from which people's interventions into our lives can be assessed. The person whose origins are genetically determined or selected by another agent can no longer see their beginning as a "contingent circumstance," as the genetic editor intervenes "*within* the field of action of the programmed person."[65] As Sandel editorializes, the "drive to mastery ... misses the part of freedom that consists in a persisting negotiation with the given."[66]

---

62. Ibid., 91.
63. Harris, *Enhancing*, 116.
64. Jürgen Habermas, *The Future of Human Nature* (Cambridge, UK: Polity, 2003), 59.
65. Ibid., 60.
66. Sandel, *Perfection*, 83.

Habermas' first worry with eugenic interventions is that they disrupt the capacity for the "authenticity" that autonomy depends upon.[67] Every parent has intentions that the child might "appropriate." Yet the intentions of over-bearing parents meet a child who is capable of resistance. The child might engage in a "critical reappraisal of the genesis of such restrictive socialization processes"—that is, they might renarrate their upbringing in ways that transform the significance of their parents' agency and actions.[68] In contrast, genetic interventions eliminate the child's opportunity to critically revise their own origins. The person at odds with their genetic programming is "hopeless": they are barred from the "spontaneous self-perception of being the undivided author of [their] own life."[69]

Habermas' argument seems to overstate the case, as even those who are born without genetic interventions cannot claim to be the undivided authors of their lives: one's genetic inheritance lies outside the scope of reappraisal, regardless of whether it was modified or not.[70] Still, the view could be rescued by more closely focusing on the directness or indirectness of the parents' agency in setting the child's genetic inheritance. The parents' choice to engage in intercourse with each other indirectly determines the child's genetic inheritance, restricting the scope of the child's possible complaints. On the other side, genetic modification determines the child's inheritance directly. As the child's genetic inheritance is immediately affected by the parents' intentional action, they have grounds for additional complaints. In that way, the worry about their autonomy being impinged seems more reasonable.

This modification of Habermas' argument shades into his second argument against eugenic interventions, which contends that they undermine the reciprocity and equality of social roles necessary to form autonomous actors. Liberal equality requires, "in principle, a reversibility to interpersonal relationships," especially when those relationships are characterized by dependency.[71] Habermas contends that genetic interventions undermine this reversibility. The non-revisability and permanence of the parents' intention establish a permanent dependence between the creator and created, which Habermas contends principally bars the created from "exchanging roles with his designer."[72] Though the relationship between creator and created is similarly permanent in ordinary procreation, the social dependence of eugenic relationships is uniquely "irreversible because it was

---

67. Sandel suggests this 'natality argument' is a *third* argument against eugenic interventions, the other two being the disruption to autonomy and equality. For Habermas, however, the description of the 'contingency' of birth forms the basis for those latter arguments and, indeed, even precedes them in the book. See Sandel, *Perfection*, 82–3.
68. Habermas, *Future*, 64.
69. Ibid., 63.
70. Sandel, *Perfection*, 81.
71. Habermas, *Future*, 63.
72. Ibid., 65.

established by ascription," rather than luck.[73] Here, again, much hangs on whether the parents' control over their children's genetic inheritance is either directly or indirectly expressed.

Still, how ordinary procreation secures the reversibility of social roles necessary for inter-generational equality remains obscure. The argument seems to turn on Habermas' claim that the genealogical dependence supplied by ordinary birth "only engages the children's existence ... not their essence"—a distinction that is "notably opaque," as Catherine Mills suggests.[74] Habermas' argument seems to be that genetic *intervention* determines a person's essence, but the genetic *inheritance* from procreation only determines the person's existence. Such an account is coherent only if "essence" is determined within the socialization process. In that case, the permanent genealogical dependence ordinary procreation establishes is compatible with equal, reciprocal social relationships between parents and children, as there is a dimension of the child's life permanently outside both the parents' and children's agency: they stand together as equals before the altar of luck.[75]

At the same time, Habermas' argument might prohibit more than he intends. Habermas attempts to limit his objection to eugenic interventions. Yet as Johnathan Pugh argues, the idea that "therapeutic modifications are morally permissible seems to be in tension with his appeal to natality." Habermas contends therapeutic modifications are permissible because we can assume consent. Yet they also would eliminate genetics as a reference point outside the socialization process, which Habermas argues is necessary for grounding equality and autonomy. As Pugh summarizes, "If the contingency of one's genome is necessary for one's sense of self continuity, and a fortiori autonomy, then this seems to imply that a child who is the subject of a therapeutic genetic intervention, and whose genome is thereby not contingent, cannot have the sense of self-continuity that is necessary for autonomy."[76] Habermas has two paths out of this problem. He could simply bite the bullet and reject the licitness of therapeutic genetic modifications. Or he could adopt a normative account of health as a corollary value with agency and autonomy, which could justify therapeutic genetic interventions while still prohibiting eugenic ones. However, invoking an understanding of health that is not determined by the socializing process would go beyond the liberal, post-metaphysical mode of reasoning Habermas employs.[77] Habermas thus does not have access to the resources he needs to overcome this worry.

---

73. Ibid.
74. Ibid., 64. Mills, *Futures*, 88.
75. This reading means Habermas anticipates Sandel's contention that Habermas does not sufficiently distinguish the determinations of genetic intervention and aggressive parenting. See Sandel, *Perfection*, 80–1.
76. Jonathan Pugh, "Autonomy, Natality and Freedom," *Bioethics* 29, no. 3 (2015): 149.
77. Ibid.

Habermas and Sandel's accounts are closely related, but not identical. Where Habermas objects to the lack of self-determination and reciprocity eugenic intervention entails, Sandel objects that the ethic of willfulness will undermine key virtues. While both attempt to name something valuable about the limits of procreative agency, they both (unlike Kass) frame their arguments without adverting to an account of "nature" or to metaphysics. While such a stance is modest, it renders their arguments less plausible than they might be otherwise. If Sandel is right that certain virtues will be diminished as we move "from chance to choice", such a risk might be worth hazarding if we can plausibly diminish suffering. And while Habermas' post-metaphysical attempt to ground the value of birth outside the "socialization process" is intriguing, it also seems to result in a total repudiation of genetic interventions.

At the same time, incorporating nature as part of the explanation for the "gift analogy" is complicated—as we saw with Leon Kass' account. While there might be something intuitively valuable about the limits on our procreative agency, the process of generating human life is intertwined with death and suffering. Parents might have reflexive, self-regarding reasons for transmitting their life to the next generation, which are undergirded by their participation in nature (Kass); and in acting on those reasons they might initiate a process over which they do not have direct control (Pruss); and the limits of that process might be conducive to their virtue and preserve the equality and autonomy of the child (Sandel and Habermas). Yet it might also involve them in the death of enough human embryos to give us pause about whether such construals of procreating and its limits are too optimistic.

Embryo Death and the Gift of Human Life

For those who think human embryos have full moral status, the problem of natural embryo death requires more finely specifying the conditions under which procreation is licit. John Harris thinks the problem so acute that anti-natalist implications emerge. Because as many as five embryos are lost for every live birth, the "sacrifice of embryos seems to be an inescapable part of the process of procreation."[78] Harris rejects appeals to the doctrine of double effect to escape this problem, arguing that, "once you know that an activity causes harm and you persist in that activity, you are responsible for the harm caused, irrespective of your intentions or hopes about whether harm will occur."[79] The "consequent

---

78. John Harris, "Stem Cells, Sex, and Procreation," *Cambridge Quarterly of Healthcare Ethics* 12, no. 4 (2003): 353–71. See also Ezio Di Nucci, "Embryo Loss and Double Effect," *Journal of Medical Ethics* 39, no. 8 (2013): 537–40.

79. Harris, "Sexual Reproduction," 77. "What matters is what the agents knowingly and voluntarily bring about." Harris, "Stem Cells," 362–3.

miscarriages are"—note the similarity to Kass' formulation above—"a price it is [not] morally justifiable to exact to achieve that end."[80]

There are a variety of paths one might take out of the puzzle.[81] Empirically, one might challenge the accuracy of claims about the rate of embryo death in ordinary procreation. A recent review of the various studies on spontaneous abortion suggests "early embryonic wastage is in the order of 50%," which is already a lower number than Harris uses.[82] But the authors go on: one half of "early spontaneous abortion specimens contain no embryonic/fetal parts. If an embryo is present at all, it is often either severely damaged or fragmented."[83] If true, then only one out of every four embryos dies, as "wastage" from incomplete fertilizations would not count morally.[84]

Yet accuracy about the rate of embryo death is only a partial response. Without further clarification, appealing to such numbers would stay wholly within Harris' blunt consequentialism. Even if we invoke the doctrine of double-effect, questions remain about whether such deaths would be proportionate. As Ezio Di Nucci writes, if "embryos are indeed persons, then it is not at all clear that the [doctrine of double-effect] proportionality condition will be met." Using a high number of

---

80. Harris, "Stem Cells," 363. Harris argues that because we find such deaths in nature, we can licitly cause them—including for embryo research. Kass explicitly repudiates this suggestion, when he contends that there "are many things that happen naturally that we ought not do deliberately." Kass, *Life*, 92.

81. I here presume the embryo has full moral status. Additionally, I set aside many of the objections to this view that I have considered elsewhere, including the role of double-effect. See Anderson, "Anti-abortionist Action Theory and the Asymmetry between Spontaneous and Induced Abortions."

82. Harris acknowledges that a more conservative estimate would be three lost embryos per live birth. See Harris, "Stem Cells," 371 n.46.

83. The authors cite one study in which 16 percent of the embryos recovered from miscarriages were normally developing, while 17 percent of them were malformed and 20 percent degenerating. Another study found that only 21 percent of lost fetuses were well-formed. See Benagiano, Farris, and Grudzinskas, "Fate," 736–7. Gavin Jarvis argues that the relevant studies are highly unreliable. While he suggests that the overall rate of pregnancy lost might be somewhere between 40 and 60 percent, he does not account for the possibility of incompletely formed embryonic material in this number. He raises the possibility that implantation failure in IVF may be related to the absence of a normal karyotype in IVF embryos, which would suggest that well-formed embryos tend to implant while malformed ones do not. See Gavin E. Jarvis, "Early Embryo Mortality in Natural Human Reproduction," *F1000Research* 5 (2016): 2765.

84. Robert George and Christopher Tollefsen take this path, arguing that "severe chromosomal defects" in embryo wastage make it "plausible to infer that in some cases, these defects are so significant that a human embryo probably failed to form." See *Embryo* (Princeton: Witherspoon Institute, 2011), 135.

embryo deaths, Di Nucci contends that ordinary procreation "kills more persons than it does not kill, for example."[85]

Assessing why this objection does not necessarily trouble optimistic approaches to procreating helps shed light on how procreative agency and reasons work.[86] Whether some number of deaths are proportionate to the end being pursued depends, in part, on the standpoint from which the question is being evaluated. For instance, the proportionality of embryo deaths might be framed retrospectively, such that one imputes blame on parents who give birth to a child *after* they suffer five spontaneous abortions. This would be a mistake, though. For one, parents make determinations of value from within partial moral bonds. Neither the miscarried embryos nor the living child are abstract, isolated individuals with whom the parents have no prior connection: they are, instead, individuals who were formed out of the parents' choices, intentions, and bodily lives. Such an account means parents resonate with the deaths of their embryos more deeply than the deaths of strangers.[87] It also restricts the strictly numerical weighing of lives that criticisms from proportionality depend upon: what parent would wish to consider whether the life of their one child is "worth" the deaths of five other embryos, whom they might have once hoped would also become a child? This reluctance to compare their child's value with the lost embryos generalizes. Comparing one life with five as Harris does implies that individuals are fungible with respect to their lives and existence. While such judgments are commonplace in contexts pertinent to public policy, they also disparage the life of the individual. Parental proximity discloses something important about personhood, namely, that individual lives cannot be weighed against each other or replaced by each other.

Alternately, the question of whether five deaths are proportionate might be put prospectively—which is the situation that prospective parents are actually in. Parents do not face a choice between one child and five dead embryos: rather, they face a series of successive choices between nothing happening, having one child, and a spontaneous abortion. While they might estimate their probability of success differently after they suffer spontaneous abortions, they would still have reason to not approach the decision through an aggregated percentage of the risk of embryo loss. For Savulescu, natural procreation gives "every embryo the greatest chance it could have of becoming a baby."[88] The couple knows that they risk causing a miscarriage by engaging in reproductive activity. But even if they have experienced five prior miscarriages, they do not know whether the next attempt will lead to another one. While procreation involves the risk of embryo

---

85. Di Nucci, "Embryo Loss," 538.

86. I have previously published this section and expanded the literature it interacts with. See "Anti-Abortionist Action Theory."

87. See the discussion on Kolodny's work in the previous chapter.

88. Julian Savulescu, "Embryo Research," *Cambridge Quarterly of Healthcare Ethics* 13, no. 1 (2004): 71.

death, such losses are not *foreseen* or *known*.[89] That alters the moral calculus, as most worthwhile activities are accompanied by risks to ourselves and others. Parents risk their children's lives by driving them to piano lessons; mothers risk their own by deciding to gestate. Risks are endemic to pursuing worthwhile ends, and the more valuable the good, the more risk we are willing to accept.

The willingness to accept such risks is intertwined with the gift analogy, then. The precariousness of procreation and the fact that success lies beyond our intentions underwrite our intuitions that life is uniquely valuable.[90] There is no room for valorizing the survival of the fittest. Instead, assessing life in terms of its fragility and vulnerability is a heuristic for assessing how and why we care about it. Prospective parents can reasonably accept the proportionality of embryo loss, because they recognize the incomparability and irreplaceability of individual lives. The cold calculation the "spontaneous abortion" objection involves misses the fact that embryos originate from within the procreative couple's life, which both gives them reason to not engage in comparative assessments of their value and puts them in a deliberative context in which they only (though not merely) risk a spontaneous miscarriage. Such a lowered threshold matters, as procreating lies beyond the scope of their intentions: the most the couple can intend is to put themselves in a situation where new life is a real possibility.

The Limits of Optimism

The idea that life is a gift ranges across a wide variety of questions and appeals to a number of deep intuitions. It names everything from the joyful identification with and transmission of bodily life in the face of mortality to the involuntariness *of* the procreative process and the luck *within* it. Those limits mean we do not bear the full weight of responsibility for our descendants' existence, and that there is a reference point outside our social relationships that enables us to stand as equals. Yet the peculiar form of procreating also illuminates what is distinctly valuable about entering parenthood in this way, as the end of a new human being stands outside or beyond what the hopeful couple can intend to accomplish. Procreators are something more than efficient causes of new "existences": we are personal agents whose descendants emerge from our bodies through an act of mutual love. The involuntariness and luck that are intrinsic to ordinary procreation mean

---

89. On the ethics of risk imposition in procreating life, see Weinberg, 2015.

90. David Wendler has argued that pro-lifers are complacent about spontaneous abortions, because they think the "natural process" of conception and development establishes the "fundamental structure" of our lives, which we are morally obligated to accept and not interrupt. While my view is related to this, it arises from the peculiarities of procreative agency—rather than the "fundamental structure" of our lives. See David Wendler, "Understanding the 'Conservative' View on Abortion," *Bioethics* 13, no. 1 (January 1999): 32–56.

those who try to conceive must repeatedly engage in a (hopefully) loving union with each other as the source of their child's existence. This luck-based dimension of procreation makes the quality of the originating relationship of paramount importance: if procreation only required one act, the internal quality of the sexual union would be less important. But as attempts increase, the importance of the couple having non-instrumentalizing, unitive reasons increases as well—at least if they are to avoid treating each other as means for the sake of a child. The parent–child relationship that animates the procreative interest thus includes the whole cluster and complex of mutual cares and concerns between male and female. Meilaender is right: procreation is a sign of the luxuriousness or lavishness at the heart of a union. Because it necessarily exceeds the intentions and abilities of individuals to bring it about, the gift of life overflows from the relationship's inner life.

Yet this does not entail procreating is beyond our outside reasoning, or that reasoning subordinates it to the will. People who stand at the threshold of parenting need some story for why they should procreate rather than adopt. One potential reason that has emerged from this discussion is that they enjoy a non-vicious gladness in their own bodily lives and in the lives of their spouses—as Kass gestured at. This affirmation would be egoistic and self-referential, yet without being individualistic or instrumentalizing. Gladness animates parents' interest in expanding their circle of concern in a way that makes visible their intrinsic and mutual affirmation of their own lives.[91] Such reflexive enjoyment need not be an invidious pride, as it is not an assertion of superiority. There is nothing about such gladness that excludes other people from being equivalently happy, or that would preclude the procreating couple from equally rejoicing at other people's joy. Indeed, insofar as gladness is a reason to bring new human life into the world *with* another, it seems uniquely *non*-proprietary and other-regarding.[92]

One might worry that such an approach risks instrumentalizing the child by reducing them to a project of the parents' own egoistic self-aggrandizement. Such a concern is doubtlessly legitimate: parents do sometimes overlook their children's uniqueness and regard them as vehicles for their own vicarious sense of glory. Yet as a normative matter, there is nothing in such an egoistic account of entering parenthood that precludes the self-denying, sacrificial, other-regarding love that parenthood itself demands. Egoism is not egocentrism: insofar as one becomes a parent, the self-regarding reasons one might have to do so overlap with the other-regarding reasons of parenthood. Egoism and altruism need not necessarily be in the competitive, exclusive relationship they are often reduced to.

Grounding reasons to procreate in partiality for one's own organic life, and for the life of one's spouse, offers a strong reason to procreate rather than adopt—

---

91. This dimension of Kass' argument seems right.

92. Such a constraint would supply grounds for questioning forms of creating life that do not include this other-regarding feature, including cloning and anonymous gamete donation. Those are implications that I am happy to accept.

without entailing that adoptive parenthood is a secondary or derivative type of parenthood. The disparate burdens of adoption and procreation are present even in the manner of entry into them: the financial, regulatory, and temporal burdens required to become adoptive parents are extraordinary compared to the relative efficiency that procreation offers most couples (though by no means all). Avoiding the inefficiencies of adoption is not a reason to enter parenthood through procreation: the gladness and knowledge about one's own life and the life of one's spouse that I have gestured at are more basic and fundamental than avoiding suffering or difficulty. The enjoyment of *one's own* supplies a reason to expand the circle of *one's own,* and to do so in ways that are directly and immediately derived from that circle. Still, insofar as adoptive parenthood uniquely exemplifies the virtues that parenthood demands, the fact that procreation remains an intelligible option is a reminder that not all are called to moral sainthood.

At the same time, pessimistic theodicy problems lurk behind attempts to specify the value or benefit of procreative parenthood. If ordinary procreation did entail that five embryos die for every one that lives, the threshold for justifying procreation would be extremely high. In that case, questions would arise about whether "nature" is itself disposed toward life. While mitigating defenses of the sort I have brought forth would doubtlessly be possible, it would be more difficult to claim that the value of procreating proportionately worthwhile given the scope of the expected destruction. However, if the ratio is inverted it begins to look like "nature" is ordered toward procreation. A ratio in which only 25 percent of embryos perish preserves the luck that is intrinsic to procreation: one still does not know whether or which gametes will combine. But it diminishes the force of the theodicy problem that embryo wastage presents from the outset.[93]

Even if the lower threshold is persuasive, though, it calls into question just how secure a pro-natalist optimism can be if it is built on such a foundation. Criticisms that the gift analogy reduces to theological claims are too strong: there are compelling reasons to value limits in our procreative agency. However, such criticisms are not wholly beside the point. "Nature" is such an expansive ground for defending the proportionality procreating that it is reasonable to wonder whether it is a placeholder for the divine. At the very least, the defense of involuntariness that renders the "gift analogy" plausible and the optimistic interpretation of nature both appeal to a complex of intuitions, arguments, and metaphysical judgments—each of which is contentious. It is hard to see how this type of procreative optimism could escape the many vulnerabilities that beset it, each of which weakens our confidence in the presumptive licitness of procreating.

Finding normative reasons to procreate that are weighty enough to overcome pessimistic or skeptical debunking arguments on philosophical terms is challenging. There is something to Anscombe's judgment that it might

---

93. Given the inherent technical difficulties of identifying the actual rate of embryo loss, it is plausible that our willingness to adopt a particular ratio is founded upon background, metaphysical commitments about 'nature' and its ends.

take "prophetical revelation or a blind belief in the care of God" to explain the normative grounds for having children.[94] The procreative neutrality embedded in The Asymmetry seems to lead to a default anti-natalism. We were no more successful by approaching the question through the lens of parenthood: the option to adopt undermined the distinctive value of procreative bonds, such that even their defenders repeatedly lowered the threshold for justifying them from proof to plausibility. The gift analogy provides a philosophically interesting way of grounding reasons to procreate, which distinguish them from the reasons to parent: yet the presuppositions of the argument (nature, the value of limited agency) are extremely contentious, and their plausibility likely dependent upon other background commitments. While the analysis offered illuminates the fault-lines for grounding an optimistic account of bringing new human life into the world, philosophical defenses of procreating still leave the practice in a precarious theoretical position. Whether the theology of Karl Barth can supply a more stable and secure answer to why we should procreate is the burden for the latter part of this volume.

---

94. Anscombe, "Why," 48.

Chapter 4

NEITHER OPTIMISM NOR PESSIMISM: KARL BARTH AMONG THE MORAL PHILOSOPHERS

Despite humanity's obvious practical commitment to carrying on the species, finding normative reasons to procreate proves harder than it might seem. At best, philosophical defenses of procreating bottom out in ambivalence: even when they recognize the value of procreating, debunking arguments are frequently invoked to qualify procreation's force. If the benefits future generations receive from procreation do not weigh in our reasons, then a *de facto* anti-natalism seems warranted. Constructivists rightly argue that parenthood is a non-reducible source of reasons, but then have little to say about why people should procreate rather than adopt. Thinkers like Leon Kass defend procreating on grounds that life is a gift—yet the force of such a view turns out to be intertwined with highly contested background commitments about nature, which take a localized form in the problem of natural embryo death. Through it all, we remain trapped in a contest of intuitions about the value of procreating and are hampered by an ineliminable ambiguity about the epistemic threshold defenses of procreating must cross in order to be persuasive.

It is tempting to throw up our hands and embrace a procreative fideism that would escape these challenges only by ignoring them. That is not Karl Barth's path, though. While Barth is explicit that there are times when the Christian community must "seriously try to maintain the race," the "homely and courageous confidence in life" he commends is still critical.[1] In a talk given while working on his doctrine of creation, Barth reiterated the importance of this confidence in the face of a European malaise: "Shall we be able, while always looking to Jesus Christ … to live in spite of everything somewhat more positively than negatively, somewhat more joyfully than sadly, patiently than impatiently, and, in spite of all the decline in Europe, to live with thankful rather than sorrowful hearts, and in confidence rather than in despair?" Barth's endorsement of hope in this context is not unqualified, though: "Anything other than 'somewhat more,'" he writes, "is scarcely possible." When we are really Christians, then we are enabled to "live a *little more* positively, joyfully, patiently, thankfully and confidently than the reverse."[2]

---

1. Barth, *Church Dogmatics* III/4, 268–9.
2. Barth, "The Christian Message in Europe Today," 179.

Even so, Barth's defense of this "confidence in life" is stronger than that which moral philosophy can offer. It is also a *complicated* confidence. It has nothing in common with straightforward pro-natalist endorsements on the basis of Genesis 1:28, and is manifestly opposed to any ethno-nationalist justifications for procreating. Barth's endorsement of a "confidence in life" and corresponding exhortation to procreate is surprising given his emphasis on the abrogation of any obligation to procreate and the relative inattention he pays to procreation's theological significance.[3] Barth is unequivocal that after the birth of Christ "the propagation of the race ('Be fruitful, and multiply,' Gen. 1:28) has ceased to be an unconditional command."[4] It is a "very heathen or even Jewish type of thought to try to make it an invariable rule" that faith should always and everywhere generate the "cheerful confidence in life" required to procreate.[5] How this nullification of the obligation to procreate and the "confidence in life" arise out of Barth's theology, and how they might be reconciled, will occupy the rest of this book.

Methodologically, this theological turn is not an attempt to persuade philosophers to adopt its conclusions or the framework that produces them. Nor is it an attempt to justify the "confidence in life" in their terms. Such an apologetic strategy would be inimical to Barth's thought, which begins the work of theological ethics from the revelation of Jesus Christ *alone*. As the "form of [God's] electing grace," the command of God as revealed in Christ is "the starting-point of every ethical question and answer." This starting point means that theological ethics cannot regard philosophical ethics as an authority to which it must answer. Theologians must not "attempt to establish and justify the theologico-ethical inquiry within the framework and on the foundation of the presuppositions and methods of non-theological, of wholly human thinking and language."[6] Barth's infamous, notorious, scandalous—the adjectives all apply—adherence to the primacy of revelation for the moral life and opposition to "natural theology" has generated considerable consternation and discussion. Even so, Barth's fideism is not anti-rational. As George Hunsinger has written, there is a "rationalism" that is internal to faith, which he describes as "reason within the limits of revelation

---

3. As Gary Deddo Writes, "Barth has not said very much about the positive significance of procreation." See Gary W. Deddo, *Karl Barth's Theology of Relations* (Eugene, OR: Wipf and Stock, 2015), 226.

4. Barth, *CD* III/4, 268.

5. Ibid., 272. William Werpehowski wonders whether "one basis of Barth's limited treatment" of parents and children "is a reluctance to endorse any but the most qualified 'pro-natalism' as over against, by his (perhaps mistaken) lights, Roman Catholic and Jewish thought." William Werpehowski, "Reading Karl Barth on Children," in *The Child in Christian Thought*, ed. Marcia J. Bunge (Grand Rapids: Eerdmans, 2001), 404.

6. Barth, *CD* II/2, 519–20.

alone."⁷ So long as theology remains true to its own task of articulating the revelation of the Word of God and does not cede its role as adjudicator of reality to philosophy, it can be "absolutely open to all that it can learn from general human ethical inquiry and reply."⁸

Nowhere does Barth practice such an openness to other disciplines more than in his doctrine of creation, which is replete with careful readings of philosophers and immanent critiques of them. Barth contends that behind every worldview lies the problem of "pure becoming," or the question of the emergence of something from nothing. Barth does not think theology closes down inquiry from other disciplines into the question: it is "quite improper for theology to assume *a priori* an attitude of scepticism" toward philosophy's answers to it, he writes.⁹ As Kenneth Oakes writes, Barth's theology means "engagements with 'non-theological' sources remain open," and that their "potential fruitfulness for theology cannot be determined beforehand."¹⁰ At the same time, the Christian doctrine of creation sets the threshold for what a satisfactory answer involves, namely, that the world is a benefit or good rather than an "event which is neutral in face of the weal and woe of the evolving and evolved cosmos."¹¹ Within those terms, theology is free to encounter and listen to philosophy—and even to direct its attention to the same questions that philosophers pursue.

Yet theology cannot direct its attention to those questions *in the same way* or in the *same direction* as moral philosophers take them up, namely, as questions to which the answer remains entirely open. As the question of good and evil has been answered decisively and revealed by Jesus Christ, theological ethics can only "attest and confirm and copy" this decision—rather than investigate it as though it were undertaking a putatively neutral enterprise like philosophy (ostensibly) does.¹² On the one side, then, Barth contends that theology can remain open to

---

7. George Hunsinger, *How to Read Karl Barth* (Oxford: Oxford University Press, 1991), 49. My later invocation of "procreative fideism" should be construed this way, namely, as an affirmation of the primacy of faith for discerning moral norms, and so a rejection of reason's status as an independent arbiter for the good life.

8. Barth, *CD* II/2, 524.

9. Barth, *CD* III/1, 341.

10. Additionally, Barth's "lasting contribution to contemporary theology is not that theologians are free to ignore the concerns and criticisms of other discourses, but that these cares can be taken up and engaged within the process of discussing Christian doctrine and practice in a way free of anxiety and pretensions to self-justification." See Kenneth Oakes, *Karl Barth on Theology and Philosophy* (Oxford: Oxford University Press, 2012), 253. See also 204–6 for an excellent discussion on "pure becoming" and Barth's use of philosophy in his doctrine of creation.

11. Barth, *CD* III/1, 342.

12. Barth, *CD* II/2, 536.

general inquiry, which can implicitly bear witness to this answer (either negatively through its failures or positively by unwittingly attesting to the truth). On the other, Barth suggests that theology "cannot adopt the questions and answers" of an ethics that attempts to investigate the foundations of the answer to good and evil.[13] Instead, ethical reflection and discussion involve faithfully repeating what God has said to us in revealing the good in Jesus Christ—and to that extent functions as a "question and summons" to philosophical inquiries into the good, a confrontation that Barth describes as "irenico-polemical."[14]

Moral theology must renounce any attempt to establish the good on terms outside the revelation of Jesus Christ, then, even while remaining open to the deliverances of "general human inquiry and reply." Whether this approach is finally tenable, much less consistent, lies beyond the scope of this book.[15] Admittedly, the order of presentation between philosophy and theology offered in these pages departs from Barth's own methodology. Because theological thinking is bound to the reality of Christ's revelation, Barth contends that it cannot "wander around in the field of other possibilities" or regard the reality of Christ's disclosure as "a mere possibility."[16] Yet listening to moral philosophy's questions about procreating is an effort to avoid assuming an "*a priori* an attitude of scepticism" toward the discipline's ability to find answers to them. More than anything, this listening has highlighted philosophy's self-conscious inadequacy to provide a meaningful account of procreating *without* articulating the foundations of good and evil and the value of the species, a task that at least some philosophers are aware takes the discipline to the limits of its powers. In this case, the turn to think (explicitly) theologically about procreating is not an attempt to offer solutions to moral philosophy's problems: again, Barth himself regards procreating as a question for his own distinctive theological reasons, as we shall see. But putting these two diverse outlooks side-by-side allows theological ethics to function as a "question and summons" to the work of moral philosophers, while also inviting theological thinking into a clarity and precision that it might lack otherwise. Giving close attention to moral philosophy need not entail either theology's wholesale repudiation or Babylonian captivity. If the order of my presentation differs from Barth's, my aim is fundamentally in keeping with his

---

13. Ibid.

14. Ibid., 537.

15. Gerald McKenny has recently criticized Barth's distinction between philosophy and theology's ways of attesting the moral norm for (among other problems) diminishing the value of our creaturely nature, undermining accountability, and leaving us without a principled basis for cooperation with those outside the church. I am hopeful, but not confident, that Barth's ethics can escape these charges. See McKenny, *Karl Barth's Moral Thought*, 33–51.

16. *CD* II/2, 536.

uses of philosophy in his doctrine of creation, namely, to elucidate the contours of the Word of God through both drawing antitheses and finding surprising points of congruence.[17]

Theological reasoning about the moral life is complicated, though, by Barth's contention that appropriate human action is conformity to God's gracious command. The immediacy and definiteness of this command, which occurs only within the encounter between humanity and God, has sometimes led to charges that Barth leaves insufficient room for moral deliberation and discernment.[18] Though Barth is clear that ethics cannot "pronounce an anticipatory judgment on the good or evil of human action in encounter with the command of God," it can "give definite instruction with regard to this event."[19] This preparation for the encounter, or "special ethics," requires both attending to the theological framework through which we are formed to hear the divine command and the social conditions into which the command reaches—both of which, as we shall see, Barth invokes in engaging in his special ethics of procreation.[20] Unpacking the theological framework within which Barth's account of procreation sits will demand attending to Christology and anthropology, creation and eschatology. As Nigel Biggar argues, the "formed reference" takes its particular shape through an affirmation of God's constancy through salvation history, which is differentiated between the spheres of creation, reconciliation, and redemption.[21] While these three spheres are united, "the one will of God, without becoming disunited within itself, has different forms; and similarly His command, while it always commands man to do one thing, has different elements."[22] This theological context means that it would be a mistake to look only to Barth's explicit treatment of parents and

---

17. As Oakes write, "It is only in Barth's doctrine of creation in CD III that he performed and embodied the kind of relationship of comprehensive listening, learning, and criticism between theology and philosophy he recommended in CD II/2." He goes on: "Barth returned to a kind of correspondence or congruence account of theology and philosophy, but one that is more sceptical of the possibility of this correspondence being of a positive kind. Nevertheless, Barth argued that philosophy can and does offer equivalences to Christian doctrine that are worthy of and demand theology's attention." Oakes, *Karl Barth on Theology and Philosophy*, 222–3.

18. Robert Willis' complaint remains paradigmatic of the charge, namely, that Barth's account leads to a "total exclusion of the necessity of *deliberation* in ethics." See Robert Willis, *The Ethics of Karl Barth* (Leiden: E.J. Brill, 1971), 183.

19. Barth, *CD* III/4, 18.

20. There is considerable disagreement among Barth interpreters about how this "formed reference" can and cannot serve theological reasoning. I prescind from weighing in on that debate until my reading of Barth's special ethics of procreation emerges.

21. Nigel Biggar, *The Hastening That Waits* (Oxford: Oxford University Press, 1993), 27–30.

22. Barth, *CD* III/4, 29.

children for his understanding of procreation: we need to see how Barth locates procreation in his broader doctrine of creation, in order to fully discern what a "formed reference" for the divine command might require here and now.[23] At the same time, discerning what sort of reasons we have to procreate will require further elaboration of how the divine command intersects with human nature and flourishing. Attending to Barth's doctrine of creation has the virtue of clarifying how reasons to procreate might (and might not) function in a doctrinally saturated ethics.

This chapter considers Barth's doctrine of creation with an eye toward three interrelated questions. First, in Barth's framework, why does God create? Second, is it possible to speak of immanent goods or ends in creation, or does Barth's

---

23. As Barth's treatment of procreation happens (understandably) in his doctrine of creation, volume III of the *Church Dogmatics* will take precedence. Other sections of Barth's corpus will be invoked as necessary—though my interest in Barth's theology is normative, rather than genealogical. While Barth's ethics has a vast secondary literature, Matthew Rose notes that it "has inspired relatively little work on individual moral problems." (See Rose, *Ethics*, 12.) One notable exception for our purposes is Gary Deddo's valuable treatment of Barth's understanding of parents and children. While Barth's understanding of sex difference has received considerable attention, Deddo's work is unique in attempting to discover a "positive theological interpretation of the meaning of procreation and parenting" in Barth's thought (Deddo, *Theology*, 347). I will affirm a number of Deddo's readings, but the analysis I offer considers aspects of Barth's thought that Deddo either ignores or gives only cursory attention to. Deddo overlooks how Barth's account of creation challenges both optimism and pessimism, and pays no heed to how such a context frames the "confidence in life" that stands beneath a society's procreative practices. Second, Deddo locates Barth's special ethics of parents and children predominately against the backdrop of *CD* III/2, which is understandable given Barth's structural parallels between it and *CD* III/4 (cf. Deddo, *Theology*, 40). Yet such a move means Barth's understanding of procreation's role in III/1 gets short shrift. A sharper account of how Barth construes the duty to procreate *ante Christum natum* helps clarify why Barth thinks the general obligation has been removed after Christ. Third, Deddo says nothing about Mary's relationship to Christ, nor about her own role in a fully formed ethic of procreation. Closer attention to Barth's understanding of Mary, though, helps build out Barth's account of the relativization of procreation in ways that not even Barth himself pursues. [Dustin Resch confirms this lacuna in *Barth's Interpretation of the Virgin Mary* (Farnham: Ashgate, 2012), 88]. Finally, and most importantly, Deddo says almost nothing about how Barth's account of humanity's constitution and limits structures procreation or its significance. Deddo suggests that because Barth's accounts of "Freedom for Life" and "Freedom in Limitation" "follow after the section of [his] central concern," neither they nor their corresponding sections of Barth's theological anthropology are "essential for [his] presentation" (Deddo, *Theology*, 40). This leaves out crucial resources for understanding both procreation's theological significance and the positive reasons Christians have to pursue it. My analysis, then, of Barth supplements and expands Deddo's work, even while occasionally correcting it.

4. Neither Optimism nor Pessimism

theocentric framework finally eviscerate the distinctiveness of creation, as has so often been alleged? And how does Barth's doctrine of creation relate to optimism and pessimism as outlooks and, by extension, help us understand the various optimisms and pessimisms about procreating we encountered in previous chapters? Barth writes his doctrine of creation in the shadow of the Second World War, which animates his concern to ground creation's goodness in God and funds his engagement with the theologies and philosophies that he thinks led to such a crisis.[24] While socio-political questions lurk everywhere, my aim here is more narrowly focused on depicting the broad theological backdrop to Barth's ethics of procreation and its ethical significance. In the end, Barth's account of our participation in creation through Christ offers us a confidence in creation's goodness that transcends the optimistic and pessimistic frameworks that moral philosophy is stuck within, though in a way that avoids an equivalence or neutrality between them.

The Trinitarian Ground of Creation

In order to know the world as *creation*, rather than as nature or existence, we must see it as a work of the Triune God. For Barth, the reality of creation begins in God's inner life. Creation is a work of God's free love, in which God's "inward glory" overflows into a reality that is distinct from Himself through an act aimed at establishing fellowship between the creature and Himself.[25] This "overflowing" is properly Trinitarian, even if Christology will have a pre-eminent place in our knowledge of creation's meaning and significance. God does not "cause" creation in the manner in which the sun causes light, much less any other type of causation we might think of: the only real analogy to creation is "in the eternal begetting of the Son by the Father, and therefore only in the inner life of God Himself."[26]

---

24. As Eberhard Busch observes, Barth contends in *CD* III/1, 414 that events since 1933 were "the bad fruit" of a "bad tree." Busch comments that it is "thus understandable that in the process of his attempt to rediscover the Creator's Yes, he grapples with modern thought more tenaciously than any other theme in his work, defining line by line that bad tree that produced such wicked fruit." See Eberhard Busch, *The Grand Passion* (Grand Rapids: Eerdmans, 2004), 177.

25. Barth, *CD* III/1, 14–15. As Barth writes in II/1, it is out of an "overflow of [God's] essence that He turns to us." "That He is God—the Godhead of God—consists in the fact that He seeks and creates fellowship with us." This seeking is God's *loving*, the "act as that of the One who loves." *CD* II/1, 273, 275. See also II/1, 283.

26. Ibid., 15. The German reads "*die nur in der ewigen Zeugung des Sohnes durch den Vater, die also nur im inneren Leben Gottes selbst.*" See *KD*, III/1, 13. It is interesting to note that Barth uses the same term here for "begetting" that he will later use to speak of human begetting as distinct from birth (*Geburt*). Cf. KD 70, 190. See also KD III/4, 473, where Barth invokes a similar distinction in the context of abortion.

As the Father, God "begets" Himself in the Son, and with the Son is the origin of the Spirit—which means that we rightly speak of the Father as Creator.[27] As Barth writes:

> In the same freedom and love in which God is not alone in Himself but is the eternal begetter of the Son, who is the eternally begotten of the Father, He also turns as Creator *ad extra* in order that absolutely and outwardly He may not be alone but the One who loves in freedom. In other words, as God in Himself is neither deaf nor dumb but speaks and hears His Word from all eternity, so outside His eternity He does not wish to be without hearing or echo, that is, without the ears and voices of the creature. The eternal fellowship between Father and Son, or between God and His Word, thus finds a correspondence in the very different but not dissimilar fellowship between God and His creature.[28]

The fellowship that God aims at with the creature in creating is founded upon the election of Jesus Christ and is brought to its completion through the covenant. In that way, Christ is the "inner divine analogy and justification of creation," and is both its noetic *and* its ontic basis.[29] Jesus Christ "is the key to the secret of creation." The divine self-witness in Jesus Christ supplies the "basis, norm and meaning" of the relationship between the Creator and creature, because creation is governed by the end of establishing fellowship with God in Him and revealed in Him.[30] The Christological basis of "God created" means the statement is not "a postulate or hypothesis," but may be confessed with "absolute certainty."[31]

While the fellowship of the Father and Son is the prototype for creation, the Holy Spirit makes possible the existence of the creature. As the Holy Spirit in God's inner life is the "communion and self-impartation" of the Father and the Son "realised and consisting between both from all eternity," there pre-exists in the Spirit "the whole reality of the fatherly compassion of God, His self-expression, His own glorification in His Son, the whole truth of the promise, the whole power of the Gospel, and therefore the whole order of the relation between God the Creator and His creatures."[32] This entails that the creature has its pre-existence in the Spirit: the Holy Spirit "makes the existence of the creature as such possible,

---

27. Ibid., 49. "As the Father, God procreates Himself [*erzeugt*] from eternity in His Son, and with His Son He is also from eternity the origin of Himself in the Holy Spirit; and as the Creator He posits the reality to all the things that are distinct from Him." See *KD*, 52.

28. Ibid., 50.

29. Ibid., 55.

30. Ibid., 25. "Jesus Christ is the Word by which the knowledge of creation is mediated to us because He is the Word by which God has fulfilled creation and continually maintains and rules it" (ibid., 29).

31. Ibid.

32. Ibid., 56.

permitting it to exist, maintaining its existence, and forming the point of reference of its existence."[33] As John Thompson writes, the Holy Spirit is the "confirmation and guarantee of [creation's] validity in the will and purpose of the Father and the Son," which is a distinct but not separate work.[34] Though the New Testament predominately speaks of the work of the Spirit in soterio-eschatological terms, Barth here describes the "deliverance effected by the Holy Spirit" as "the confirmation of creation when God first gave to man the life which he then lost." As the giver of the *new* life of salvation, the Spirit is indirectly revealed to be the "*conditio sine qua non* of creaturely existence, i.e., of its glorification, its hope, its adaptability for its appointed existence and activity."[35]

As creation comes from God, so its direction and end is God. "The aim of creation is history," Barth writes, a history in which God "has patience with the creature and with its creation gives it time—time which acquires content through these events [of reconciliation and redemption] and which is finally to be 'fulfilled' and made ripe for its end by their conclusion."[36] The time that humanity is given is ordered by the covenant, which, as the theme of history, encloses and provides a reference point for all other history.[37] In Barth's formulation, creation is the "external

---

33. Ibid.

34. John Thompson, *The Holy Spirit in the Theology of Karl Barth* (Allison Park: Pickwick Publications, 1991), 160-1. As Philip Rosato writes, Barth "in effect proposes a theology of man's pre-existence in the Holy Spirit from eternity, which perfectly parallels his understanding of Christian faith as pre-existing in the eternal divine election of Jesus Christ." See Rosato, *The Spirit as Lord* (Edinburgh: T&T Clark, 1981), 103. Andrew Gabriel contends that Barth's doctrine of creation has a "binary character" between the Father and the Son, which arises from his lack of an explicit endorsement of the Holy Spirit's *creative* activity in creation. The lack of emphasis on the Spirit's creative activity stems from Barth's doctrine of the Trinity, and his emphasis on the Spirit as the love between the Father and the Son. See Andrew Gabriel, *Barth's Doctrine of Creation* (Eugene: Cascade Books, 2014), 78-80. I suspect whether we think Barth has adequately accounted for the role of the Spirit in creating depends on the value we place on the pre-existence, confirmation, and maintenance of creation itself.

35. Barth, CD III/1, 57-8. "In this indirect way, by expecting life—life in the new aeon which is true life for them—from the work of the Spirit, and from Him alone, [the New Testament writers] also bear witness that there could be no creature, nor any creation, if God were not also the Holy Spirit and active as such, just as He is also the Father and the Son and active as such." It is remarkable how similar Barth's account of the Holy Spirit's relation to creation is to his discussion in I/I, where he also points to the New Testament's use of "making alive" to describe the work of the Spirit as primarily indicating salvation, but indirectly referring to creation. "The Holy Spirit is the Creator God," Barth writes there, "with the Father and the Son in so far as God as Creator creates life as well as existence." CD I/1, 472.

36. Ibid., 59.

37. Ibid., 60.

basis of the covenant" and the covenant is the "internal basis of creation."[38] While creation "precedes and prepares for" God's work of reconciliation in the covenant, the covenant is creation's "indispensable basis and presupposition"—and as such, creation "follows" the covenant.[39] Though creation might be first in the order of time, the covenant is first in the order of explanation: the covenant is the basis and grounds for creation's existence.[40] The end of the covenant is not immanent to creation, but remains extrinsic to it. Creation does not *cause* the covenant out of its own immanent resources, nor can creation's significance or goodness be understood without God's revelation of the covenant to us.[41]

Beneath Barth's doctrine of creation lies an account of God's love and glory, which has significant implications for how we understand the role human well-being plays in his ethics. God's love is the "inner basis of the covenant," which provides the ultimate answer to why God creates.[42] The extrinsic basis of creation in the covenant means that "there is no inherent reason for the creature's existence and nature, no independent teleology of the creature introduced with its creation and made its own."[43] Instead, creation means that "world itself, in respect of its existence and essence, is an absolute gift of God," and the creature's "existence and nature ... are the work of the grace of God."[44] God's love is a sufficient and complete explanation for the existence of creation: God "wills and posits the creature neither out of caprice or necessity, but because He has loved it from eternity, because He wills to demonstrate His love for it, and because He wills, not to limit His glory by its existence and being, but to reveal and manifest it in His own co-existence with it."[45] God's love is unique, though, in its ability to create the object of love. While human love is *responsive* to the other's being and nature, divine love "does not rest on a presupposition of this kind, but creates the presupposition." For that reason, God's love in giving the gift of our creation is the "inaccessible prototype and true basis" of creaturely love. On this basis, Barth describes creation as the "presupposition of the realization of the divine purpose of love in relation to the creature."[46]

---

38. These two statements are not reducible to each other; the benefit or goodness of creation can only be understood when they are each allowed to stand on their own terms.

39. *CD* III/1, 44, 46. See also 232, where Barth describes creation as the "formal presupposition" of the covenant, and the covenant as the "material presupposition" of creation.

40. Barth, *CD* III/1, 76. "If creation takes precedence historically, the covenant does so in substance." (231).

41. Ibid., 95.
42. Ibid., 97.
43. Ibid., 95.
44. Ibid., 15, 96.
45. Ibid., 96.
46. Ibid.

While there is no reason for creation beyond the free demonstration of God's love in electing to be with the creature, God's love in creating is ordered toward and governed by the manifestation of His glory in time. The reality of creation in space and time is a mark of God's patience, which Barth suggests exists "where space and time are given with a definite intention, where freedom is allowed in expectation of a response."[47] In God's patience, He allows another "space and time for the development of its own existence, thus conceding to this existence a reality side by side with His own," such that he "accompanies and sustains it and allows it to develop in freedom."[48] Space and time are even the "the form of God's being for us."[49] Indeed, because time has a beginning and end, "ethics must be a problem for us," as our knowledge of the good "depends upon the command of the supratemporal God" who is "bound to no time, and therefore [is] the Lord of all times."[50]

The space and time of creaturely life are ordered toward the glorification of God with the creature in Jesus Christ. While God's inward glory is complete, the creation, reconciliation, and redemption of the world "magnifies and enhances the glory of God outwardly."[51] God's outward glory is the "answer evoked by Him of the worship offered Him by His creatures."[52] The *gloria Dei* gives rise to *glorificatio*, as the complete, immanent life of God engenders an answer among creation in Jesus Christ through the Holy Spirit—who Barth describes as the "unity between the creature and God, the bond between eternity and time."[53] Barth is explicit that Jesus Christ has answered the question of what we ought do and completed the

---

47. Ibid., 408.
48. Ibid., 610.
49. Ibid., 612.
50. Ibid., 638.
51. Barth, *CD* II/1, 513. Cf. *CD* II/2, 121, 166, 168. Barth writes that God's glory is His "dignity and right not only to maintain, but to prove and declare, to denote and almost as it were to make Himself conspicuous and everywhere apparent as the One He is." II/1, 641.
52. Ibid., 647.
53. Ibid., 668–9. It is through the Holy Spirit that the creature may serve the glorification of God, and so have "its part in His glory and therefore in the glory of God." Ibid., 670. To this extent, Tyler Wittman is exactly right that we "must not seek for a higher motive, purpose, or end, than God's love in Christ, even if we attempt to locate that purpose in God's inner life … Whatever God's love means, it must enable us to say that God communicates himself to another as an intrinsically purposeful act without any higher end or greater good." However, insofar as Barth's account of ethics is shaped by the reality of time, the 'good' to which humanity is ordered is fellowship with God specified in a particular way, namely, as participation in the glory of God in the limits of space and time established in creation. Such a modification will prove necessary for seeing how Barth can preserve aspects of a teleological conception of ethics and the creaturely goods it is responsive to in his divine command theory. Tyler Wittman, *God and Creation in the Theology of Thomas Aquinas and Karl Barth* (Cambridge: Cambridge University Press, 2019), 172. See especially Wittman's excellent discussion of Barth's account of love on pages 151 ff.

obedience that we owe, which means we "have actually nothing to add, but only have to endorse this event by our action." Yet this endorsement has *not* happened in space and time: humanity has not yet given God the glory, or the honour, that He is due. As the ethical problem arises because of time, so the "ethical problem of Church dogmatics can consist only in the question whether and to what extent human action is a glorification of the grace of Christ."[54] The "answer" of the creature to God's self-glorification through Christ is constituted by participating in that glory through thanksgiving and honour, service, and praise.[55] At the same time, this "answer" is inextricable from our own glorification with Christ. It would be a strange sort of love, Barth observes, that "was satisfied with the mere existence and nature of the other." Instead, God's love in creating aims beyond the creature's mere existence toward its "preservation and glorification …"[56] Our creatureliness consists in being "prepared for the place where [God's] honour dwells," a place that

---

54. Barth, *CD* II/2, 540. I should here register a tentative and partial dissent to Gerald McKenny's recent criticism of Barth. In *Barth's Moral Thought*, McKenny worries about whether Barth is able to give creation and human nature its due, so long as they not only exist by grace, but *for* God's grace. "Can God's action," he asks, "truly be *for* the human creature as such if the human creature as such is, and is what it is, solely so that God can be for it?" (24). I am inclined to simply answer: "Yes." McKenny thinks that creation's status as the presupposition to the covenant entails that the "creature itself is the work of grace, brought into existence so that grace may have material for its work." God "creates the creature for whom God can act." But if the creature is real and God's action for the creature happens with the creature's (real) action, then Barth seems to escape McKenny's worry. There may be a circle here (that Barth is acutely aware of, as we shall have occasion to note below). But it is hard to see how it is a vicious one. God's work for the creature is inclusive of the creature's good, as it is teleologically ordered toward the creature's glorification in Christ. I suspect McKenny's worry is tied to how little he says across either of his two books about the glorification of the creature that the disclosure of Christ aims at. Barth never finished his doctrine of redemption, wherein he doubtlessly would have written much more about the significance of this glorification for ethics. Yet Barth also makes clear in his existing work that the creature is glorified as the creature, and that in answering God in gratitude the creature participates in God's glory (cf. *CD* II/2, 670, 674). This glorification is inextricable from the work of the Spirit. As JinHyok Kim rightly observes, for Barth God "is glorified by the creature's worship and praise in its utter creatureliness," and the creature is glorified through the Spirit: the "Spirit glorifies the creature in order that it can enter into the glory of God, and God is glorified in return by the creature's participation in the Trinitarian fellowship." See JinHyok Kim, *The Spirit of God and the Christian Life* (Minneapolis: Fortress Press, 2014), 213, 215. The extrinsic nature of grace is compatible for Barth with the perfection of our nature through our share in the glorification of God in Christ through the Spirit. It is difficult to see, in this light, what is self-defeating about Barth's contention that God creates the creature so that He might glorify Himself in and with and through us.

55. Ibid., 670–7.

56. Ibid.

is (as we shall see later) inextricable from the honour we have as creatures by virtue of being recipients of God's grace.[57] As Barth notes, while our existence remains a creaturely existence, it is "fulfilled in the co-existence with God."[58]

The self-glorification of God in creation and the glorification of the creature through the Holy Spirit are centered on Jesus Christ, who as the revelation of the covenant God makes with humanity in election is the source of our knowledge of creation and its goodness.[59] As an article of faith, the doctrine of creation has Jesus Christ as both its noetic and ontic basis.[60] Tying creation together with the covenant this way has long led to worries that Barth does not give creation its due, but that its instrumentalization for the sake of the covenant in Christ effectively hollows out its goodness and significance, leaving Barth with a docetic account of creation (despite his protests to the contrary).[61] Barth's rhetoric does not help matters: he

---

57. Barth, *CD* III/1, 364. This theme of glory has received more attention in recent years. JinHyok Kim's treatment of glory in *The Spirit of God and the Christian Life* is magnificent—see especially Chapter 5. See also Andrew Dunstan's *Karl Barth's Analogy of Beauty* (London: Routledge, 2022). Jason Fout offers a critical reading of Barth's treatment of honour, arguing that Barth is unable to "affirm that God's honour itself honours the creation, either through being witness to God's honour or through participation in the honouring of God" (7). I have several substantive disagreements with Fout's reading, which I will return to in Chapter 8. See Jason Fout, *Fully Alive* (London: Bloomsbury T&T Clark, 2015).

58. Barth, *CD* II/1, 673. The "glorifying of God consists simply in the life-obedience of the creature which knows God," which means thanking and praising God and so becoming in its existence a "reflection of the perfection of the divine being." "In this sense the way and theatre of the glorification of God is neither more nor less than the total existence of the creature who knows God and offers Him his life-obedience." This is the purpose of the creature's existence. Barth, *CD* II/1, 674–5.

59. See Barth *CD* II/1, 661–4. As Joseph Mangina notes, the concrete answer for why God made the world is so that "God can shower grace upon his creature in the person of his Son." See Joseph Mangina, *Karl Barth: Theologian of Christian Witness* (Louisville: Westminster John Knox, 2004), 88. See also Gabriel, *Barth's Doctrine of Creation*, 34 ff.

60. Barth, *CD* III/1, 24–31.

61. Syd Hielema writes that "the significance of the creation is completely enveloped by its covenantal character." Syd Hielema, "Searching for 'Disconnected Wires,'" *Calvin Theological Journal* 30, no. 1 (1995): 79. Richard Roberts describes Barth's account as the "most profound and systematically consistent theological alienation of the natural order ever achieved." See Richard H. Roberts, "Karl Barth's Doctrine of Time," in *A Theology on Its Way* (Edinburgh: T&T Clark, 1991), 37. G.C. Berkouwer contends that Barth's doctrine that creation is determined for the covenant (of reconciliation and redemption) and his rejection of their 'step-wise' character risks a monistic conception of God's works and entails that there is no room in Barth's theology for "a goodness which does *not yet* stand in need of *reconciling* grace." See G. C. Berkouwer, *The Triumph of Grace in the Theology of Karl Barth* (Grand Rapids: Eerdmans, 1956), 259.

is explicit that creation only makes the covenant "technically possible."[62] Even if the agency of the creature means it is not an "instrument" in the sense of being a passive tool, creation is still the "establishment of the ground and sphere and object and instrument" of the covenant.[63] The extrinsic basis of creation's goodness in Christ threatens to leave creation bereft of its own immanent value.

Creation's Christological determination does not entail that its form is void of any meaning or goodness, though, or that it is simply an empty receptacle without the disclosure of Christ. When we look at creation from the standpoint of the covenant, we discover that it "is itself already a unique sign of the covenant and a true sacrament …"[64] The time, space, and opportunity creation affords humanity to glorify God are a set stage, a theater with imagery that points toward Jesus Christ—even if we cannot recognize such imagery *as* pointing without seeing the one to whom it points. Creation is good because it is "*adapted* to be a theatre of the covenant which is the purpose of the divine volition and accomplishment; and because, *in virtue of its nature*, it is radically incapable of serving any other purpose, but placed from the very first at the disposal of his grace."[65] The adaptability of creation for the covenant does not entail a shared participation in "being" between it and God, nor does it mean that creation's significance for the covenant can simply be "read off" of it directly. Yet it means that creation is not in itself *neutral* for the covenant, but that it "is the reality which is *appropriate* to the *covenant*," as Eberhard Busch has written.[66]

We can see glimpses of Barth's use of the non-neutrality of creation in his reading of Genesis 1. Barth suggests the light of the stars is "the symbol of the revelation of grace."[67] Light's goodness is based on its "correspondence to the goodness of His creative will and acts," which makes it a "witness and sign" against darkness and chaos.[68] The signs and symbols of creation are not static, inert images, but are intertwined with the history of salvation. Barth associates the sea in Genesis 1:9-13 with the "evil powers which oppose and resist the salvation intended for the people of Israel."[69] However, this is not a "mere image." Instead, the seas "fully participate as an image in the actuality of a higher order which

---

62. Ibid., 22. See also 230: The creature is the "exponent of [God's] intention, plan and order," and the "revelation of God's glory in the act of creation."

63. *CD* III/1, 47. In III/3, 46–7, Barth invokes the language of instrumentalization as one imperfect analogy for creation, and affirms the agency of the creature.

64. *CD* III/1, 232.

65. Ibid., 99, emphases mine. See also *CD* II/1, 674. In II/1, 118, Barth writes that the creation story is the "promise of revelation and reconciliation, the designation and characterisation of the world as a 'good' world, i.e., a world determined and adapted as the theatre of revelation."

66. Busch, *The Great Passion*, 184.

67. *CD* III/1, 119.

68. Ibid., 122.

69. Ibid., 147.

is the theme of the history of Israel."⁷⁰ The covenant of grace is "prefigured" in nature, and the "beginning of natural history ... is both a precursory type and also a substratum of the history of the covenant of grace."⁷¹ This entails, though, that creation is "one long preparation, and therefore the being and existence of the creature one long readiness, for what God will intend and do with it in the history of the covenant." Its "nature" is its "equipment for grace." The creature is thus "intrinsically determined as the exponent of [God's] glory and for the corresponding service."⁷²

While creation's goodness is extrinsically revealed in Christ, Barth is still capable of speaking of "nature" as a theological category, even if it is not an independent theme from grace. Barth argues that the Bible begins with the history of creation in order to disclose that "the question about the origin, existence and nature of things cannot be withdrawn from the sphere of grace." While there is a "realm of nature which as such is different from the realm of grace," there is "in it nothing which does not point to grace and therefore already come from grace; nothing which can enjoy independent life or exercise independent dominion." At the same time, though, there is "no place in [the realm of grace] for anything unnatural, but from the creation everything is also nature."⁷³ While Barth carefully cordons off "nature"

---

70. Ibid., 149.

71. Ibid., 144, 154.

72. Ibid., 231. In I/2, Barth argues that the subjective reality of God's revelation consists in the Holy Spirit using "certain definite events and relations and orders within the world" as signs that attest and point to revelation itself. Crucially, their "nature as signs does not rest upon a capacity resident in these particular creaturely realities as such, either to be or to become testimonies to revelation," 223–4. The 'adaptability' of creation to being instruments of God does not rest upon or reinsert an *analogia entis* where Barth would have none. The disclosure of the nature of signs happens only after the fact of revelation reveals them to us as such.

73. Ibid., 62. How much continuity is there between Barth's Christology in I/2 and that which he develops in Volume IV? The question is crucial, and is intertwined with broader disputes about whether Barth's theology is programmatically anti-metaphysical and whether it is possible to speak of nature as a substantive category in theology. At the very least, Barth's emphases seem to have shifted between the volumes. In I/2, Barth critiques the "spiritualistic moralism" of liberal Protestantism for its aversion to "nature," and with it externality and corporeality. Barth wonders what such a view would have to say "to Jesus' bodily resurrection, or to *natus ex virgine*," but this is a secondary worry. His primary concern is that such opposition contains a "horror of the being in God in His revelation." In "refusing to acknowledge a 'natural' element in revelation, it refused to acknowledge an ontological element"—which stripped away the realism of the Bible and emptied it of its authority to command us (I/2, 130). At the outset of IV/2, though, Barth objects to the use of "nature" in Christology, arguing that it is "fatally easy to read out of the word 'nature' a reference to the generally known or at any rate conceivable disposition of being, so that by the concept 'divine nature' we are led to think of a generally known or knowable essence of

from being invoked in any generalized, non- or pre-theological manner to explain or function as a point of contact for theological concepts, once we stand within the purview of the covenant we can rightly see creation as an order that is typologically

deity, and by that of 'human nature' of a known or knowable essence of man—for this is our present concern—being thus determined by a general anthropology, a doctrine of man in general and as such." Barth subsequently opts against using "nature" in his Christology (IV/2, 26). Yet there is strong reason to think that Barth's decision in this matter is pedagogical, rather than programmatic: it protects us against importing our pre-determined conception of "nature" into Christology, and preserves the uniqueness of Christ's humanity in the Incarnation—a move that Barth had made in his theological anthropology, and that he confirms in this context (IV/2, 27). Moreover, even in raising his concern, Barth suggests that the danger of its abuse "does not mean we have to abandon it." While Barth's concern is not strictly linguistic—though note, he worries about reading out of "*the word* 'nature'"—his method is commensurate with how he approaches *causa* in his doctrine of providence, namely, by purging it of sub-theological content while also sanctioning its appropriate use in theology (cf. III/3, 98–104). In IV/2, Barth speaks of "nature" to establish what Christ has in common with us. "Jesus Christ is like us in our creaturely form, but also in its determination by sin and death; in our human nature, but also in its concealment under the human 'un-nature' which results from the opposition of man to God" (cf. IV/2, 27). As with I/2, Barth seems especially concerned to affirm human corporeality in contexts where he defends the role of nature. In the "existence of the man Jesus we have to do with the true and normal form of human nature, and therefore with authentically human life" (IV/2, 452). The German reads: "Wir setzen neu ein mit der Feststellung, daß wir es in der Existenz des Menschen Jesus mit der echten, der normalen Gestalt der menschlichen Natur und also mit dem authentisch menschlichen Leben zu tun haben" (*KD*, IV/2, 513). What immediately follows recapitulates Barth's account of humanity's constitution, albeit from the negative standpoint of its fragmentation and dissolution through sin. The "conflict, the inversion of the order in which man is the soul of his body, is continually shown to be unnatural" (IV/2, 452-3). None of this entails that nature is freestanding, much less that our knowledge of it can ground definite and concrete moral norms (though, as I will note later, Barth does grant that everyone has some knowledge of the wrongness of killing on the basis of nature). "There is no law and commandment inherent in the creatureliness of man as such, or written and revealed in the stars as a law of the cosmos, so that the transgression of it makes man a sinner" (IV/1, 140). Yet it does indicate continuity between I/2 and Volume IV, and offers some grounds for thinking that Barth is not so systemically post-metaphysical as some have claimed. As Darren Sumner writes, rather than "offering an alternate form of ontology, Barth aims at *de-securing* our ontology—at undermining the theologian's confidence in her own reasonable concepts." Darren Sumner, *Karl Barth and the Incarnation: Christology and the Humility of God* (London: Bloomsbury, 2014), 15. Having done this work, though, Barth seems to give those concepts back to us for our use—at least in theological anthropology and, subsequently, ethics. See also Sumner's discussion of "nature" on pages 170–4.

differentiated, in which humans have a nature that animals do not.[74] This "nature" is the "sum of [the human's] possibilities and destiny and nothing more."[75]

The knowledge of creation we are given in Christ is mediated to us by Scripture. Our knowledge of the covenant, creation, and Scripture lives together in a threefold bond, such that to disrupt or distort their inner relationship would be

---

74. Ibid., 236-7. Barth's actualism and its emphasis on events and relationships have sometimes been pitted against essentialist or substantialist ontologies, turning Barth into a programmatic anti-metaphysical or post-metaphysical thinker. In interpretations of Barth's ethics, readers like Nigel Biggar, Matthew Rose, Gerald McKenny, and Donna Neal have brought Barth into closer contact with something like Thomism, by defending the relevance and constancy of "nature" for ethics. Prior to his turn away from Barth, McKenny elegantly articulated the role nature plays in Barth's theological ethics in "Karl Barth and the Plight of Protestant Ethics," *The Freedom of a Christian Ethicist* (London: Bloomsbury T&T Clark, 2016), 17-38. Donna Neal argues that the covenantal determination of creation does not absorb creation into the covenant, undermining its ontological distinctness, but rather that "Barth's ontology of creation is specifically *covenantal in structure*, but is not equivalent to Christology." See *Be Who You Are* (PhD diss., University of Notre Dame, 2010), 5. By contrast, James Cassidy argues that Neal "fails to realize that classical metaphysics is precisely what Barth attacks on his way to a more radically reconstructed doctrine of creation. See *God's Time for Us: Barth's Reconciliation of Eternity and Time in Jesus Christ* (Bellingham: Lexham Press, 2016), 58ff. More judiciously, Alexander Massmann reads Barth's ethics predominately through the lens of his actualism, over and against Biggar's (and von Balthasar's) emphasis on the orders of creation. See Alexander Massmann, *Citizenship in Heaven and on Earth* (Minneapolis: Fortress Press, 2015), xxxviii. Paul Nimmo's *Being in Action* is the most substantive and pervasive account of how Barth's actualism informs his ethics (Edinburgh: T&T Clark, 2007). My foregrounding of "nature" here as a theologically relevant concept for Barth's doctrine of creation shows my cards: while I will try to give full honour to Barth's actualism through my discussion of the divine command as it relates to "borderline" cases, Barth's willingness to make specific practical judgments about special ethics (as in his treatment of abortion) seems to belie a willingness to let creation and its immanent orders shape his special ethics, which prepares people to hear and recognize the divine command. More broadly, I have found George Hunsinger's critique of allowing actualism to become an architectonic principle for interpreting Barth persuasive. See George Hunsinger, *Reading Barth with Charity* (Grand Rapids: Baker, 2015). Shao Kai Tseng's careful assessment of how Barth revises, but does not abandon or historicize, substantialist terms seems right: "What [Barth] seeks to avoid is the metaphysical (be it substantialist or historicist) attempt to define human nature in the framework of a general anthropology, and divine nature from the starting point of some general notion of divinity. Yet he retains the traditional grammatical definition of 'nature' as the formal-causal aspect of different *kinds* of substances." Shao Kai Tseng, *Barth's Ontology of Sin and Grace* (London: Routledge, 2019), 6.

75. Barth, *CD* IV/1, 140.

to lose the knowledge of all three. Honouring God's status as "Creator" within the Christian confession means adhering "to the biblical witness in its context of Old Testament and New Testament, of promise and fulfillment."[76] At the same time, positing a knowledge of creation "alongside or outside the Christian knowledge of the covenant," or allowing a "special knowledge of the covenant alongside or outside the Christian knowledge of creation" both weakens the affirmation of creation and undermines our confidence in Scripture.[77] Creation and covenant are not "two intrinsically separate spheres" that proceed one after the other in a step-like fashion. Treating them as such nominalizes creation and reduces its goodness to a "mere hypothesis," while also undermining our understanding of Scripture, which is a witness that "lives in virtue of this inner connexion [of creation and covenant], and cannot be heard where the view of this connexion is fundamentally repudiated and disappears."[78] Maintaining a proper relationship between the Old and New Testaments is uniquely important for a doctrine of creation: dividing the Testaments imperils the order of creation and covenant, and distorting the order of creation and covenant undermines the relationship of the two Testaments.[79] Marcion, for instance, looked wholly and exclusively to the covenant and denied creation's status as a benefit—which ended in a docetic Christology that was intertwined with his rejection of the Old Testament. As Barth summarizes his view, "Where the humanity of Christ is denied and by implication the covenant, Israel and the Old Testament, the Creator and creation, are all necessarily placed on the left hand and cast into outer darkness."[80]

Within this threefold bond, we must conclude that creation is good in its own right—even if its goodness is constituted by its correspondence to and conformity with the covenant. As Barth writes, "The created world is, therefore, right as it is, because in its essence and structure it is an appropriate sphere and instrument of the divine activity, and because man at the heart of it is the true object of the divine work which has its beginning, centre and end in Jesus Christ." This rightness and goodness of creation "spring from its correspondence to the work of God's own Son as resolved from all eternity and fulfilled in time." The fact that creation's goodness arises from its serviceability to God's glory means that it is "not evil but

---

76. Barth, *CD* III/1, ibid., 11. It is because of Scripture that we know the Creator as Father, rather than as an abstract 'world-cause.' Cf. 12–13. This is also a theme that Barth sounds in I/2, where he suggests that the Protestant doctrine of *sola scriptura* is intertwined with the assertion of the "single absolute fundamental and indestructible priority," which is the "priority of God as Creator over the totality of His creatures and each of them without exception." This absolute priority is learned only through Scripture, though, and Scripture itself speaks from the side of the absolute. See I/2, 497–9.

77. Ibid., 333.
78. Ibid., 333–4.
79. Ibid.
80. Ibid.

good, and not imperfectly but perfectly good."[81] Creation's existence is subordinate to the good of God's disclosure in Jesus Christ, but also has a "direct and immanent goodness" that God's self-disclosure obligates one to recognize.[82] As Barth writes, "Even [creation's] future glorification presupposes that it is already perfectly justified by the mere fact of its creation."[83] The affirmation of creation as good is "not only permitted," but "commanded," as creation "carries with it the Yes of God to that which He creates."[84]

Barth's doctrine of creation turns on the inner connection between form and content, between the "nature" that creation is composed of and its teleological determination in Christ. While creation is good in and by Christ, when we grasp it in this connection through Scripture's revelation, we are able to affirm that it has its own (non-independent) goodness. Creation stands as a sign, symbol, and witness to the covenant—the meanings of which are unintelligible without the covenant. The covenant is primary: it "already characterises creation itself and as such, and therefore the being and existence of the creature."[85] But as the "necessary preparation" which "genuinely points to grace," creation is also itself grace.[86]

The Doctrine of Creation against Pessimism and Optimism

Our knowledge of creation in Barth's theology is unremittingly fideistic, a position that Barth animates by invoking *ethical* or *existential* criteria. As we have seen, creation's goodness is only discerned in light of our knowledge of the covenant. Yet Barth also takes Christ as the ontic basis of creation with utmost seriousness, arguing that Christ also grounds our knowledge of the world's existence as an independent reality. We need the "divine self-witness" if the reality of the world is going to be more than an "an indemonstrable and contestable hypothesis."[87] Barth adopts a maximally high justificatory threshold for our knowledge of creation's existence, which he justifies on practical grounds: we must "make up our minds to think and live and die on the basis of this hypothesis."[88] In his interaction with Descartes, Barth acknowledges that we "assume being and not appearance or non-being," but contends with Descartes that this assumption is "in itself is not better

---

81. Ibid., 370.
82. Ibid., 371.
83. Ibid., 366. "The only thing which can be better than creaturely existence is the goal of the covenant for which the creature is determined in and with its creation. But in the order of created existence as such there can be nothing better than what is."
84. Ibid., 331.
85. Ibid., 231.
86. Ibid., 97.
87. Ibid., 5.
88. Ibid., 5, 8.

founded than the morbid idea that we are not, and that nothing is."[89] The nihilism "implicit and often enough explicit in the human mode of life" makes the idea that we live as if we exist nothing more than a hypothesis. No attempt at self-persuasion can escape the "vicious circle of consciousness and being."[90] Instead, we must be "authorised and compelled" to say we exist, which we can only do "because it has first been said to us."[91] Any proof of God's existence must be constituted by "the self-demonstration of the One whose existence is to be proved." Otherwise, "God" remains within the realm of human ideas. Again, ethical considerations are pre-eminent in the rejoinder to Descartes: the proof of God's existence is the lives of those who have heard God's self-demonstration.[92] The only escape from the vicious circle of consciousness that traps Descartes is to believe "the word of God who evinces Himself authoritatively in His revelation" and subjects "[one] to His commands and prohibition." Only through obedience does one "prove and confirm [one's] awareness of the divine character of the being whose existence is to be demonstrated."[93] Yet this ethically saturated knowledge of creation's existence *heightens* our confidence in its reality, rather than diminishes it: the "wretchedness of life" is "bound up with the fact that sound common sense and the *natura docet* have no power at all firmly to plant our feet on the ground of the confidence that the created world is real." Only God's self-disclosure has that power.[94]

The litmus test for a doctrine of creation, and for our knowledge of its goodness, is our capacity to "live and die" based upon it, which requires taking both the goods *and* evils of the world with utmost seriousness. Neither optimism nor pessimism—which "embody the two classical views of life which have always divided men"—is capable of doing so, as each of them dissociates creation from the covenant.[95] Christianity simultaneously transcends optimism and pessimism and

---

89. Ibid., 345. See Fergus Kerr, "Cartesianism According to Karl Barth," *New Blackfriars* 77, no. 906 (July 1996): 358–68.

90. Ibid., 346.

91. Ibid., 348.

92. Ibid., 360. While one might be commanded to offer proofs of God's existence like Anselm did, it is only "by his obedient activity" that one can "show that he is aware of the divine existence and can prove it." Anselm's proof is specifically a proof of the God "who is revealed and believed in the Christian Church," and makes it "logically *and morally* impossible" to think such a God does not exist (emphasis mine).

93. Ibid., 361.

94. Ibid., 362.

95. *CD* III/2, 543. In *CD* I/2, Barth argues that pessimism and optimism both arise when the particular nature of God's constancy toward the world is forgotten in favor of a dualism that pits the mutability of the world against God's mutability. In one form, the emphasis on God's immutability and humanity's inability to participate in it leaves humanity with a "bad conscience, helpless, tortured by the immutability of God"—and so disposed to the pessimistic practical conclusion that "death is God or that God is death." In the other form, the emphasis on the world's mutability becomes an affirmation of it, as the independence

(paradoxically) deepens them, allowing us to approach the evils of the world with a practical seriousness that pessimism cannot muster, and to have a confidence about its fundamental goodness that optimism can merely mimic.

Barth distills his critique of pessimism through a critical reading of Schopenhauer, whose exclusive attention to creation without attention to the covenant generates an outlook that is "inevitably as godless as Marcion's view of God is world-less." For Schopenhauer, humanity "has to thank himself alone, and is responsible only to himself, for the existence and apprehension of the world and himself."[96] Isolating creation from God shrouds its goodness in darkness. On Schopenhauer's unsparing anthropocentrism, humanity is condemned: "the fault of this creator-god [humanity] with all his fictions and illusions is to have been born at all."[97] This honesty about humanity's plight without God is Schopenhauer's "greatness," as "the creation from which God is excluded can only be evil."[98] Every philosophical attempt to explain creation's status as benefit ultimately becomes either the Christian doctrine of creation or reduces to Schopenhauerian pessimism. Philosophical answers to the *whence* of the universe must be "able to show as unequivocally as is the case in the Christian doctrine of creation that this pure becoming is *pure divine benefit* preceding all knowledge and being and underlying all knowledge and being."[99] In other words: philosophy must demonstrate creation's fundamental and ineradicable character as good for it to offer a plausible explanation of the world's origins. Barth supplies no basis or grounds for such a methodological requirement, and it is not clear—besides a reassertion of the primacy of Jesus Christ, or the practical requirement that we must be able to *live* on the basis of an outlook—what sort of explanation might be given. Yet any attempt to answer the question of creation's "pure becoming" on a basis other than the covenant "is logically doomed to end up with Marcion or Schopenhauer," or "must itself become theology" and thus cease to be true to itself.[100] There is only the Christian doctrine of creation or pessimism.

---

of the world generates its own self-affirmation. This pessimism and optimism in practice "continually meet and interchange and complement one another," even while they have a "common failure to see that the divine love is that which has freely posited creation." As Barth concludes, "Pessimism and optimism can arise and be expounded only if men forget the relationship which exists in virtue of the constancy of God and in which creaturely life is lived," 501–2. See also the discussion of optimism and pessimism in Timothy Gorringe, *Karl Barth against Hegemony* (Oxford: Oxford University Press, 1999), 171 ff.

96. *CD* III/1 339.
97. Ibid.
98. Ibid., 340.
99. Ibid., 342. Emphasis mine.
100. Ibid. Correspondingly, theology is reduced to "a type of philosophical thinking … if it concerns itself with the problem of pure becoming without this character [that creation is benefit]." (343).

Barth underscores this instability of positive accounts of the world in his critique of optimism, especially as it is crystallized in Leibniz. Trying to secure creation's goodness by positing a "kindly God" might only be the "last and supreme expression" of our scheme of valuation. As such, it cannot deliver anything besides the "comforting and expressive underlining to convictions already formed and established."[101] As a projection of our values, optimism is inherently unstable: it can "easily turn into pessimism and even indifference." Optimism cannot secure an "unequivocal Yes with the certitude necessary for a life lived in faith."[102] This fundamental instability means that the confidence that Leibniz and other eighteenth-century optimists dress their outlooks in is a façade. It "cannot be denied that Leibniz and all his stronger and weaker followers proclaim glad tidings, and thus display a formal affinity to the proclamation of the Gospel," Barth writes.[103] But such linguistic similarities mask fundamental insecurities in their optimism. Leibniz pushes the shadow side of creation to the margins, but the gladness of eighteenth century proves hollow: "Incapable of weeping with them that weep," he writes, "it is also incapable at bottom of rejoicing with them that rejoice, i.e., profoundly, calmly and definitively." The school's excessive dependence on superlatives and its moralizing tone are marks of its frailty, a weakness that stems from its belief that the "goodness which justifies creation must be intrinsic to it, and as such amenable to human judgment." There remains a "question of the goodness of this good," which precludes Leibniz from being "as certain of goodness as so obviously desired."[104] What appears to be the height of confidence fundamentally lacks it.

The frail confidence that besets optimism derives from the same circularity Barth had challenged Descartes' view with—and suffers from similar ethical problems. The eighteenth century optimists thought they could infer God's character from the "character of the world." But the reliability of this inference is precisely what is in question. Their argument assumes as "given and known that which is to be proved—the perfection of existence." There is a vicious circle of God and nature in such natural theologies and the only point of entry is ourselves, which is "purely and simply an act of human self-confidence."[105] For the optimist, "existence is rational as and to the extent that he himself is rational. Once he doubts himself, the abyss yawns."[106] In contrast, Christian optimism has "nothing whatever to do with that sort of self-confidence," as it is based "unequivocally on the judgment of the Creator God."[107] As an echo of the gospel, optimism is confused and practically impotent. Optimists become mere spectators of the world, so that they "do not

---

101. Ibid., 368.
102. Ibid.
103. Ibid., 405.
104. Ibid., 408.
105. Ibid., 410.
106. Ibid.
107. Ibid., 411.

4. Neither Optimism nor Pessimism

allow themselves to be personally affected." Such a distant reserve is a mark of optimism's insecurity. It is, on this basis, "symbolical and symptomatic" that the Lisbon earthquake of 1755 overturned optimism. "Real certainty," he contends, "depends on whether the ground on which we see and think is solid or unstable." Christians affirm creation not as "spectators but sworn witnesses to the perfection of the created world."[108]

The Christological orientation of creation means that Christianity can give the intuitions beneath both optimism and pessimism their due.[109] The revelation of Christ means there is a "more profound and more radical" form of joy *and* misery that determine the creature. Creation has not only a positive meaning that corresponds to Christ's elevation of humanity, but a negative meaning that naturally corresponds to our wretchedness and alienation through sin. While existence as such is justified and good just as such, it is also bordered at every point by non-existence and is incapable on its own of maintaining existence.[110] In that respect, the joy and misery of life have "their root in the will of God and in the truth of being."[111] The non-existence that borders humanity is not sinful *per se*—rather, as the lights in the heavens are signs and witnesses to God's grace, so darkness and the wilderness are proleptic indicators of the chaos and barrenness that come from humanity's rebellion against God. From the standpoint of the covenant, the Christian can take creation's "shadow side" more seriously than Schopenhauer: as the atonement is the confirmation of creation's goodness, we can do "justice to the reality of the created world even on its darker aspect," and "accept its silent or negative testimony."[112]

At the same time, transcending optimism and pessimism's basic judgments entails neither indifference nor a symmetry between them. Because both the light and darkness of creation are assumed by God, "we are unambiguously summoned to take life seriously in its twofold determination." The "indolence and neutrality" into which we might retreat is "so plainly forbidden us" that it is "the most impossible of all courses." "Indifference alone—if the accursed were capable of it—would be genuine ungodliness."[113] Neither can we simply coordinate the goods and

---

108. Ibid., 412. Barth names the Lisbon earthquake as the definitive end of optimism in a variety of places. See, among others, II/1, 114.

109. The disclosure of Christ permits the "confirmation of these two aspects and judgments (as opposed to their neutralization by doubt)." Ibid., 375.

110. The creature "is destined for God as certainly as it is actual by Him alone; yet it is not incapable of being unfaithful to its origin and destiny and becoming the instrument of sin. It has subsistence; yet it does not have such subsistence as it can secure and maintain for itself. It lives; yet it does not live in such a way that its life is guaranteed in its own strength against destruction and death." Ibid., 376.

111. Ibid.

112. Ibid., 372.

113. Ibid., 377-8. The doctrine of creation requires repudiating a "false attitude of resignation or neutrality in the face of the question of [creation's] goodness." (370).

evils of the world, which can only be done at the "expense of the full seriousness of one or the other aspect."[114] Goodness is primary and fundamental, and evil derivative—or, alternately, goodness is durable while sorrow is transient. Christ "pronounced the Yes and No with differing emphases."[115] As Barth says elsewhere, "the cross is followed by the resurrection … and the latter is the true, definitive and eternal form of the incarnate Son of God."[116] The resurrection grounds the asymmetry between the light and the darkness, and reveals that the creature's perfection consists in "contesting and overcoming of the imperfection of the creature by God's own intervention on its behalf." The Yes of creation "conforms to this archetype [of the resurrection]."[117]

In seeing creation in terms of the covenant, the Christian inherits a confidence in life that is founded upon God's action in Christ. Christianity acknowledges that assessments of well-being are unreliable better than pessimism can, even while the Christian No is "never addressed to creation as such but to the nothingness by which creation is surrounded and menaced …"[118] In the same way, Christianity "realises better than any optimism that the final Word about creation is positive and not negative." This enables it to "take in all seriousness the penultimate negative word which is also true in this connexion, but only within its limits …" Yet that negative word is only (though not *merely*) penultimate. When we encounter God through the divine command, we are blocked both from being either pessimists or optimists, and from regarding creation as neutral. In the encounter with God, we enter into a circle in which "we can only [move] in one direction, and which we can no longer leave"—the circle of *God's* confidence in creation's reality and its goodness.[119]

Within an anthropological context, Barth reiterates his approach of distancing the Gospel from pessimistic and optimistic attitudes even while he again admits the covenant does not negate them. The linchpin of the argument is again confidence. In the face of death, Barth writes, we might be "unreflective and frivolous … or

---

114. Ibid., 378.

115. Ibid., 383. On IV/1, 349–50, Barth argues that the death of Christ happens "in exact correspondence with what He did as Creator when He separated light from darkness and elected the creature to being and rejected the possibility of chaos and nothingness." Yet here, too, there is an asymmetry between the positive and negative aspects of the atonement: "The No pronounced in the cross of Jesus Christ can and should be heard and accepted only as the necessary and in the true sense redemptive form of His Yes."

116. Ibid., 384.

117. From the standpoint of Jesus Christ, his death and resurrection, the creature's "justification and perfection will be infallibly perceived, and it will be seen to be the best of all possible worlds." (385).

118. Ibid., 386.

119. Ibid., 388. The knowledge of creation's goodness is "unshakeable," as the creature's confidence in reality is the "necessary and therefore sure confidence of those whom God has first drawn into His confidence …"

reflective and preoccupied," "optimists or pessimists …"[120] However theoretically pure these attitudes might be, though, we invariably adopt an amalgam of both in practice. There is "something healthy and brave about" an unreflective optimism in the face of death. Yet this cannot account for all the facts: a "broad shadow of uncertainty lies over all the time we have," which induces a reflectiveness about life we "stifle or suppress" but cannot extinguish.[121] Instead, the Christian should face the future with an unreflectiveness that is marked by the "confidence that the future is that which God gives, and this confidence alone."[122] Neither is the pessimistic confrontation with death any more complete. "Because of its ostensible honesty and realism," pessimism is "often compared favourably with its opposite."[123] It has the appearances of being the view of the "mature man, of one who has plumbed life to the depths." Yet nobody can be a "pure pessimist." Schopenhauer was only one "on paper," and the one who commits suicide indicates that "in spite of everything he is trying to make a better future."[124] Instead, we are summoned to reflectiveness animated by God's "judgment which will be pronounced over us at the end." The question of whether we have really lived our lives with God reveals how "comical and empty all optimism" is. The knowledge that death means meeting God, then, both banishes "all false fears of the future, enabling us to live unreflectively" and "evokes and inspires the necessary and serious fear of God Himself."[125]

Barth famously heard in Mozart's music the appropriate coordination of light and darkness in creation, in which the "shadow side" is present but not pre-eminent.[126] As he writes, Mozart "heard the harmony of creation to which the shadow also belongs, but in which shadow is not darkness, deficiency is not defeat, sadness cannot become despair, trouble cannot degenerate into tragedy and infinite melancholy is not ultimately forced to claim undisputed sway."[127] Barth's account of creation's goodness has sometimes been charged with failing to give suffering its due—a charge (ironically) parallel to that which he made against Leibniz and other heirs of optimism when he objected that they lack the compulsion to "face this [shadowy, tragic] aspect of life without running away."[128] What it means, precisely, to adequately leave room for sorrow and misery in the face of evils is an underspecified

120. *CD* III/2, 542.
121. Ibid., 543.
122. Ibid., 548.
123. Ibid., 544.
124. Ibid.
125. Ibid.
126. This paragraph distills and echoes themes in my essay "Giving Thanks for the Gift of Life: Karl Barth on Gratitude to God for One's Own Life," *Religions* 13, no. 10 (2022): 959.
127. Barth *CD* III/3, 298.
128. Barth, *CD* III/1, 406. As Joseph Mangina writes, "The danger in Barth's approach to suffering may be that it moves too quickly into the mode of affirmation. Mozart's music is beautiful, but our lives very often are not." Joseph Mangina, *Karl Barth: Theologian of Christian Witness* (Milton, UK: Routledge, 2017), 112.

question. Yet the miracle of Mozart's music is that it includes the negative, without placing it on a par with the positive. Thus, Barth writes, "the cheerfulness in this harmony *is not without its limits*."[129] Limits are at the heart of Barth's doctrine of creation: there is "no light which does not also know dark, no joy which does not also have within it sorrow." At the same time, the center of Mozart's music is one in which "the light rises and the shadows fall, though without disappearing, in which joy overtakes sorrow without extinguishing it, in which the Yea rings louder than the ever-present Nay." These forces are never brought into an equilibrium, with the "uncertainty and doubt" that such an equivocation would entail.[130] To that extent, Barth is acutely aware of the difficulty of Christian optimism: given the shadow around us, our affirmation of creation's goodness needs to be secured for us by the grace of God in Christ. On life's own terms, outside of grace, we would be trapped in a perpetual ambivalence and oscillation between optimism and pessimism.

Barth's Doctrine of Creation among the Analytic Moral Philosophers

Karl Barth's "Christian optimism" is pervasively theological.[131] The primacy of the covenant and of Jesus Christ in the history of God's actions toward humanity means creation has a Christological center and form. On Barth's view, creation's extrinsic basis and grounds in Christ does not *weaken* our confidence in its goodness, but definitively establishes it and heightens it. If *God* has deemed the creation good, and good just as it is, who are we to say otherwise? Through faith, we are drawn into the circle of God's confidence, which gives us a confidence in the actuality and goodness of the created world that is impossible if we remain trapped in the self-enclosed circle of rationality or experience. This confidence is uniquely ethical or existential: we can "live and die" in it, unlike any other hypothesis about creation's existence or goodness.

This "Christian optimism," though, does not entail that *philosophical* optimism and pessimism are on a par. On the one side, Barth commends Schopenhauer for his "honesty," as any philosophical optimism founded inescapably bottoms out into his pessimism. At the same time, Barth recognizes that the meaning of the world's negative aspects is ambivalent: life's "disquietudes, objectively considered, are never so great and crushing as to make us ultimately disturbed and therefore

---

129. Barth *CD* III/3, 298, emphasis mine.
130. Karl Barth, *Wolfgang Amadeus Mozart* (Eugene: Wipf and Stock, 2003), 55–6.
131. Andrew Gabriel distills his view this way: "By focusing on Jesus Christ, Christian 'optimism' does not eliminate but assimilates the shadow side of creation. It affirms that creation has an imperfection. Hence, unlike optimism, it does not base its positive judgment on the world. In Barth's mind, such a judgment has no authority and wrongly supposes a goodness intrinsic to creation; by contrast, Christian optimism regarding the goodness of creation is based on a recognition of the Yes of the Creator as revealed in Jesus Christ." Gabriel, *Barth's Doctrine of Creation*, 48.

ready to find peace in God," as they are so often followed by "pacifications" that allow us to recover our poise.[132] Pessimism is ultimately wrong because it is practically self-defeating: the human proclivity to carry on despite the trauma and suffering life can bring is a phenomenon in want of an explanation. On the other side, philosophical optimism seems to have a formal affinity with the Gospel. For Barth, the goods of creation are fundamental and recalcitrant, while evils and suffering are transient—and the Yes of Christian optimism is primary, while its No is secondary and derivative. This primacy of goodness means that Schopenhauer might be honest, but Leibniz's optimism has a commonality with Christianity that pessimism does not enjoy. Leibniz "must be taken seriously in dogmatics," Barth suggests, "because he too ... in his own way did in fact sing, the unqualified praise of God the Creator in His relationship to the creature."[133] Barth goes on: "In the whole history of ideas," he writes, "there is hardly a single verdict which verbally corresponds so closely to the Christian verdict as that of 18th century optimism."[134]

The formal affinity between philosophical optimism and the Gospel is not an endorsement of natural theology. Neither is it a license to optimistically infer God's action or blessing from the events of history.[135] Yet Barth's rejection of the inference from the goodness of this world to God's goodness must be set alongside his endorsement of creation's non-neutrality *vis a vis* the covenant. That creation is adapted and serviceable to God's purposes can only be known from within the covenant. From that standpoint, we discover that it *is* so adapted, and that it has its justification from God on the basis of this adaptation—and not only through its use by God. There is one order of God, the reconciliation of the world in Jesus Christ. Yet this order is "also the confirmation and restoration of the order of creation," such that in the life of Jesus Christ "there takes place, with the establishment of the new order, the reconstitution of the old."[136] God does not withdraw from creation the "time, space and opportunity" that he gives it, but rather as the "Guarantor, Sustainer, and Protector of His creaturely world, of the cosmos or nature," gives to it "constancy in the being with which He endowed it at creation."[137] The goodness of creation is secured by God and is constituted by its correspondence to God's work in the covenant.

Barth's doctrine of creation thus has more points of contact with the philosophical attempts to justify procreating than we might have expected given

---

132. Barth *CD* III/1, 374.

133. Ibid., 405.

134. Ibid. The "whole of Christendom," Barth contends, "must think and feel and speak more or less plainly and tastefully according to the insights, expression and tone of the 18th century."

135. In IV/3.2, Barth writes that the doctrine of providence "has nothing whatever to do with an optimistic evaluation of the world." Barth, *CD* IV/3.2, 692.

136. Barth *CD* IV/3.1, 43.

137. Ibid., 138.

its Christological orientation. Barth's defense of creation's goodness is apologetic in the sense that it demonstrates the necessity of fideism through immanent critiques of moral philosophers. The limits of philosophy only emerge through an encounter with it: there is no *a priori* determination in Barth about what philosophy can do. Instead, Barth makes time for dissenting opinions in his doctrine of creation. These interactions do not distract from his theological work, but clarify and deepen his dogmatic account by highlighting the antitheses between it and its philosophical alternatives.

There is a formal similarity between the optimism and pessimism that Barth repudiates and the various accounts of procreation that the first part of this work considered. Barth's contention that philosophical attempts to coordinate the light and shadow sides of creation will fail to give one side their due cuts hard against both philosophical pro- and anti-natalism. Benatar must debunk countervailing evidence about life's benefits in order to maintain his thoroughgoing anti-natalism, while optimistic accounts must minimize the seriousness of pessimistic concerns (like Sandel's defense of limited responsibility seems to do). Like eighteenth-century optimism, procreative optimisms are too unstable, too insecure to live, or give life, based upon them. Methodologically, Barth thinks that the moral field is unremittingly opaque until it has been clarified by revelation: the Word of God rescues us out of a "clash of opinions."[138] Barth's judgment concurs with David Heyd's contention that we need an independent, external reference point to determine whether we ought be optimists or pessimists about procreating—only where Heyd prescinds from claiming such a standpoint, Barth thinks revelation makes it available to us. Without it, the contest of intuitions that emerged in the first chapter seems like a structural feature of moral philosophy (indicating that Jeff McMahan is right to worry that realism might be the cost of consistency).

Substantively, Barth's asymmetrical priority of goods over evils in creation changes the landscape against which we might assess the risks of procreative activity. Barth's ethical framework is not far from Kass' teleological, evolutionary understanding of nature, in that the presuppositions of moral judgments (nature for Kass, creation for Barth) dispose us to act in certain ways without themselves being the grounds or basis for moral judgments. For Barth, creation is adapted to be the instrument of God and the theater of the covenant. Though it does not determine or produce the covenant, its form is neither dispensable nor arbitrary, but allows us to speak of signs and witnesses to God's grace when we recognize them as corresponding to God's action in Christ. If God's action in creating is primarily oriented toward life, then it might be reasonable from this standpoint to expect a lower rate of embryo loss than Kass invokes—even while endorsing one does not permit someone to blithely, optimistically wave the problem away. Insofar as the weight or significance of one's reasons to procreate is affected by such background considerations, then the broadly optimistic account of creation Barth supplies might make procreation presumptively permissible.

---

138. *CD* III/1, 367.

4. Neither Optimism nor Pessimism

God creates out of the freedom of His love—and in creating, orders the world toward the display of His glory in time through establishing fellowship with humanity. There is no reason for God's creation beyond God's love—but this love aims beyond the mere existence of creation toward its glorification. Such a framework delicately preserves a teleology in God's creative work without invidiously instrumentalizing creatures for ends that do not include their own well-being or flourishing.[139] Yet Barth blocks any direct derivation from God's reasons for creation to our reasons to procreate. As noted above, the mutuality of human love responds to existing individuals, which does not account for the asymmetry between parents and children procreating creates. By contrast, God's love does not "rest on a presupposition of this kind, but creates the presupposition."[140]

The gap between what God is doing in creating and what we do in procreating means the theological question of procreation can be approached from two (interrelated) levels. On one level, there is a question about the theological significance of procreation as a practice: why does God permit the species to continue, especially after the birth of Christ? On another level, there is a question about what reasons individual couples might have to pursue forming human life. These two planes are intertwined, yet distinct: the theological significance of procreation forms the broad backdrop against which reasons to procreate are assessed, and out of which the church can responsibly base her exhortations to procreate.

Subsequent chapters will consider each of these questions, though not necessarily in direct linear fashion. Barth's contention that the obligation to procreate ceases after the birth of Christ means we must assess more carefully how he situates procreation in his account of creation and the covenant and, correspondingly, between the relationship of the Old and New Testaments. Barth argues that Marcion's docetism corresponds to his repudiation of the Old Testament. However, there is a question about whether Barth's Christological focus leaves sufficient room for the Old Testament's witness to the good of procreation. These themes occupy Chapter 5, which will attend more specifically to the theological significance of procreation (if any) in Barth's theology. Chapter 6 takes a more localized focus, attending to how Barth's anthropological account of "life" and his construal of humanity's constitution underwrite his procreative ethics. As we saw in Chapter 3, the moral value of procreative bonds is tied to the significance of biology to personal identity. Barth's account of "life" requires us to affirm our own constitution, which offers a path toward giving prospective couples discrete reasons to generate life. Still, any Barthian pro-natalism must account for the primacy of Christ for both anthropology and ethics. While Christ did not have children himself, he was born of a woman—and his birth has some bearing on how we understand our own participation in making human life. Chapter 7 thus introduces Barth's Mariology to assess how Barth's worries about ascribing Mary

---

139. I elaborate more on the place of eudaimonism in Barth's moral theory in Chapter 8.
140. *CD* III/1, 96.

agency structures his special ethics of procreation—and also invokes Barth's ethics of parenthood to reconfigure Barth's treatment of Mary. Chapter 8 extends this reconstruction by developing Barth's (often overlooked) treatment of honour at the end of his doctrine of creation, which offers an affirmation of procreative action that also extends the reasons prospective parents have to procreate.

The strength of Barth's account of creation is that it engenders a strong confidence about facing the future—though not, as we saw in the introduction to this chapter, as brash a confidence as one might expect from Barth's reputation. Barth's argument that pessimism and optimism are neither deep nor comprehensive enough to live upon is attractive. In the face of suffering and the debunking arguments that draw upon it, mitigating strategies by pro-natalists seem wanting. Yet humans keep generating new life, forgetting the traumas and horrors of the past out of a resilient belief that goodness will prevail. Neither pessimism nor Pollyannish optimism are able to account for this strange set of affairs. Yet Barth's doctrine of creation, with its prioritization of the covenant and the asymmetrical acknowledgment of both creation's light and darkness, offers an escape from the interminably vague contest of intuitions, opinions, and hypotheses that otherwise besets us. Only faith in God the Creator offers us the "necessary and therefore sure confidence of those whom God has first drawn into His confidence, by the revelation of His activity, in view of which this confidence is continually renewed and its certainty continually achieved and confirmed."[141]

---

141. Ibid., 388.

Chapter 5

BIRTH BETWEEN THE TIMES: PROCREATION IN BARTH'S DOCTRINE OF CREATION

Barth's insistence that the birth of Christ means the "the propagation of the race … has ceased to be an unconditional command" raises questions about what sort of obligation it was and why Christ's birth has dissolved it.[1] Assessing whether and why procreating might be an appropriate response to the goodness of God and of creation requires understanding its meaning and significance in God's economy of the world—an economy structured not only by God's creative work, but by the fulfillment of the covenant in Jesus Christ.

The question of procreation's significance in Barth's theology is a species of the broader concern that his theology has an inadequate account of the meaning of creation and of human action. While others have pointed to Christ's fulfillment of our action and Barth's repudiation of deification as undermining the significance of human action, I will suggest that the pressure against the moral and theological significance of procreating comes from elsewhere in Barth's thought—namely, his account of eternity and the dissolution of time and human existence Barth thinks comes with it.[2] Understanding Barth's ethics of procreation requires looking behind his special ethics of parenthood and procreation in III/4 of the *Church Dogmatics* to his whole doctrine of creation, which includes his anthropology and doctrine of

---

1. Barth, *CD* III/4, 268.
2. Gerald McKenny frames his worry about Barth's ethics as, in part, a question about the "moral significance of our being as creatures." See *Karl Barth's Moral Thought*, page 46. In *The Analogy of Grace*, McKenny puts his worry similarly. While concurring with Webster and others that there is ample room for human action in his theology, McKenny contends that the fact that Jesus Christ accomplishes the good in our place means "it is unclear what meaning and status our moral action can have for Barth even if we are not in doubt regarding the reality of human action in his theology." See McKenny, *The Analogy of Grace*, 202. There, McKenny's verdict on Barth's theology is ambivalent: he contends that Barth's denial of sacramentalism and of deification cannot make adequate sense of our participation in God's action through the Spirit. See *The Analogy of Grace*, 201–23. I reserve the full response to McKenny's concern until the end of Chapter 7.

providence. Adopting a wide scope on Barth's view of procreation will clarify the tensions in his doctrine of creation that emerged in the previous chapter, namely, between the Christocentric basis for creation and its immanent or intrinsic goodness (or lack thereof). At the same time, such an excavation will show how Barth's account of procreation intersects with his understanding of life, the *imago Dei*, and marriage. This chapter generally proceeds chronologically, from the earlier volumes of Barth's doctrine of creation to the later. Yet the movement might also be described as one from the external to the internal, or from the third-person point of view to the first-person point of view. Insofar as ethics is preparation to hear the command of God, rather than a strict derivation of a practical norm from a theological description, such a movement is necessary—as ethics does not leave the question of procreation free-floating in an otherwise abstract doctrine of creation but brings it within the perspective and outlook of the couple whose decision it ultimately must be.

Procreation in the Doctrine of Creation (III/1)

Barth's first and only substantive discussion of Genesis 1:28's "command" to "be fruitful and multiply" happens in II/2's discussion of the covenantal character of the divine command, rather than in the doctrine of creation he develops in Volume III. In it, Barth argues that Scripture does not offer a general or universal moral code. Instead, God commands characters in the text so that they might be equipped to bear witness to the unique history of the covenant of grace. Such an approach might seem to leave Genesis 1:28 in a precarious position, as its content seems universally applicable. While Barth argues that it is, he also notes that it "does not seem to reckon with the possibility of sin." The themes that Barth later develops in his doctrine of creation are all present here, including framing the command to procreate around the affirmation of life: "The grace of God wills that man should live …, but live without question or discussion and not as his own judge." Sin's invasion into the world means the "command to live must now be repeated under the sign of the divine patience, and from now on it must be heard under this sign and with this caveat."[3] While Barth seems to think that there is a general obligation to perpetuate the species, the intrusion of sin means such an obligation should not—or cannot—be disconnected from the faithfulness of God in the covenant. Moreover, God's patience with humanity becomes the pre-eminent theological referent for procreative activity (rather than His glory, beatitude, joy, or love).

When Barth turns to his doctrine of creation, he expands his account of life to tie together Genesis 1:28 with the development of a "natural history" that indicates the history of the covenant. In his discussion of vegetation, Barth associates life

---

3. *CD* II/2, 679.

with reproduction: a "creature is alive," he suggests, when "through its seed it can continue in the existence of similar creatures, and in addition can bear fruit."[4] The existence of living vegetation is not a result of the earth's immanent powers: vegetation is created in response to hearing the Word of God, and so is "an archetype of the capacity for obedience on the part of the creature as the Bible understands it."[5] At the same time, vegetation's reproductive potential entails that "what is produced by the Word of God is itself something that produces."[6] Because it bears seed and is alive, vegetation begins "natural history," which is "both a precursor type and also a substratum of the history of the covenant of grace."[7] Barth correlates the "natural history" indicated by the livingness of vegetation with God's command to "be fruitful and multiply." In forming the basis for a natural history, the significance of the command is only made manifest in this "commission which constitutes the Messiah [as] the beginning and goal of human history."[8]

The blessing given to birds and fish on the fifth day has similar typological content as vegetation, but underscores the limits on human agency in fulfilling the command to procreate. While vegetation "already possesses [the power required to reproduce] by reason of its nature," the autonomous movement of animals requires a special blessing to reproduce.[9] God's blessing authorizes and empowers animals to be successful in the unique act of reproducing themselves. For Barth, reproduction is "a definite venture where it has the form of a spontaneous act of a creature qualified for the purpose." And "because of its similarity with the divine activity, it requires divine permission and the divine promise if it is not to be arrogant and purposeless."[10] The need for God's special blessing to form new life brings generation into the sphere of divine action, and thus introduces for the first time the problem of "history proper as a continuation of creation." Such a problem takes as its original form "the problem of the sequence of procreation, of fatherhood and sonship," which Barth thinks is central to the biblical history of the covenant.[11] The need for divine blessing in procreation means the fifth day thus functions as an "introductory prologue" to the covenant.

"What happens here to fish and fowl prefigures the divine promise to Abraham which initiates the whole history of salvation, namely, that through a son God will make of

---

4. *CD* III/1, 143. "Beasts and men will also be creatures which bear seed and are therefore alive." Ibid., 154.

5. Ibid., 153.

6. Ibid., "The living creature" is, "without being untrue to its nature, able to reproduce itself in the form of seed, which without being untrue to itself can again be productive."

7. Ibid., 154.

8. Ibid.

9. Ibid., 174.

10. Ibid., 170.

11. Ibid.

him a great nation, as numerous as the stars of heaven and as the sand by the seashore, 'and thy seed shall possess the gate of thy enemies'. (Gen. 12:1, 151, 22:15)"

This "involves the multiplication and replenishment of the earth, and therefore the fulfilment of the blessing pronounced on fish and birds as well as man."[12]

Ordering procreation to the covenant secures it in the face of the ongoing threat of evil and nothingness, rather than diminishing our confidence in it. The "prologue" of God's blessing of the animals reveals that God wills the creature to be fruitful, which means God will "bear and surround and rule it in the exercise of the freedom granted to it."[13] Anticipating his doctrine of providence, Barth writes that the blessing means the animal needs "the accompaniment of the powerful Word of God," by whom it is "empowered to accomplish its own living acts."[14] Such divine accompaniment means the "history of the preservation and renewal of created life as such is to take its course," even in the face of the threats of chaos and nothingness.[15] On this basis humanity "may therefore live, not in fear but in trust and confidence."[16]

When Barth turns explicitly to humanity in his reading of the first creation account, he puts procreation in continuity with the theological significance he affords animal and vegetative reproduction—yet also qualifies that significance through Genesis 1:26's claim that humanity is created in the "image of God." On Barth's view, Christ is the image of God, while humanity is created "in correspondence with the image of God."[17] Barth notoriously ties the content of the image, though, to the sexual differentiation that is prototypically revealed

---

12. Ibid., 174. This is not to say that the procreation of animals and humans is equivalent. Barth underscores on 179 that the blessing of humanity is "something new." The distinction between humanity and the animals is partially ethical: animals may function as a "spectacle of submission," but only humanity hears the Word of God "mediately, reflectively and deliberatively." We are "ordained to meet the divine reason with reason." That humanity can be disobedient is the converse of the fact that we are "summoned to decision by the divine address," giving us a freedom as an "actively participating witness" to God's grace that other animals do not enjoy. Ibid., 175.

13. Ibid., 170.

14. Ibid., 174.

15. Ibid.

16. Ibid., 171. "Daß Gott auch diesen Kreis gut geschaffen und daß der Mensch Anlaß hat, auch im Blick auf ihn nicht in Furcht, sondern im Vertrauen und mit Mut zu leben, dieser Bericht und diese Mahnung der Sage hat offenbar jetzt erst, indem sie auch von diesem Segen berichtet, spezifischen Gehalt und überzeugende Kraft gewonnen." KD III/1, 191. Land animals are a "dumb but eloquent type" of the "theme of human history," which is the "mystery of fatherhood and sonship," but also introduce the possibility of sacrifice—and thus indicate the "indispensable offering of the promised Son of Man." Ibid., 178.

17. Ibid., 197. The covenant reveals that the "divine likeness" can only exist for humanity in the one who "will actually be God's image," who is "real man on his behalf," namely, "Jesus

in Christ's relationship to the Church. The "creaturely repetition" or "copy and imitation" of God's inner life that makes humanity the fitting counterpart to God is constituted by the structural differentiation of male and female.[18] The duality of man and woman indicates that humanity is a creature, but also "distinct and free" and thus to "reflect God's image." The "true *humanum*" of male and female is the "great paradigm" of the history of divine action, a "type of the history of the covenant and salvation."[19] However, this *humanum* is only the presupposition for human action. To engage in spontaneous and independent movement, humans need the divine blessing.[20] This movement takes two basic forms: procreation and lordship over other animals. While Barth's treatment of the blessing of the animals had suggested human procreation needed such a blessing because of its similarity to divine activity, Barth here *diminishes* its divine-like character. Human procreation is "animal-like," but our lordly stance toward the world "assumes a dangerous proximity to God's activity as Creator" and thus stands in particular need of God's "permission and promise for his activity."[21] Here, already, Barth seems to be engaging in a tacit deprioritization of procreative activity in favor of other forms of labor, a move that will become explicit in his reading of the second creation account.

Despite this minimization of procreation's intrinsic significance, Barth contends that it is an expression of our hope in God—at least before the birth of Christ.[22] New individuals who are created will "be blessed with the blessing addressed to the first man in and with his creation." The permission and promise God gives in blessing the first man are confirmed by the covenant—which means that everything that happens in the generational line of humanity "will essentially and properly be salvation history."[23] While humanity is unable to maintain our species through our own initiative, the extrinsic basis of our lives in Christ secures our hope and confidence in its continuation. God's action in the covenant will "confirm and fulfil the blessing given to man in relation to the act of his propagation and in relation to the assumption of his position of power and dignity as compared with other creatures."[24] Humanity has the "divine permission and promise" to procreate

---

Christ and His community." Ibid., 190. The "creation saga is careful not to say of Adam that he either was or in some way possessed the image of God," which can be said only of Christ alone. Ibid., 202.

18. Ibid., 183.
19. Ibid., 186.
20. Ibid., 188.
21. Ibid., 188–9.
22. Ibid., 191.
23. Ibid., 189. This also anticipates Barth's doctrine of providence, where he argues that salvation and natural history are one. See III/3, 132.
24. Ibid., 190.

because our existence is "only the external basis of the existence of this other man [Christ] but as the existence of this other man may really be an existence in genuine hope on God." Through their exercise of the twin powers of procreation and lordship, humans "continually realise in themselves the sign of this hope," and even participate in that to which they point, namely "the sign of the Son of Man and of His community."[25] Indeed, Barth contends that human activity *only* has meaning insofar as it is a realization of this sign of hope—but at the same time our "natural being and activity" are signs that God has made Himself our hope.[26] While Barth generalizes this significance, so that everyone who procreates participates in this hope even if they do not know Christ, tying procreation to natural history raises a question about whether the hope procreation expresses has the same valence once Christ is born. Barth contends the genealogical tables of the Old Testament are a "sign of the patience in which God fulfills his blessing of the human race and makes possible its history (as a natural history within all other natural history)."[27] Yet once the end and goal of that natural history are revealed through the birth of Christ, and procreating no longer has its "external basis" in the future Messiah, whether it can continue to be a sign of our hope for further divine action remains an open question.

Barth's insistence that procreating is (only, but by no means merely) a sign of our hope in God extends to his description of what we are doing in creating human life, which also further circumscribes procreating as a natural phenomenon. Children do not inherit the *imago Dei* from their parents; instead, God directly and immediately secures the next generation's status as created in the *imago Dei*. The "repetition of [humanity's] being in this image and after this likeness cannot be his own concern, but only that of a divine restoration and renewal."[28] The divine likeness is the "pledge and promise with which God accompanies the physical sequence of the generations and gives it meaning." The fulfillment of God's pledge is not found in the "course of any natural compulsion, and therefore not merely in and with generation."[29] Only "the existence of the human race as such" is preserved in procreating: the generation of a new human being only establishes the physical *possibility* of the *imago Dei*, not its reality. Adam's begetting of Seth is a separate act from God's creating of Adam—which means the "the likeness of Adam to God and the likeness of Seth to Adam" are two different things.[30] As Barth emphasizes, it is "not at all the case that God's activity now finds as it were renewal and continuation in Adam's procreation."[31] Because the covenant requires divine action, the "possibility and continuity" of human history are "not assured

---

25. Ibid., 190–1.
26. Ibid., 191.
27. Ibid., 199.
28. Ibid., 189.
29. Ibid., 200.
30. Ibid., 193.
31. Ibid., 198.

by the fact Adam can be reflected in Seth; that man can become a father and have a son."[32] Instead, the most we can do is "hope" that the Creator will "so acknowledge the new creature," that the "son he has begotten may like himself be created in and after the image of God." Children do not inherit the *imago Dei* from their progenitors: rather, their reception of it is "the realization of a hope which can be fulfilled only in a direct decision and action on the part of God Himself."[33]

Barth thus attempts to hold together the human act of procreating with the need for special, divine action in creating individuals. On the one side, procreation is a sign of hope in God and the sequence of generations is an indication of His patience. On the other side, procreation only makes the advent of Christ technically or physically possible and divine action is needed for the child to be created in the *imago Dei*. God has promised to hold these two sides together and, as He is faithful to His promises, they are more secure than if they were only grounded in nature. Still, it is striking that Barth contends humanity's lordship over other animals places him in "dangerous proximity" to the Creator, while he simultaneously dissociates human begetting from the divine action of creating. The fact that procreation appears to be so near to creating a human being in God's image animates Barth to emphatically distinguish the physical act of procreating from God's work of creating a human being in His image, even while holding them together. Barth's position that the *imago Dei* is not a possession or intrinsic capacity of humanity, but is instead an external referent to which humanity's existence and action correspond (namely, Christ), entails that the means of securing a genealogy of descendants in the *imago Dei* lies not in humanity, but God.

While Barth's reading of the first creation account distinguishes procreation from the perpetuation of individuals created in the *imago Dei*, his reading of the second makes procreation independent of marriage. Such a move is exegetically animated: unlike the first creation account, the second lacks an explicit blessing on humanity's procreative powers. Yet Barth's treatment of life in the second creation account also eclipses its reproductive dimension, reorienting humanity's "fruitfulness" away from fertility toward service and (non-procreative) work. On Barth's reading, the second creation account regards the flourishing of vegetation and animals as its own end, which humanity is oriented toward. The crisis of creation in this account is internal to it: the threat is barrenness or aridity, rather than the external threat of chaos. The creaturely world "moves from death to life," a drama which is signified by the original barrenness of the earth until the mist goes up from it and the human is created.[34] The question of creation is whether "God should have created the earth in vain, denying it a future and hope."[35] Adam is the answer to that question, though only insofar as the human is uniquely and immediately dependent upon God. The creation of the human from the dust is a

---

32. Ibid., 199.
33. Ibid.
34. Ibid., 237. Cf. also 235.
35. Ibid., 241.

"sign of the courage and confidence" that creation's existence will not be left barren or meaningless—not because we are created from the dust *per se*, but because unlike any other animal, God directly animates us with His own breath. This "most direct and personal and most special" act of breathing life into humanity's nostrils means humanity is able to function as a sign of the "courage and confidence" that creation be fruitful.[36] As Barth writes, the "realisation of this hope waits for man as the being which, earthy by nature, will triumph over the aridity, barrenness and deadness of the earth because God is his refuge and hope, because God has constituted Himself as such." Though Barth contends that humanity is a sign of hope in our "existence," work is the end and purpose of existence.[37] Humanity's creation from the dust means that "man is destined for the earth, for its service, i.e. its cultivation."[38] In tilling and keeping the ground, humanity "is responsible to both God and the creature" and "fulfils the meaning of his own existence."[39]

At the same time, the creation of the woman is necessary to fulfill and complete the man, just as the covenant completes creation. Humanity's existence "must be an anticipation or type"—the image—of the "form of God's relationship to it ... in the coming covenant between them."[40] Male and female together thus function as an image of the covenant. Yet the creation of male and female is also patterned upon creation and its completion in the covenant, which means the creation of the woman is "not only one secret but *the* secret, the heart of all the secrets of God the Creator." God's covenant with humanity is "prefigured in this event, in the completing of man's emergence by the coming of woman to man."[41] On this basis, Barth recapitulates his stance that the covenant is not caused by creation's immanent powers or capabilities, but through divine action. Adam is incapable of bringing about the woman: he does not "actively participate" in the "completion of his own creation."[42] Nor does Eve's formation from Adam's rib indicate that his flesh is an intrinsically suitable instrument for God's creative-redemptive action. Instead, Adam becomes for Eve what the earth and dust were to his own creation—"the material which quite apart from its merits or suitability is used by God for His work and impressed into His service."[43] If there is a preparation for the covenant in humans, it is "the secret of God."[44]

---

36. Ibid., 237.

37. Barth writes that humanity is permitted to erect a sign of this confidence in "his existence and work and service, and even in his necessary return to dust." Ibid., 238.

38. Ibid., 244.

39. Ibid., 237.

40. Ibid., 290.

41. Ibid., 295.

42. Ibid., 294.

43. Ibid., 302.

44. Ibid., 295. The completion of creation takes a Christological shape: the removal of Adam's rib indicates that a "grievous wound inflicted on him but also healed." The creation of Eve as his completion is an indicator to Adam of the "nearness of death but also—and much more so—of protection from death." Ibid., 299.

However, the completion of creation by the covenant has no *further* referent or completion to which it might be ordered—a position that has significant implications for Barth's understanding of procreation. The woman's silence indicates that as the completion of man the woman "has no need of a further completion of her own."[45] Barth's reading of the first creation account distanced procreation from any kind of continuation of or participation in God's creation. Here, he regards marriage as the completion of humanity. The "therefore" that marks the transition from Eve's creation to the explanation that a man "shall cleave unto his wife" is not arbitrary: marriage, not procreation, is "conformable to what begins in creation," and so is an anticipation and recapitulation of God's action in completing the covenant with humanity. Barth discovers in the passage an "account of the divine basis of love and marriage as the fulfillment of the relationship between man and wife," which reveals the "mystery of the divine covenant of grace."[46]

The eschatological reconfiguration of love and marriage that Christ's advent brings about introduces the possibility of a marital union that has no reference to children. The second creation account lacks "what the rest of the Old Testament regards as the heart of the matter," namely, the "problem of posterity, human fatherhood and motherhood, the family, the child and above all the son." The Old Testament predominately frames this "problem of posterity" as the reason for marriage; marriage is sacred because it makes possible the "procreation of the holy seed and therefore the hope of Israel."[47] Only Genesis 2 and the Song of Songs know of male and female apart from their status as potential fathers and mothers.[48] The *eros* these texts depict appears only because the Old Testament is able to see (in a glass darkly) outside itself toward the covenant's fulfillment.[49] "Because the election of God is real," Barth writes, "there is such a thing as love and marriage."[50] But because the Israelites wait for the Messiah, the Old Testament mainly depicts "man and woman in the role of father and mother, begetting and bearing posterity, i.e. not directed toward themselves but towards the future Son."[51] Such a position comes near to framing the procreative interest as responsive to conditions of sin, a position that Charlotte von Kirschbaum seems to make explicit.[52] Sin ruined

---

45. Ibid., 303.
46. Ibid., 305.
47. Ibid., 312.
48. Ibid., 313.
49. Ibid., 314.
50. Ibid., 318.
51. Ibid., 320.
52. Von Kirschbaum suggests that the Israelite author of Genesis 2 "perceives the man-woman relationship as in essence destroyed … but dependent on hope in a future eventuality." As such, "he sees man and woman basically as oriented toward their progeny." As the "mother of all living," Eve becomes "for [the man] bearer of hope." It is notable how little Barth discusses Genesis 3:20, Adam's description of Eve as the "mother of all

the relationship of male and female *per se*, which is why it is spoken of in the Old Testament only in Genesis 2 and the Song of Solomon: "For it can be ventured only in relation to God's creation, and then again in the eschatological context of the portrayal of Solomon's royal glory."[53] The fulfillment of creation through Christ's action in the covenant means "for the first time the relationship between man and woman is honoured as such, and not merely in the light of fatherhood or motherhood or posterity—which fade into the background in the New Testament."[54]

Barth's construal of procreation across both accounts of creation underscores that it is a sign of hope in God—but also leaves open questions about how it can be a sign of hope after the advent of Christ. The first creation account indicated that the fruitfulness of humanity is the "external basis" of the birth of the Messiah and set sharp limits on what sort of continuity procreation is able to secure. And while Barth says animal reproduction needs divine blessing because it is similar to divine activity, he emphasizes the animality of human reproduction when it is set alongside our "lordship." The second creation account frames our work and service as the meaning of our existence, subordinating existence toward those ends. And perhaps most significantly, the absence of children marks Barth's understanding of the eschatological reconfiguration of marriage—rather than their presence. The completion of the man by the woman seems to generate fruit only accidentally, as there is nothing intrinsic in the relationship of male and female that requires anything further. Barth's account does not entail that the paradigmatic marriage is barren or sterile. Yet it does seem to qualify the sense in which procreation can be a sign of hope after the advent of Christ, which brings to an end the necessity of the "sequence of generations" that demonstrated God's patience through the Old Testament. Together, these readings leave procreation in a precarious theological condition.

Procreation in Barth's Anthropology (III/2)

Barth's anthropology confirms and extends his discussion of procreation from his doctrine of creation. Barth contends in the preface to his volume on anthropology that his exposition of the being and nature of humanity through a(n ostensibly) strict Christological lens "deviates even more widely from dogmatic tradition"

---

living": the index to the *Dogmatics* lists precisely one reference to the text, and that is a quotation of someone else (IV/1, 667). It also seems to be a fairly ambivalent term for von Kirschbaum. Like Barth, she seems to only speak of motherhood emerging in response to the intensification of desire for one's husband as a result of the fall (Genesis 3:16). See Charlotte von Kirschbaum, *The Question of Woman*, 61. See also 116 and 121–2, where Eve's name is a promise that overcomes the judgment of Genesis 3:16.

53. Ibid., 314.
54. Ibid., 323.

than his landmark treatment of predestination.[55] Deriving the content of a general human nature from Jesus Christ is by no means straightforward, as his humanity is "determined by a relationship between God and Himself such as has never existed between God and us, and never will exist."[56] Christ's union with the Father is not the abrogation or transcendence of His humanity, but its foundation. As Barth writes, it is Christ's "very participation in the divine which is the basis of His humanity."[57] This entails that we know the contents of human nature by looking at Christ's work and history as the Savior. There is "no neutral humanity in Jesus," and there is no place outside of Christ's determination for the covenant from which we might discover the contents of human nature.[58] Christ's work as Savior "reveals and explains human nature with all its possibilities."[59]

The theocentric orientation of Christ's life as a human enables Barth to begin his general anthropology with the claim that "basically and comprehensively ... to be a man is to be with God," which we can do only insofar as we are with Jesus.[60] Our nature and essence are extrinsically ordered, which means a true description of our humanity requires us to see it in an explicitly Christological frame. Barth's personalism, which stresses that our being is constituted by our encounter with God, moves (covenantal) history to the forefront of his theological anthropology. For Barth, history begins when "something new and other than its own nature befalls" a creature. It is not the creature's self-motivated action through time that makes history possible, but an encounter with something that transcends it so that it is "compelled and enabled to transcend itself in response and in relation to this new factor."[61] This entails, though, that the creature does not *have* a history but rather "*is* in the history itself."[62] While our nature does not make us capable of being with God, the history of humanity's encounter with God in Jesus (which has its prototype in God's election) reveals the essence of our being.[63] As Barth distills the two main principles around which our humanity is organized, our humanity is summoned by God because we have been elected with Christ, and we have heard God's gracious summons in Christ and so are to answer in gratitude, honour, and responsibility.[64]

The primacy of the history of our encounter with God does not eclipse humanity's constitution—even if it does relativize it in a way past treatments of

---

55. Barth, *CD* III/2, ix.
56. Ibid., 49.
57. Ibid., 66.
58. Ibid., 56.
59. Ibid., 59.
60. Ibid., 135.
61. Ibid., 158.
62. Ibid.
63. Ibid., 163.
64. This distills—too quickly!—Barth's work on pages 142–202.

theological anthropology failed to do. While I will reserve the substance of my discussion about Barth's treatment of humanity's organic life in time for the next chapter, it is worth noting here that his theological anthropology runs on parallel tracks to his doctrine of creation by integrating the covenantal and creaturely dimensions of humanity without dividing or confusing them. As the covenant precedes and explains creation, so humanity's "endowment merely follows as part of the summons, his constitution being his equipment."[65] While being "summoned includes, and therefore has as a presupposition [humanity's] constitution, his existence as a natural and spiritual being," in relation to his "awakened being" this presupposition is only a "*materia inhabilis et indispositia,*" like the dust from which Adam was formed.[66] At the same time, our humanity (including our constitution) is not *neutral vis a vis* the covenant. As Barth writes, the "creatureliness of man, his human nature, his humanity, cannot be alien to this grace of God (no matter how inconceivable its address to it) but must necessarily confront it as it were with a certain familiarity." As the theater of God's creation is adapted to His service, so the creature is "serviceable, adapted, and well-pleasing" to be God's covenant-partner.[67] As Barth distills humanity's being and nature in its relationship to the covenant, humanity is "orientated towards that which he is determined."[68]

There is no minimization in Barth's work of the form of human life and existence. Indeed, Barth contends that if we do not consider humanity "from below," as it were, in the creaturely form of our humanity, then we "shall certainly have seen and understood the content of [humanity's] being, but not the form inseparable from the content."[69] Humanity's divine determination for the covenant corresponds to our creaturely form "indissolubly and indestructibly."[70] This form includes our constitution and our life in time, but the "supreme constant" is the "mystery of the correspondence and similarity between the determination of man

---

65. Ibid., 152.

66. Ibid. Finally, the doctrine discloses that "even the potentiality of [humanity's] being does not lie within but outside himself."

67. Ibid., 224. See also 243, where Barth suggests the "manner of [humanity's] being is a likeness of its purpose and therefore of the fact that it is created by God for God." This "determination" of human being for the covenant is "parabolic." In his treatment of the 'basic form' of humanity, Barth argues that the form is distinct from humanity's determination for the covenant and that it persists even outside the covenant. While the covenant gives our existence and nature meaning, male and female are "covenant-partners by nature" but not "the covenant-partners *of God* by nature." Unlike becoming covenant-partners with God, being male and female is "something which is our own, and is inviolable and indestructible." That we are created in this way "*as* mutual partners ... leaves open the further possibility that we are created to be the partners of God." Ibid., 320.

68. Ibid., 319.

69. Ibid., 204.

70. Ibid., 206.

[for God] and his humanity."[71] This correspondence is constituted by the fact that Jesus in his humanity "repeats and reflects the inner being or essence of God and this confirms His being for God" by being *for* humanity. While the "divinity of the man Jesus" is constituted by His being "man for God," his humanity "can and must be described no less succinctly in the proposition that He is man for man, for other men, His fellows."[72] In this, the humanity of Jesus is the *imago Dei*.[73] All this entails that we see the humanity of Jesus only insofar as we see Him as with and for humanity. Yet this latter preposition is irreversible: only Jesus's humanity can be "absolutely and exclusively described as a being for man." By contrast, the human summoned by God "is a being of man with others," which is not an abstraction but takes its most basic form through the personalistic, I–Thou encounter in which "I am as Thou art."[74] This encounter requires reciprocity, even in its origin: "as" cannot mean that "Thou art" is the "cause, even the instrumental cause, or the true substance of the 'I am,'" as that causation would undermine the reciprocity that marks the relationship. While each side of the I–Thou relationship has its "own validity, dignity and self-certainty," they are not static existences but instead a history of dynamic and active relations. The origin of the I and Thou is thus "two-sided."[75]

While the I–Thou dynamic governs all of human relationships, its paradigmatic form is the relationship of male and female, which is the only "structural differentiation of human existence."[76] In putting male and female at the center, Barth inherently relativizes parenthood and, with it, procreation. Barth recapitulates his argument from Genesis 2 that the "basic form of humanity" can be sketched "without the usual expansion or restriction" to "father and mother and therefore child as the third thing proceeding from the other two."[77] While the rest of the Old Testament is almost exclusively concerned with the question of progeny, Genesis 2's silence about children means that the "relationship of man and woman has its own reality and dignity," and as such is the "basic relationship involving

---

71. Ibid.

72. Ibid., 208.

73. Ibid., 219. Barth goes on: "The humanity of Jesus, His fellow-humanity, His being for man as the direct correlative of His being for God, indicates, attests and reveals this correspondence and similarity" between the relationship of God and humanity and the prior relationship of God to Himself. Ibid., 220.

74. Ibid., 243.

75. Ibid., 248.

76. Ibid., 286. The I–Thou dynamic must be "explained as coincident with that of male and female" (293). Barth's treatment of the relationship between the sexes has been subject to considerable scrutiny. As my focus in this work is narrowly on the question of reasons to procreate, I do not here consider the broader questions of gender that Barth has often been criticized on.

77. Ibid., 293.

all others."⁷⁸ The eschatological announcement of the New Testament makes this independence of marriage from procreation and parenthood explicit. For Israel, the covenant with God is a "promise and preparation" for Christ's advent, and as such its completion must come to them from beyond. Because Israel is on the way in the "middle stretch between creation and the end," it must "display that sober interest in man and woman in their quality as father and mother."⁷⁹ However, the eschatological completion the New Testament announces means the "whole concern for marrying and giving in marriage and the raising up of children" can "no longer occupy men in the resurrection when according to Luke 20:38 they cannot 'die any more.'"⁸⁰ The mystery disclosed by the marital relation of male and female is "Christ and the community"—a correspondence that raises questions about the analogical value of procreation in Barth's framework.⁸¹

Barth's decision to bracket procreation from the *imago Dei* and so from having any place in the mystery of Christ and the church is consistent with his broader theological anthropology, even if critics object to it.⁸² Salai Hla Aung has suggested that Barth's omission fails for being insufficiently Trinitarian: "If Barth had seriously taken the place of the child in the structure of human relationship and interpreted the trinitarian model of human creation in the image of God as a creation in the form of I–Thou–He/It relationship ... it would make his trinitarian model a truly trinitarian one."⁸³ Such an amendment need be neither arbitrary nor founded upon natural theology, as Andrew Gabriel suggests.⁸⁴ Consider: the parent–child relationship is constituted by an asymmetry of origin. The child is from the parents, not vice versa. It is possible to see a correspondence to this asymmetry in the Triune God's inner life: the Father begets the Son, not vice versa.⁸⁵ Moreover, the covenant's role as the prototype for marriage makes it seem reasonable to want to give children a more robust position *vis a vis* the *imago*. Christ is begotten by the Father with the same

---

78. Ibid.

79. Ibid.

80. Ibid., 295.

81. Ibid., 317. As Faye Bodley-Dangelo observes, Barth "disentangles the sexual relationship from a reproductive framework, secures its christocentric reference in the Ephesians 5 bridal metaphor for Christ's relationship to the church, and locates in the Song of Songs the seeking, speaking, confessing (ecclesial) bride who is absent in Genesis 2." See Faye Bodley-Dangelo, *Sexual Difference, Gender, and Agency in Karl Barth's Church Dogmatics*, T&T Clark Explorations in Reformed Theology (London: Bloomsbury T&T Clark, 2021), 106.

82. See Elizabeth Frykberg, *Karl Barth's Theological Anthropology* (Princeton: Princeton Theological Seminary, 1993).

83. Salai Hla Aung, *The Doctrine of Creation in the Theology of Barth, Moltmann and Pannenberg* (Regensburg: Roderer Verlag, 1998), 269.

84. Gabriel, *Barth's Doctrine*, 69.

85. Gary Deddo notes that Richard St. Victor makes such a parallel in his work on the Trinity. See Deddo, *Theology*, 351 n.75.

love that he demonstrates to the church in the covenant. If Christ and the church are the prototype for marriage, then the Father-Son relationship into which the church is adopted would be the prototype for the fulfillment of marriage—and so children would have a role in the *imago*.

Yet Barth's concern to not let the *imago Dei* run over the distinction between the Creator and creature means other theological commitments block him from including children within the structure of the *imago*. For one, Barth's contention that creation corresponds to the Father's begetting of the Son places a stopping point in the correspondence between marriage and the Triune life. On his view, creation is a completed act that has no precise creaturely analogue (including procreation).[86] While marriage might embody the covenant in which God elects humanity in Christ, it can supply no analogy to creation. The only analogy to creation is the "eternal begetting of the Son by the Father."[87] Second, Barth emphasizes a number of asymmetries between God's covenant with us in Christ and the corresponding covenant of marriage. There is an asymmetry in the union we have with each other in virtue of our nature and the union God has with creatures in virtue of the covenant. There is also an asymmetry in our determination: humanity is with other humans, but God is also *for* humans in a way we cannot be. And there is an asymmetry of equality: male and female have a reciprocity and equal dignity the Creator–creature relationship lacks (at least if we take Barth's explicit statement about the matter as accurate).[88] Though Barth does not make it explicit, this asymmetry seems to include origination. For Barth, the female is the source of the male and *vice versa* in the I–Thou encounter. Similarly, there is a sense in which humanity is the source of Christ, who allows His humanity to be "prescribed and dictated and determined by an alien human being (that of His more near and distant fellows), and by the need and infinite peril of this being."[89] Barth goes on to suggest that if there "is indeed a powerful I of Jesus, it is only from this Thou, this fallen Adam" and from the "sequence of generations" that springs from Him. Christ is pleased to have His life "only from His apostles."[90] This symmetry of origins in the I–Thou encounter is obscured, though, when a third person who is

---

86. Aung's desire to see children included within the *imago* is, in this way, tied to her reading that Barth thinks "creation is not a reality which has been completed once and for all. Rather, creation is an ongoing work of God, and we ought to name it *creatio continua*." Aung, *The Doctrine of Creation*, 81. This collapses together providence and creation, though, which Barth emphatically distinguishes. See Barth, *CD* III/1, 44, 60 and *III/2*, 6 ff.

87. Creation "denotes the divine action which has a real analogy, a genuine point of comparison, only in the eternal begetting of the Son by the Father, and therefore only in the inner life of God Himself, and *not at all in the life of the creature*." Barth, *CD* III/1, 14, emphasis mine.

88. *CD* III/2, 321.

89. Ibid., 214.

90. Ibid., 215.

asymmetrically dependent upon them is included.[91] While male and female's love for each other is mutual, God's love uniquely "creates the presupposition" of the person—a move that secures the Creator/creature distinction, even at the cost of leaving children outside the relational structure of the *imago Dei*.

Procreation and Providence

Barth's naturalization of procreation in both his doctrines of creation and anthropology leaves it bereft of any analogical correspondence to either creation or the eschaton. Generating new human life seems to participate in God's work only insofar as God providentially secures the continuation of human existence for His purposes. On Barth's account, God's providence "guarantees and confirms the work of creation," but does not continually create it afresh. While creation is a complete and concluded act of God, it opens up to the history of the covenant, in which God reconciles the world to Himself. Yet as creation needed an external basis, so the history of the covenant needs an external basis—namely, the ongoing life and history of the creature in space and time.[92] While the grace of the covenant is wholly God's, the "one indispensable presupposition" to the covenant is the fact that the creature "has time, space and opportunity both to exist and to do so for God's glory." In the theater of God's glory, we may be God's servant, instrument, and material—and our creaturely occurrence can be a mirror and likeness to God's working in the covenant.[93]

God's constancy and faithfulness are the basis for our preservation as creatures, rather than any feature intrinsic to our existence. The fact that God is the Creator, rather than a "mere manufacturer," means there is a connection which "makes it impossible for the Creator to leave His work to itself." The creature's preservation is secured in the "majestic freedom" of God. As Barth writes, the "eternity of God is the pledge that He will give [the creature] time so long as He wills."[94] The election of God in Jesus Christ means that Christ "represents our right to existence and the necessity of our existence, and of the existence of the whole creaturely world."[95]

God's preservation of the creature happens through creaturely means and also (crucially) within creaturely limits. Barth notes that "God Himself sustains

---

91. James Mumford has rightly criticized Barth's understanding of humanity as 'being in encounter' for its inability to understand procreation, as the reciprocity and equality inherent within it fail to capture the asymmetrical relationship that a mother has with her embryo. See James Mumford, *Ethics at the Beginning of Life* (Oxford: Oxford University Press, 2013).
92. Barth, *Church Dogmatics* III/3, 6–7.
93. Ibid., 47, 47–9.
94. Ibid., 9–10.
95. Ibid., 59. See also 10.

the creature, but He sustains it in the context in which He has created it and ordains that it should exist." In between creation and redemption, God acts freely and mediately, through the creature.⁹⁶ This mediated preservation includes the preservation of the "race as a whole and all the species of beasts and plants by natural propagation."⁹⁷ In pursuing this preservation, the creature becomes the "witness and herald and proclaimer" of the grace of the covenant: the "spiritual relationship of the creature in the covenant of grace is the dominant pattern or type of what God does when He preserves creation as such in being." Barth goes on: "God maintains its existence in a way which is not parallel but corresponds to the significance which it acquires in this covenant."⁹⁸ God indirectly preserves the creature through means of the creature.⁹⁹

At the same time, God's preservation of the creature is not endless, but remains within the "limits which correspond to its creaturely existence." "Everything has its own time," Barth writes, and "no more than that time."¹⁰⁰ God's eternal preservation of the creature is not an indefinite extension of the time, space, or existence that we currently enjoy. In the final act of salvation history, the history of creation "will not need to progress any further," as it will have "fulfilled its purpose." While Barth repudiates pantheism and the corresponding claim that God will be "alone again" in the eschaton, the eternal preservation of the creature does *not* include the existence that makes human action possible. The life of the creature "will then be over," as it will not "need any continuance of temporal existence." Time itself will be eliminated, even while in some sense God preserves the creature and all that has existed.¹⁰¹

Barth's doctrine of providence offers a way, then, of giving meaning to procreation—but also strictly qualifies its significance. Positively, God's providential preserving of the species is not only teleologically ordered toward the covenant as a stage is to a play, but is a mirror and likeness of the contents of the covenant. This claim is underspecified, though, and Barth issues strict warnings against seeing creaturely occurrences as anything more than indications of divine action.¹⁰²

---

96. Ibid., 63–4.
97. Ibid., 63.
98. Ibid., 64–5.
99. Ibid., 64.
100. Ibid., 62. I discuss Barth's treatment of limits in Chapter 7.
101. Ibid., 86–8. See the discussion in Christopher C. Green, *Doxological Theology* (Edinburgh: T&T Clark, 2011), 47–8, and the accompanying literature. Green notes that Barth does incorporate an "afterlife" into his theology later, as in IV/3, 924–8. There, Barth indeed speaks of the "true beginning in reconstitution" of all things and humanity in the exaltation of our temporal existence to eternal life (928). Yet there he maintains the same position he adopts here in III/3, namely, that this exaltation (while just) means the "end of time generally" and the "conclusion of the temporal existence of those still living" (924).
102. Ibid., 51. "Each is merely an imperfect indication of what is here to be described, namely, the divine rule operative in creaturely occurrence."

Moreover, we cannot infer directly from any qualities or features of a creaturely occurrence that God has done it, but can only conclude so if God does in fact do it. It is too strong to say "creation *is* God's servant and instrument, the theatre, mirror and likeness of His gracious and saving action." Rather, creation "may become" all of this. Its goodness consists in being prepared to be all this, in standing "ready for God, or more exactly for God's action in the covenant of grace and kingdom of Christ."[103] To this now familiar qualification on the meaning of procreation, though, Barth adds a third: the existence that procreation perpetuates is limited. The eschatological preservation of the creature by God does not include either time or existence. What this means for Barth's account of procreation will become clearer as we turn to his ethics.

The Relativization of Procreation (III/4)

Barth's special ethics of marriage and parenthood recapitulates themes that are by now familiar, yet in a preparatory mode for those who must make ethical decisions. As the discursive aim of special ethics is to offer a "formed reference" by which the agent can stand ready to receive the command of God, Barth extends his theological reflections beyond pure description and offers hesitating (and sometimes not-so-hesitating) judgments about what form the divine command might take in different contexts.[104] Substantively, Barth makes his verdict explicit that marriage's analogical relationship to Christ and the church gives it an eschatological consecration and confirmation, reifying it as a form (even while still a creaturely form). By contrast, procreation's Christological significance seems to come to an end after the birth of Christ. This alteration does not entail an anti-natalism for Barth, even though it does turn procreation into a question for couples as they prepare to hear the divine command. And while it does seem to limit procreation's theological significance to the continuation of natural history, Barth also hesitates to describe it as a purely "natural" event. Instead, as we shall see, a Barthian pro-natalism must appeal to *life*.

In his special ethics of marriage, Barth argues that the male–female relationship is subject to the twofold relativization of being subject to the command of God and the disclosure of celibacy in the kingdom of God. While the I–Thou encounter between male and female remains the paradigmatic form of human relationships, Barth objects to apotheosizing the erotic impulse into a form of natural

---

103. Ibid., 52.
104. As Barth writes, the function of ethical inquiry is "not to pronounce an anticipatory judgment on the good or evil of human action in encounter with the command of God, but to give definite instruction with regard to this event." Barth, *Church Dogmatics* III/4, 18. Gerald McKenny's analysis of the preparatory quality of ethical instruction is helpful. See *Karl Barth's Moral Theology*, 262–4.

transcendence. Marriage and sexuality are realms governed by the command of God, which demythologizes them and directs humanity toward its creaturely freedom. This subjects the male–female encounter to a "radical relativisation," rather than its "negation or destruction."[105] Views that apotheosize marriage—like Schleiermacher's—go awry by collapsing the distinction between Christ and the church. The analogical relation of the Church instead becomes an "identity," leaving humanity without an independent referent "to whom he can look and from whom he can expect help as man expects it from God."[106] Marriage must remain a matter of creatureliness, rather than being exalted into "something metaphysical and absolute."[107] At the same time, the command of God as revealed in Christ relativizes marriage by introducing celibacy as a possible vocation. Marriage remains the *telos* of the sphere of male and female, even if it is not the only form of life the command allows. Everything in the sphere of male and female "must be judged by the criteria which apply to the married state," so that what is good or bad in the narrow sphere of marriage must also be good or bad in the broader social relations between the sexes. The relativization of marriage that celibacy introduces does not "mean the suspension of this rule."[108] The two vocations are instead mutually complementary, as humans are "oriented to marriage and determined for it even though temporarily or even finally they do not contract it."[109]

The eschatological relativization of marriage that celibacy introduces goes hand-in-hand with the dissolution of the obligation to procreate that the hope of the Messiah imposed upon Israel. The unmarried state in Israel was "a terrible disgrace for both male and female," because they would not partake in the "procreation of children." The burden of posterity that animated Israel was *not* the "general one that man is obliged to share creatively in the process of making new life," but rather the "special" reason that the "hope of Israel must be carried forward from one generation to another."[110] In Israel, marriage and procreation are bound together by the role they have in salvation history—both by mirroring the covenant between God and His people and by carrying the lineage forward to the birth of the Messiah. The birth of Christ, though, means "the clamp which made marriage a necessity for man and woman from their creation is not removed but it is certainly loosened. Marriage is no longer an absolute but a relative necessity. It is now one possibility among others."[111] While Barth points positively to Christ's

---

105. Barth, *Church Dogmatics* III/4 121.
106. Ibid., 125.
107. Ibid., 124–5.
108. Ibid., 140.
109. Ibid., 142.
110. Ibid.
111. Ibid., 143. Faye Bodley-Dangelo rightly notes that Barth did not make this admission explicit in his figural reading of Genesis 2 in III/2, and that Barth's target here is a Protestant ethics of marriage that (following Luther) reduces marriage's aim to the procreation of children. See *Sexual Difference, Gender, and Agency in Karl Barth's Church Dogmatics*, 154.

celibacy as the positive basis for this loosening, its negative grounds are that the "necessity to procreate imposed by the history of salvation prior to the appearance of the Messiah" has been dissolved.[112] The theological significance of marriage and procreation, then, stands and falls together: while Christ's celibacy reveals that marriage is now optional, Christ's birth also makes procreation optional.

At the same time, Barth argues the birth of Christ means marriage and procreation have a distinct theological significance *vis a vis* the eschatological life. On the one side, the Old Testament "problem of posterity and heirs" does not have the importance for the church that it has for Israel "and for other reasons in other nations."[113] The dawning of the Kingdom of God means that what "really counts" is being born of God. Barth raises the question of the "meaning and content of this time between the resurrection of Jesus Christ and His return," which he argues is "simply the message about Him and the way of life of the Church whose function is to proclaim this message in expectation of His final manifestation." The birth of Christ means that birth no longer has anything to do with the history of salvation: "No child conceived and born in this last time will bring anything that is fundamentally and decisively new." Barth insists that this relativization does not entail a "subordination and devaluation of procreation and marriage," which remain a "natural possibility."[114] As with his doctrine of providence, Barth seems to reduce procreation and marriage to the ongoing existence of the species, suggesting that even "in the light of the final decision of God, there are still human beings in this passing world which now moves toward its end." Procreation is a way in which Christians can participate "in the nature in which God has created man, male and female."[115] But its theological significance as a participation in the hope of the coming advent of the Christ has come to an end. On the other side, the disclosure of marriage's prototype in Christ and the church gives it "quite a new consecration" as a "representation of humanity's determination as the covenant-partner of God."[116] The eschatological disclosure of Christ reveals that marriage belongs to the passing world, which makes it "a special spiritual gift and vocation" alongside celibacy.[117] Yet this eschatological standpoint also reveals marriage's true

---

Charlotte von Kirschbaum's reflections on celibacy emphasize that it is an eschatological sign of the church's union with Christ, and so a reminder to those who are married that it is a form of life that "belongs to the transitoriness of the world and will pass away along with it," rather than framing it in the context of the "burden of posterity" as Barth does. See von Kirschbaum, *The Question of Woman*, 91–4.

112. Ibid., 143.

113. Ibid. Barth's inclusion of "other nations" here is likely an allusion to the ethnonationalist pro-natalism practiced by the Nazis. If so, his correlation with Israel is fascinating and disturbing.

114. Ibid.

115. Ibid.

116. Ibid.

117. Ibid., 144, 148.

ground and determination—conferring upon it its "true Christian meaning" and giving it a theological significance as a sign and symbol that procreation lacks.[118]

While Barth underscores that marriage is not strictly for the sake of procreation, it is also not an impermeable, self-enclosed sphere. The marital union is exclusive, but the establishment of a home makes it possible for third parties to enter and leave. In this way, marriage is "fruitful outwards and also richer and more active within."[119] Such an external dimension is a requirement, as marriage is "not permission to establish an egoistic partnership of two persons," but rather a commitment to "active participation" in the external world. In this way, the marriage "may and must be significant and fruitful, an outward witness and help, as the inner fellowship of these two persons, and in which it may in its own place and manner be a factor in human history."[120] However, procreation is only one form such a fruitful marriage takes. While marriages must build up a "common world," there is no internal necessity that would impel a couple to procreate. Marriage "implies" an "inner readiness for children," but is "in no way conditioned by the co-existence of children." The absence of children in Genesis 2 and the fact that the question of posterity "has lost its decisive significance in the time of the new covenant" are crucial for understanding that "husband and wife form a sphere of fellowship independent of child or family."[121]

Barth's ethics of parents and children continues his emphasis on the relativization of procreation and family bonds, but also comes nearer to establishing a presumptive pro-natalism than his ethics of marriage. At the outset of his treatment, Barth suggests that being born and bearing others is a part of humanity's "creaturely status."[122] Parents and children stand in a relationship that is, on both sides, "special,

---

118. Ibid.
119. Ibid., 195.
120. Ibid., 225. Barth's assertion that those who enter marriage must take this responsibility to be externally "fruitful in all seriousness" animates him to reflect on the public act of marriage, which he differentiates from weddings on grounds that the "institution in itself offers not the smallest guarantee that a marriage is concluded in responsibility before God." To the extent that Barth refers to children in this context, he considers the limits of parental authority over their child's marriage and says nothing about whether this public act should have any reference to the emergence of a similar parent–child relationship.
121. Ibid., 189. The full German text reads: "Der Text Gen. 2, 18–22, in welchem vom Kind und von der Familie nun einmal mit keinem Wort, wohl aber von der Beziehung zwischen Mann und Frau mit höchstem Nachdruck die Rede ist, aber auch die Erinnerung, daß die Frage nach der Nachkommenschaft in der Zeit des neuen Bundes ihre ausschlaggebende Bedeutung verloren hat, dürften entscheidend sein für die Erkenntnis, daß Mann und Frau gegenüber dem Kind und also gegenüber der Familie einen eigenen Gemeinschaftsbereich bilden."—KD III/4, 214.
122. Ibid., 240. Barth will later suggest that fatherhood and motherhood "always confer a *character indelibis,* introduce an irrevocable turning point in the life of the individual and bring about an indissoluble relationship to the third party, i.e., the child now born." Ibid., 277.

exclusive and lasting." Once the relationship exists, it cannot be annulled.[123] The parents are the "presupposition and starting-point" of the life-history of the child, and the child is "a symbol of their own life-history."[124] Yet while humans are necessarily children, they are only contingently parents.[125] The child's relationship to the parents is involuntary, while the parents' relationship to the child is (typically) chosen. Sexual intercourse is "the *conditio sine qua non*" of procreation, but is also "not a sufficient ground for the conception and birth of a child."[126] This asymmetry entails that the standpoint of the child has "more direct [theological] significance" than the question of whether we will conceive and bear children.[127]

Barth's discussion of whether couples should become parents happens in between his development of the ethics of parents and children from each respective standpoint.[128] Barth draws on distinct theological resources in considering the "two preliminary questions" to the ethics of parenthood, namely the questions of childlessness and birth control.[129] With respect to the first, Barth draws heavily on the abrogation the obligation to procreate and the corresponding destabilization of physical "fruitfulness" to argue that childless couples should "be comforted and cheerful."[130] Barth acknowledges that childless couples will to "some degree all feel their childlessness to be a lack, a gap in the circle of what nature obviously intends for man, the absence of an important, desirable and hoped for good." Such a feeling will be proportionate to how grateful they are "for the gift of children."[131] Yet this is as much as we can say about childlessness. We may not say it is a "misfortune," as it might still be "fruitful" in a non-physical sense. More significantly, Barth suggests that in the sphere of the New Testament the general obligation to perpetuate the species from Genesis 1 is dissolved: in the New

---

123. Ibid. On 241, Barth writes that if a couple does become parents, a "relationship arises between them and their child which in its particularity, exclusiveness and permanence corresponds *exactly to the relationship of the child to them*" (emphasis mine).

124. Ibid., 240–1.

125. While the necessity of being a child might incline one to think it should be a "structural differentiation" between types of humans, Barth rejects this. The "necessity with which he is a child, and a son or daughter … is bound up in the fact that he is male or female, and the one or the other on the basis of this structural differentiation." *CD* III/2, 286.

126. Barth, *CD* III/4, 241. Barth's suggestion that procreation is impossible without sexual intercourse is a moment that betrays his limited technological imagination.

127. Ibid., 243.

128. Barth develops the ethics of childhood from pages 243–65, and considers the ethics of parenthood from pages 276–85. The latter raises the "same complex of problems from a different angle" as the former (265). I reserve discussion of the content of Barth's account of parenthood (and childhood) for a later chapter.

129. Ibid., 265.

130. Ibid., 267.

131. Ibid., 265–6.

Testament there is "no necessity, no general command, to continue the human race as such and therefore to procreate children." Procreation continues that the "joy of parenthood may still have a place, [and] that new generations may constantly follow those which precede," but this is "all that can be said in light of the fact that ... the kingdom of God comes and this world is passing away." It is "one of the consolations of the coming kingdom and expiring time that this anxiety about posterity" is "removed from us all by the fact that the Son on whose birth alone everything seriously and ultimately depended has now been born and has now become our Brother." In this way, parenthood is simply a "free and in some sense optional gift of the goodness of God."[132] Bringing up children is "a beautiful and promising thing," but the "meaning of this activity is only earthly and temporal."[133]

Barth's discussion of birth control both affirms the responsible use of contraception and defends a qualified, theologically animated pro-natalism that is attentive to the social and political dynamics that arise when people are encouraged to procreate. After reiterating his claim that the "unconditional command" to procreate has been undone by Christ, he suggests procreation happens under "God's longsuffering and patience, and is due to His mercy, that in these last days it may still take place."[134] As such, Barth argues that it may sometimes be the "duty of the Christian community to awaken either a people or section of a people which has grown tired of life and despairs of the future, to the conscientious realisation that to avoid arbitrary decay they should make use of this merciful divine permission and seriously try to maintain the race."[135] Barth's analysis of this contingent duty is attentive to social circumstances. He raises a worry about overpopulation and emphasizes the political dangers of pro-natalist policies, noting that the "most recent encouragement to the utmost possible procreation and increase of population had a definitely heathen and nationalistic character" and was perversely related to "military aims and therefore the projected slaughter of whole masses of people."[136] At the same time,

---

132. Ibid., 266. Barth's understanding of the relativization of procreation has two attitudinal correlates for those without children. Their lament "can have no justification in the community of the new covenant." And they are forbidden an attitude of neutral resignation. Instead, they "must set their hope on God and therefore be comforted and cheerful." Barth's pastoral recommendation, which he suggests will be heard only where the "great message of divine comfort is known and received," is that childless couples should recognize they are "all the more called and empowered to build up their life-companionship with particular care both outwardly and inwardly." Barth also raises the possibility of a 'fatherliness' and 'motherliness' that are available to all, regardless of whether they are parents or not.

133. Ibid., 267.
134. Ibid., 268.
135. Ibid., 268–9.
136. Ibid., 269.

Barth seems to correlate an unwillingness to procreate with the dissolution of faith. "It may be," Barth writes, "that in a given case the faith of a man and a woman will assume the form and character of a homely and courageous confidence in life." When a husband and wife agree that the prospect of giving birth is not a threat but a promise, and think they are equal to the task of raising children, then "in all seriousness they should seek to have a child in the name of God, and what happens, even if they are mistaken, will at least happen in responsibility and therefore in a right relation to the divine command."[137] Barth observes that many people in his day do not "seem able to command this confidence in life," and suggests that a "certain degeneration and impoverishment of faith rather than outward circumstances undoubtedly plays some part" in the problem. Barth's exhortation lies in a pronatalist direction, though: there "can be no doubt that a positive choice and decision ought to be made far more often than they are to-day on the basis of this confidence in life grounded in faith."[138]

Behind Barth's qualified, fideistic pro-natalism lies an account of sexual intercourse that makes room for divine action in creating life, even if there is no mention of the grammar of "blessing" that Barth developed in his reading of the first creation account. As Barth thinks marriage is a form of life-fellowship independent from children, so he suggests sexual intercourse has a value independent of procreation. Sexual intercourse can indicate "love relationship of the two partners and exclude the conception and birth of children."[139] The possibility of procreation is a "natural consequence," even while prospective parents have the "technical possibility of so guiding their sexual activity that it does not have this consequence."[140] Yet while Barth regularly correlates the meaning of procreation with the extension of humanity's natural history, the act of sexual intercourse puts us into close proximity with God's action. Sexual intercourse can be "not merely human action, but an offer of divine goodness made by the One who even in this last time does not will that it should be all up with us."[141] This is the only consideration that weighs against the licitness of birth control: contracepting is "a refusal of this divine offer" and "a renunciation of the widening and enriching of married fellowship which is divinely made possible by the fact that under the

---

137. Ibid., 272.

138. Ibid. Barth's sociological observations about the correlation of economic prosperity and the decline of faith with birth rates have received considerable empirical confirmation in recent years. See, among many other places, Jonathan Last's *What to Expect When No One's Expecting* (New York: Encounter Books, 2013) and Phillip Jenkins, *Fertility and Faith: The Demographic Revolution and the World's Religions* (Waco: Baylor University Press, 2020).

139. Ibid., 269.

140. Ibid., 269, 270.

141. Ibid., 269.

command of God this fellowship includes sexual intercourse."[142] As an action, sexual intercourse not only makes the perpetuation of the species technically possible, but invites unique divine action in the formation of a person who is created in the *imago Dei*.

These heightened stakes for sexual intercourse mean that couples should have a presumptive readiness for children: a couple "must have valid reasons if the gravity of this renunciation and seriousness of this threat are to be dispelled …" Whether to procreate is a decision about which there can be no "frivolity and expediency."[143] The question of procreation is distinct from the question of marriage. Because procreation is not "merely the *inevitable* consequence of the physical intercourse which forms the climax of [marriage]," it requires a responsible "choice and decision between Yes and No."[144] Barth distinguishes the "course of nature" from the "providence of God," such that the latter has to be "freshly discovered" in the former by the "believer who hears and obeys His word, and apprehended and put into operation by him in personal responsibility, in the freedom of choice and decision." This decision requires a response to the specific question "May I try to have a child?"[145] In other words, wrongdoing in the realm of making human life is possible. Negatively, an "actual divine gift may be refused," and a child "who might have been the light and joy of its parents is not generated and conceived and come into existence."[146] Positively, a "child may be generated of whom it might well be said from the parents' standpoint that they would have been better without it."[147] Barth does not specify on what basis parents might know whether or not they are wrong to pursue a child—such specificity is difficult to attain on any account—but several times he alludes to the dangers procreation poses to women.[148]

The weight of Barth's special ethics of marriage and procreation falls on three complementary claims. First, the advent of the Christ destabilizes both marriage and procreation, making both optional for Christians. Second, marriage and procreation are now two independent spheres; the former can be entered into without being conditioned by the latter. Third, while the birth of Christ dissolves both marriage and procreation alike, marriage has a theological referent in

---

142. Ibid. As Anna Louise Poulson notes, this reason to reject contraception seems to tie together the good of new life with the good of the marriage. Though she does not note it, it potentially undermines Barth's contention that marriage and procreation are independent spheres. See "An Examination of the Ethics of Contraception with Reference to Recent Protestant and Roman Catholic Thought," 173–4.

143. Ibid., 270, italics mine.

144. Ibid.

145. Ibid., 271.

146. Ibid.

147. Ibid.

148. These dangers include both the risks to her "physical and psychological health." Ibid., 272. I return to Barth's discussion of the asymmetrical burdens of procreation in Chapter 8.

typologically signifying Christ's relationship to the church that procreation lacks: only marriage receives a "new consecration." Procreation remains a "natural possibility" for the couple—but it is by no means inevitable, much less obligatory, that a couple will pursue it. While marriage must be an expanding circle of fellowship, Barth's emphatic interest in the I-Thou quality of the union, his understanding of the *imago,* and his suggestion that there is no further completion beyond the climax of the covenant means children have a gratuitous quality when understood theologically. As Jonathan Tran writes, "Children serve no purpose [for Barth], in that they of themselves do not offer meaning; they simply exist as God's goodness; God does not signify his blessings through children, since Christ sacramentally denotes the infinite endurance of God's presence and blessing as displayed in the church."[149]

At the same time, procreation's position as an independent sphere from marriage clearly does not mean it lies beyond the command of God or that a general Christian anti-natalism is warranted. Marriage is a union that must be outwardly fruitful, even if not physically generative. While the decision for or against procreating must not be left to chance, the possibility of an "offer" from God in sexual intercourse means that a couple must have "valid reasons" for rejecting it through the use of (negative) birth control. To this account of divine action Barth adds his invocation of the "confidence in life," which takes seriously the empirical conditions of being able to maintain a child's life, but is also "grounded in faith." Whether Barth adequately correlates the divine and human dimensions of sexual intercourse is, for now, an open question. Yet in bracketing procreation from having any theological significance beyond extending the natural conditions for the church's work, Barth seems to put the entire weight of reasons to procreate on the life that couples have confidence in through faith.

Procreation in Barth (So Far): Appreciation and Critique

Barth's understanding of procreation consistently subordinates it to other theological concerns. Sexual intercourse makes divine action technically possible—but the generation of human life has no theological significance after the birth of Christ. Procreation does not intrinsically engender an individual made in the *imago Dei,* but only creates the possibility for one. In III/1, Barth argues that animal procreation needs divine blessing—but then stresses that human procreation is (only) animal-like while our lordly governance of creation needs God's unique permission. This sits uncomfortably (at best) alongside his intensification of our responsibility for procreating in III/4, which brings sexual intercourse into close proximity with God's creative power by framing it as a potential "offer" from God. The subordination of fertility to other forms of labor that is tacitly present in his

---

149. Jonathan Tran, "The Otherness of Children as a Hint of an Outside," *Theology and Sexuality* 15, no. 2 (2015): 207.

reading of the first creation account becomes explicit in his reading of the second, where the absence of any explicit mention of children animates him to frame human life in terms of service and work. The only "structural differentiation" of humanity is male and female—and while the relationship between parents and children is subordinated to it, the standpoint of the child is more "theologically significant" because parenthood is conditional on our choice. When the woman comes to the male in Genesis 2, there is no need of a "further completion." As a type of the covenant, marriage is complete in itself, without reference to children, who exist in an independent sphere. The advent of the Christ nullifies both the "burden" of genealogy that Israel is under as those who witness to the covenant and the general obligation to procreate that Genesis 1:28 seems to place on humanity. Marriage receives a new consecration in light of the eschatological union of Christ and the church—but procreation does not. Gary Deddo suggests Barth fails "to bring out the interpersonal dimensions of procreation which give it its relativized value," considering it instead "almost exclusively in terms of the biological event."[150] Given where Barth locates procreation in his theology, such a judgment seems right. While Barth protests that procreation does not have a diminished value *post Christum natum*, it is hard to avoid the anti-natalist pressures within his thought.

At the same time, procreating does continue. While Barth's reading of the first creation account had framed procreating as a participation in hope for the coming Messiah, the Son's advent means that it is "under God's longsuffering and patience, and is due to His mercy, that in these last days [procreation] may still take place."[151] Though such a description is surprisingly pallid, Barth does regard patience as a "special perfection of the love and therefore the being of God."[152] Specifically, God's patience is His will to allow another "space and time for the development of its own existence."[153] God's intervention on behalf of the creature does not mean (yet) the nullification of space, time, and existence, but their preservation.[154] As Barth had suggested in II/2, the presence of sin means the "command" to live in Genesis 1:28 must "now be repeated under the sin of the divne patience, and from now on it must be heard under this sign and with this caveat."[155] Here as well, though, we encounter sharp limits on what procreation signifies. The meaning of the time between now and Christ's return is "simply the message about [Christ] and the way of life of the church."[156] While procreation was once an expression of hope, Christ's second advent will bring about the dissolution of the existence that procreation secures, rather than its extension—even if the creature will somehow be preserved

---

150. Deddo, *Theology*, 349.
151. *CD* III/4, 268.
152. *CD* II/1, 407.
153. Ibid., 409.
154. Ibid., 411.
155. *CD* II/2, 679.
156. *CD* III/4, 143.

in God.[157] The Church's witness is partially structured by a future in which there will be no more time—which correlates with the fact that the consummation of redemption is witnessed by the union of male and female in marriage just as such, without any further relationship to children. As Barth says, it is "one of the consolations of the coming kingdom and *expiring time*" that the "anxiety about posterity" has been removed from us.[158]

Such is the broader theological landscape in which Barth situates his ethics of procreation. Despite its anti-natalist pressures, Barth affirms a presumptive pro-natalism that requires weighty reasons to say "no" to the possibility of children in marriage. Barth's appeal to the "confidence in life grounded in faith" and to sexual intercourse's character as "divine offer" of human life together underscore that Christians who marry should be ready for children. At the same time, this presumption does not entail that one may procreate without reasons. While contracepting might be a refusal of the "divine offer" of parenthood, procreating still requires a positive reason that does not reduce to the blind acceptance of chance, nature, or providence. Barth's claim that procreation must be a decision demands an openness to saying Yes, but also an openness to saying No to making human life—even if the deliberating agent is not neutral between such possibilities, as though the reasons for and against procreating were equally weighted.

Barth's description of the attitude underlying a Christian pro-natalism as a "confidence in life" both builds upon and deepens the dialectic of optimism and pessimism the previous chapter explored. As we saw there, Barth contrasts the self-confidence of Leibniz and other optimists with the confidence of those "whom God has first drawn into his confidence," a confidence "continually renewed" with a certainty "continually achieved and confirmed."[159] Only this Christologically grounded confidence can take the shadow side of creation seriously without devolving into a pessimistic nihilism like Schopenhauer's. Similarly, Barth's "confidence in life" is not an optimistic or vitalistic endorsement of humanity's capabilities, which would risk bottoming out in the social conditions of prosperity that Barth observes are often correlated with a reluctance to have children. Rather, it is a confidence in life grounded *in faith*, which is finally underwritten by the knowledge that human life is ordered to and determined by the disclosure of God in Jesus Christ.

This correlation of optimism and pro-natalism becomes sharper when we see that Barth attributed both to Judaism. For Barth, reducing the "confidence in life" into an inviolable obligation to procreate is a "very heathen or even Jewish type of thought."[160] Similarly, Barth had disavowed the "ancient Hebrew optimism whose

---

157. See the above discussion of procreation in Barth's doctrine of providence, and III/3, 86–8.
158. *CD* III/4, 266.
159. *CD* III/1, 388, 411.
160. *CD* III/4, 272.

triumphant song could later give way to pessimism (like that of the followers of Leibniz after the Lisbon earthquake)."[161] Barth's association of optimistic (natural) theologies with pro-natalism is understandable given the social and political context surrounding his development of the doctrine of creation. Yet while Barth's account of the goodness of creation critiques the Marcionite tendency to divide the Old and New Testaments, his procreative ethics thrives upon a sharp distinction between their respective understandings of parenthood and children—which constitutes perhaps the most acute practical and ethical difference Barth highlights between Israel and the church. Whether Barth is able to sufficiently fund confidence in life on theological grounds might turn upon whether he is able to avoid reducing the eschatological "relativization" of the (purportedly) Jewish optimistic pro-natalism into an abrogation of it.[162]

One reason to be skeptical of Barth's view is that his depiction of the Old Testament's understanding of procreation potentially rests upon distorted emphases, which empower a sharper discontinuity between the Testaments than would otherwise exist. The interplay of blessing, reproduction, and life that emerged in Barth's analysis of the first creation account plays a marginal role (at best) in his special ethics of marriage and parenthood. There is good reason to think that fertility was predominately associated with blessing in the Old Testament, but Barth replaces the concept with his intense focus on the Old Testaments' description of procreation and posterity as an obligation, burden, or problem.[163] Additionally, Barth's emphatic depiction of the birth of the Christ as an end-point of Israel's procreative activity potentially truncates Israel's vision. They looked for a Messiah that would fulfill the promise that Abraham would be the "father of many nations." Such a formula indicates that there may be a completion for Israel *beyond* her union with the Messiah, a fruitfulness that is not arbitrary or a surd but intrinsically grounded in the union of the bride and groom. Such alternate depictions would minimize the discontinuity between the Jewish and Christian outlooks on procreation—and potentially provide more robust

---

161. *CD* III/1, 122.

162. Barth's relationship to the Jews and to Jewish theology lies beyond the scope of this work, even though it has substantive and important implications for how we might understand his broader theology of procreation. On the subject, see Mark Lindsay's excellent and sympathetic summation of many of the key data points, and the accompanying literature, in Mark Lindsay, "Barth and the Jews," in *The Wiley Blackwell Companion to Karl Barth*, ed. George Hunsinger and Keith L. Johnson, 1st ed. (Hoboken: Wiley Blackwell, 2019), 881–92. On Barth and supersessionism, see Jennifer M. Rosner, *Healing the Schism: Karl Barth, Franz Rosenzweig, and the New Jewish-Christian Encounter*, Studies in Historical and Systematic Theology (Bellingham, WA: Lexham Academic, 2021).

163. For a comprehensive treatment of the use of the fertility blessing in Genesis 1:26 by the rest of the Old Testament, see Jamie Viands' excellent *I Will Surely Multiply Your Offspring* (Eugene, OR: Pickwick Publications, 2014).

theological grounds for affirming a pro-natalist outlook *post natum Christum* than Barth has access to.

Barth's suggestion that a "confidence in life grounded in faith" stands beneath a pro-natalist outlook calls for closer investigation into his ethics of life, which we shall undertake in the subsequent chapter. As we saw in Chapter 2, there are significant questions about the relationship between biological relatedness and parenthood. Barth's ethics of parents and children frames procreation as happening under the mercy and patience of God, but also indicates—in a phrase I did not develop above—that it happens so that the "joy of parenthood may still have a place." Given Barth's stance that posterity no longer has theological significance, the dilemma of procreative bonds reasserts itself: why should parenthood be undertaken procreatively, rather than through means of adoption? Addressing such questions from the standpoint of life will help deepen our understanding of the place humanity's biological constitution has in Barth's ethics—and subsequently the significance of procreation as well.

Such an exploration will draw upon and deepen a number of themes that have emerged in this chapter. Specifically, it will query whether the intrinsically reproductive quality of life that Barth develops in his reading of the first creation account has any purchase on his theological anthropology—or whether it disappears beneath the weight of the phenomenological I–Thou framework. It will also reconsider how life in time can be an "offer" from God, in order to more precisely determine what sort of significance such a claim has in Barth's ethics. Methodologically, such an expansion of our focus is warranted not only by Barth's explicit invocation of "life" in his ethics of procreation, but by his own acknowledgment that his special ethics build on each other. Barth's discussion of "Freedom for Life" in §55 presupposes humanity's freedom for God (§53) and freedom within community (§54), the latter of which includes his treatments of marriage and parenthood (§54.1 and §54.2).[164] As Barth later suggests, the single command of God is a living commanding, which means to understand it we must "be prepared to see that it continually discloses new and apparently opposing aspects, like successive steps along the same path or ensuing pages of a single book, which certainly limit, supersede and supplement, though they do not, of course, negate those which precede."[165] Which is to say, a full treatment of Barth's account of procreation must attend not only to its explicit treatment in his doctrine of creation, but his ethics of life and—as we go farther—the ethics of limits he develops in §56, and especially his treatment of honour in §56.3.

---

164. *CD* III/4, 324.
165. Ibid., 470.

Chapter 6

RESPECT FOR LIFE AS A REASON TO CREATE

A theological ethics of procreating must account for both its significance as a practice and the immanent reasons that couples might have to pursue it. As we have seen, Barth's answer to the former is that God's patience and mercy continue to give creation time, space, and opportunity to develop and to turn to Him. The meaning and content of the time between Christ's resurrection and return are simply the work of the church, which entails procreation is strictly (though perhaps not *merely*) a natural event. With respect to the latter, Barth appeals to the "confidence in life grounded in faith." These two domains are not wholly independent: procreation's theological significance certainly bears on how the church might seek to encourage couples to pursue that confidence in life and shapes how people's work as procreators and parents fits the ecclesiastical community's mission. Moreover, procreation's theological framework matters for deliberating couples insofar as Barth's account of it means they must look elsewhere for reasons to procreate besides participation in the hope for the coming Messiah, as was the case *ante Christum natum*. A different account of procreation's theological significance might open up additional reasons for couples deliberating about whether to participate in the work of making new human life.

While Chapter 7 will revisit the broader theological framework that Barth locates procreation in, this chapter examines his appeal to "life" as a basis for couples' confidence in pursuing procreation. Behind Barth's invocation of the "confidence in life grounded in faith" for his (modest) pro-natalism lies a thick, theologically saturated account of how humanity's organic, material constitution in time relates to our personal identity. Barth's invocation of life does not commit him to vitalism, in which the moral significance of our life is self-interpreting. Yet the primacy of the divine command for assessing how we should act includes, as we shall see, honouring the intrinsic capabilities and powers that come with being a living human animal in time. The confidence required to be ready to procreate is a confidence *in life*, which is *grounded* in faith—which seems to give God's command a self-reflexive, egoistic dimension that is easy to overlook in Barth's ethics.[1] At the same time, Barth's appeal to life requires some account for

---

1. There has been a debate in recent years among Barth's interpreters about the extent to which eudaimonism guides his ethics. On the one side are those like Nigel Biggar and Matthew Rose, who argue that humanity's flourishing has a constitutive role in discerning

the role "nature" and human ontology plays in his ethics, as procreation for Barth is a participation in it. Barth's account of human life in time does not give up his Christologically centered method—yet, as we shall see, it simultaneously pushes his opposition to natural theology to its limit and reifies nature's contents as a theater adapted to the covenant.

First, then, I take up Barth's theological construal of the human constitution, which Barth's ethics of life is built on. Barth's pneumatological anthropology preserves humanity's extrinsic, eccentric orientation even within the inner dimensions of our organic existence. I then consider our life in time. While the limits of our life heighten its value, I will suggest that Barth's account of the eternalizing of our lives maximally consecrates its creaturely form. Finally, I turn to the special ethics of life in III/4. Barth's account of life there offers a way of expanding the grounds for understanding Barth as offering a presumptive endorsement of our procreative powers, but Barth's equivocation about procreation makes such a reading tenuous.[2]

Theological Anthropology and the Human Constitution

Barth's theological anthropology locates Christ's physical body in a secondary position to His office as Messiah and Savior—though, as has been the case with Barth's account of creation and nature, he is insistent that this does not entail any diminution of its value. While the New Testament unequivocally presents Jesus as a "whole man" who is "embodied soul and besouled body," we are not "given a complete, much less a concrete, picture" of His bodiliness.[3] Barth suggests that the New Testament pays no attention to Jesus' health or celibacy, and surprisingly cites John 4:27 to suggest that an "impenetrable veil of silence lies over the fact

---

the divine command. Biggar writes that we "should obey God's command, not out of spineless deference to the capricious wishes of an almighty despot, but out of regard for our own best good, which this gracious God alone truly understands and which he intends with all his heart." See Biggar, "Barth's Trinitarian Ethic," 215. Rose echoes Biggar, suggesting that God "ought to be obeyed not out of mindless obedience but out of regard for our own good and true happiness." Cf. Rose, *Ethics with Barth*, 10. On the other side are readers like Jennifer Herdt, who contends that Barth's divine command theory is not eudaimonist in the 'reason-giving' sense. On her view, Barth's ethics is an 'agent-perfective' eudaimonism, in which "my own good is not necessarily that for the sake of which I desire all else that I desire." See Herdt, "Sleepers Wake!," 163. As she puts it, while "'for me it is good to cleave to God', it is not in order to realize my good that I cleave to God ..." (166) The reading I offer here tries to split this difference between these—but this will not be clear until the final chapter.

2. This chapter adapts and modifies readings first offered in my essay "Giving Thanks for the Gift of Life," 959.

3. Barth, *Church Dogmatics* III/2, 327, 330.

that [Jesus] was a male."[4] While Christ is a whole man, He exists as a "cosmos, a formed and ordered totality."[5] There is thus a higher and a lower in Christ: soul and body are asymmetrically related, so that human action occurs "from soul to body and not *vice versa*."[6] But body and soul cannot be separated or evaluated independently of the other. While Christ's body never receives special attention in the New Testament, it also "never plays an independent role."[7] As such, there is "no logic" in Christology that "is not as such physics, no cure of souls which is not as such bound up with cure of bodies."[8]

Christ's perfect union with the Holy Spirit entails that the differentiated order and wholeness of His human constitution is "structured and governed from within" and thus belongs to Him in an unrepeatable way. As Barth puts it, the order of Christ's body and soul "derives from Himself."[9] That Christ possesses life entails He can bestow it upon "many others without it ceasing to belong to Him and to be His life, without its being diminished or lost to Him."[10] As the perfect recipient and bearer of the Holy Spirit, Christ has "life in its fullness," which ensures His "soul and body is personal life, permeated and determined by His I, by Himself."[11] Such a permeation begins at the conception of Christ by the Spirit, which indicates that Christ's whole being is one "in which chaos is left behind and cosmos is realized, and in which the flesh is slain in its old form and is quickened and comes alive in its new—and all this by and from out of itself."[12] It is this union with the Spirit as the Messiah that is the fundamental ground for the wholeness of the man Jesus; the asymmetrical union of body and soul is only analogous to it.

Other humans do not have life as the immanent possession of the Spirit like Christ does, yet our constitution is still extrinsically and eccentrically determined by the ongoing activity of the Spirit toward us. While Christ's union with the Holy Spirit is total, humanity receives only a "transitory and partial bestowal" of the Spirit.[13] Three axioms govern Barth's general anthropology: humanity is not God, we are not without God, and we only exist as we are "grounded, constituted, and

---

4. Ibid., 330. Barth's citation could plausibly read as indicating the opposite of what he concludes, namely, that the New Testament is acutely conscious of Jesus' maleness but that it highlights the sometimes subversive ways he enacts it. The fact that John records the disciples' surprise that Jesus is speaking with the woman at the well suggests his maleness in fact matters for the interaction, if only as supplying the context that makes his conduct seem scandalous.

5. Ibid., 327, 332.
6. Ibid., 327.
7. Ibid., 339.
8. Ibid., 328.
9. Ibid., 332.
10. Ibid.
11. Ibid., 335.
12. Ibid., 337.
13. Ibid., 334.

maintained by God."[14] Spirit names this final reality. What Christ has of Himself, humanity has of God: humanity has Spirit, without being Spirit. The Spirit is the "the operation of God upon His creation, and especially the movement of God towards man."[15] This Spirit means that God is "there for" humanity, and that humanity stands in need of a "freedom to live which is not immanent in him but comes to him."[16] That the Spirit forms the basis of humanity's life means that humanity lives only insofar as we are the recipients of grace.[17] Because the Spirit is the "event of the gift of life whose subject is God," it "must be continually repeated as God's act if man is to live." In that way, "Spirit is the *conditio sine qua non* of the being of man as soul of his body."[18] As the Spirit makes "possible [humanity's] being as soul of his body," he performs *ad extra* the role Barth had ascribed to Him *ad intra*, namely providing the "pre-existence" of the creature in God's life.[19]

While human life is dependent upon the ongoing encounter between God and the creature, as "embodied souls and ensouled bodies" humans still *have life*. On Barth's understanding, life names the non-autonomous independence as God's creatures: it is the "capacity for action, self-movement, self-activity, self-determination" that arises, especially, from the fact that humans have soul.[20] Soul and body are two asymmetrically ordered "moments," which analogously repeat

14. Ibid., 346.
15. Ibid., 356.
16. Ibid., 362.
17. "Man himself exists as, consciously or unconsciously, … he is a kind of receipt for the creative word of God." III/4, 73.
18. *CD* III/2, 359. It is worth noting that in II/1, when Barth describes the being of God as act, his first specification of God's being is as *life*. Barth is intent to both distinguish God's disclosure of Himself in His act from anything that would be natural and hold them together: the "event of revelation as described for us in Scripture," Barth writes, "has everywhere a natural, bodily, outward and visible component." This component "cannot be a matter of indifference for the description of the being of God." II/1, 263, 265.
19. Ibid., 363. Barth notes that the non-identical intimacy of the Spirit with humanity does not relate to his body and soul in the same way. See 364–5.
20. Ibid., 350. Philip Rosato rightly observes that Barth must both distinguish and unify the concepts of *Spiritus Creator* and *Spiritus Redemptor*. As Rosato notes, "Christian existence in the Word through the power of the Spirit discloses that the same Spirit made of his creatureliness the perquisite foundation of what he was to become through grace." In doing so, Barth draws an analogy between the Spirit in His creative capacity and His prophetic role (cf. III/2, 396). See Rosato, *Spirit as Lord,* 99 and 97–101. Rosato argues that Barth subsumes the Spirit's function as Creator beneath its soteriological mission and does not give the Spirit an adequate eschatological orientation. Together, those flaws eviscerate human action of its significance. See Rosato, 139–40. Yet this follows only if Barth does collapse together what he seems to distinguish, namely, the work of the Spirit in creation and redemption. On Rosato's reading, because the Spirit is the "sole point of contact between God and man in time …, autonomous human actions lose their right to play even a subordinate part in divine-human interaction" (139). While Barth unequivocally rejects

the person's dependence upon God. To say humanity is "soul" is to say that "he is the life which is essentially necessary for his body."[21] And as we are "essentially and existentially in time as well," outward as well as inward, we are also body.[22] Life is the life of the embodied soul and the besouled body. As Barth writes, "Life is life of the body, and while it is this it is more than this." Specifically, it is "freedom, apprehension and control of the body."[23] Humanity never ceases to be dependent upon Spirit. The soul is not an intermediary or independent substance between God and humanity: "As he really lives, and is thus soul of his body, [humanity] is always and immediately of God."[24] Yet the life of an ensouled body gives us a type of independent agency: human life is a "spatio-material system of relations … which is lived and quickened by [soul], and which by the self-contained life of this subject is alive for its own part, i.e. one in which the self-movement, self-activity and self-formation of this subject fulfils and realises itself, and which thus acquires a share in this life of which in itself is not participant."[25] On this basis, Barth distinguishes between the material body and the organic body, the latter of which is "besouled and filled and controlled by independent life."[26]

The prioritization of the Spirit for Barth's understanding of humanity's constitution corresponds to his methodological prioritization of the covenant over creation and entails that humanity's ontology is adapted to and structured by the covenant.[27] As Marc Cortez writes, humans are constituted as body-soul entities "specifically *because* they have been created for covenantal relationships."[28] Humanity "is determined by the one grace, that of his creation, for the other grace, that of the covenant; and he is referred by the one to the other."[29] But the

---

'autonomous' human actions in the sense Rosato wants, his conception of life affirms that there is a sense in which human action is independent. As JinHyok Kim notes, Barth's invocation of the Spirit in his theological anthropology gives it "eschatological tones." See *The Spirit of God and the Christian Life,* 176–81 for his excellent discussion.

21. Ibid., 350.
22. Ibid., 351.
23. Ibid., 353.
24. Ibid.
25. Ibid., 376.
26. Ibid., 378.
27. Barth writes near the beginning of his treatment of the "basic form of humanity" that human beings have no intrinsic capability to become a covenant partner with God. At the same time, our "creaturely essence cannot be alien or opposed to this grace of God, but must confront it with a certain familiarity." Theological anthropology, then, is considering that "which makes [humanity] as the work of His Creator possible, serviceable, adapted and well-pleasing as His covenant-partner before all other creatures, and to that extent capable of entering into covenant." Ibid., 224.
28. Marc Cortez, *Embodied Souls, Ensouled Bodies* (London: T&T Clark, 2011), 99. I am in broad agreement with Cortez's reading, especially pages 92–9.
29. Barth *CD* III/2, 349.

Spirit indicates that the covenant is the "original and model to which the natural constitution of man must succeed and correspond," rather than the other way around.[30] Because of this, the extrinsic basis of humanity's life is distinct from a general creaturely dependence upon God: other animals "lack that second determination by the Spirit which is primary and peculiar." Or, as Barth puts it, "Men and beasts can be born, but men alone can be baptised."[31]

Humanity's adaptation to the covenant secures our constitution's constancy, and even seems to give it an intrinsic content that brings Barth's theology to the edge of admitting a "natural theology." As the "likeness and promise of the divine covenant of grace," humanity's "special constitution corresponding to this calling is determined by the fact that he owes it to the God who is the Lord of this covenant of grace."[32] Because our constitution derives from God, it is a "saving fact" and therefore "unshakeable."[33] This account entails that humanity cannot permanently alter its constitution in such a way that it becomes a different kind of creature, and that humanity's constitution has an intrinsic content—even if we cannot recognize it without revelation. Just as our being as man and woman represents the covenant, so our constitution is a sign of God's turning to humanity. As Barth writes,

> For from [our constitution's] origin from God, like the being of man as man and woman, [our constitution] has an inner relation to God's turning towards man and to the salvation which God intends for him; for man cannot be what he is, soul and body in ordered unity, without representing in himself—long before he understands it, and even when he will not understand it—the good intention of God towards him, without himself being guarantor for this good intention of God.[34]

As those who procreate were unwittingly signs of hope in the coming Messiah, so humanity's constitution is itself a mute sign of the covenant, which can only be perceived and understood as such through the disclosure of Christ. The interconnection of soul and body, which makes us a single subject, is even "one

---

30. Ibid., 357.

31. Ibid.

32. Ibid., 347.

33. "This God as such gives him his creatureliness. This God as such establishes him as soul and body, constituting the unity and order of this being, and maintaining him in this being in its unity and order. Because He is this God in the constitution of man we have to do with an unshakeable but also a saving fact. Since his constitution derives from this God, from Him who is faithful and does not repent of His goodness, it is therefore unshakeable." III/2, 347.

34. Ibid.

of the natural points of contact for the covenant of grace," and in fact "it is the basic one."[35]

Humanity's adaptation for the covenant also gives our constitution an ethical dimension, as the body is folded into Barth's theologically ordered rationality. Barth acknowledges the similarities between human and animal life, but contends that only the "life of man, and man alone, is for us the object of a true and direct knowledge."[36] This self-reflexive aspect of our knowledge does not entail human self-knowledge is a closed circle. Instead, humanity is aware that he can "be responsible for himself" only because "he is capable of meeting God."[37] While animals *might* have such responsibility, the distinctiveness of the human form "emerges only in the fact that the continuation of the story is the history of the covenant and salvation, not between God and animals, but between God and man."[38] Because we can be covenant-partners with God, humanity is also a "subject of his own decision" as one who "posits himself in relation to God."[39] As the "essence of human nature," soul and body are the "presupposition and precondition, the potentiality, which underlies the actuality of [humanity's] being in the Word of God."[40] Soul and body are related as center and periphery; they are indivisible and together in our actualization, even while the soul has a certain precedence over the body. They "are distinguished from each other as subject and object, as operation and work."[41] Barth names two aspects of our creaturely nature that our encounter with God reveals, namely, perception and action, the latter of which Barth divides between desiring and willing.[42] The rationality that marks humanity off from other creatures is unremittingly theocentric: humanity, writes Barth, is a "rational being because he is addressed as such by God." The only stable proof and demonstration of humanity's rationality consists in the "call and summons that man, to be man, should value and respect the obvious fact of his rational nature and therefore of that order, that in his being and conduct he should take account of this nature of his and therefore of the law of his better self."[43] Such a command requires "the affirmation concerning his being or non-being," so that humanity cannot stand in

---

35. Ibid., 371. Knowing that we have this status as a single subject in common with God, though, "presupposes the covenant of grace and therefore God's revelation to man." Yet it is a fact prior to this knowledge.

36. *CD* III/2, 374.

37. Ibid., 396.

38. Ibid.

39. Ibid., 396–7.

40. Ibid., 396.

41. Ibid., 398. The self-reflexive awareness in which humanity grasps their life is "wholly and at the same time both a soulful and a corporeal act, or, more accurately, a soulful act which directly includes a corporeal." (376).

42. Ibid., 399–416.

43. Ibid., 422.

"neutrality" between them but faces a choice "between life and death."[44] Though the soul has precedence in the reception of this command and summons, Barth strikes a strong Aristotelian note in contending that "[an individual's] body also has a full participation in his rationality" by virtue of his soul.[45]

Barth's "covenantal ontology," as it has been called, offers a pneumatologically grounded, covenantally determined construal of humanity's life as the soul of our body and the body of our soul. As the subject of our own acts, humanity's life is inextricable from its bodily presuppositions and preconditions. The precedence that Barth ascribes to the soul as the life and freedom of the body is not a freedom *from* the body. Soul and body are not "two factors" that must be coordinated, but rather "two moments" of a single subject, such that the individual is "just as much soul from head to foot as he is body."[46] The soul rules, and the body serves—but the body is the "locus, even the subject, of man's capability and activity as soul."[47] This extends to the function of specific organs, like the heart, which Scripture simultaneously invokes to refer to anatomy and to the human subject.[48] Barth's account of human life thus treats bodiliness as an essential, if secondary, aspect of humanity's constitution.

Though Barth's account of the body makes it possible to evaluate our reproductive possibilities theologically, Barth does not take that step—at least not explicitly. Barth argues it is "intrinsically a bodily process that I desire, wish or long for (or negatively fear, shun or avoid) another, or a certain relation between me and another, or it arouses my liking (or dislike)."[49] Bodily urges form the raw material for our self-conscious affirmations and aversions, as it were.[50] Barth does not describe the content of these urges, much less draw them into a discussion of our reproductive powers. Yet Barth's contention that human desire and action are unremittingly corporeal seems to entail that sex differentiation and our procreative powers have a theological significance that other aspects of his theological anthropology might resist. Barth had proposed that an "impenetrable veil of silence" lies over Jesus' maleness in the New Testament. Yet the reality of Christ's humanity is indicated by the fact that he is "born of a woman."[51] The reproductive powers inherent in humanity's bodily, animal capabilities are no more than a presupposition for our actualization as individuals in response to the divine command, to be sure, and to that extent cannot claim precedence or priority in any theological anthropology. At the same time, Barth's contention that our constitution is a "saving fact" seems to give it a durability and constancy

---

44. Ibid., 423.
45. Ibid., 419.
46. Ibid., 425.
47. Ibid., 435.
48. Ibid.
49. Ibid., 408.
50. Ibid.
51. Ibid., 329.

that establishes limits on how we live in the body—or rather, on how God will command us to live in the body.[52] Those limits are not intrinsic, in the sense

52. Paul Dafyyd Jones suggests that Barth's account of sex and gender is a failure on its own terms. On his reading, "Barth's anthropological actualism, which imagines the human as 'opened' towards historical existence and propelled towards an identity defined by the newness of grace, encourages an understanding of the self that escapes the pull of various kinds of 'essentialism'" (402). See Paul Dafyyd Jones, "Human Being," in *Oxford Handbook of Karl Barth* (Oxford: Oxford University Press, 2020), 389–406. Jones' worry is similar to critiques that Barth illegitimately appeals to a natural theology in the realm of sex and gender, which are at this point, legion. Graham Ward contends that Barth's failure to permit same-sex sexual acts is founded on an illicit appeal to natural theology. See Graham Ward, "The Erotics of Redemption—After Karl Barth," *Theology and Sexuality* 4, no. 8 (1998): 52–72. For an early version of this worry, see Jaime Balboa, "'Church Dogmatics,' Natural Theology, and the Slippery Slope of 'Geschlecht,'" *Journal of the American Academy of Religion* 66, no. 4 (1998): 771–89. Gerald McKenny worries that it "cannot be denied that Barth's descriptions of the domains of creaturely life in *Church Dogmatics* III/4 reflect the conventions of mid-twentieth-century bourgeois society, and this raises the question of how decisive scripture has been in their identification and formulation." McKenny, *Analogy*, 255. Faye Bodley-Dangelo's critique of Barth on this score is the most substantive. She objects to Christopher Roberts' use of "biological differences" and "biology" to explain the theological significance of sex-differentiation. According to Faye-Dangelo, Barth's detaching of the "theological significance of men and women from sexual reproduction" opens up critical reconstructions like the one she offers. Against Roberts, Bodley-Dangelo argues that "Barth never names 'biology' as the material presupposition of the covenant, but rather creation, and 'creation' is a history, a sequence of divine acts that include God's production of a human actor whose own sequence of activities (seeking, recognizing, electing, and naming Eve ... but notably and explicitly not sexually reproducing himself via Eve) are central to Barth's theological framing of sexual difference and male precedence" (cf. 139 ff.). (For Roberts, see Christopher Roberts, *Creation and Covenant* (New York: T&T Clark, 2007).) It is true that Barth does not appeal to biology *per se* to explain sex differentiation. At the same time, his contention that humanity's constitution is adapted to the covenant and is durable suggests that his account of sexuality may not be as driven by a natural theology as Bodley-Dangelo and others suggest—if, that is, Barth sufficiently substantiates the claim that our humanity is inextricable from our bodies. Barth's critics have understandably trained their sights on Barth's explicit treatment of sex and gender and given only scant attention to his construal of humanity's constitution. Yet Barth's theological anthropology is an integrated whole, and his treatment of humanity's constitution and life in time builds upon and deepens the earlier sections. While Barth might never appeal to "biology," he says enough in his discussion of humanity's life to warrant biology's use in ethics—which Barth himself does, as I note below. Whether Barth's account of humanity's constitution succeeds in avoiding an illegitimate natural theology, though, depends upon whether Barth successfully grounds his account of humanity's constitution in Scripture. The challenge is especially acute for Barth, as on his reading the New Testament is exclusively interested in Jesus' office and work—which

that we can know them without reference to our encounter with God. Yet they are present in our constitution, regardless of whether we recognize them for what they are.[53]

leaves us with only indirect attestation and confirmation of those aspects of his humanity and nature which a theological defense of humanity's basic form as male and female, and our constitution as soul and body depend upon (cf. III/2, 56-9). On III/2 325-6, Barth suggests that the "New Testament witnesses to revelation apparently took no very great interest in the questions [of humanity's constitution] here to be answered, but took up their position towards them only incidentally and with a certain carefree inexactness, thus giving the impression that they were to be regarded rather as formal." The irony is that Scripture's incidental presentation must be clarified, as a gap "would be intolerable, would have the most fatal consequences, and would give free entrance to the most varied ambiguities and errors." Though Barth does not draw heavily from the Gospels, I am persuaded he does enough to vindicate his reading of our constitution.

53. In his reading of Aquinas and Barth's respective accounts of the body, David Kelsey suggests that Karl Barth's "concrete monism" might come "even closer to a 'naturalistic' view of the human subject than ... Thomas's Aristotelian view" (677). Kelsey rightly contends that the "hallmark of distinctively human life is that it is at once a bodily life and in charge of that bodily life," and suggests that there are an "indefinitely large number of degrees and of ways in which to be in charge of one's life"—including those that are distorted by sin (688). The question for Barth's account is whether the body sets limits on the appropriate ways we can live in it, and whether those limits are constant. Kelsey's contention that Barth's pneumatological account of humanity leaves no room for distinctly human action echoes Rosato's above. As Kelsey writes, because "God the Holy Spirit is understood to engage our bodily acts directly and individually," it is "very difficult not to get the picture that our living bodies are puppets under the Spirit's control or sluices channeling the Spirit's power"—leaving our bodies to be "mere instruments of the Spirit, not genuine covenant partners." Like Rosato, though, Kelsey collapses the Spirit's work in creation and redemption together, even though Barth goes to pains to keep them distinct. He also fails to distinguish between body and soul in their relation to the Spirit. On Barth's view, "As body [humanity] does not go beyond himself, for it is not as body but as soul that he is immediate to the Spirit and therefore to God" (III/2, 425). By contrast, Kelsey contends that, for Barth, grace engages "our bodily action directly." Kelsey goes on: "Because [Barth] holds consummation to be prior to creation even in the formal order, he has no grounds for holding that our 'what' is a form ordered to ends independent of covenant fellowship with God" (685). While it is true that God's grace engages us bodily, it is not the case that the Spirit gives life to our bodies directly. The immediacy of the Spirit's sustaining power is limited to our souls, which keep our bodies alive—that is, which give them the capability for independent action, even action that is not in conformity with the ends for which God has created us. Moreover, if we are not created for "ends independent of covenant fellowship with God," our covenant fellowship with God *includes* other ends as well. See David Kelsey, "Aquinas and Barth on the Human Body," *The Thomist: A Speculative Quarterly Review* 50, no. 4 (October 1986): 643-89.

Human Life as Life in Time

Human beings are not only alive: we have a life in time, which Barth describes as the "form of the existence of the creature."[54] The life of the human as "soul of his body" presupposes that "he is temporal." While time is not the only basis for human life, without time we would "have no life."[55] The nature and content of this time are neither self-evident nor known through immediate reflection on human nature or action, but are disclosed to us in the person of Jesus Christ. Because Christ's life is for God and for humanity, His time is the center of all other times.[56] Barth rejects any temporal docetism that might emerge from an account of God's eternality, arguing that the Incarnation entails that the "eternal content" of God's disclosure is inextricable from its form in time: "If we abstract [Christ] from His time, we also lose this content of his life. If we retain the content, we must needs retain the form as well, and therefore His temporality."[57] In addition to sacralizing time, the Incarnation is an affirmation of humanity's being in time. Christ's incarnation means that "God takes and has time for us."[58] The incarnation thus registers a protest against the "loss of time" that characterizes our life in time after the fall and gives us a confidence in time's reality that would be unavailable otherwise.[59] The "existence of the man Jesus in time is our guarantee that time as the form of human existence is in any case willed and created by God, is given by God to man, and is therefore real."[60] Our life in time continues only because of the ongoing gift of God's presence—whether we recognize and give thanks for this or not. God's "presence as such is the gift of my time. He himself pledges both its reality and goodness," Barth writes.[61]

As the gift of God, time has a pervasiveness and durability that also comes near to grounding a natural theology. If humanity's constitution is one of the "basic points of contact" for the covenant of grace, our embeddedness in time forms another. Humanity's inability to take possession of time—we cannot make the future past, or the past future—indicates that we are "ordained by a higher

---

54. *CD* III/1, 69. The fact that time is the *form* of the creature's existence does not entail that time *is* the existence of the creature. The movement required for creaturely life requires time. Richard Roberts thus overstates things from the outset of his notorious critique of Barth when he suggests that "time is a surrogate for substance in general" in Barth's theology. See Roberts, "Karl Barth's Doctrine of Time," 2. Cf. III/2, 520 ff.

55. *CD* III/2, 437.

56. On the 'Today' of Christ's time, see ibid., 466–73.

57. Ibid., 440.

58. Ibid., 519.

59. Ibid., 518.

60. Ibid., 520.

61. Ibid., 530. Barth goes on: "For our time is the dimension of our whole life. If our whole time is the gift of God, then God also pledges to maintain its reality as a whole."

power than existence itself," that we do not "have [this] existence and nature autonomously, but as they are given by God." In this way, time functions as an "exact parallel" to the role the Spirit plays in humanity's constitution.[62] Barth contends that interpreting the temporality of humanity *positively* requires either illusions or "secret borrowings from theology."[63] Yet the inevitability of time bears witness to God, such that to say "'man' or 'time' is first and basically, even if unwillingly and unwittingly, to say 'God.'"[64] Whatever damage humanity does to our being in time, we cannot destroy it. "Time as the form of human existence is always in itself and as such a silent but persistent song of praise to God," Barth writes. While it has this quality because it makes the covenant possible, the fact that the creature has time "speaks of God's faithfulness to Himself and His creature." Hours and days are the "declaration of the acts of God's righteousness and mercy, of His wisdom and patience, whose witness and object he is privileged to be in virtue of his existence in time." Time is the "secret rustling of the Holy Spirit," which means in the "form of our existence" we are "actually confronted by the presence and gift of God's grace." In his astonishing conclusion, Barth suggests that if "we are to speak of prevenient grace it is difficult to see in what better form it may be perceived and grasped than in the simple fact that time is given to us men."[65]

The time God gives humanity is bounded by birth and death. Just as having a body requires a definite place, human life exists in an "allotted span," which is the "limited space, which he needs for this fulfillment [of his life] and which is given him for this purpose." Human life is ordered by both our resistance to and affirmation of such limits. On the one side, the "abstract desire for life, life hungering for life" protests against limits. Though a naturalized account of life cannot justify a desire for more time, humanity's determination for God and other humans means it would be an "unwarrantable denial of itself" for the creature "not to demand duration."[66] At the same time, this theologically determined desire for life must respect the limit of death. While the eternal life of God is "self-grounded and self-creative, welling up from within itself," the extrinsic basis of human life requires that it have a life in which its "beginning and end are distinct, and therefore constitute its boundaries."[67]

We can only affirm the boundaries of our life at birth and death as benefits if we see *God* at our limits, rather than an abstract conception of non-existence.[68] Birth and death uniquely clarify God's gracious action to us. The longing for infinite

---

62. Ibid., 525.
63. Ibid., 514.
64. Ibid., 525.
65. Ibid. As Gorringe notes, if "there is an analogy to the role of prevenient grace in Barth's theology then it is surely in the role time plays, especially in his anthropology." See Gorringe, *Karl Barth against Hegemony*, 183.
66. Ibid., 557.
67. Ibid., 559.
68. Ibid., 564.

duration is only completely extirpated when we realize that limits are necessary if God is to be our "Counterpart and our Neighbor." Such limits thus become an "expression of the divine affirmation under which we stand."[69] Reflecting about our limits forces a stark binary upon us: either "the gracious God (and He alone) is for us, or nothingness is the abyss from which we have emerged and to which we shall return." That God is *for us* is "clear and essential" to us at these limits.[70] Human nature is thus intrinsically limited, and these limits disclose the "proximity of [God's] free grace in this clarity."[71]

Yet our confrontation with God at life's limits also intensifies life's significance by making clear that our life is a definite, unrepeatable "offer" from God. The reality of God's presence in our time makes "our present not only real but weighty and therefore important." Specifically, it "encloses the opportunity [*Gelegenheit*] which He wills to be realized in and through us now."[72] That "opportunity" is singular and unrepeatable, and as such it corresponds to the singularity and unrepeatability of God in Jesus Christ. As Barth says in his doctrine of providence, "The fact that [the creature] is here and now, that it exists in one way and not another, is its opportunity; the one opportunity which does not recur; an opportunity which corresponds to the oneness of God and the uniqueness of the work of liberation which He accomplished in Jesus Christ."[73] At the same time, this "opportunity" of life has a transcendent orientation and determination, which prevents us from simply pursuing the endless duration that could only give us permanent unrest rather than real satisfaction.[74] When situated against the background of God, our limits lose their character as threats and even provide an assurance humanity will find what it seeks. Such a reconfiguration means life is not simply a "series of opportunities" with only the "possibility of satisfaction." Instead, Barth suggests that "an offer [*angebot*] must be made which is greater and more powerful than its deepest need or the most urgent question to which it is an answer." When life becomes such an "offer," it is "upheld and sustained ... and finally satisfied." Only when life takes on this definite, irreversible, and guaranteed character as a limited life from God can one have "full satisfaction" in the "realisation of its determination" for the covenant.[75]

As moments that make the limits of our agency transparent, birth and death are unique signs and witnesses to God's life. In his doctrine of providence, Barth argues that the limits of human life are among the "certain constant elements" that stand in a "special relationship to the history of the covenant and salvation."[76] Such

---

69. Ibid., 567.
70. Ibid., 569.
71. Ibid.
72. Ibid., 531. *KD* 645.
73. *CD* III/3, 85. It is this "time, space, and opportunity" that God gives to the creature in creation and preserves in His providence.
74. Ibid., 562.
75. Ibid., 563. *KD* 684.
76. *CD* III/3, 199.

constants—which include the history of the church, of the Jews, and of Scripture—are "signs and witnesses" that the world is really ruled by God.[77] Unlike the other constants, though, birth and death are immanent in the life of every individual. Barth frames their theological significance conditionally, so as to ensure that they do not open a pathway toward an illegitimate natural theology: *if* humanity's limits bear witness to the Triune God, they can be "contemplated directly," while the other constants are not "present to any of us so continuously and naturally and self-evidently."[78] Yet whether we realize it or not, "each individual man as such is a sign and testimony in this respect."[79] Birth and death are "unique and incomparable," Barth writes, because they "reflect the two great acts of God at the beginning and end of all things, the creation and the consummation."[80] They also indicate that God's Lordship bounds human freedom, as life is "something which I myself cannot take, or give, or maintain; something which is ordained and given to me."[81] The fact that human life is "disposed and limited" reveals that "there are divine decrees."[82] And, finally, they underscore the unrepeatable character of each individual. In both birth and death, the individual is "utterly himself, absolutely original, and absolutely alone."[83] Such limits reveal the "once-for-allness" of life, in that they set the "particular place and function" that belong to an "irreplaceable, indispensable and non-interchangeable" individual. Such unrepeatability, Barth contends, reflects the "eternal singleness of God Himself."[84]

At every step, Barth's construal of life in its limits seeks to avoid diminishing or devaluing the form in which humanity knows God. Acknowledging the reality of birth and death clarifies the unique opportunity we have, while seeing God at each of those limits intensifies life's significance as an offer from God. Locating the individual against the backdrop of God rather than non-existence means there is no neutrality beneath or behind humanity's life: the status of every human being as given by God means their life is fundamentally and ineradicably a distinct benefit or good. As a sign of God's uniqueness and non-repeatability, the life that happens between birth and death is irreplaceable and, as such, deeply important. As Barth says when he turns to his special ethics of life in its limits in III/4, because "this unique being in temporal limitation is an offer made to man" by God, it is "surely worthy of honour, attention and reflection, even though its significance may not be immediately apparent."[85]

---

77. Ibid.
78. Ibid., 227.
79. Ibid., 228.
80. Ibid., 230.
81. Ibid.
82. Ibid., 231.
83. Ibid.
84. Ibid., 232.
85. *CD* III/4, 572.

Respect for Life as Reason to Create

While Barth's account of life in its limits intensifies its value, his special ethics of God's command to respect life can be read as grounding a presumptive willingness to procreate by honouring our animal nature, our life as embodied souls and ensouled bodies. The theocentric character of life entails that it is not self-interpreting: life cannot be the basis for ethics as Albert Schweitzer thought it should be. "Where Schweitzer places life," Barth writes, "we see the command of God." At the same time, obedience to God the Creator means "man's freedom to exist as a living being of this particular, i.e., human structure."[86] This freedom presupposes our freedom for God and for our fellow-humanity, yet accentuates the particularity of the individual and their constitution (which is the presupposition of their encounter with God). Freedom for life preserves the other freedoms from remaining "singularly majestic but also singularly problematic and docetic." In other words, the command of God reaches "all the way down" into humanity's constitution: it includes humanity's "psycho-physical act of being as such," the "act of [humanity's] existence." Were that not the case, there would be a private realm into which humanity might retreat, creating an ethical vacuum.[87] Barth's actualistic ontology and his corresponding ethics of divine command mean that one cannot read off norms from "biology"—yet neither can they be separated. Insisting on "the separation of the moral from natural volition and action," and "therefore of natural from moral," undermines the ability to "ward off the danger that, in so far as the life of man is below that point, however excellent the ethics above it, it is surrendered to a naturalistic ethics of opportunism and expediency."[88]

Barth's ethics of life carefully builds in a self-referential, egoistic dimension to the divine command—yet without allowing it to become untethered from other-regarding concerns. In the *Leitsatz* to §55, Barth writes that humanity is ordered to "honour his own life and that of every other man as a loan."[89] Barth's theocentric account of life means that there is no independent basis for affirming or willing our own existence. Each particular human life has its origins in God, is determined to return to God, and is animated at each moment by God. Life's status as a loan from God depends "entirely on the fact that God addresses him." God's address gives us confidence in our structure as rational creatures, as the "quickening Spirit" necessarily holds together our structure as soul of our bodies and makes our lives real across time.[90] And God's address "acknowledges and reveals" an individual person in their particularity. While the Word of God presupposes both a "life-process" and "many specific life-acts" that are different

---

86. *CD* III/4, 324.
87. Ibid., 325.
88. Ibid., 326.
89. Ibid., 324.
90. Ibid., 328–9.

from itself, it relates to "to individual and unique rational creatures." In holding individuals responsible for the loan of life, the Word of God "confirms him in the particularity of his creatureliness by claiming him in this particularity."[91] Our particularity as individuals is inextricable from our universality as human beings, though. Hearing the divine command as humans necessarily entails our recognition and solidarity with all others like ourselves. Human life "by its very nature consists in solidarity with those who have also to live it in their own way as it is lent to them." While God might address others "with a different emphasis, content and commission," what God says to the individual "applies to him only as a creature that has others of his kind." As such, the individual addressed by God "recognizes himself in the other." The "natural and historical relations" are only the "concrete conditions in which this solidarity achieves form, and is visible, and becomes a problem, to him and them."[92] While we are commanded to honour our own life, then, its determinations for God and our fellow humans mean we cannot regard it as a self-contained, independent end in itself. As we live eccentrically from and through God's gift of life to us, we are "called from the isolation and self-sufficiency of a life for life's sake."[93] Our participation in freedom as God's creatures only happens "to the extent that it does not have its aim in itself, and cannot therefore be lived in self-concentration and self-centredness, but only in a relationship which moves outwards and upwards to another."[94]

Life's status as a gift and loan from God gives us reason to affirm its ongoing significance beneath the eschatological relativization of Christ's revelation. The theocentric character of human life means that our good is teleologically ordered toward God: limited life is "good and worthwhile" because it gives us the "one great opportunity of meeting God and rejoicing in his praise."[95] Yet the grace of this encounter does not eliminate the prior grace of creation, which has significance independently (in a sense) of its orientation toward the covenant. While God summons humanity to service for Himself, Barth argues that humanity is not "merely a kind of great X on which God wills to magnify His glory and which is itself to be glorified." God does glorify Himself in creation, but humanity is "not merely the *tabula rasa* on which everything that has been factually and objectively decreed will be inscribed." God permits humanity to go on living, not "merely out of concern for His own [honour] and man's salvation, but in connexion therewith,

---

91. Ibid., 328.

92. In this, Barth has some surprising commonality with John Finnis, for whom the initial perception of the basic goods of life, friendship, knowledge, etc. means seeing that they are "good not only for me or thee, but for 'anyone.'" Such a "childish" insight is then deepened by reflecting on the metaphysical capacities individuals have to actualize those goods, and by the evaluative judgment of the worth of those persons. See Finnis 2011, 35, 39.

93. Ibid., 476–7.
94. Ibid., 478.
95. Ibid., 336.

yet also independently, for his existence."[96] The pursuit of the "great cause" of redemptive history means that God "continually creates and offers [humanity] space to live."[97] God has given humanity everlasting life, which Barth argues that in "this new mode it will still be life, and indeed human life." Though Barth does not commit himself to the continuation of life, he suggests that eternal life means "a proper evaluation even of this corruptible and mortal life," and that whatever our new life is it "will be a matter of this life which is lent." The basis and grounds for the divine command for "freedom for life" are not, then, based on life itself, but on the "fact that little man with his existence may in the biblical message stand directly before God and in the centre of all things and occurrence." This revelation happens "finally and decisively in the fact that the Word became flesh."[98]

The birth of Christ at Christmas is the disclosure of the divine command to respect life. In the Incarnation, humanity meets something superior which gives human life "even in the most doubtful form the character of something singular, unique, unrepeatable and irreplaceable," and reveals human life's character as the "incomparable and non-recurrent opportunity to praise God."[99] The incarnation excludes disregarding human life through either intellectualistic or materialistic construals of humanity and prohibits us from over-valuing human nature by enjoining us to humility. Respect for life is, in the first place, an attitude of awe, "an adoption of the distance proper in face of a mystery." Though humanity lives in the limits established by God, in these limits it "must always be honoured with new wonder."[100]

Yet respect for life also has a practical character—and on this score, Barth's ethics of life echoes the "confidence in life" he endorses in his procreative ethics. Respect demands that life must be "affirmed and willed by man," which takes the form of a "determination and readiness for action in the direction of its confirmation." This confirmation necessarily includes the lives of others: "egoism and altruism are false antitheses when the question is that of the required will to live."[101] Indeed, whether we consider the existence of others together with our own is the main criterion Barth lays down for discerning whether we have the proper form of respect for life.[102] Even in our solidarity with others, though, we

---

96. Ibid., 337. Note that I revised the translation of *Ehre* to "honour," for purposes of consistency with Barth's meaning elsewhere. The reasons for this will become clear in Chapter 8. While I have left "independently," it should be noted that Barth's term is "besonderen Interesse," or "special interest." See *KD* III/4, 388.

97. Ibid. In this respect, Barth seems to anticipate McKenny's worry in *The Ethics of Karl Barth* that God's creation of humanity for the sake of being gracious to us in the covenant empties out creation's significance. See above, Chapter 4, note 54.

98. Ibid., 338.
99. Ibid.
100. Ibid.
101. Ibid., 341.
102. Ibid.

are required to perceive and affirm our own life as divine loan, which consists in "our making the use [of our life] prescribed by its nature as seen in these points."[103] The will affirms the value of life through responsible obedience, which must be intentional: we cannot live "accidentally, irresolutely, without plan or responsibility." In other words, we "cannot and must not seriously tire of life" [*des Lebens nicht ernstlich müde warden*]—a formulation that echoes Barth's wording in his ethics of procreation. Where he suggests it is sometimes the "duty of the Christian community to awaken … people [who have] grown tired of life …" [*bestimmten lebensmüden*] to the value of procreation.[104] We are not permitted to tire of life, Barth goes on to say, because it is an "offer [*Angebot*] waiting for man's will, determination and readiness for action," a formulation that recapitulates Barth's contention that the value of human life intensifies when situated in its theocentric context.[105]

This practical affirmation of life includes and extends to humanity's sexual impulses and powers, in such a way that might ground a presumptive pro-natalism by married couples. While Barth's anthropological investigation bracketed humanity's reproductive powers from consideration, his ethics of life seems to reintroduce them. Positively, respect for life means respecting the "requirements of metabolism and the impulses of sexuality."[106] These impulsive or vegetative aspects of life must be affirmed humanly: they are not absolute and have no "independent right and dignity."[107] Instead, they must be exercised "only in co-ordination with the rational actions of the human soul; … as shaped by human individuality; … in the power of human spontaneity; … [and] in relation to man's natural orientation on God and solidarity with his fellow men."[108] With these qualifications, though, the command of God means that a life humanly lived not only "may but should" be lived in such a way that the animal impulses are "lived and not denied." Crucially, the affirmation of life in these limits takes a presumptive form for Barth: we can assume we are free to use our animalistic impulses unless we are told otherwise. The command to respect our animal impulses is not an unconditional norm. God might demand asceticism. But our animal impulses deserve "conditional respect," which means life "can claim validity within those limits and *until a clear command to the contrary is heard from the One who really knows and rules it.*"[109] The fact that

---

103. Ibid., 341.
104. Ibid./Ibid., 268. *KD* III/4, 387/*KD* III/4, 301.
105. Ibid., 341.
106. Ibid., 344.
107. Ibid., 345.
108. Ibid. Emphasis mine.
109. Ibid., 346. *KD* III/4, 398. Barth uses *Befehl* here to name the "command to the contrary" (*Gegenbefehl*), rather than his customary *Gebot*. Does anything substantive hang on it? I think not, as Barth seems to regard the terms as interchangeable. It is possible Barth is nodding to what he suggests is true about Brunner's account of creation. In his

our animal impulses are natural, part of our creaturely equipment, gives their use a *pro tanto* licitness.[110]

At the same time, Barth's silence about the reproductive dimension of these animalistic impulses should give us pause. Barth's treatment of our animal impulses in this context recapitulates his reading of the first creation account, which makes it plausible to think he includes our reproductive powers within their scope. As he notes immediately after affirming that God "offers [humanity] space to life," the "creation story in Genesis 1 right up to the creation of man is one long account of how God ensured and fashioned this space for man to live on earth."[111] Yet Barth omits reproduction from his list of vegetative life's features: "Indeed," he writes, "The Old and New Testaments generally have an extraordinary amount to say about such things as man's dwelling, food, drink and sleep, labour and rest, health and sickness, in short about his life and its limitation by death; nor are these statements incidental only, nor overshadowed by the greater and more decisive matters at issue."[112] There are, as we have seen, reasons why procreation might not appear on such a list, including Barth's contention that the New Testament places an "impenetrable veil of silence over the fact that [Jesus] was a male," his corresponding relativization of procreation in his theological anthropology, and his contention that the New and Old Testaments come apart in their respective accounts of the importance of procreation.[113]

---

discussion of Brunner in III/4, Barth commends his "basic idea" as sound, namely, that the command of God (*Gebot*) does not hover over our existence but arises from it. Barth objects that he does not know how Brunner claims to know the "orders" of creation. On Barth's account of Brunner, reality bears witness to these orders, and the "command of God [*Gebot*] for the moment, His order [*Befehl*], comes to us from this reality" (ibid., 20; KD III/4, 24). Barth wonders whether we are on sound footing, though, in claiming to "hear a divine command" [*Befehl*] from this reality and its embedded "orders." As such, I take it that Barth's terms are equivalent.

110. Barth reiterates this standard on 347 in his summary: "Respect for life means then, especially when it is a matter of others and not ourselves, to admit that the animal impulses should be given their rights within their essential limitations and until there is a clear command to the contrary." Introducing the idea of 'presumptive' licitness or reasons in Barth's ethics of life raises questions about how he understands the divine command and the "boundary," or *Grenzfall* case. While I reserve additional discussion of the case until the final chapter, it is worth noting here that Gerald McKenny's exposition of the "boundary case" in the ethics of *protecting* life confirms this reading of Barth's construal of the ethics of *affirming* life. As he reads Barth, the "surrender or sacrifice of life bears a very strong burden of proof" to be considered a boundary case. See McKenny, *The Analogy of Grace*, 259.

111. Ibid., 337.

112. Ibid., 338.

113. CD III/2, 330. The "substance and nature" of Jesus' corporeality "remain fundamentally hidden," and can only be supplied by "an imagination whose methods have nothing in common with what the New Testament has to say to us."

Even with this qualification, though, invoking Barth's account of respect for life to defend a presumptive pro-natalism might only make explicit what Barth leaves implicit. Barth argues humanity's constitution is adapted to the covenant, that it is a saving fact, and that it "has an inner relation to God's turning towards man and to the salvation which God intends for him."[114] Our affirmation of this life beneath the command of God means resisting weariness about it, by honouring its singularity and unrepeatability as an offer from God. The "offer" of life within God's limits corresponds to the "offer" that God sometimes makes in sexual intercourse—a possibility that requires us to have serious and weighty reasons to use contraception, lest we refuse the offer illegitimately.[115] While Barth's account does not permit us to reify life on its own terms, our practical affirmation of it beneath the divine command is specifically governed by what happens at Christmas, namely, the birth of Christ and our recognition that "little man" has the opportunity to live in service and praise to God. Such a disposition might require us to affirm, presumptively, the value of procreating and give us a basis for exhorting others to pursue it when their confidence in life begins to wane.

The Prospects and Limits of Barth's Account of Life

Barth's account of the nature and theological value of human life helps sharpen the argument for a presumptive, theologically animated pro-natalism *post Christum natum*—and also demonstrates the limits of Barth's resources for that task. Humanity's organic existence is dependent upon the gracious gift of the animating Holy Spirit, who makes possible human life as such. The affirmation that humanity must give to life is not founded on our appreciation or enjoyment of its immanent powers or benefits (contra Kass), but the command of God, which is disclosed to us in the incarnation of Jesus Christ. As God has affirmed human life even down to its organic presuppositions, so we must revere life and respect our own lives and the lives of those like us. If such an account does include humanity's procreative powers, then Barth's view could be martialed to defend a presumptive affirmation of procreation by those who are married, so that it would take a special command of God in order to remain voluntarily childless.

This reading of Barth must lean heavily on his incorporation of something like "nature" into his theological ethics. Such a move is both controversial and dangerous, yet seems in keeping with Barth's ethics of procreation and life. Procreation must be a moment for responsible decision, rather than simply an indifferent matter of luck or chance. But the readiness for children that Barth exhorts for married couples seems to arise, theologically, out of a presumptive licitness of the natural consequences of sexual intercourse. The abrogation of the obligation to procreate

---

114. *CD* III/2, 347.
115. *CD* III/4, 269; cf. above, pp. 132–3.

after the advent of Christ putatively does not mean its devaluation or subordination, as it remains a "natural possibility which the Christian may exploit," and Christians are "participants in the nature in which God has created, male and female."[116] For Barth, nature is never a free-standing entity that has its own independent moral salience. As he had said in the first volume of his doctrine of creation, while there is a "realm of nature which as such is different from the realm of grace," there is "in it nothing which does not point to grace and therefore already come from grace; nothing which can enjoy independent life or exercise independent dominion." Yet neither can grace be understood apart from nature: there is "no place in [the realm of grace] for anything unnatural, but from the creation everything is also nature."[117] While Barth interprets life theologically and leaves room for divine commands that qualify its claims upon us, his opposition to natural theology seems commensurate with allowing nature to ground presumptive moral commitments. In addition to his claim that our animal impulses "can claim validity" until "a clear command to the contrary is heard from God," Barth argues that everyone has some knowledge from nature that murder is wrong. The impetus to kill, Barth writes, is not "the nature" of the criminal, but "belongs to the corruption of his nature." Barth then adds an epistemic component to his argument: "All men know," he writes about killing, "either in an obscure and feeble or perhaps a clear and forceful way, that they are ordained and disposed to respect human life, and this in a far more original form than can be said of the evil readiness to kill."[118] Barth's opposition to natural theology does not preclude appealing to nature when defending moral norms, provided that the account of nature one offers is itself animated theologically and tied together with the covenant. In a letter to Pope Paul VI after *Humanae Vitae* was published, Barth avoided raising material concerns about contraception and instead focused on its "momentous" appeal to natural law, "or rather, its estimate of natural law as a kind of second source of revelation, and on the side of critics of your text, ascribing a similar function to the conscience of the individual and the individual Christian."[119] Nature and conscience are realms that attest to God's

---

116. Ibid., 143. "Sie blieb eine natürliche Möglichkeit, die auch der Christ ergreifen, ein natürlicher Weg, den auch er gehen durfte." *KD* III/4, 163.

117. *CD* III/1, 62.

118. *CD* III/4, 414. Barth suggests that the lust to kill is "not [the criminal's] nature," but "belongs to the corruption of his nature." Similarly, Barth invokes the Incarnation to justify his opposition to abortion, suggesting that the "true light of the world shines already in the darkness of the mother's womb." This theological claim sits alongside Barth's explicit appeal to embryology in order to argue that the unborn child has independent life which is "affected by [the life] of the mother" and also affects hers. His account of humanity's constitution allows him to invoke what would otherwise merely be "phenomena of the human" as morally salient facts. Ibid., 416.

119. Karl Barth, *Letters: 1961–1968*, trans. Geoffrey Bromily (Edinburgh: T&T Clark, 1981), 314.

revelation, Barth elsewhere argues, but as they are mute they are in "absolute need of elevation by God's free grace if they are to be the means of attestation of his Word." Nature and conscience contain both a Yes *and* a No, unlike God's promises. Barth did not object to the invocation of nature *per se*, but rather its use in an abstract, unevangelical way, which eclipsed its ambivalence without the Word of God clarifying its demands on us.[120]

Moreover, Barth's ethics of life allows for an affirmation of our organic powers that is explicitly self-referential or self-regarding. I suggested in Chapter 3 that the reasons to enter parenthood through procreation (rather than adoption) need not be viciously egotistical, even if they might be egoistic. While the full flowering of my reading of Barth's ethics must wait until the final chapter, the theocentric account of life described here offers a way toward requiring individuals to affirm their own lives while incorporating other-regarding concerns into their own sense of flourishing or well-being. The affirmation of life beneath the divine command requires us to seek the space, time, and opportunity to meet God and rejoice in His praise in the manner to which God calls us. This affirmation happens within life's limits, crucially, which do not permit us to demand an infinite duration of time. Yet the Yes that God says to creation in the covenant is rightly answered through our Yes to ourselves *with* each other, in God—a Yes that might animate a presumptive, qualified pro-natalism.

At the least, Barth's theocentric account of humanity's constitution and life requires qualifying Gary Deddo's critique that Barth frames procreation "almost exclusively in terms of the biological event."[121] Such a description fits Barth's account of procreation in his doctrine of creation, his formal anthropology, and even his doctrine of sex and marriage. Yet from the standpoint of the covenant and the command there can be no hint of it being "*merely*" a biological event. Humanity's organic life in time is a "saving fact," a "silent but persistent song of praise to God," an indicator of God's prevenient grace. From the standpoint of the covenant, human life in its limits takes on the character of an "offer" from God—as can sexual intercourse. This quality of human life is intrinsic to it: Barth repeatedly argues limited human life is an unwitting sign of the uniqueness and unrepeatability of God's life, as those who procreated were unintentional signs of hope in the coming Messiah. However, the significance of this witness is only known as such in light of the revelation of the Word of God in Jesus Christ.

At the same time, the theological foundation that Barth builds his ethics of life upon continues to leave any pro-natalism in an unsteady position. If such an ethic is present in Barth, it only emerges by making explicit what he left implicit and by emphasizing minor themes in his work over and against its dominant chords. Barth's reading of the first creation account asserted an inextricable relationship between life and reproduction. Though the link emerged first in a vegetative

---

120. Ibid., 335. Intriguingly, Barth suggests that if the document had been written in such a way, it would have "been received with joyful applause by the whole episcopate and all serious Christians of all churches."

121. Deddo, *Theology*, 349.

context, Barth allowed that it was a precedent for human procreation.[122] Yet his treatment of humanity's constitution and organic life downplays this intrinsically reproductive dimension, a move that is buttressed by Barth's suggestion that the New Testament is uninterested in Jesus' maleness and that the New Testament abrogates procreation's theological significance. While Barth's reintroduction of our sexual impulses in his special ethics comes near to locating life in a genealogical matrix of reception and transmission, it is not clear that Barth had such an aim in mind—or whether the independence of marriage and procreation he elsewhere defends generates a corresponding independence of our sexual impulses and procreation. Moreover, while Barth insists that God gives humanity time (in His patience) to go on living, not "merely out of concern for His own glory and man's salvation, but in connexion therewith, yet also independently, for his existence," we have seen that it is a time oriented toward a future in which there will be no more time or human existence.[123] While procreation as a participation in nature might be presumptively licit, its lack of an eschatological correlate seems to leave it still without theological significance.

Much hangs, then, on Barth's argument that the eschatological disclosure of Christ gives a new consecration to marriage but abrogates procreation. The resurrection reveals that life in its limits is penultimate, rather than ultimate. But Barth's insistence that such a disclosure means the intensification of life's value might have been extended to the value of humanity's reproductive powers—rather than being invoked to diminish them. That Barth does not take this path is intertwined with his account of Christ's birth dissolving any putative burden of genealogy. Paradoxically, though procreation does not have an eschatological correspondence, the birth of Christ is the disclosure of the command of God to respect life. Such an account raises questions about the theological status of the organic and volitional presuppositions of Christ's birth, namely, the person of Mary and the role she might play, if any, in offering a more robust theological framework for childbirth and procreation in the New Testament than Barth's theology otherwise has resources for. As such, Chapter 7 revisits the question of the theological significance of procreation in Barth's theology and argues that his account of the Virgin Birth and parenthood forms a model for how the eschatological disclosure of Christ might simultaneously relativize *and* confirm or intensify procreative bonds and the acts that generate them. The final chapter focuses on procreation as a peculiar form of human action and agency, which clarifies how a practical affirmation of life might generate reasons for particular individuals to pursue parenthood through procreating even when they might licitly become parents through other means.

---

122. It is notable that while Barth regards our impulses as predominately tied to our animality in his discussion of respect for life, he also associates them with our vegetative nature. See III/4, 345–56. "The satisfaction of the needs of the impulses corresponding to man's vegetative and animal nature is one thing, but health, although connected with it, is quite another." Ibid., 356.

123. Ibid., 337.

Chapter 7

MARY AND THE ESCHATOLOGICAL CONFIRMATION OF PROCREATIVE BONDS

Barth's theological account of procreation emphasizes that any obligation to bring human life into the world has been dissolved because Christ has been born. While Barth's construal of life offers a way of grounding a presumptive willingness to procreate on the part of married couples, his contention that marriage receives an eschatological consecration that procreation lacks weakens the force of procreation's theological significance: ultimately, prospective parents deciding to procreate only have recourse to the logic of nature and the "space, time, and opportunity" that God gives to humanity in His providential patience in order to make a positive decision to try to procreate. This limits procreation to establishing the physical or technical opportunity for God to act in the world, even though this (ostensibly) does not minimize life's significance: the life of humans in space and time bears secret and silent witness to God's own life.

For Barth, though, we learn the contents of what is natural for humanity from Christ—which poses an immediate problem for any theological account of procreation. Barth's minimization of procreation's significance is animated by his decision to foreground Christ's life for both theological anthropology and ethics. Whether an "impenetrable vile of silence lies over the fact that [Jesus] was a male" in the New Testament, Jesus clearly does not father His own children.[1] But if Christ does not procreate, He is conceived by the Holy Spirit and born of the Virgin Mary—a fact that distinguishes Him from Adam, whose origins lie exclusively in God and the earth. Barth never makes the links between his account of procreation and Mariology explicit. In his treatment of the Virgin Birth, Barth observes that it would have been simpler and more valuable for Christian ethics had Christ become incarnate as the "natural fruit of an elect and specially blessed" married couple.[2] As Dustin Resch suggests, though, Barth "does not address the difficulties that he suggests the Virgin Birth presents" for an ethics of parents

---

1. *CD* III/2, 330.
2. *CD* I/2, 190.

and children (much less procreation) when he turns to his formal treatment of the subject.³ Barth does contend that the child's standpoint has "more direct [theological] significance" than prospective parents', which arises out of the fact that we are necessarily children (omitting Adam) but contingently parents.⁴ Yet Barth also might have deeper, more theological reasons for this asymmetry, as treating parenthood and childhood's theological significance alike might risk placing Christology and Mariology on an equal plane. Such a move would make the equivalence between Jewish and Roman Catholic pro-natalism more explicit and undermine Barth's efforts to develop a robust account of human agency without endorsing Mariology or the Roman Catholic theological apparatus that he associated with it.⁵

In order to understand the significance procreation has in Barth's theological framework, then, we must revisit (and potentially reconstruct) Mary's role in the economy of God's creative and salvific work. Mary's labor in childbirth raises crucial questions about whether the "eschatological" irruption of Christ relativizes or confirms ordinary means of bringing human life into the world. The conception and birth of Christ from a virgin is a miracle: but is it a miracle that puts an end to procreation's theological significance, as Barth contends, or one that offers procreation an eschatological consecration like that which marriage receives? Such a question hangs on how we construe the analogy between Mary's peculiar,

---

3. Resch, *Interpretation*, 88. While Christ's conception by the Holy Spirit could plausibly be used to fund a critique of abortion, Barth instead argues the embryo is independent based on embryology. The nearest he comes to mentioning Christ's conception is his claim the "true light of the world shines already in the darkness of the mother's womb" (III/4, 416).

4. *CD* III/4, 241.

5. As quoted earlier, Werpehowski makes the association between Roman Catholicism and Jewish accounts of procreating, suggesting that Barth's "limited treatment is a reluctance to endorse any but the most qualified 'pro-natalism' as over against, by his (perhaps mistaken) lights, Roman Catholic and Jewish thought." See "Reading," 404. My aim in this chapter, as in this book, is more systematic than genealogical. As such, the complex, even tortured relationship between Barth and Roman Catholicism lies beyond its scope. Keith Johnson's entry on the subject in the *Oxford Handbook* provides a helpful concise overview of Barth's development from polemicist to ecumenical participant, a transformation that Hans Urs von Balthasar was doubtlessly instrumental in—regardless of whether his reading of Barth was accurate or not. See Keith Johnson, "Barth and Roman Catholicism," in *Oxford Handbook of Karl Barth* (Oxford: Oxford University Press, 2020), 147–68. D. Stephen Long's excellent volume *Saving Karl Barth: Hans Urs von Balthasar's Preoccupation* carefully rehabilitates von Balthasar's reading of Barth, in ways that preserve Barth's theology as an ecumenical resource. The reading of Barth I have offered here is commensurate with his. See D. Stephen Long, *Saving Karl Barth: Hans Urs von Balthasar's Preoccupation* (Minneapolis: Fortress Press, 2014). See D. Stephen Long, "Responses to My Reviewers: Identifying What Matters Most," *Pro Ecclesia* 24-2 (May 2015): 154–61.

sui generis act of giving birth with ordinary moments of procreation, on the one hand. And, on the other, it entangles us in how Barth construes the time, space, and opportunity that the church will have—or, perhaps, will *not* have—when united in the consummation of her union with Christ. These dimensions of Mary's role will occupy us in this chapter; I reserve questions about Mary's agency that Barth moves to the foreground in his treatment of the subject for the next.

In reconstructing Barth's Mariology, I read Barth against himself by invoking resources from his doctrine of creation. His ethics of parents and children offers a pattern for construing the miracle of the Virgin Birth as a confirmation and reification of ordinary procreation, even in the eschatologically governed life of the church. I begin by considering Barth's concern to bracket Mary from having any capacity for God and his analysis of the twin claims that Christ was *born* and born *of a virgin* in *Church Dogmatics* I/2. Barth's interest in protecting the primacy of Christ's conception for the Virgin Birth's theological significance keeps Mariology in a subordinate position to Christology.[6] I then turn to Barth's account of humanity's *whence* from *Dogmatics* III/2, which demonstrates the lengths to which Barth takes the relativization of the natural in favor of our ecclesiastical, baptismal identity. Barth's treatment of our origins and the value of time clarifies why he thinks the obligation to procreate has been dissolved after Christ and sets the stage for Barth's treatment of parents and children in *Dogmatics* III/4. I do not offer a full ethics of parenthood in turning to Barth's treatment of the subject in III/4, but suggest that his construal of the "boundary" case or *Grenzfall* in his ethics of parents and children intensifies the creational norm of natural parenthood, rather than dissolves it—just as the eschatological disclosure intensifies the value of life. If this is right, then Barth's account of parenthood offers a pattern for treating Mary's procreative work as a clarification and confirmation of the norms of ordinary procreation. If Mary is the first member of the new creation, then procreation might have an eschatological significance Barth thinks it lacks. This approach would require revising Barth's account of the end of time, but would also give procreation more theological significance than Barth's account otherwise allows.

The Primacy of Christology for Mariology

Barth's construal of Mary's relation to Christology in I/2 is illustrative of the challenge he faces in founding anthropology upon Christology without either admitting an illicit natural theology into his dogmatics or affirming a

---

6. In his preface to *CD* IV/2, Barth describes the volume as an "attempted Evangelical answer to the Marian dogma of Romanism—both old and new." On his view, the exaltation of Christ's humanity renders Mariology superfluous. As Barth writes, the "fact that the man Jesus is the whole basis and power and guarantee of our exaltation means that there can be no place for any other in this function." Barth, *CD* IV/2, ix. I have outlined my reasons for thinking that there is more continuity between *CD* I/2 and IV/2 than some have thought above. See Chapter 4 note 73.

corresponding preparation in human nature for God's grace. For Barth, the use of *theotokos* is a litmus test for whether theologians have properly understood the *vere Deus vere homo* of the incarnation. So long as the appellation does not give rise to an "independent Mariology," it is "sensible, permissible and necessary as an auxiliary Christological proposition."[7] The "mother of God" correlates with the "Word became flesh" in two ways. First, Mary's designation as the *mother* of God means in the Incarnation we are "not concerned with a creation out of nothing." That the Word became flesh simply means that Christ was born. Second, that Mary is the mother *of God* indicates that He "who was here born in time is the very same who in eternity is born of the Father"—that the *Word* became flesh.[8]

Barth's rejection of an independent Mariology stems from his concern that she might become an exemplar of humanity's intrinsic capacity for God's revelation and so be given honour that is rightly owed to God alone. With John the Baptist, Mary is at the same time the climax of the Old Testament and "the first man of the New Testament."[9] Yet her witness is pronounced precisely because her attention is "directed away from herself to the Lord." She represents humanity, but "in his reception of God." She is the one to "whom the miracle of revelation happens." But she has no intrinsic capacity that prepares her for this reception.[10] Barth argues that Roman Catholic Mariology regards her as the "principle, type and essence of the human creature co-operating servantlike (*ministerialiter*) in its own redemption on the basis of prevenient grace, and to that extent the principle, type and essence of the Church."[11] The Roman Catholic interpretation of Mary's *fiat mihi* indicates that humanity is "capable, by prevenient grace, of preparing himself for genuine sanctifying grace."[12] Barth goes on: "For it is to the creature creatively co-operating in the work of God that there really applies the irresistible ascription to Mary of that dignity, of those privileges, of those assertions about her *co-operatio* in our salvation, which involve a relative rivalry with Christ."[13] As God's agency in redemption precludes Mary's, so the honour we owe to Christ excludes giving honour to her (or humanity)—a point that is crucial for our purposes. Jesus Christ rules over the world and church in "such a way that at every point He is always Himself the Lord, and man, like the Church, can give honour only to Him and never, however indirectly, to himself as well."[14] No matter how

---

7. *CD* I/2, 138.
8. Ibid.
9. Ibid., 140.
10. Ibid., 141.
11. Ibid., 143.
12. Ibid., 144.
13. Ibid., 145.

14. Ibid., 146. Barth reiterates this judgment in IV/2: "It was to safeguard this unity of the person of Jesus Christ as the Son of God and Son of Man (as was necessary against Nestorious) that the title 'mother of God') ... was ascribed to Mary—not to her own honour, but to that of Jesus Christ—at the Council of Ephesus in 431." (IV/2, 71).

many precautions or safeguards we build in, the honour we give God is strictly non-reciprocal.[15]

Barth amplifies humanity's passivity and potentiality with respect to God when he turns to his Christology. As Mary's humanity is constituted solely by her response to God, so Christ's humanity is solely constituted by its union with God—a point Barth emphasizes by invoking its *enhypostatic/anhypostatic* character. Barth contends that Christ assumes "human essence and existence, human kind and nature," that which makes humanity human. Yet Christ's humanity never exists independently. The only presupposition to Christ's incarnation is the "potentiality of being in the flesh, being as a man."[16] Human nature is thus *anhypostatically* related to God, in that it has no subsistence, existence, or (even) content independently of its union with God in Christ.[17] Alternately, and affirmatively, human nature is *enhypostatically* ordered to God, as it assumes its "existence (subsistence) in the existence of God."[18] Human nature is not a universal, which has an existence independent from any particular person, as the uniqueness and particularity of being an individual is partially constitutive of it.[19] On one side, there is no generally known "human nature," no *humanum* that we have independent access to outside Christ. On the other, God assumes the *humanum* in Christ, the "being and essence, the nature and kind, which is that of all men, which characterises them all as men, and distinguishes them from other creatures."[20]

---

15. Ibid. "Faith in particular is not an act of reciprocity, but the act of renouncing all reciprocity."

16. Ibid., 149.

17. In both I/2 and IV/2, Barth uses the *anhypostatic/enhypostatic* distinction to focus attention on the fact that Christ's humanity lacks subsistence or existence apart from its union with Christ—rather than on the unavailability of the content of that humanity apart from Christ. That claim is derived more from Barth's theological anthropology, where the true content of human being and nature is known only through Christ.

18. Ibid., 163. Von Balthasar suggests this notion of 'presupposition' is "the central problem in Barth's theology" at this stage of his writing. On von Balthasar's understanding, there must be a capability for God that "does not adversely affect Christ's prototypicality." God's original act of positing requires that he "must presuppose something else *[voraussetz]* in that very act." See Hans Urs von Balthasar, *The Theology of Karl Barth*, trans. Edward T. Oakes (San Francisco: Ignatius, 1992), 119.

19. Barth contends that "the individuality and uniqueness of human existence belong to the concept of human essence and existence." Ibid., 149.

20. *CD* IV/2, 48. Barth adds the qualifier that we might use "human nature," provided that we are careful to "keep the expression free from any idea of a generally known *humanum*." The substance of his description here and his treatment of the *anhypostatic/enhypostatic* character of Christ's humanity seem otherwise indistinguishable from that which he gives in I/2, 163. See above, Chapter 4 note 73, for additional discussion about the continuity between I/2 and IV/2. Dustin Resch has suggested that in Barth's Christology, the Logos "unites himself with human *nature*, not a human *person*." By contrast, Darren Sumner

While Barth's theological anthropology might preserve an independent Mariology from arising, it raises questions about whether Mary's agency in labor and birth is strictly or exclusively physical, and what, if anything, Christ inherits from her. Mary's humanity is constituted by her response to God, which is why Barth's narrative "centers on the narrative of the Annunciation, in which [Mary's] passivity is particularly evident," as Dustin Resch observes.[21] Christ's humanity is constituted exclusively by its *anhypostatic/enhypostatic* union with God. What then does Christ receive from Mary, if anything? Barth insists the incarnation is not a second *creatio ex nihilo*. Yet does bracketing Mary as the presupposition to Christ's humanity bring the incarnation nearer to a *creatio ex nihilo* than he admits? As he says in his later treatment of the doctrine, *creatio ex nihilo* discloses that "even the potentiality of [humanity's] being does not lie within but outside himself."[22] Is that not what we learn at the Incarnation, though? And what are the implications of this for Mary's agency? We are thrown again into the cluster of questions that beset Barth's doctrine of creation and theological anthropology, namely, whether the external, extrinsic means of God's action in creation have been given sufficient weight or honour. Does Mary *merely* give birth to our Lord? To make progress on these questions, we must consider how Barth construes the sign of the Virgin Birth.

The Virgin Birth as a Sign

The Virgin Birth is only a sign of God's revelation in Jesus Christ—but it is an indispensable sign. Its significance is not reducible to its biological or historical oddities, yet neither can it be understood without those features. Though *vere Deus vere homo* is Christology's primary substance, the Virgin Birth points to the "mystery of that reality, the inconceivability of it"; it clarifies our need for a "spiritual understanding" of the incarnation, the "understanding in which God's own work is seen in God's own light."[23] Specifically, the Virgin Birth underscores the independence and freedom of God's action in salvation: as the Virgin Birth is

---

suggests that the "Son did not take up a human nature (particularly one substantially construed), but rather actualized the *concrete possibility* of existing as the man Jesus." Sumner goes on: "The existence of God the Son as Jesus Christ is not a general reality that is already part of the created order, which He merely acquired, but is creatively sourced—a new thing born from the power of God." We can split the difference between these by saying that "human nature" is not an abstraction or generic that is known independently of Christ, but that it is real nonetheless insofar as it exists only in particulars, as being unique and irreplaceable is a constituent part of human *nature*, not only of particular human *persons*. See Resch, *Intrepretation*, 44 and Sumner, *Karl Barth and the Incarnation*, 173.

21. Resch, *Interpretation*, 203.
22. *CD* III/2, 152.
23. *CD* I/2, 177.

enacted by God "solely and directly," it is a "sign of the freedom and immediacy, the mystery of His action," and a "preliminary sign of the coming of His Kingdom."[24] It indicates that "God does it all Himself," that "God Himself has the initiative."[25]

In order to be a sign, though, there must be some kind of connection between the form and substance: the sign must "have in itself something of the kind of thing it signifies; it must be in analogy with it noetically and ontically."[26] The Virgin Birth happens "in the unity of the psychical with the physical, in time and in space, in noetic and ontic reality," but its significance is not reducible to its historical or biological features.[27] Instead, the Virgin Birth is a "pointer" to the new beginning of Christ's birth and "not a conditioning of it."[28] The sign and substance are held together by God, rather than out of any causal or ontological necessity, which means that we can distinguish them without dividing them. Though God willed to be *vere Deus vere homo* in this form, we "shall not say that God could not have given it quite a different form." Barth goes on: "We can therefore juxtapose form and content, sign and object, but we cannot undertake to derive them from each other by any method of calculation," before concluding, "This as little as we can separate one from the other!"[29] The fact that God unites form and substance entails both that the sign is epistemically significant, and that it does not have a constitutive or ontological role in Christology.[30] As Dustin Resch argues, Barth

---

24. Ibid., 181.
25. Ibid., 182. On the side of continuity in Barth's account of Christology, it is worth noting that Barth's invocation of the Virgin Birth in *CD* IV/1 more or less recapitulates his treatment from I/2 without loss or emendation. Cf. IV/1, 207.
26. Ibid., 182.
27. Ibid., 181.
28. Ibid., 189.
29. Ibid., 189. Translation revised. The original reads: "Therefore we can separate form and content, sign and thing signified. But we cannot derive them from each other, any more than we can separate them from each other, by any method of calculation." The German: "Wir können also Form und Inhalt, Zeichen und Sache, wohl gegeneinander halten, aber nicht in einer rechnerischen Pragmatik auseinander abzuleiten unternehmen. Dies so wenig, wie wir das eine vom anderen trennen können!" (*KD* I/2, 206). I have opted to use 'juxtapose' over 'divide', as the latter implies a separation that Barth rejects.
30. Ibid., 179. In *Credo*, Barth argues that the doubt thrown upon the Virgin Birth stems from the failure to recognize its quality as a sign. As it might be "impossible to separate this content from this form, this form from this content," it is the "better course" to simply leave the dogma uncriticized (72). In *The Faith of the Church*, Barth suggests the sign does not prove the substance of the doctrine but only communicates it, while raising the possibility that "God could have chosen another process, even as Jesus could have done other miracles to signify the same Word." Yet he maintains we cannot have the substance without the sign. Karl Barth, *The Faith of the Church*, trans. Gabriel Vahanian (Zürich: Theologischer Verlag Zürich, 1958), 85.

thinks the sign bears "epistemological significance for the person and work of Christ," but does not ontologically affect either the "identity of Jesus Christ" or alter the significance of His work.[31]

Barth's formulation of the content of the sign of Christ's birth from the Virgin Mary has significant implications for his construal of the agency involved in ordinary procreation. Christ's birth from Mary indicates His solidarity with humanity. The *natus* "states that the person Jesus Christ is the real son of a real mother, the son born of the body, flesh and blood of his mother, both of them as real as all the other sons of other mothers."[32] Barth's construal of birth in this context anticipates his later argument that the *imago Dei* is only indicated by being born, not established through it.[33] In an excursus, Barth distances his view from the "gnostic and docetic ideas" of those like Valentinus, which presuppose that Christ "had received nothing from His human mother." His birth from Mary underscores His common humanity—a theme Barth repeats elsewhere.[34] It means, more fundamentally, that humanity is one of the elements in the miracle of Christmas, that he is present "at the event as one of the principals; not as a cipher or as a phantom, but as the real man that he is."[35] However, as Resch notes, Barth is "careful to keep from stating that a human birth is itself constitutive of true humanity or even suggesting that it is the decisive factor." Instead, a human birth "is only an indication of genuine humanity."[36]

---

31. Resch, *Interpretation*, 5. Resch leans on Barth's treatment of the Virgin Birth in *Credo*, where Barth writes that the "miracle of the Virgin Birth has no ontic but noetic significance." Karl Barth, *Credo*, trans. J. Strathearn McNab (New York: C. Scribner's Sons, 1936), 69.

32. *CD* I/2, 185.

33. See above, Chapter 5, Section 1.

34. In his theological anthropology, Barth argues that the New Testament is "unambiguously and emphatically clear that we have to do with a real man" on the grounds that Christ's birth from a woman is the "self-evident presupposition of all the New Testament writers." Cf. III/2, 329. Similarly, while Barth does not think one's parents are a determination of a person, he opens his treatment of parents and children by arguing that "It is part of the creaturely status of man in his relationship with other men that he is conceived and born and is thus the child of a father and mother, and that he himself in his turn can conceive and thus become the father or mother of children." See *CD* III/4, 240.

35. *CD* I/2, 186.

36. Resch, *Interpretation*, 84. Barth notes in I/2 that living as a human means to "be related to man, to differ from him and to agree with him, to come from man and depend on man." However, he immediately brackets the *from* as part of the definition of humanity because we "do not exist for our fellow-man, we exist for God." Such a move seems predicated on a broader principle that Barth sometimes employs, namely, that we return to our origins. While Barth thus frames the *from* as indicative of humanity, it is by no means essential (*CD* I/2, 42).

At the same time, Christ's birth from a virgin underscores humanity's incapacity for God under the conditions of sin. Mary's significance is determined by the "extremely concrete negative" of her virginity. Mary's virginity signifies that human nature "undergoes a very definite limitation," that the grace which is imparted to humanity comes with judgment.[37] The event "approaches nature in the biological sense," yet is also a real event: humanity receives a grace that makes us not only a spectator, but entangled in an event that "contradicts and withstands" us.[38] However, Mary is emphatically not a partner to God's action in this event: she is the "old natural humanity" that prevents the incarnation from being a *creatio ex nihilo*. Ascribing to Mary unfallen humanity would establish her as "God's partner" and admit a "creaturely self-glorification" and corresponding natural theology into dogmatics. Mary's virginity and its "positive background" of Christ's conception by the Spirit provide the "necessary safeguard" against this happening.[39] The Virgin Birth is the denial that humanity has any "power, attribute, or capacity within him for God."[40] Barth here suggests disobedience goes

---

37. *CD* I/2, 187. "By the *ex virgine* the essential point is plainly expressed that by the Word being made flesh, by God's Son assuming 'human nature,' this human nature undergoes a very definite limitation" ("widerfährt dieser menschlichen Natur eine ganz bestimmte Begrenzung.") *KD* I/2, 204.

38. Ibid., 187. The translation here is revised. The original reads: "Manifestly the *natus ex virgine* according to these texts not only runs counter to nature in the biological sense, but deals positively with a genuine experience belonging to man as such. In that grace is imparted to him he is given not simply to be the spectator of an unusual event, but to participate in an event which contradicts and withstands him." (*CD* I/2, 187). However, 'counter' signifies that Barth thinks the miracle contradicts nature, when in fact he writes that it *entgegengeht*—approaches—nature. The second sentence does not indicate that humanity participates in the event, at least not if 'participates' indicates some kind of concursus with God's action. Rather, it stresses that humanity meets this event with opposition. The full German: "Es ist offenkundig, daß das *natus ex virgine* nach diesen Texten nicht nur im biologischen Sinn der Natur entgegengeht, sondern daß es sich dabei sachlich um ein echtes Widerfahrnis handelt, das dem Menschen als solchem zuteil wird. Er bekommt, indem ihm Gnade zuteil wird, nicht nur als Zuschauer eines ungewohnten Ereignisses etwas zu staunen, sondern dieses Ereignis widerspricht und widersteht ihm selbst" (*KD* I/2, 204). The only other place, I believe, where the couplet of 'contradicts and withstands' appears in the *Dogmatics* is in Barth's treatment of the 'nothingness' that opposes God in III/3: "That which rendered necessary the birth of His Son in the stable of Bethlehem and His death upon the cross of Calvary, that which by this birth and death He smote, defeated and destroyed, is that which primarily opposes and resists [*widerspricht und widersteht*] Himself, and therefore all creation" (*CD* III/3, 304; *KD* III/3, 346).

39. Ibid.

40. Ibid., 188. Barth goes on to suggest that this negation is strictly tied to sin, engaging in a moment of abstraction to consider humanity outside the context of the redemptive history that we know. Such a move is incommensurate with his theological method. Yet even in

to the "roots of [humanity's] being" and structures human nature. It is this fallen human nature that is "limited and contradicted by the *natus ex virgine.*"[41] Christ's "existence in our old human nature" posits a conquest over original sin.[42] But the Virgin Birth is not the cause of Christ's triumph over original sin. It is only a sign and "pointer" to the new beginning offered in Christ and supplies no "technical proof" of that conquest.[43]

Even so, Barth's construal of the exclusion of sex as the sign of God's triumph over original sin threatens to strip Mary of her agency and affects how Barth depicts natural generation. God's exclusion of fallen humanity in the Virgin Birth cannot float free of the event's form: dividing them would imperil the interconnection of sign and substance Barth defends. To preserve divine freedom, then, Barth argues Mary is involved in God's act only as "non-willing, non-achieving, non-creative, non-sovereign man, only in the form who can merely receive, merely be ready, merely let something be done to and with himself."[44] Mary's "readiness" is not an intrinsic property that is indicated by either her virginity or willingness. Instead, when the Word becomes flesh Mary concurrently "becomes the possibility, becomes the mother of God's Son in the flesh."[45] Note that Mary does not have the capability to be this possibility intrinsically, but acquires it through God's act of becoming flesh. In positing Himself in the incarnation, God also posits its presupposition in Mary's capacity for God.[46] Mary's "adaptability for God" is thus extrinsic to her: whatever readiness Mary has for God is a response to the Word's assumption of humanity in His conception by the Spirit, rather than being founded upon her virginity or any other property she possesses. This way of approaching the Virgin Birth forces Barth to intensify the work-like character of human procreation: "every natural generation is the work of willing,

---

this context, Barth does not affirm that humanity has a *capacity* for God beyond sin—only that we would have had the *possibility* of God. Barth's suggestion that humanity under sin lacks "power, attribute or capacity" for God (Möglichkeit, Eignung, Fähigkeit) is narrowed to the affirmation that humanity in Paradise would have the possibility (Mölichkeit) for God. "Der Mensch als Geschöpf—wenn wir vom Menschen in dieser Abstraktion einen Augenblick zu reden versuchen—hätte wohl die Möglichkeit für Gott und würde sich in dieser Möglichkeit auch verstehen können" (*KD* I/2, 205).

41. Ibid., 189.

42. Ibid.

43. Ibid. Barth's account of the Virgin Birth accepts the fallenness of Christ's humanity, and thus his solidarity with Mary and with us.

44. Ibid., 191.

45. Ibid.

46. In this formulation, then, Barth regards the Virgin Birth as the restoration of nature, namely, through the re-establishment of humanity's possibility (Möglichkeit) for God. "Dieser Mensch, die *virgo*, wird die Möglichkeit, wird die Mutter des Gottessohnes im Fleische. Wohlverstanden: sie ist es nicht, sie wird es; und sie wird es nicht aus eigener Fähigkeit, sondern indem der Gottessohn Fleisch annimmt, bekommt sie sie" (*KD* I/2, 209).

achieving, creative, sovereign man," he writes. While sex is not sinful *per se,* it "cannot be considered at all as the sign of the divine *agape* which seeks not its own and never fails." Such a stance both leaves little room for Barth's later depiction of humanity's natural generation as a "gift" and would, if true, inflate the importance of natural parents in ways that also cut against his later view.[47]

Barth buttresses this depiction of Mary's virginity as indicating a non-willing, non-striving (sinful) humanity by introducing a gendered distinction into the agency of natural generation. The "human creaturely *eros*" the Virgin Birth contradicts is associated with the male. Barth's discussion of why the Virgin Birth uniquely brackets the male combines his understanding of the *enhypostatic* character of Christ's humanity with a (dubious) principle of male prerogative that he derives from "world history." On his *enhypostatic* Christology, Christ's humanity has existence only in the "eternal mode of being of the Word or Son of God." In that sense, His being in time is identical to His existence as the eternal Son of the Father. Such a principle excludes having a human father, though, because it is "precisely the human father whom a human son has to thank for everything that marks his existence as belonging to him."[48] As such, a sign that describes the mystery of the *enhypostasis* requires the "actual elimination" of the sign of a human father. It is the male who cannot be the "participator in God's work," as the male is the "father of man in the sexual act which man has to thank for his earthly existence."[49] The elimination of the male in the Virgin Birth indicates that Christ's origin is in God alone.[50] While woman has a share in this active, willing dimension of human erotic life, Barth argues there is no equality between the sexes in this respect. Male action is uniquely significant for the "world history with which we are acquainted." While Barth contends the biblical witness assumes such a principle, he also (here) grounds the super- and subordination of male and female it depends upon in the sphere of the Fall.[51] The male's putative pre-eminence is a "divine ordinance valid in the sphere of the Fall," rather than an "order of creation." The Virgin Birth functions as a countersign to this principle, as the absence of the male means the "limitation of man and his sin" and so the "limitation of male pre-eminence."[52] Barth's emphasis on the negation of the male does not generate a corresponding affirmation of female superiority, even though

---

47. Necessarily, then, sex points "elsewhere than to the majesty of the divine pity." Ibid., 192.
48. Ibid., 193.
49. Ibid.
50. Barth writes in *CD* IV/1, 207, that "conceived by the Holy Ghost" means that "God Himself—acting directly in His own and not in a human fashion—stands at the beginning of this human existence as its direct author."
51. *CD* I/2, 194. "Thus, not because of an original mark of distinction, but because of the common Fall of man and woman, in which both step out of a relationship in which there is no word of super—or sub-ordination, there arises the unlikeness, and man becomes the lord of woman and therefore significant for world history."
52. Ibid.

women alone are capable of gestating and giving birth to human life.[53] The female is not "readier for God's work than the male-human." Barth does nod approvingly (and begrudgingly) toward Roman Catholic Mariology, as it renders the female "as significant for human nature as such as the male is for human history," so that if the male must withdraw, the female "can and must be there, there for God, if God on His part wishes to act on man and with man."[54] Yet it is only through an "act of divine justification and sanctification (at this very point, too) that human nature becomes a partaker of the divine nature."[55] Mary's theological significance remains exclusively founded upon the annunciation of the Word of God and the subsequent conception of Christ by the Holy Spirit, two divine events that encompass and determine her virginity and procreative work.

Given such a backdrop, it is easy to see how Barth argues Christ's conception by the Spirit indicates the "ground and content" of the miracle of Christmas, while the Virgin Birth indicates the "form and sign."[56] Neither Mary's virginity nor her human nature has any independent meaning from the conception of Christ by the Spirit. While Barth had spoken of Mary's sinful human nature as the presupposition of the Incarnation, the Holy Spirit's role in the conception of Jesus means that we have to do here with a "pure divine beginning."[57] The Holy Spirit," Barth writes, "is God Himself in His freedom exercised in revelation to be present to His creature, even to dwell in him personally and thereby to achieve his meeting with Himself in HIs word and by this achievement to make it possible.[58] The "very possibility of human nature's being adopted into unity with the Son of God is the Holy Ghost."[59] In this way, the Virgin Birth forms the prototype for Christians' new birth through the Spirit and of the baptism that indicates it.[60] However, this conception does not

---

53. Faye Bodley-Dangelo argues that Barth's Christocentrism allows for only one pattern of human action, which is a "male prerogative, and consequently eviscerates the would-be female agent." She suggests that the 'barrenness' of the waters in Barth's reading of Genesis 1 is akin to Barth's treatment of the Virgin Birth, namely, that the "capacity of a woman's body to conceive might suggest a capacity of creaturely material for the creative work God does with it, which in turn might lend support to an anthropology in which human beings have a capacity for (or a point of contact with) the revelatory and redemptive work of God." See Bodley-Dangelo, *Veiled*, 121. This seems exactly right. Jess Wyatt's defense of Barth's account of female agency against Bodley-Dangelo's criticisms is worth attending to, even if not (I think) fully persuasive. See Jess Wyatt, "Does Barth's Understanding of Sexual Difference Conflict with His Theological Anthropology?," *Scottish Journal of Theology* 76, no. 1 (February 2023): 44–55.

54. Ibid., 195.

55. Ibid., 196.

56. Ibid.

57. Ibid., 198.

58. Ibid.

59. Ibid., 199.

60. Ibid. Barth reiterates this point in a variety of places throughout the *Dogmatics*. See, for instance, *CD* IV/4, 15: "Christmas Day is the birthday of every Christian."

happen on any analogy with marriage or ordinary conception: the Holy Spirit is not akin to the human father of Jesus. Instead, Christ's conception by the Spirit indicates the "inconceivable act of creative omnipotence in which [God] imparts to human nature a capacity, a power for Himself, which it does not possess of itself and which it could not devise for itself …"[61]

Though Barth's treatment of procreation and parenthood in *Dogmatics* III/4 makes no explicit use of the Virgin Birth, his treatment of the subject in I/2 prepares the ground for his relativization of procreation throughout his doctrine of creation. Though Mary is the "first man" of the New Testament, her witness is self-abnegating. While Christ's celibacy and childlessness necessarily complicate any theological affirmation of procreation, Barth's aversion to Roman Catholic Mariology leads him to construe Mary as a representative of (fallen) humanity's passivity and incapacity before God. At the same time, Barth stresses the male's role in procreation—even though the female is the one burdened with the work of gestation, labor, and childbirth. All of this is animated by his effort to ensure Mariology does not become an independent locus of reflection, and thus the basis for an illegitimate natural theology. Barth's attempt to hold together the Virgin Birth's form and substance is subject to the same tensions and difficulties he faces in holding form and content together elsewhere, but is even more strained than his efforts in his doctrine of creation: Barth allows that Christ could have become human through other means to secure divine freedom, but then argues that Mary's virginity indicates that one could not become the Mother of the Lord through ordinary procreation.[62] The notion of divine freedom in this account is closer to an abstract possibility of acting otherwise, rather than God's conformity to His nature and essence as disclosed in creation.[63] Even so, the form of the Virgin Birth is not antithetical to ordinary procreation, but is a miracle that (for Barth) approaches what happens naturally and sheds light on its distortions by sin.

The Ecclesiastical Whence and Natural Parenthood

If Barth's treatment of the Virgin Birth lays the groundwork for his subordination of the role of parents to the standpoint of the child, his treatment of humanity's *whence* in the theological anthropology of *Dogmatics* III/2 makes his minimization of natural parentage after (and in) the advent of Christ even more explicit. Barth's account of life in its limits is guided by Christology, but his account of the

---

61. Ibid., 201.

62. Mary's virginity declares "that in any other way, i.e. by the natural way in which a human wife becomes a mother, there can be no motherhood of the Lord and so no entrance gate of revelation into our world." Ibid., 188.

63. This is a similar objection that Matthew Puffer puts to John Howard Yoder's construal of God's freedom in his understanding of the 'borderline' case. See Puffer, "Taking Exception to the *Grenzfall*'s Reception," *Modern Theology* 28, no. 3 (2012): 491.

individual's origins only implicitly raises the question of Mary's role and agency. Barth argues that Christ's Incarnation displaces the role of natural parents as the answer to our origins, while he transposes Genesis 1's correlation of blessing and fruitfulness into an explicitly ecclesiastical register.

Evaluating our origins as individuals confronts us with the fact that "even from my origin I am threatened by annihilation, being marked as a being which can advance towards non-existence."[64] This anxiety animates our interest in history, which exploration of the past can fully satisfy: the only answer to humanity's *whence* is that we "derive from this God." We "certainly come from non-being," Barth writes, "but we do not come from nothing"—that is, from the chaos that stands in hostile opposition to God because God has negated it by uttering His Yes to creation.[65] Instead, we come from the "being, speaking and action of the eternal God who has preceded us" in time.[66] In this way, the "inner life as Father, Son, and Holy Spirit" is the "content of the time before our time, the meaning of the pre-history before our history."[67] The nature of our beginning becomes a kind of promise, which indicates God will "surely guarantee the whole of our life."[68] Neither our constitution nor our parentage can serve as a presupposition that inclines or disposes us to meet God. On Barth's reading, the doctrine of *creatio ex nihilo* is rendered necessary by anthropology, rather than creation: the only thing that "precedes human being as a being summoned by the Word of God is simply ... God in the existence of the man Jesus."[69] While there is a "real pre-existence" of humanity in the "counsel of God," *creatio ex nihilo* means humanity's existence is "not grounded upon nothingness and chaos," but "derives from God and no other source."[70] The question of a creaturely presupposition of this summons arises only on the basis of a non-theological anthropology, so that attempting to know a beginning behind humanity's summons in Jesus Christ is the anthropological equivalent of attempting to know the God who is "known to us only in this absence of any other presupposition or not at all."[71]

---

64. Ibid., 574. Barth's attempt to prescind from any judgment about the details of the individual's origins seems to be animated, in part, by a theological actualism that is one step removed from the biological conditions of life. However, his description of creationism, in which God is both the primary *and* sole cause of the body and soul of the new human being seems to comport best with Barth's description of humanity's origins.

65. Ibid., 576.

66. Ibid., 577.

67. Ibid.

68. Ibid.

69. Ibid., 151.

70. Ibid., 155.

71. Ibid., 151. Christiane Tietz notes that Barth began his draft autobiography with these lines from Paul Gerhardt: "What have we here or what are we/Of good what can earth give/ That we do not alone from Thee/Our Father, aye receive?" As Tietz notes, these lines could function as a "summary of Barth's theology: human beings are what they are solely through

As our knowledge of our origins is governed by revelation, it is mediated by the people of God—rather than by biology or our parentage. Barth's prioritization of the covenant thrusts his account of humanity's *whence* into the dialectic of continuity and discontinuity between the Old and New Testaments. On one side, Barth's treatment of Christ's time emphasizes the continuity of the two communities' posture of hope. The New Testament confirms and ratifies Israel's expectant waiting for the Messiah, the "Yesterday" of Christ's life.[72] The resurrection provides the apostolic community a "foretaste of their inheritance and a glimpse of the new creation." Christian hope thus grasps the "promise implicit in the origin of their existence," and from this beginning lives "with a view to its continuation and completion." The church is necessarily, then, a "gathering in this hope."[73] The apostles who saw the hope of Israel fulfilled "began to wait as never before, together with the fathers of the old covenant, hoping and living wholly and utterly in Advent"[74] The Christian thus stands between "two choirs singing antiphonally— the apostles on one side and the prophets on the other."[75] For the church, that song is one of "patient joy and joyful patience" as it awaits the coming of the Lord.[76]

On the other side, Barth's emphasis on the church's continuity with Israel disappears in his discussion of the individual's *whence*, as the New Testament transposes the Old Testament's depiction of parents as mediators and progenitors into an ecclesiastical key. For Israel, mothers and fathers have an exalted position because they are either "the direct witnesses or the accredited narrators" of Israel's calling by God.[77] They "serve as [the Israelite's] sureties." Natural parents stand between the individual and God in the Old Testament: while life in the land depends on "the *prius* of [God's] election and covenant ... father and mother are the concrete, visible embodiments of this divine *prius*."[78] The individual thus finds meaning and significance in their "participation in this history and in the accompanying mediation of the divine promise and command from generation to generation."[79] Crucially, this security is not founded on natural generation *per se*. If it were, procreating would intrinsically secure the *imago Dei*, which Barth

---

God." She also suggests, though, that Barth's decision to begin his autobiography with his parents and grandparents indicates that "person's life does not start with himself." While that might be true, Barth's theological treatment of humanity's *whence* sits uneasily (at best) with such a conclusion, as it underscores the only appropriate theological answer to our origins is: God. See Tietz, *Karl Barth*, 1.

72. Ibid., 475.
73. Ibid., 489.
74. Ibid., 493.
75. Ibid., 496.
76. Ibid., 492.
77. Ibid., 579.
78. Ibid.
79. Ibid., 583.

rejects. Instead, parents bestow an Abrahamic blessing, which indicates "the word, spoken in power as God's own Word, of election, covenant, salvation and hope" stands behind every Israelite's life.[80] Such a blessing is "never a self-evident reality or natural condition," but must (alongside circumcision) "be declared afresh with every generation." This freedom to bless and receive blessing is the "Old Testament's answer to the *whence* of humanity's natural life."[81]

The church, by contrast, relativizes the status of natural parents and emphasizes ecclesiology in their place by replacing the blessing with baptism. Despite the apostolic communities' intense interest in Christ's "Yesterday" of the Old Testament, the "divine word of blessing, as the New Testament sees it, has been uttered once and for all in the incarnation of the Word of God ... and therefore cannot be repeated."[82] No Christian can bless another the way Hebrew parents blessed children. The individual Christian thus "lives directly by the beginning" of Christ's advent, and the church mediates only this beginning without building on its antiquity—as Israel's transmission of the Abrahamic blessing does.[83] The completion of the covenant in Jesus Christ is "now the *prius* for every human life," rather than mother and father.[84] The baptism that displaces the blessing is an exclusively individual affair, as it identifies a "direct relationship of the individual Christian to Jesus." In salvation, "no man can stand proxy for him."[85] Barth's wariness about infant baptism is founded in this context on the individual's immediate origins in God: such a practice confuses the Church with a "natural and historical entity like Israel."[86]

Barth's ecclesiastical reconfiguration of the Abrahamic blessing corresponds to his transposition of fruitfulness into an ecclesiastical register. While Barth had (understandably) considered the category in his discussion of creation in III/1, it otherwise disappears from his account until his treatment of humanity's origins at the end of III/2. Barth contends that the church's life is marked by whether it "understands and takes seriously and turns to good account"—makes *fruitful*— its "present existence under the lordship of Jesus in the form of the Spirit as

---

80. Ibid, 580.

81. Ibid. Charlotte von Kirschbaum distills the thought nicely when she argues that "natural propagation of Israelite lines of descent is no guarantee as such that God will fulfill the promise to his covenant people." Instead, fulfillment "remains an act of God's free choice, as he summons whom he will to be the bearers of living hope." See Charlotte von Kirschbaum, *The Question of Woman*, 123. Note that von Kirschbaum stresses the importance of mothers in the question of descendants, which is a clear contrast to Barth's patriarchalist emphases.

82. Ibid., 582.
83. Ibid., 584.
84. Ibid.
85. Ibid., 585.
86. Ibid.

considered in relation to the future."[87] However, such fruitfulness does not become the Church's possession, as the blessing is Israel's. Instead, the Church mediates the individual's origins in Jesus Christ's resurrection without standing between God and the individual.[88] Barth's curious near-silence about the blessing of fertility in his ethics of procreation in III/4 has its roots here: such categories have become the domain of the church, properly, and only in that light can they be extended to parents (if at all).[89]

Barth's construal of humanity's *whence* simultaneously relativizes genealogical bonds after the advent of the Christ and intensifies the significance of the life we are given as individuals by God. Israel and the church have more in common than it might seem: neither is an exclusively "natural" community (though the church is not a natural community *at all*). The blessing secures continuity across generations in the Old Testament, rather than procreation *per se*—which is consistent with Barth's claim that the *imago Dei* is not transmitted through procreation. As Barth observes in his account of the Virgin Birth, the genealogies of Jesus indicate their authors understood "the idea of descent quite differently from the way in which we do," namely, as including non-procreative bonds.[90] If the power to bless sacralizes natural parenthood in the Old Testament, though, the displacement of the blessing by baptism in the New Testament imperils it. As parents no longer transmit the blessing, they can no longer stand as surety for children. At the same time, the same theological framework that relativizes parenthood intensifies the significance of our individual lives. As noted in Chapter 6, evaluating life at its limits underscores that it is an offer made by God, and so is "surely worthy of honour, attention and reflection, even though its significance may not be immediately apparent."[91] Seeing our life at its origin means eclipsing our parents and history, and directly and immediately encountering God.[92] While Barth is explicitly concerned that

---

87. Ibid., 505. Barth's appeal to Matthew 26:29 here suggests he is using organic rather than procreative imagery. However, the association of ecclesiastical fruit in such close context to the language of blessing also corresponds to his description of the fruitfulness of vegetative life as a precedence for human procreation in III/1.

88. As Travis McMaken writes, the church "points individuals back to their eternal election in Jesus Christ," but the "mode of mediation is different" from Israel. Eberhard Jüngel writes that the "Church represents Christ by renouncing any self-representation." W. Travis Mcmaken, *The Sign of the Gospel* (Minneapolis: Fortress Press, 2013), 126, quoting Jüngel. McMacken's broader discussion is invaluable. Cf. pages 124–30.

89. The nearest Barth comes there to discussing children as a "blessing" is in his full endorsement of Ernst Michel's suggestion that revealing the "full potentiality [of children] as blessing" requires the "responsible Yes of parents …" (III/4, 271).

90. As Barth suggests, Romans 1:3's "being born of the seed of David according to the flesh" "need not altogether signify biological provenance." *CD* I/2, 175–6.

91. *CD* III/4, 572.

92. John Webster proposes that Barth's repudiation of inherited sin in IV/1 is "ultimately because an inheritance cannot be one's own act." Such a move is not obviously incompatible

reinserting natural parents as part of the theological explanation of humanity's *whence* would revive an (ostensibly) Jewish way of thinking, it would also threaten to collapse into a Roman Catholic reverence for Mary. The theological answer to humanity's whence that Barth supplies comports perfectly with his prioritization of the *conceptus de Spiritu sancto* over *natus ex Maria Virgine* in his account of the Virgin Birth, which locates Christ's human origins immediately in the life of God and keeps Mary's role firmly in a secondary position. Barth develops the answer to humanity's origins almost exclusively along two lines: the individual and the church, with nothing in between.

The Weight and Dignity of Biological Parenthood

The fact that genealogical bonds no longer have theological significance in Barth's framework does not entail we can dispense with them. Barth's treatment of parenthood in *Dogmatics* III/4 argues that procreative bonds have a weight and dignity that require respect and honour.[93] His defense of the value of "biological bonds" and his ethics of the "boundary case" of deliberate orphanhood together offer a model for how the command of God might intensify the value of procreating and the bonds it gives rise to. Barth's wariness about Roman Catholic Mariology keeps him from making such an argument outright. Yet his discussion of parenthood and procreative agency in his ethics of "Parents and Children" offers a path toward reconstructing Mary's role in the economy of salvation in terms that Barth might accept and provides additional resources for identifying reasons to procreate.

Barth's discussion of the importance of procreative bonds is located in a theological context that concentrates our attention on the relationship between parents and children, rather than the more expansive categories of family, genealogies, or peoples. Family became a "fundamental concept for Christian

---

with Barth's account of the Virgin Birth, as the doctrine of *enhypostatis/anhypostsis* might call into question whether Jesus inherited a human nature from Mary at all. Yet it raises a question about what, precisely, Jesus did inherit from Mary—or, if he did not inherit anything, why we should not adopt the Valentinian heresies that Barth repudiates in I/2. While the dismissal of inherited sin might be animated by Barth's actualism, as Webster suggests, and so indicate a shift in emphasis from I/2, it is also plausible that Barth is worried about restoring natural parents to a position of primacy in an account of generations. See Webster, *Barth's Moral Theology*, 72 ff, and *CD* IV/1, 499–501.

93. Gary Deddo describes this as "perhaps the finest theological discussion of parenting available in the English language." (Deddo, *Theology*, xv). Matthew Rose demurs: "One comes to these sections of the Dogmatics with great anticipation; one often leaves with disappointment. Despite the unplumbable theological depths of this relationship, Barth's commentary must be counted among the most unsatisfying of his excurses." (Rose, *Ethics*, 161).

ethics" only through the "Christianized heathen."⁹⁴ The "determinations" of human nature are limited to male and female, parents and children—which means the command of God uniquely bears upon them.⁹⁵ One's national and ethnic identity is only "a presupposition of the divine command," rather than a "constant determination."⁹⁶ These presuppositions must be taken seriously, as they help us specify the content of the command. We must "seriously accept [the presupposition] as a direction to the place which we must occupy," lest we "fail to hear the command of God."⁹⁷ Yet parents and children are marked by an asymmetry, exclusiveness, and permanence that national identity lacks. Unlike parental bonds, relationships to neighbors are "fluid"—that is, non-exclusive—and impermanent.⁹⁸

In this concentrated field of vision, Barth argues the authority and honour of parents are founded upon their correspondence to the being and action of God. For the child, parents are "God's primary and natural representatives," such that children are "directed to assume a very definite attitude of subordination in relation to their parents." Parents have a "Godward aspect" for the child that is grounded not in any physical or moral relationship, but is a light that "falls and rests upon them from outside, from above—the light of the free grace of the Creator turned towards them as parents."⁹⁹ The correspondence of parents to God grounds the "meaning and dignity" of parenthood and entitles them to respect and honour.¹⁰⁰ This correspondence includes parents' precedence and seniority in time over their children, which reminds the child of the "eternity and prior time of God from

---

94. *CD* III/4, 242. Barth reiterates this critique in IV/2, arguing that the "coming of the kingdom of God means an end of the absolute of family no less than that of possession or fame." Barth does not question the relationships of husband and wife, parents and children, and so on, as such. Rather, what is "questioned is [humanity's] self-sufficiency in the warmth of these relationships, the revolving of their problems and the sphere of their joys and sorrows." Cf. IV/2, 550-1.

95. Ibid., 304-5. The "necessary determination of human nature by creation has its limit in the relationship between man and woman and parents and children."

96. Ibid.

97. Ibid., 295, 305.

98. Ibid., 299-305. Barth reaches here for the language of 'creation orders' to mark the difference. Peoples are founded on God's "dispositions and ordinances," but they are not "permanent orders (ordines) of creation like the being of man and woman or parents and children" (301). Barth's use of 'creation orders' is sharply contested. For a substantive overview of the various positions and critical examination, see Paul Nimmo, "The Orders of Creation in the Theological Ethics of Karl Barth," *Scottish Journal of Theology* 60, no. 1 (2007): 24-35.

99. Ibid., 243, 245.

100. "And the fact that the [human fatherhood] may symbolise the fatherhood of God in a human and creaturely form is what lends it its meaning and value [*Sinn und Würde*] and entitles it to respect." *CD* III/4, 245; *KD*, III/4, 275.

which they come."¹⁰¹ Yet this precedence is not an explanation of the child's origins: whatever causal role parents play, no "human father is the creator of his child, the controller of his destiny, or its saviour from sin, guilt and death."¹⁰² Instead, God is "real whence of [the child's] life."¹⁰³

While Barth's construal of parents as God's representatives thus seems to inflate their role, it also sharply qualifies it. Parents' status as God's representatives remains extrinsic to them, which means they are prohibited from asserting their status to their children. Their correspondence to God is constituted by their witness to God's life: the "decisive action" children need is God's action, which their parents can only bear witness to.¹⁰⁴ The Old Testament's prioritization of parents as mediators of the covenantal blessing meant the fatherhood of God had only an "indirect significance" to the Israelite and entailed there could never be a gap between honouring God and parents. However, the immediacy of our origin in God through Christ makes God's fatherhood "an independent fact alongside the existence of their earthly parents" and allows (apparent) conflicts to arise between our responsibilities as parents or children and our obedience to God.¹⁰⁵ As parents are now only the indirect representatives of God, we must consider the child's "own immediate relationship to God" to understand means to honour God through honouring parents.¹⁰⁶

Barth's construal of parenthood as imitating God's action doubly relativizes the value of biological kinship. The grounds and source of the parental relationship lie outside the biological presuppositions that accompany it, in God.¹⁰⁷ As with Barth's broader anthropology, procreative bonds are not an independent basis or grounds for moral norms. Moreover, parental responsibility is not concerned with the physical relationship *per se* but "with a certain [privilege and mission] with regard to the children which this physical relationship implies for the parents."¹⁰⁸ Such an oversight belongs to the "historical order," wherein parents really are elders

---

101. Ibid., 246.

102. Ibid., 245. Barth's emphasis on fathers throughout this chapter is perhaps not surprising, given the account of patrilineage he adopts in his treatment of the Virgin Birth. While Barth's conception of inheritance obscures the female's agency in procreating, I will return to his description of that agency in the next chapter.

103. Ibid., 246.

104. Ibid., 247.

105. Ibid., 248.

106. Ibid., 278.

107. The superiority of parents is "the brightness of a light which falls and rests upon them from outside, from above"—the light of grace. *CD* III/4, 245.

108. Ibid., 243. We shall return to the basis for this 'honour' in the next chapter. The translators here render "*Vorzug und Auftrag*" as "responsibility and oversight," but only a few pages later render them "superiority" and "mission." See *CD* III/4, 241–3, *KD* III/4, 272 and 274. I have opted for terms that I take are closer to Barth's own.

7. Mary and the Eschatological Confirmation

and children are "apprentices."[109] The biological dimensions of the parent–child relationship are only the occasion in which the historical relationship emerges.

But the same logic that relativizes biological bonds also establishes and confirms them. Biological fatherhood, Barth writes, has "a weight and honour which physical sons must respect in the fact that it has as such a spiritual mission in execution of which it finds fulfillment."[110] This "weight" is not an intrinsic property of procreative parenthood, but is grounded in the revelation of God's fatherhood through Jesus Christ. The New Testament presents God's "characteristic action as Father" as a "single whole," while the work of human birth and rearing are "two different things."[111] While regeneration through the Spirit gives us immediate access to the inner benefits of the Triune life that Christ enjoys, the creature lay benefits that come from human parenthood are conditioned by time and development. Our new birth as children of God is the "original process in the relation between God and man," which shows that the generation of a child and the parents' task of instructing that child belong together.[112] The mission of parenthood is "given and put into effect" when God creates a child and is thus "to be respected by the children."[113] Baptism does not weaken the biological bond, but strengthens it by disclosing its origins in God rather than in biology *per se*.

Barth's confirmation of natural parenthood in light of the eschatological disclosure of Christ extends into his discussion of how the divine command relates to parenthood. For Barth, the "direct confrontation" between God's fatherhood and natural parents in the New Testament means an intensification of the honour

---

109. Ibid. Barth's removal of the basis of parenthood from the properties intrinsic to it is partly explanatory of his later exhortation that children cannot be released from the command to obey failed parents. Barth even goes so far as to call into question the empirical basis of such a judgment, suggesting that children can have nothing more than the "strong impression" that their failures mean they are not parents—but not be certain they do so. See 256-7.

110. Ibid., 244.

111. Ibid., 247. This move anticipates Barth's treating justification and sanctification as a unified work of God which "consists of different 'moments' with a different bearing," or as "two different aspects of the one event of salvation." *CD* IV/2, 501, 503.

112. Ibid., 247.

113. Ibid. Translation mine. The original reads that "in the mission of procreation this task [of the parents' mission] is implied and established, and is thus to be respected by the children." However, I take it that Barth's use of *gegeben* indicates that the mission is given by God *with* the procreative relationship, rather than that it arises independently from such a relationship (as "implied and established") suggests. The German reads: "Aber gerade das dürfte dieser unnachahmliche Originalvorgang zwischen Gott und Mensch in größter Schlüssigkeit deutlich machen, daß Zeugen und Gebären einerseits und der Auftrag zu diesem Tun andererseits zusammengehören, daß mit dem durch Zeugung und Geburt begründeten Verhältnis auch dieser Auftrag gegeben und in Kraft gesetzt und also von Seiten der Kinder zu respektieren ist" (*KD* III/4, 277).

owed to parents, rather than its abrogation. Barth reads Jesus' interaction with Mary and Joseph in Luke 2 as indicating a stronger and more firm union between them, rather than a break. Though Jesus had acted "apart from and against them," He had not "really dishonoured but honoured them."[114] On this basis, Barth frames God's command not as the "weakening or suspension" of the responsibility to honour parents, but as indicating the individual "should obey his parents all the more seriously."[115]

This intensification of parental bonds in light of the eschatological disclosure of Christ structures Barth's discussion of the *Grenzfall,* or boundary case, in his treatment of parents and children.[116] While sin might disrupt the relationship

---

114. *CD* III/4, 250.
115. Ibid., 250–1.
116. The *Grenzfall* has attracted significant commentary from Barth's English-speaking interpreters, but almost all of it has focused on Barth's use of it in the ethics of war (which is understandable, as that is Barth's most substantive employment of the concept). I am not interested in offering a full-scale defense of Barth's employment of the category. While I have opted to translate it as 'boundary case', many of Barth's uses arise when considering human life and goods at its limits—which, as I noted above, means an immediate encounter with God. Keeping this in mind is important for seeing how the boundary case clarifies and confirms creaturely goods, even while paradoxically seeming to undermine them. For instance, Barth's introduction of the *Grenzfall* in his treatment of "The Protection of Life" in §55.2 begins by underscoring the limited and relative value of life, which Barth had developed at the end of III/2 and recapitulated in his treatment of "Respect for Life" in §55.1. Again, in §55.1 Barth had argued that the affirmation of our life through the use of our animal instincts was permissible within their distinctively human limits "and until a clear command to the contrary is heard from the One who really knows and rules it" (III/4, 346). The protection of life is already the negative form of the more fundamental, more basic affirmation of life—which means the logic of the boundary or limit case in that context will necessarily be distinct from the logic of the boundary case in the affirmative context. Barth does not explicitly invoke an asymmetry between positive and negative norms, but it seems to be assumed. As the command to respect life is prior and more fundamental to the command to protect life, the "boundary case" and our conditions for discernment of it would be similarly asymmetrical for each situation. Barth invokes the "boundary case" in §54.3's treatment of parents and children to mark the eschatological disruption of the ties between parents and children, but also to evaluate single parents (III/4, 277). In this latter case, the irregular form of parenting does not free parents from embracing their responsibilities or honour. The "boundary case" in this context is not so much a paradoxical form of the command, but the preservation of the command—and with it, the underlying goods of the parent–child relationship—in a situation where others might think it no longer applies. In the case of killing, Gerald McKenny's reading seems precisely right: "There is ... a requirement to protect life that is always in force in God's commands regarding life and must be met in every instance in which God addresses a command regarding life. The *Grenzfall* is a strange or paradoxical instance of this requirement

between children and parents, the New Testament also indicates that the Law which governs such relationships is only provisional. The fulfillment of the Law by Jesus Christ means that "the kingdom of God has come from heaven

to protect life which, according to Barth, remains in force in the command to take life." As McKenny notes, Barth uses "paradox" twice to describe such borderline situations in the context of "respect for life," even if he does not in his treatment of "defense of life." See McKenny, *Karl Barth's Moral Thought*, 100. McKenny objects that Barth's construal of protection of life fails, as Barth does not adequately explain how one can rightly protect life by killing someone else's life. McKenny contends that Barth obfuscates the fact that "one is protecting one life by taking another life that is not protected," and suggests that Barth's qualification of the protection of human life by its twofold creaturely and eschatological limitation is incompatible with his contention that the "protection of life is unconditionally required." The "twofold limitation serves to weaken the requirement to protect life so that, far from being valid unconditionally, it may be revoked when God commands that one life be taken to protect another life." See McKenny, *Karl Barth's Moral Thought*, 103. While I am not especially sympathetic to Barth's account here, I take it that his view is not as misleading as McKenny suggests. At the outset of his discussion, Barth contends that the command is only unconditional or absolute in the limits God places upon it, and that the "protection of life required of us is not unlimited nor absolute." (III/4, 398). The "required protection of life," Barth goes on, "must take into account its limitation in relation to that which is to be protected." As such, its protection might have to consist in "its surrender or sacrifice." McKenny contends that the aborted child does not carry out a "service to God" as the suicide might, which means Barth's attempt at qualifying the claims other lives make on us for their protection fails. Yet this is precisely how Barth frames the choice in a licit abortion: "a choice must be made for the protection of life, one life being balanced against another, i.e., the life of the unborn child against the life or health of the mother, *the sacrifice of one or the other being unavoidable*" (III/4, 421, emphasis mine). Behind this lies Barth's contention that, in fact, God has deemed that the child has reached the limits of their life: "If [God] can will that this germinating life should die in some other way, might He not occasionally do so in a way as to involve the active participation of these other men?" (III/4, 420). The one who kills therefore does so in service to God—and the one who is killed is sacrificed to protect the life of another. It is not clear, though, that Barth ever lays out the requirement that the protection of life through killing is only merited where the one killed conceives of their death as an act of service or sacrifice, as McKenny seems to presume. That is, Barth's conception of the "sacrifice" that might be required seems to include the passive voice: the child in a justified abortion *is sacrificed*. Barth says enough elsewhere about the ways our lives can unwittingly testify to God's grace (even within their biological dimensions) to perhaps build a case that he has something like that in mind here—though it might require rejecting a strongly actualist reading of Barth that treats the only ethically significant event as that which a mature agent deliberates about and chooses. At the least, it might be "simply not credible" that one "protects life in a strange way by taking it," as McKenny suggest. But Barth does not obfuscate about what sometimes might be required. See McKenny, *Karl Barth's Moral Thought*, 101.

to earth, that it has taken solid shape among us, and that it has foreshadowed the end of all human history and therefore of the parent–child relationship."[117] Because of this, some people might be called to bear witness to this grace that "hastens to its future revelation and consummation" by effectively embracing a voluntary orphanhood. Obedience to Jesus Christ, Barth writes, can mean "that certain men find themselves in some sense claimed, engaged and committed by His special calling in a very different sphere, i.e., in an immediate relationship to Himself in which they must accept their commitment without regard to the fact that they are also children of their parents."[118] In the same way that celibacy is now possible because of the eschatological life, so there might be "an orphaned state required for the sake of the kingdom of heaven." Such a person "must symbolize with his being and action ... the new creation in relation to which the old has already passed away."[119] This sign of the prophetic renunciation of earthly parents on the basis of the command will doubtlessly clash with "the biological and social conventions of the framework in which this commandment is pronounced."[120] In obeying the divine command this way, an individual both embodies obedience to their parents and issues a "general and generally authoritative clarification" of the parent–child relationship's basis and grounds by revealing its creational and eschatological limits. In this way, the boundary case does not function as an exception to a general norm. Jesus' exhortation to hate one's parents in Luke 14:26 indicates that the peace between parents and children is provisional—but this relativization of the parent–child relationship is not Barth's final word. Paradoxically, the eschatological disclosure of the boundary case constitutes an affirmation of the parent–child relationship. Barth observes that the final word of the Old Testament and the first word of the New are that God will turn the hearts of fathers and children to each other (Malachi 4:6 and Luke 1:17)—a striking departure from his reading of Luke 1:17 earlier in his career and an affirmation that, however much Jesus troubles the relationship between parents and children, His final word will be peace and reconciliation.[121] As such, the possibility of the boundary case that Jesus introduces is "not a question of the destruction but of the radical renewal of the child–parent relationship, not of the separation of these kinsfolk but of their genuine reconciliation, not merely in the peace of this transient world, but in the prospect of the perfection of the kingdom."[122] While the

---

117. *CD* III/4, 260.
118. Ibid.
119. Ibid., 261.
120. Ibid., 262.
121. In *The Great Promise,* Barth suggests this phrase is "not easily comprehended." He reads it as meaning that those who enter the kingdom of God must become like children—but says quite literally nothing about parenthood and childhood. See Barth, *The Great Promise*, trans. Hans Freund (New York: Philosophical Library, 1963), 14.
122. *CD* III/4, 262.

eschaton will bring the "end of the parent–child relationship," it also re-establishes and intensifies its significance for the moral life here and now.[123]

Barth's account of parents and children provides a model for how the eschatological relativization of a form of life can paradoxically reinscribe and reinforce the same relationship. In the same manner that Barth's account of life beneath the horizon of the eschaton heightens its urgency and significance, so his treatment of parents and children does the same. Barth does not invoke this structure with respect to procreation: his emphasis on the dissolution of any obligation to procreate has no counterbalance in the eschatological life, which means any theologically animated exhortation to procreate can only appeal to God's patience. Such an aversion is, I suspect, at least partially motivated by his concern to avoid granting Mary too significant a position in the economy of salvation. Yet Barth's description of procreative agency in III/4 also opens up the door to reconstructing Mary's role in the economy of salvation, and with it, the theological significance of procreation—or so I will argue in the next chapter.

Conclusion: First Steps toward a Protestant, Barthian Mariology

Barth's contention in *Church Dogmatics* III/4 that the standpoint of the child is of primary theological significance comports with his prioritization of Christology over Mariology. For Barth, the conception of Jesus Christ from the Holy Spirit is the primary fact on which Mary's virginity is based. It is not because Mary is a virgin that she is apt to be the mother of God. Rather, it is because God announces the conception of the Messiah to her that she is a virgin. Such an argument follows Barth's broader method that what comes second in the divine economy is primary in its importance, as the covenant is the inner basis of creation. Mary's "becoming" in her human nature is a response to the Word's "becoming" flesh. The downside of such a framework is that it risks framing both Mary's virginity and agency in negative or passive terms: the male is excluded as a sign of Christ's *enhypostatic* nature, yet Mary is only present as non-desiring, non-willing, non-achieving human. In bracketing Mary from having any kind of co-operation in the Incarnation, Barth risks reducing her to a merely technical "host" for Christ.

However, Barth's argument that the eschatological disclosure both troubles and reaffirms natural parenthood also provides the basis to reappraise his treatment of Mary and so move toward an alternate account of the theological significance of procreation and procreative agency. In Barth's ethics, the "boundary cases" can arise when the command of God contradicts ordinary, bourgeois conventions and the goods of creation they are founded upon. Yet as Barth makes clear in his discussion of vocational orphanhood, the command's eschatological dimension disrupts those conventions in a way that intensifies and deepens the value of creaturely life: there is no "weakening or suspension" of the command to honour

123. Ibid.

parents, but rather a requirement to honour them in a more serious way. In the same way, Barth's treatment of life in its limits in III/2 underscores that the eschatological conditioning of creaturely life in the resurrection does not undermine life's value but deepens and intensifies it. This provides warrant for arguing that the atypical, "eschatological" form of birth in the Incarnation is a clarification and endorsement of the value of ordinary procreation. Barth defends the Virgin Birth's form, which he regards as counteracting and disrupting the (sinful) pattern of male domination. Yet he does not take the step I am suggesting, even though his account of the boundary cases supplies reason to do so. As a miraculous disclosure of divine action, the Virgin Birth may be alien to the biological and social conventions of procreation—but it is a complementary clarification of procreation's true basis and grounds, and an intensification of its value.[124]

124. We might also consider Barth's discussion of miracles for additional warrant for this reading. In IV/2, Barth frames miracles as something more than an antithesis between the old and the new, or between the natural and the supernatural, or the ordinary and the extraordinary. The antithesis between the kingdom of God and humanity that Jesus' miracles reveal is unique and concrete, situated as it is within the history of the covenant. Barth contends that the light that shines on humanity in these miracles confronts the human in our entirety, but especially in our "natural" or physical existence. The miracles of Jesus mean that the human's "existence as a creature in the natural cosmos is normalised" (IV/2, 222). In healing humanity, God "does not negate but affirms the natural existence of man." (IV/2, 225). In III/3, Barth distances the miracle from an 'exception', with an argument that is similar in form to his treatment of the "boundary cases." Barth contends that God is the law of all occurrence, and that His order is not bound to our concepts of order. It is thus natural that "mention has to be made of events which can be understood only as an activity *supra et contra naturam*" in the advent of Christ. Barth contends the final revelation of Christ will be an event like this, as the creation of the world was. Yet he contends that we "must be quite clear in our minds that what is revealed in these events is not a *miraculous* exception but the *rule* of divine activity, the free good-will of God Himself, i.e., the law at which we are aiming with our concept of law." (CD III/3, 130). Barth goes so far as to make the correlation between miracles and the "boundary case" explicit: "The marvels of natural phenomena, the inscrutabilities of physico-psychic individuality, the border-line cases of moral conduct and action, the freedom which defies all expectation or prevision in the wider or narrower coherences of history—all these are obviously the work of [God's] rule." Yet we are not free to think of God only as the "God of the exception, the incident, the individual case," as "God honours law as well as freedom." In a delightful sentence, Barth writes that to the revelation of God's wisdom "there belongs the wonderful revelation which is particularly dear to His Holy Spirit that two and two make four and not five." (*CD* III/3, 161). This structure remains more or less consistent into IV/2. There, Barth reaffirms that the Spirit's work has form and contour, and that it has "far more affinities to the comfortable truth that two and two make for than to the most conceivable, bitter-sweet irruptions from the sphere of the numinous." (*CD* IV/2, 129). He reasserts the rational character of distinctive and miraculous power of

While Barth emphasizes that Mary's witness directs all the attention away from herself and toward the Lord, he minimizes the fact that her willingness to give birth to Christ is a positive response to Christ's eschatological disclosure to the world—not as an indicator of prevenient grace at work, but proleptically beneath the justification for sin Christ's death brings about. Framing Mary in this light would put her in close proximity to those who undertake celibacy in bearing direct witness to the kingdom. There are hints Barth would be amenable to such a view, provided that it does not allow Mary to become an independent locus of theological reflection. In *Church Dogmatics* I/2, he locates Mary with John the Baptist between the Testaments: she is the "personal climax of the Old Testament" and the "first man of the New Testament."[125] Moreover, Barth suggests in *The Great Promise* that in her response to God in asking "how can these things be," Mary stands "representatively at the head of the whole Advent community and of the whole Church."[126] In IV/2, Barth contends that the fact that the "man Jesus is the whole basis and power and guarantee of our exaltation means there can be no place for any other in this function, not even for the mother of Jesus."[127] Mary's *fiat* might precede Christ's work in time, but it is second to it in priority: "Even the *fiat mihi*," Barth writes, "is preceded by the resolve and promise of God." Her response "confirmed" God's work, and only in that light can be said to be a participation in God's work.[128] The angel's word precedes Mary's response: it is "only in her willingness and readiness to accept what is told her by the angel that she is the handmaid of the Lord and may describe herself as such."[129] As Barth attempts to found a generalized anthropology upon the *sui generis* nature of Christ's

---

the resurrection in the Christian life in an even stronger way, suggesting that we "can think and say with absolutely unshakeable confidence that two and two make four and will never make five" (*CD* IV/2, 314). We gain a "new determination" in the resurrection, but this is an elevation of our earthiness and our vegetative impulses through their freedom from the forces of death, rather than their negation or destruction. (*CD* IV/2, 316-19). Thinking of the Virgin Birth as a miracle which establishes, confirms, and deepens our understanding of the ordinary, bourgeois manner of procreation by situating it immediately beneath the revelation of God thus has warrant in Barth's broader theological framework. While this context will by no means resolve debates about Barth's employment of boundary cases, it does supply reason to affirm Nigel Biggar's reading of the *Grenzfall*: "It baffles moral reason; but it baffles it into learning. It is not, therefore, irreducibly exceptional. It startles systematic ethics with something that it has not comprehended; but it does so in order that the ethical system might yet extend or refine its grasp." See Biggar, *Hastening*, 34.

125. *CD* I/2, 140.

126. Barth, *Promise*, 32.

127. Barth, *CD* IV/2, ix.

128. Ibid., 45.

129. Barth, *CD* IV/3.2, 605. Barth notes here that humanity can "participate only passively" in Christ's action for the world, "in pure faith in Him, love for Him and hope in Him, without making even the slightest or most incidental contribution." Barth had

humanity, so incorporating Mary's virginity as something besides a negation of humanity's sinful incapacity for God would allow it to bear positive—though not independent—weight for theological anthropology, and thus also for ethics.[130]

If Mary does disclose the fitting human response to God's work in Jesus Christ, rather than the human preparation for it, it seems significant she gives birth. Barth views the birth of the Christ as the terminus of Israel's (putative) burden of posterity. But if the eschatological disclosure of Christ is a confirmation and clarification of creaturely life, giving birth could be one form—and perhaps a preeminent form—the Church's reception of God's Word might take. In bringing the burden of posterity to an end, the birth of Christ would also reaffirm and intensify the value of procreation itself. As with the above, there is at least one hint in Barth's thought such a construal is not unknown to him: in *The Great Promise*, Barth writes the story of Elizabeth's blessing of Mary and John's leaping in the womb must be told because wherever "there are such people who have received the promise, such a Mary and such an Elizabeth, where the *Church* is, there is what is called pregnancy in physical life, there is expectancy and the presence of what is expected; there is not only a knowledge of grace, but there is grace itself."[131]

Framing Mary as the first member of the new creation this way has a number of important implications and would require at least one substantive revision to

---

opposed any contention that Mary had a "readiness" for God in I/2 based on her natural aptitude or capacity. Here he suggests that it is "only in her willingness and readiness to accept what is told her by the angel that she is the handmaid of the Lord and may describe herself as such."

130. Barth suggests that Thomas Aquinas' view of Mary makes her the "first to be redeemed by her divine Son." As such, her dignity is "like to that of the humanity of Christ, surpassing all other creatures." (*CD* I/2, 142) Barth's depiction of Mary as the "first man" of the New Testament comes near this, yet if Mary is the "first redeemed," that does not entail she indicates humanity is "capable, by prevenient grace, of preparing himself for genuine sanctifying grace, by uttering this *fiat*." (144). While Mary might signify an active, affirmative reception of divine grace, it does not follow that her response indicates a readiness for grace that is endemic to a fallen creation as such—or, at least, it does not follow on Barth's account. Yet Barth's polemic against Catholic theology in I/2 seems to lead him into conflating Mary's active response in the *fiat mihi* with the whole architecture of natural theology that he rejects. One advantage of making Mary nearer to the witness of celibacy is that it would supply grounds for affirming Mary's perpetual virginity, a position once common in Protestantism, and do so without the rest of the Marian dogmas accompanying it. (143 ff.)

131. Barth emphasizes in this passage taking Elizabeth's greeting of Mary literally. The church has *what is called* pregnancy—not pregnancy in physical life itself, which is reserved to families. Yet through having the primary referent, the church affirms the natural form: Mary's natural pregnancy and Christ's natural birth. *The Great Promise* was given in 1934. Given Barth's later critiques of the Nazi ethnonationalist emphasis on procreation, it is not surprising that this thread disappeared from his thought.

7. Mary and the Eschatological Confirmation

Barth's broader theological framework. First, it more closely connects the theme of blessing in the New Testament with the Old Testament's association of blessing and fertility. As I observed above, Barth's construal of Israel's practice of blessing frames it as an answer to humanity's *whence*; while it is not reducible to procreation, it is also inseparable from it. The New Testament replaces this form of blessing with (non-infant) baptism. This reading allows Barth to heighten the contrasts between the Old and New Testaments' treatment of procreation—yet it also allows him to downplay the significance of Elizabeth's "blessing" of Mary in Luke 1:42 and Mary's claim that "all generations will call me blessed" in the Magnificat. Barth argues that Mary is blessed "in the light of her faith, yet not because of her faith, but because of what was told her by the Lord and what she believed, and in relation to its accomplishment."[132] Similarly, Elizabeth does not bless Mary, but "recognizes and acknowledges her as an object of blessing."[133] While Jesus says in Luke 11:27 that people are blessed because they "hear the word of God, and keep it," Mary's blessing by God manifests itself in her procreative work. In that respect, Mary's role as "blessed" by all generations comes nearer to how Barth construes blessing in his exegesis of the first creation story, which underscores the need for divine blessing in order for humans to reproduce.[134] Making this dimension of Mary's role more explicit would underscore the continuity between the two Testaments and give Barth more resources to articulate why giving birth remains theologically significant than he otherwise has access to.[135]

Such an account comes near to the way Charlotte von Kirschbaum frames both procreation and Mary in *The Question of Woman*. Von Kirschbaum adopts Barth's emphasis on the relativization of procreation and procreative bonds after the birth of Christ, but makes the theme of procreation being a "blessing" much more prominent.[136] While barrenness in Israel is a "sign that God did not behold

---

132. *CD* IV/2, 189.
133. *CD* III/2, 582.
134. See above, pages 107 ff.
135. The nearest Barth comes in his ethics of parents and children to describing children as a "blessing" is in his endorsement of Ernst Michel's suggestion that revealing the "full potentiality [of children] as blessing" requires the "responsible Yes of parents." However, his emphasis is not on the blessing that children are—but on the necessity of responsibility in order to fully receive that blessing. (*CD* III/4, 271).

136. Von Kirschbaum suggests that 1 Timothy 2:15's line that women might be "saved through childbearing" indicates that the "the Christian women at Ephesus, following the birth of *the* child, no longer regarded conceiving and giving birth to children as 'keeping with the times,' and rebelled against the natural destiny of woman. Our text tells them that the only thing that matters is their salvation, and that this can happen even when they are quite simply mothers, 'provided they continue in faith and love and holiness, with modesty.'" As such, she thinks it is a mistake to claim that childbearing is "*the* work demanded of them." Such an argument is keeping with Barth's contention that the birth of Christ relativizes procreation. See von Kirschbaum, *The Question of Woman*, 116.

this woman favorably," it is also "not the biological reality that produced fruit—it was a miracle of the Lord."[137] Children in Israel are "not only the fulfillment of maternal longing, but the sign of divine blessing," as God "intervenes in the begetting and bearing." This is compatible for her with a "form of motherhood that transcends biological motherhood," namely, "prophetic women who become spiritual mothers."[138] Even so, in the New Testament the figure of the mother "retreats into the background, and her task in salvation has ended." As such, the question of whether Christians may or should have children "is a justified one." Von Kirschbaum gives the same answer to it that Barth does, though with a stronger accent on blessing, joy, and hope: "For as long as it may please God to preserve this world and its people, children may be begotten and born as a sign of his patience, and mothers may rejoice in them as an assurance that God blesses them in their action if they are imbued with living hope." Crucially, biological motherhood is justified in the New Testament not directly or immediately, but only with reference to Mary. "That it pleased God," she writes, "to become man in a woman's womb, that Mary can rightly be called "Mother of God," is the glory of the promise resting over every human mother, and at the same time is an unambiguous warning never to glorify biological processes as such."[139]

In addition, treating Mary as the first member of the new creation might supply grounds for giving procreation an eschatological correspondence in the way that Barth contends marriage has. On such a view, Christ's advent would give marriage and procreation both the same relativization and confirming consecration—uniting them in their theological significance, even if still keeping them distinct. If marriage and procreation are on the same plane, then the marriage of Mary and Joseph would be the presupposition of Christ's birth—rather than Mary's virginity *per se*.[140] Barth rejects this in his discussion of the Virgin Birth, as it might make it seem possible that Christ could come into the world through means of a sanctified act of sexual intercourse. At the same time, Barth also thought Joseph had not received his due with respect to ecclesiology and welcomed Vatican II's decision to include him in the canon of the mass.[141] By treating Mary and Joseph's marriage

---

137. Ibid., 125. Compare above, note 127.

138. Ibid., 128.

139. Ibid., 129-30. See the Suzanne Selinger's discussion as well in *Charlotte von Kirschbaum and Karl Barth*, 108-15.

140. Barth contends that the "virginity of Mary, and not the wedlock of Joseph and Mary, is the sign of revelation and of the knowledge of the mystery of Christmas." This claim arises from his hard distinction between the *eros* which is at work in sex (and presumably, therefore, in marriage) and the divine *agape* that the Virgin Birth indicates. This abstracts the significance of Mary's virginity from its biblical context, in which her betrothal to Joseph looms large.

141. For Barth, Joseph was more suited as an image of the church than Mary, because his role was clearly and unambiguously that of servant. As Dustin Resch observes, Joseph

as the presupposition of Christ's birth, there would be grounds for viewing Mary and Joseph as representing distinct yet equally important facets of ecclesiology. As Barth argues the sphere of male and female's relationships is not independent of marriage, so the procreation of children is not independent of marriage.

To be clear, ascribing Mary's act of giving birth an eschatological correlate would require modifying Barth's contention that eternity means the end of time and existence for humanity. In his discussion of humanity's *whence*, Barth underscores that the church's fruitfulness is limited by time, as it is self-consciously caught between God's patience toward the creature and the dissolution of time in the consummation of creation. The resurrection that founds the church announces that "time is at an end." Barth goes on: "The sole purpose for the extension of time after this decisive event is to allow space before the kingdom comes to repent and believe the Gospel (Mk. 1:15) on the basis of this event and its indication."[142] Barth even describes the resurrection as inaugurating a "present without a future," as creation was an "event without a past.[143] When Christ returns the "secret of Calvary will be revealed," but "nothing further will follow from this happening …"[144] Barth maintains this position throughout the Dogmatics. In IV/3, he writes that humanity's exaltation means "the end of time generally" and the "conclusion of the temporal existence of those still living."[145] The Christian community lives in the unique knowledge of the last time, which is given through the presence of the Spirit.[146] The dissolution of time in the eschaton does not empty time of

---

stands in no danger of being construed as having an "innate capacity that qualified [him] for mutual cooperation with God." See Resch, *Interpretation*, 174 ff. As Barth writes, Joseph's "function as foster-father of Christ makes him a much more appropriate patron of the church than the *theotokos*, who is usually mentioned in this connection." Karl Barth, *Letters: 1961–1968*, trans. Geoffrey Bromily (Edinburgh: T&T Clark, 1981), 84.

142. *CD* III/2, 622.

143. Ibid., 624. The "Easter story," Barth writes in I/2, speaks of "a present without any future, of an eternal presence of God in time" (*CD* I/2, 114).

144. Ibid.

145. Barth, *CD* IV/3, 924. While Barth here adds the qualifier "temporal," only a few paragraphs later he describes the triumph of hope as happening in the face of "the ineluctable end of human and therefore Christian existence" (ibid., 925). Cf. *KD* IV/3, 1062–3.

146. Barth regards the resurrection, the outpouring of the Spirit, and the final return of Jesus Christ as forms of the same event. In IV/1, Barth notes that the time of the resurrection ended with Christ's ascension—but that this began the "time of another form of His *arousia*, His living present—no less complete and sufficient in itself, but quite different." In this time, God is "revealed and active in the community by His Spirit, the power of His accomplished resurrection" (IV/1, 318). The church thus looks backwards to its origin in the resurrection of Jesus Christ, but also forward to the final form of the *arousia*. In this way, the church is strong "because it knows what time it is," Barth writes, namely, the time between the resurrection and the consummation (IV/1, 726–7). This time is demarcated by

its meaning: the present is not an empty placeholder between the resurrection of Jesus and His return. If anything, the eternalization of time maximally heightens its significance. As Barth writes in III/1, "Even in eternal life [the human] will be still in his time. For he will then be the one who, when there is no time but only God's eternity, and he is finally hidden in God, will have been in his time."[147] Though time will be dissolved in the eschaton, God's patience gives time after the Resurrection its own distinctive meaning. Barth notes that God has "spoken His final Word, but He has not yet finished speaking it," which means that "there is still space for humanity, and in that space it can still exist—surplus space, and a surplus existence, but still a possibility of being, and actual being."[148] The fact that

life in the Spirit, which makes the church's life fruitful (cf. 726, 733). Yet Barth also seems inconsistent in his treatment of the form of the final coming. In IV/1, Barth writes that the community knows its goal and end "only in the form of its beginning. It knows the returning Lord only in the form in which He came then according to the record." (IV/1, 731) Barth writes in IV/3.1 that the resurrection of Jesus does not mean the prolongation of His temporal existence, but the "appearance of this terminated existence in its participation in the sovereign life of God, in its endowment with eternity, in the transcendence, incorruptibility and immortality given and appropriated to it in virtue of this participation for all its this-worldliness." At the same time, Barth affirms that the resurrection was Christ's "new appearance in the psycho-physical totality of His temporal existence familiar from His first coming," one in which he participated "in [humanity's] concrete temporal existence and in the concrete temporal existence of all creation" (IV/3.1, 312). The fact that Christ in his resurrection participates in humanity's time (even if transfiguring it) seems to be an argument for extending time in the eschaton, not dissolving it—and with time, also our existence. Crucially, Barth distinguishes between "temporal existence" (*zeitlichen Existenz*) from the "being" (*Dasein*) that is preserved with God in the eschaton. It is the former that procreation extends in III/3 63–5 (*KD* III/3, 75–6).

147. Barth, *CD* III/1, 521. Cf. Barth, *CD* IV/3.2, 928. As Nathan Hitchcock writes, "If *this* life, this bodily life, is the life slated for eternalization, then one must invest in the here and now, knowing it to be eternally significant." See *Karl Barth and the Resurrection of the Flesh* (Eugene: Wipf and Stock, 2013), 105. Here we have the full rejoinder to McKenny's worry about the meaning and moral significance of our being and action as creatures, which I flagged up in note 2 at the outset of Chapter 5. As McKenny puts it in *The Analogy of Grace*, the fact that Jesus Christ accomplishes the good in our place means "it is unclear what meaning and status our moral action can have for Barth even if we are not in doubt regarding the reality of human action in his theology." See McKenny, *The Analogy of Grace*, 202. I take it that Barth's account that God accomplishes the good in our place does not entail that God answers that accomplishment through our own action in time, except insofar as he accompanies, guides and directs us to its accomplishment through the Holy Spirit. Our action in this life not only has moral significance for Barth: it has maximal moral significance, as it will be eternally elevated and reified with God.

148. Barth, *CD* IV/1, 737.

7. Mary and the Eschatological Confirmation

time continues after Christ's resurrection means that our creaturely existence has a teleology, so that "in itself it cannot be without meaning, plan or purpose."[149] In fact, Barth argues that the presence of Jesus Christ in the promise of the Spirit gives the time between Christ's resurrection and the eschaton its "own specific glory." God demonstrates His power in this time through developing grace under the "conditions and in the limitations and problems of our present, and in the vulnerability of our existence."[150] We should be glad for the extended opportunity God has given us to live:

> Unreservedly joyful praise and sincere thanksgiving must be given Him for the fact that He willed and arranged that we should have time and place and opportunity not merely for the expression of our creaturely freedom but for life in hope in Him as the hope of all men, for life under the promise of God and in the power of this promise.[151]

Procreation thus might be able to contribute to the distinct or unique glory of the temporal life that is elevated with God's eternal life—yet it also contradicts the dissolution of time in the eschaton.[152] If procreation is to have an eschatological

---

149. Barth, *CD* IV/3.1, 336. While creaturely freedom is "in analogy to the teleology of the revelation of accomplished reconciliation," it "thus follows a direction which is not condemned but confirmed from this standpoint." Barth's discussion of the significance of the incomplete declaration of God's reconciliation for both non-Christians and for Christians on the subsequent pages notes that the Christian knowledge of the end of time requires solidarity with non-Christians. Cf. 340–1. See also IV/3.2, 793–5.

150. Ibid., 361.

151. Ibid., 362.

152. Criticisms that Barth's account of time and eternity hollow out his doctrine of creation have a long and distinguished history. G. C. Berkouwer contends that Barth's "eternalizing" arises from Barth's conception of the limitation of human life, an anthropology that "dominated Barth's thinking *from the beginning*" (emphasis his). See *The Triumph of Grace in the Theology of Karl Barth*, 340. Robert Song similarly ties it to Barth's opposition to the immortality of the soul in his theological anthropology, but contends that his motivation there is soteriological, as "abandoning a doctrine of natural immortality removes an opening to a doctrine of natural human divinity." See "Technological Immortalization and Original Mortality: Karl Barth on the Celebration of Finitude," in *Eternal God, Eternal Life*, ed. Philip Ziegler (London: Bloomsbury T&T Clark, 2016), 202. We should not discount the moral and pedagogical arguments that Barth gives for the view in III/2's discussion of 'Allotted Time', though. His positive argument for limits is that they are good for us, as they prevent our lives from being "centrifugal," and preserve our reality as a concrete subject with whom God "can enjoy communication and intercourse" (*CD* III/2, 565). While this seems true, Barth's arguments for a defined span as necessary for our reality as subjects tacitly elevate our being limited by time over and above our being limited by God, and place our beginning and end as on a par. Were it the case that God gives us a

consecration, and not only contribute to the unique glory of the Spirit's presence now, then we must reject Barth's account of the eternalizing of human life and the corresponding cessation of time and temporal existence.

If Mary's response to the Annunciation does ground an "eschatological consecration" of procreation, then procreation might have more theological

beginning, but not an end, our lives would still not be "centrifugal"—and, *post mortem*, our being would still be limited by the conditionality of our existence that our *whence* indicates and, more fundamentally, by the immediacy of God's presence with us. Barth contends that we are "right to ask for duration and perfection in our life; and to exist in this respect" (*CD* III/2, 566). Asking for duration is our determination as humans, a creaturely determination that comes near to how Barth speaks of *eros*. We are wrong to remain dissatisfied with the "set span God has given us and want unrestricted space." The "genuine unrest" with our limited life looks "beyond itself to realisation and therefore to the peace of a permanent life under God and with other men" (*CD* III/2, 562). Yet Barth contends that we are wrong if we think that this desire can be satisfied anywhere but in God (*CD* III/2, 566). Barth's final contention that it is "good and salutary for us to have a limited life in restricted time because here the grace of God is near and clear to us" might apply to our lives prior to their being taken up into eternal life with God—either through death, or through God's direct act (*CD* III/2, 571). However, it does not entail the eternalizing account and the cessation of time and humanity's existence that Barth seems to defend necessitates a lifespan: after all, God's grace could be made perfectly clear to us in our eschatological union with Him ("face to face") *without* us needing the outer definition or limit of the end of our time in the way that Barth presupposes. I do not quite share Nathan Hitchcock's worries that Barth's account of the eschaton yields "bodies weirdly lighter *and* denser than flesh." I worry that Barth's stress on the dissolution of time and existence means the dissolution of bodies *outright*, along with the capability for distinctively human agency that accompanies them. Hitchcock cites Barth's lines from III/2 as indicating his commitment to the "flesh": "[One] does not hope for redemption from the this-sidedness, finitude and mortality of His existence. He hopes positively for the revelation of its redemption in Jesus Christ, namely, the redemption of his this-sided, finite and mortal existence. This psycho-physical being in its time is he himself" (*CD* III/2, 633). From this, Hitchcock concludes that for Barth the "resurrection cannot be anything less than psychosomatic, for what is raised is the life of the whole person, the soul of a body, the body-soul." While Barth affirms this of Christ's resurrection, he is hazy about the timeline of our resurrection in its relationship to Christ's *parousia* and the end of time. What Barth affirms on III/2, 633 is that the *content* (*Inhalt*) of our lives that is raised is not a liberation from our bodies, but that which we have only within and through our bodies (*KD* III/2, 755). On Hitchcock's reading, Barth's construal of the limits of our time is motivated by his actualist ontology. However, the notion that one's "being can be identified directly, even entirely, with the extent of one's actions and enacted relations" does not clearly entail that one's time must be limited (Hitchcock, *Resurrection*, 97). Hitchcock sees Barth's account of participation in God as being similarly problematic (Hitchcock 142–5). Though Hitchcock acknowledges the careful constraints that Barth puts on the concept (143), he also suggests that, for Barth, the creature "*as such is meant to exceed itself* through

significance than indicating God's patience (which is how Barth predominately frames it). As I suggested above, Barth contends that it is "under God's longsuffering and patience, and is due to His mercy, that in these last days [procreation] may

divine participation," which wipes out our creaturely nature (143). This is a surprising reading, given Barth's rejection of infant baptism on grounds that it fails to appropriately honour creaturely agency in the fragment of IV/4. Hitchcock worries (with Douglas Farrow and others) that Barth's Christology ends up being Eutychian. While those tendencies in Barth's thought might be there, the reading of Barth's theological anthropology and doctrine of creation offered above indicates that Barth was acutely aware of them and their docetic implications. He sought at every turn to counteract such implications—except in his eschatology and the final dissolution of time he affirms. Similarly, while Barth's concept of election might have the "panentheistic thrust" that Hitchcock suggests it has, Hitchcock's own aversion to speaking of humans as "in" Christ must face up to the Pauline warrant for the phrase (167). Hitchcock's reading of Barth's doctrine of creation is, I think, indicative of his overreading of Barth: he treats Barth's view as Platonic, in which the physical world becomes "an appendage, an accessory, a derivation which in the end may or may not be needed by the higher stratum governing it in the first place" (174). While I do not think Barth's conception of the dissolution of time is isolated from the broader currents of his theology, I also think it is severable from Barth's doctrine of creation in a way that would leave the latter mostly intact. A similar rejoinder could be made against James Cassidy's argument that Barth's account of time resolves into "Christopanism." Cassidy more or less updates Richard Roberts' contention that time replaces substance in Barth's theology by adopting the claim that Barth's actualism entails that "All essentialism is gone in Barth's thought" (5). Cassidy contends that the covenant not only absorbs creation, but that "Jesus Christ is himself creation" (59). If this is what actualism requires for reading Barth, then it is hard to make sense of his great many claims across both Volumes III and IV of the *Church Dogmatics* that creation has its own existence, even if not an independent one. If nothing else, Barth's discussion of the actualization of creation at the end of III/1 (§42.2) is devoted to the claim that creation has a reality distinct from God. As Barth says in IV/3.1, the cosmos "is real in its own way, which is distinct from that of God but genuine within its limits." Existence (*Dasein*) does make itself known and so "is secure and secures itself." "In this sense," Barth goes on, existence "has and is its own basis. This basis is certainly given it by God at its creation. It does not derive from itself. Yet it is its own basis which could then be taken away only if God were to revoke His will and choice that it should be created and have this existence. So long as time endures, He has obviously not done this, and therefore we cannot doubt the power of its basis, or its reality" (*CD* IV/3.1, 143; *KD* IV/3.1, 164). The constancy of God might secure creation—but the gift is really given, and is really distinct from God. By suggesting that God's eternal preservation of the limited creature means "the creature has an eternal existence, yet it is limited by its own time," Cassidy conflates what Barth holds apart (86). While I am dissatisfied with Barth's account of the end of the existence of the creature, Barth thinks it is consistent with affirming the reality of creation as such—over and against Cassidy, Hitchcock, and others who collapse together what Barth holds distinct. See Cassidy, *God's Time for Us*.

still take place."¹⁵³ While God's patience is not simply a negation or privation for Barth, ascribing procreation eschatological significance would indicate a surplus and abundance of life and existence even after creation's consummation. Such an eschatological consecration need not entail that there is intercourse and generation in the eschaton, any more than marriage's eschatological consecration contradicts Christ's claim that there is neither marrying nor being given in marriage in heaven (Matthew 22:30). Rather, whatever form of union that celibacy inaugurates will be commensurate with a form of fruitfulness that transposes procreation into a new key. Procreation now indicates that the church will have more time then, in the fullness of her union with God. Insofar as Mary's response is a proleptic "yes" in answer to God's eschatological disclosure, her procreative activity is not only an ending, but a new beginning: responding to God's disclosure in Christ can take the form of a procreative willingness that is the occasion for the special, unique divine action of generating human life and giving humanity more time.¹⁵⁴

These alterations to Barth's account of the Virgin Birth do not require granting Mary an intrinsic ability or capacity to be the mother of the Lord in a way that would open the door to Roman Catholicism's Marian dogmas—a conclusion that would not simply reconfigure Barth's theology, but replace it with an alien scheme. In fact, they turn on treating Mary as asymmetrically dependent upon Christ, so that what is true of the former cannot be known or understood without prior reference to the latter. To that extent, this reconstruction reaffirms Barth's prioritization of the child's standpoint over the parents' and depends on Barth's prioritization of the covenant for creation and his corresponding account of embodiment. Barth repudiates Thomas' understanding of Mary's unique dignity as indicating that humanity is "capable, by prevenient grace, of preparing himself for genuine sanctifying grace, by uttering this *fiat*."¹⁵⁵ It is Mary's will that establishes the basis of Roman Catholic Mariology.¹⁵⁶ On Andrew Louth's reading, Barth's account falls prey to thinking of Mary in "merely physical terms," bifurcating the physical conditions of Mary's pregnancy and her bridal relationship with God.¹⁵⁷ Yet if Barth does not frame Mary's willingness as a natural capacity for God, he need not assume the reductionistic physicalism that seems to animate his reading of her in the *Dogmatics*. Barth's later defense of the inextricability of soul and body and his suggestion that prevenient grace comes in the form of time given to humanity together raise the possibility that Mary's procreative powers and her bodily virginity make her ready for God's acts—as creation is ready for

153. *CD* III/4, 268.
154. Ibid., 586.
155. *CD* I/2, 144.
156. Ibid. Roman Catholic Mariology bases Mary's dignity not on her physical act, but on the "the accompanying bridal relationship to God expressed in her 'Behold the handmaid of the Lord. Be it unto me according to thy word.'"
157. Andrew Louth, *Mary and the Mystery of Incarnation* (Oxford: SLG Press, 1977), 16, 18.

7. Mary and the Eschatological Confirmation

the covenant, even though it has no immanent power or natural capacity for it.[158] The primacy of the latter discloses the content of the former, just as the primacy of Christ discloses Mary's willingness to be a response to God's election as revealed in the Annunciation, rather than an indicator of humanity's natural capacity for God.[159] As Paul Fiddes writes, Mary indicates that human beings are "open and receptive to God because he is always opening himself to them, and in this constituting their very humanity."[160] Though Fiddes turns to Barth's account of faith to defend this conception of prevenient grace, it has more resonance with Barth's construal of time and bodiliness, which stand as witnesses to God's action in the covenant regardless of whether humanity consciously acknowledges or realizes it.[161] Moreover, if the conception and birth of Christ are proto-salvific acts, there is no need to suggest that Mary's response somehow happens from behind the fallenness of creation. Her giving birth happens because she is first redeemed, not because the new creation begins the history of creation over again.

Mary and Christ remain asymmetrically ordered, then, as do parenthood and childhood. If the Virgin Birth represents an intensification and clarification of the natural aspects of creaturely life by disclosing that their operation depends upon divine action, Mary remains in the second place to the conception and work of Christ Jesus. In this she stands for all human beings, who are in a similarly responsive and responsible position toward the divine address. Yet this account

---

158. *CD* III/2, 525.

159. As George Hunsinger writes, "If divine precedence and human subsequence are complete ... then the human partner receives a capacity it did not bring to the event. It receives a capacity that is not given except in the event by which it is actualized. The capacity is therefore a consequence of, and in no sense a condition on, grace." (Hunsinger, *How to Read Karl Barth*, 216).

160. Paul S. Fiddes, "Mary in the Theology of Karl Barth," in *Mary in Doctrine and Devotion*, ed. Alberic Stacpoole (Collegeville, MN: Liturgical Press, 1990), 119–20. Fiddes founds his suggestion upon a purported "pre-history" of Mary, in which God is secretly bearing witness to her. Tim Perry, however, critiques this as unnecessary, suggesting that Barth's understanding of election is sufficient. My own account is an attempt to reconcile these two approaches, by framing the biological dimensions of Mary's readiness for God as visible manifestations of God's election—such that the sign of Christmas and the substance are interconnected. See Tim Perry, "'What Is Little Mary Here For?' Barth, Mary, and Election," *Pro Ecclesia* 19, no. 1 (2010): 63 ff. Barth's discussion of Mary's *fiat mihi* on page 45 of IV/2 is crucial. There, Barth suggests that the "*fiat mihi* of Mary is preceded by the resolve and promise of God. It confirmed His work, but it did not add anything at all to it." Even if true, such electing work requires a form that is apt for it, namely, Mary's virginity.

161. Philip Rosato argues that any "natural capacity man has for being in a special relationship with God is the gift of the Spirit and not his natural possession." Humanity's ability to respond to God's command is the "work of the Holy Spirit who establishes the creature's being as body and soul." My reading of the Virgin Birth comports closely with this view. See Rosato, *The Spirit as Lord*, 99.

parts ways with Barth's treatment in I/2 precisely at the point where Barth argues that honour cannot reciprocally redound from Christ to Mary. For Barth, the honour children are obligated to show their parents includes the relationship's biological dimensions—which Christ shares with Mary.[162] Barth's understanding of the *Grenzfall* as deliberate orphanhood makes it clear honour is not identical to obedience and rejects making parents the visible, concrete embodiments of God's election (as in Israel). At the same time, children really do owe honour to their parents. As Barth says, while parents are called to imitate God, their children are "summoned to honour God by honouring [them]."[163] Such an account opens up the possibility, though, of vicariously extending the responsibilities to show honour to third parties: if Christ honours His mother for giving Him birth, should third parties do likewise?

While reconstructing Barth's account of Mary this way would deepen procreation's theological meaning and significance, considering the language of honour Barth uses in his treatment of parents and children might expand the reasons Barth has to offer prospective parents to pursue parenthood through procreative means. Though the above discussion attempts to reconfigure Barth's understanding of Mary in light of his later account of the value of bodily ties, it does not address the central matter in Barth's account of the Virginal Conception, namely, Mary's agency *vis a vis* the birth of the Savior. Overcoming such a gap is essential for grounding the reasons to procreate theologically: it is one thing to say that parents are owed honour when procreative bonds exist, but another to say the honour parents are owed establishes a reason to enter parenthood in a procreative way. For Barth, honour designates the intensified importance of creaturely life and agency when they are set in the nexus of the eschatological light of God's revelation in Christ. Exploring Barth's account of honour will provide further grounds for reconfiguring Mary's role in moral theology, while also clarifying how procreation might be grounded theologically even *post Christum natum* in a broadly Barthian framework.

---

162. Or, at least, Barth's view must affirm this in order to avoid the Valentinian Docetism that he rejects in I/2.

163. Barth, *CD* III/4, 247.

Chapter 8

HONOUR, AGENCY, AND REASONS TO PROCREATE

Reconfiguring Barth's account of Mary offers a path toward grounding procreation in the eschatological irruption of Christ's revelation, rather than limiting its theological significance to the doctrines of creation and providence. Yet deepening procreation's theological significance this way does not obviously supply couples with reasons to procreate that intersect with their well-being. The cheerful "confidence in life grounded in faith" that Barth sets forward as a basis for the church's exhortation to extend humanity's time arises in response to the disclosure of Jesus Christ. While one can defend a presumptive pro-natalism from Barth's theology by affirming the animal impulses toward reproduction that he correlates with "life," those reasons fail to clarify how an individual or couple's good might be expanded and increased through procreating. There are worries on both sides: why should anyone want to procreate for the kingdom of God, and what kind of good it is for humanity to embrace our corporeality and the generation of life that might come from it?

Such questions come together in Barth's account of honour, a category that both philosophical and theological ethics have almost entirely abandoned.[1] Honour is

---

1. In III/4, Barth suggests that the "the significance of the term [honour] has been missed and it has not been regarded as of true theological import, being mentioned only incidentally and superficially or not at all (cf. even Bonhoeffer) ..." (653). Barth saw its import and made much of the category, which pervades his theological ethics. The centrality of honour for Barth is tied to his acute emphasis on being "children of God," a motif that begins his discussions of the Christian life in the *Church Dogmatics* (I/2, §18, "The Life of the Children of God") and that structures his posthumously published work on the subject (*The Christian Life*). Despite this, Barth's English-language interpreters have had little more to say of honour than Barth's contemporaries. Stanley Hauerwas provides a brief distillation of Barth's account and critiques him for failing to articulate the "kind of societal ethos, the concrete community, that is capable of producing" honour in agents. As my argument here uses honour for different ends, I do not take up Hauerwas' critique. For Hauerwas' essay, see Stanley Hauerwas, "On Honour," in *Reckoning with Barth*, ed. Nigel Biggar (London: Mowbray, 1988), 145–69. Jason Fout's *Fully Alive* is a welcome contribution on the theme, as it is the most substantive reading of Barth's account of honour to date. I reckon with it below.

Barth's final word of the doctrine of creation: it names the intensified value creaturely life has in its limits and transposes our recognition of those limits into an ethical and deliberative key. The honour of God at stake in creation is secured for us by the honour that God shows humanity in the Incarnation, and is answered by the honour that humanity gives back to God by living in correspondence with him. While Barth's treatment of honour does not dissolve the many questions that arise from his ethics of the divine command, it ensures that the command is not dislocated from its proper context in the immanent, immediate relationship that humanity has with the gracious God. In that way, Barth's treatment of honour offers a way of incorporating humanity's flourishing and good into his theological ethics—a move that Barth makes explicit, as we shall see. Barth places sharp limits on an egoistic pursuit of honour in order to possess it as our own, yet concurrently opens a crack for vicariously honouring those who honour God. At the same time, Barth's construal of honour as extrinsically given by God in Christ structures his understanding of procreative agency in ways that allow us to extend the Barthian reconfiguration of Mary that the last chapter began: the honour that God gives to humans includes the unique form of agency they enact when they stand ready together for new life from God.

I begin this final chapter, then, by exploring how Barth's understanding of honour affirms the dignity of human agency in response to the divine command. I then turn to how honour structures Barth's understanding of procreative parenthood. I consider whether the uniqueness of the human action in procreative parenthood makes it a moment of distinct theological significance, which allows parents to be honoured for their role in God's creation of human life. As this understanding of human agency and honour is incompatible with Barth's Mariology, I then extend the reconfiguration that began in the previous chapter. This brings together the theological significance that procreation might have with the reasons couples might have to procreate: parents procreate for the honour of generating new life, and are rightly honoured by the child and third parties for their agency. The social dimensions of this understanding of honour allow for a vicarious and reciprocal relationship between parents and children, as the child's life redounds to the parents as the parents' honour falls upon the child. Despite its dangers, the constraints Barth builds into honour prevent it from being used to instrumentalize children for their parents' self-glorification.

The Honour of Human Life and Agency

Behind Barth's explicit account of honour at the conclusion of *Church Dogmatics* III/4 lies his broader doctrine of creation and his account of God's glorification of humanity.[2] For Barth, our glorification as creatures is distilled through our

---

2. While I addressed this at the outset of my treatment of Barth's doctrine of creation, I expand and recapitulate on the theme here in order to more formally tease out its ethical dimensions.

status as "children of God," a category that brings together gratitude and honour as the fundamental dispositions of the Christian life.[3] In II/1, Barth frames human participation in God's glory through these twin lenses. On Barth's account, God's glory is "his dignity and right not only to maintain, but to prove and declare, to denote and almost as it were to make Himself conspicuous and everywhere apparent as the One He is."[4] In making Himself manifest in Jesus Christ, God loves: "God's glory is the indwelling joy of His divine being which as such shines out from Him, which overflows in its richness, which in its super-abundance is not satisfied with itself but communicates itself."[5] This glorious revelation of Jesus Christ gives

---

3. In his ethics lectures at Münster in 1928 and 1929, Barth distills the command of God under the doctrines of creation and reconciliation into the formula "Be what you are, namely, my creature" and "do this, and do it in such a way as is appropriate to one who is reconciled to me" (Barth, *Ethics,* 461). Yet this, he argues, leaves out the goal to which we are headed, the "future man whom I cannot be in and of myself but whom I truly am through God." For Barth, this eschatological dimension permits us uniquely to speak of the fact that we are God's children, which "can be said … only in the light of the *goal* of creation, of completed creation, to which the present creation only points" (463). The futurity of our status as children of God preserves the eccentric, extrinsic basis of Christian action while enjoining the Christian to obey as children of the Father. The "being and having of God's children cannot be described or affirmed except as those to which we are—in the present, yet in the present with reference to our own future—*directed*" (466). While the Christians' final state is a unity of those who are "one with God as children are with their father," this unity remains an encounter—and as such, it is "not an intrinsic or an attained possession of man but a most actual affair of divine giving" (499). This emphasis on the givenness of God's grace gives rise to gratitude, which in coming to us as a command means that we must "honestly be what we are" (499). Gratitude goes beyond the orderliness and humility required by the doctrines of creation and reconciliation by specifying that "I am *gladly,* i.e., voluntarily and cheerfully, ready for what God wills of me in acknowledgment of what is given to me by God and as my necessary response to God's gift" (499–500). While this can only be known properly from an eschatological standpoint, the recognition that God has won us establishes us as individuals: in renewing us in God's image, the Holy Spirit reveals the "eschatological reality of our divine sonship in which the 'I am' is possible" and liberates us to confirm God's command with our own affirmation of it (500–1). As Barth notes, gratitude "cannot be commanded. I must really command it of myself." But such a command can only be issued if the individual confronts himself "as I do when seen from the standpoint of eternity in my divine sonship, in my participation in the divine nature" (501). While Barth does not develop the theme of honour here, his correlation of being "children of God" with gratitude sets the stage for incorporating honour accordingly, given the biblical injunction to children to honour their parents. Indeed, Barth invokes many of these themes in his treatment of honour in the *Church Dogmatics,* as I point out below in note 7.

4. Barth, *CD* II/1, 641.

5. Ibid. "In the fact that He is glorious He loves."

rise to "a *glorificatio* which itself springs from the *gloria Dei* and has a share in it."[6] On the one side, our response to God's glory is constituted by our gratitude, which preserves the eccentric, extrinsic character of grace and ensures that our participation in God's glory remains creaturely. Gratitude is the pre-eminent descriptor for humanity's right relationship to God: it is not only "a quality and an activity," nor is it "merely a change of temper or sentiment or conduct and action," but is "the very being and essence of this creature." The creature *is* gratitude, rather than being "merely grateful."[7] On the other side, our participation in God's life is

---

6. Ibid., 668.

7. Ibid., 669. Gratitude and honour both take form for Barth through the imagery of being "children of God," which is Barth's primary motif for the Christian life and which structured his ethics lectures at Münster in 1928 and 1929 (above, note 3). Barth's first substantive discussion of gratitude in the *Dogmatics* occurs in II/1, §27.2. There, Barth argues that our knowledge of God is participation in His revelation and, as such, consists in our offering thanks to God. Barth emphasizes that such an offering must be voluntary. In revealing Himself, God both offers us knowledge of Himself and gives permission to have Him as the basis for our actions—a permission that is "so great and strong that it becomes in us an imperative which breaks through all indolence and dilatoriness" (*CD* II/1, 216). The extrinsic basis of our gratitude preserves the asymmetry between humanity and God. Yet Barth fills out gratitude with its own ethical content, developing it in terms of a subordination that is characterized in terms of childhood rather than servitude. Barth contends that the revelation of God not only comes to us, but comes into us: "It does not cease to transcend us, but we become immanent to it, so that obedience to it is our free will." This joyful gratitude involves our "our elevation above ourselves," as the God who comes to us remains transcendent. Joyful action is thus an "exuberance of movement" in which humanity remains human, and yet "at least as a sign reaches out above himself" and, "in this very sphere of his human capacity, witnesses to what transcends all his possibilities." This "sober exuberance," though, is "not the undertaking of a slave but of a child." Barth suggests that it is "childlike" both in the concrete, specific sense of the term and in "such a way that the very limitation of that which is childlike is also the earmark of the peculiar freedom here bestowed upon man." That is to say, it is both 'childlike' in the familiar sense, and also in the sense that the limits that mark humanity as humanity are constitutive of our freedom (*CD* II/1, 219). It is not insignificant that Barth's first full statement on ethics in the *Dogmatics* in I/2 is titled *The Life of the Children of God* (borrowing from Adolph von Harnack). Even prior to that, in I/1, Barth's discussion of the filioque underscores that the Holy Spirit's work in revelation in begetting children of God has a correspondence to the inner life of God: "It is rather a confirmation of what has been said already, namely, that as the Holy Spirit in revelation unites God and man, Creator and creature, the Holy One and sinners, so that they become Father and child, in the same way He is in Himself the communion, the love, which unites the Father to the Son and the Son to the Father." Barth distills the work of the Holy Spirit in revelation through two expressions, which allude to biblical claims: "He is 'the Lord who sets us free'

constituted by the honour we give Him, which is our answer to display of His glory and the honour He gives humanity in Christ.[8] If deification is one danger, saying too little of our glorification is another. As Barth observes, *doxa* in the New Testament means "not only the honour which God Himself has or prepares for Himself, but also that which the creature gives Him, as well as finally the honour which He for His part gives to the creature." This "coincidence of what appears to be opposite meanings in the same concept is absolutely necessary." If God prepares Himself honour, then the creature "may pay Him Honour, and as it does so it acquires and takes a share in the glory of God."[9] Our glorification is always "wholly and utterly a gift given" to us: it is "always God's self-glorification which is accomplished even in his glorification by the creature."[10] Yet God's self-glorification is constituted by the "over-flowing of the divine existence into co-existence with the creature," which permits human existence to be a "creaturely testimony to God's existence," a "confirmation of the divine existence."[11] The "whole point of creation is that God should have a reflection in which He reflects Himself and in which the image of God as the Creator is revealed, so that through it God is attested, confirmed and proclaimed." The meaning and purpose of creation have been realized in Jesus Christ, but through our correspondence to Him, the children of God can "become an image, *the* image of God" and so become "reflections of the divine glory."[12] Honour thus becomes the hinge between divine and human action, which brings about their fundamental coexistence and compatibility: "Self-determination

and 'by receiving Him we become the children of God.'" The second claim comprehends the first: as Barth writes, "He is the child of God. As such he is free, he can believe. And he is God's child as he receives the Holy Ghost. One can and should also say conversely: He receives the Holy Ghost as he is God's child" (*CD* I/1, 459–60). These claims are pervasively eschatological for Barth: "In the New Testament sense everything that is to be said about the man who receives the Holy Spirit and is constrained and filled by the Holy Spirit is an eschatological statement" (*CD* I/1, 465).

8. JinHyok Kim regards Barth's uses of honour (*Ehre*) and glory (*Herrlichkeit*) as interchangeable, noting Barth's preference for the former in the *Göttingen Dogmatics* and his use of both terms in the *Church Dogmatics*. See Kim, *The Spirit of God and the Christian Life*, 208–10. It seems significant, though, that when Barth turns to speak of God's attributes in II/1, he uses *Herrlichkeit* instead of *Ehre*. I parse the difference this way: glory is what God has in Himself and that in which the church participates in eschatologically; it is hidden now, but will be revealed later. Honour is the public form this glory takes when it overflows into creation and in Christ's redemptive work. As we will see, Barth's treatment of honour in III/4 supplies some reason to think he regards them as distinct categories.

9. Ibid., 670.
10. Ibid., 672.
11. Ibid., 673.
12. Ibid., 673.

comes about when God is honoured by the creature in harmony with God's predetermination instead of in opposition to it."[13]

The mutually entailing character of gratitude and honour becomes even more pronounced in Barth's theological anthropology in III/2. There, Barth contends that being grateful means "to recognise and honour as a benefactor the one who has conferred" a benefit that "one could not take for oneself … but which has nevertheless happened to one."[14] The peculiar character of honour ensures the relationship between gift and giver is not dissolved by the expression of thanks. Gifts incur a type of "debt" that cannot be absolved through repayment. The "fact that the grace of God finds gratitude, that the God who is gracious to his creature is honoured in the world of creation, is the being of man, and this being engaged in its characteristic activity." In this way, gratitude itself "can … be understood only as grace."[15] Honouring God means giving Him due weight and reverence as our

---

13. Ibid., 674. Whatever developments in Barth's theology II/2 heralds, his specification of ethics as a response to the divine command largely retains and recapitulates the account of gratitude he develops in II/1. As Barth writes there, "God chooses the individual in order that his existence may become simply gratitude. That he may achieve this gratitude and be this gratitude in his whole person is the determination of the elect." Materially, Barth describes gratitude as "participation in the life of God in a human existence and action in which there is a representation and illustration of the glory of God Himself and its work." Such a stance arises because of the singularity of the benefit: "Gratitude is the response to a kindness which cannot itself be repeated or returned, which therefore can only be recognised and confirmed as such by an answer that corresponds to it and reflects it. Gratitude is the establishment of this correspondence." This correspondence means imitation: "The elect man is chosen in order to respond to the gracious God, to be His creaturely image, His imitator." See II/2, 413–15.

14. III/2, 167.

15. III/2, 168. Gerald McKenny's discussion of the inseparability of responsibility and gratitude rightfully notes that Barth escapes the aporia of the gift through a conception of grace that avoids being an economic exchange: gratitude is "the form in which the recipient participates in the benefit." Without minimizing the importance of responsibility for Barth's thought, it is surprising that McKenny fails to mention honour, which seems to be Barth's own way of describing how humanity returns the gift of grace to God. See McKenny, *Analogy of Grace*, 17–18. While Herdt rightly notes that it is because God gives us the gift of Himself that there is an "absolute claim on us," she argues the "heart of Barth's understanding of the basis of the divine command has not to do with debt as such, but with responsibility." If we are "bound because we are infinitely indebted—that we have somehow to pay God back for grace received," that would entail we are "obliged *prior* to being commanded, simply reproducing the vicious circle that has always haunted theological voluntarism" (Herdt, "Sleepers Awake!," 166–7). Herdt's corrective is helpful. Yet a narrow focus on the command eclipses the pervasive role gratitude and honour play in Barth's account of the Christian life and, in a sense, the way they structure our recognition of the divine command. While the same disclosure of grace that animates gratitude and honour

8. Honour, Agency, and Reasons to Procreate

Creator and Redeemer, which requires living in responsible conformity to Him.[16] There can be no honour to God if we "do something which we think will honour him." Instead, to "honour God is to meet Him as He gives Himself to us, to be responsible before Him as the One He truly is." God has laid down the manner in which He is to be honoured. God has "already glorified Himself and does so even before man decides to participate in this action," Barth writes. Our knowledge of God consists in honouring God in the way that is appropriate to Him.[17]

Honour has a peculiar motivational salience for Barth, then, which is distinct from the obligations of necessity or compulsion that a strictly Kantian framework might lead to.[18] God stakes His honour on creation, which underwrites the constancy of His love as manifested through His redemptive work in Jesus

---

gives us the divine command, grace impels us to honour God. In that way, there is a sense of "debt" at the heart of the divine command that precedes responsibility—but it is non-economic and cannot be repaid. Not every form of debt is created equal. Jenae Nelson has developed an account of what she has termed "transcendent indebtedness," which is a sense of indebtedness that is accompanied by gratitude and an eagerness to repay. Barth's account of honour functions similarly, though I would describe the form of "debt" as a *bonding* indebtedness—as the "debt" of honour ties together humanity with God. See Jenae Nelson et al., "Transcendent Indebtedness to God: A New Construct in the Psychology of Religion and Spirituality," *Psychology of Religion and Spirituality* 15, no. 1 (2013): 105–17. This paragraph revises the same point in my essay "Giving Thanks for the Gift of Life," 959.

16. In Barth's specifications of gratitude, he argues that humanity fulfills our true being only as we give thanks to God. In giving thanks, "he gives honour to the One to whom alone it is due, and the honour which alone is worthy of Him." Such an action "may assume many forms." But only when human action is a form of giving thanks does humanity "do justice to that in which his being is rooted, to the Word of God which declares that God is gracious to him." Ibid., 171.

17. III/2, 185. Barth argues here that "true and correct knowledge of God is that in which God is honoured," such that "where this knowledge is found, there the honour due from man to God is shown Him."

18. The formal similarity between Barth and Kant's ethics has long been noted. Yet Barth's incorporation of honour (and gratitude) into the center of his ethics gives his view a material and substantive similarity to Kant, as well, whose ethic of honour sits alongside his account of the categorical imperative. As Elizabeth Anderson argues, the "genealogy of commanding value originates in the ethic of honour," rather than exclusively in the categorical imperative as Kant claimed (124). On Anderson's reading, Kant modified the honour tradition by making esteem "dependent on the respect the agent showed for everyone—including herself" (133). Barth modifies this, by grounding our self-esteem and honour in God's honouring of us in Christ. See Elizabeth Anderson, "Emotions in Kant's Later Moral Philosophy: Honour and the Phenomenology of Moral Value," in *Kant's Ethics of Virtue*, ed. Monika Beltzer (Berlin: Walter de Gruyter, 2008), 123–46.

Christ.[19] As Barth writes in his doctrine of creation, God "does not dishonour Himself, but does Himself honour, by being the God of man, of this man." God and the creature's honour are thus mutually involved and implicated.[20] In sin, humanity "robs the gracious God of His honour, and in so doing he casts into the dust his own honour, the honour of the creature whom this God has created."[21] Beneath the history of salvation lies "not merely a question of the creature, but also of the Creator's own cause and honour."[22] In redeeming the world from the negation of sin, God "makes Himself responsible for the preservation of being, and in so doing, He vindicates His own honour as the Creator."[23] God "was and is under no obligation to the creature" to save us.[24] Instead, God's honour binds Him to Himself and animates Him to undertake the work of redemption.[25] That is not to say the atonement is efficacious *because* God's honour is satisfied in Christ. Barth follows Anselm in affirming that humanity "owes the subjection of our wills to God, which is the one great honour which he can render to God and which he is indeed committed to render to Him as man." Those who sin rob God of this honour. But Barth rejects the Anselmian thought that forgiveness must be founded upon the restitution of this lost honour: for Barth, God's honour is confirmed and preserved in the act of forgiving, rather than through repayment.

---

19. This theme runs throughout the entire *Church Dogmatics*. One representative sample: "Against the aggression of the shadow-world of Satan which is negated by [God] and which exists only in virtue of this negation, God must and will maintain the honour of His creation, the honour of man as created and ordained for Him, and His own honour." *CD*, II/2, 124. At the end of his doctrine of creation and his treatment of honour, Barth writes that the "honour of God, and therefore the origin and true home of all human honour, is the One in whom He has created all things and reconciled them to Himself." Cf. III/4, 685.

20. *CD* III/1, 364. God "honours and approves this other within the limits of its distinct being." "Creation is blessing because it has unchangeably the character of an action in which the divine joy, honour and affirmation are turned toward another."

21. *CD* III/2, 35.

22. Ibid., 69.

23. Ibid., 149.

24. Barth, *CD* II/1, 506. God's work of reconciliation is not "necessitated by creation or the existence of the world."

25. At the outset of Barth's doctrine of reconciliation, Barth writes: "He does not permit that that which He willed as Creator—the inner meaning and purpose and basis of the creation—should be perverted or arrested by the transgression of man. He honours it and finally fulfils it in this conflict with the transgression and overcoming of it." See *CD* IV/1, 37. Elsewhere, Barth argues that for Anselm the "unchangeability of God's honour" is the "improper" necessity that governs God's acts. See Karl Barth, *Anselm: Fides Quaerens Intellectum* (Eugene: Pickwick Publications, 2009), 51, n.1. My thanks to Tyler Wittman for flagging this. See Wittman, *God and Creation in the Theology of Thomas Aquinas and Karl Barth*, 140.

Even so, God's preservation of His honour is the basis and grounds for salvation: if God is not obligated by anything intrinsic to the creature to act in salvation, it is still fitting to defend His honour. The obligations of honour are thus distinct from any obligations of necessity.

The grammar of honour surrounds Barth's ethics of divine command, tying it to the immanent relationship of father and children while at the same time imbuing it with an eudaimonistic flavor. The former notion, first: when Barth turns to his substantive treatment of honour at the end of his doctrine of creation, he wonders whether the structure of command and obedience means humanity experiences a subordination and humiliation in which "God is active and man passive."[26] Barth argues it does not, so long as we invert its terms: hearing God's commands is humanity's great honour, not our humiliation. It is the "wonderful condescension in God" that is "man's wonderful exaltation and honouring in the demand for obedience addressed to him."[27] Through God's summons, humanity

---

26. *CD* III/4, 647.
27. Ibid., 649. I should note here my disagreement with Jason Fout's criticisms of Barth's account of glory in *Fully Alive*. Fout claims that Barth "was unable to affirm that God's honour itself honours the creation, either through being witness to God's honour or through participation in the honouring of God" (Fout, *Fully Alive*, 7). Fout hangs much of his critique on a tendentious reading of Barth's discussion of God's glory in II/1. He acknowledges that Barth is "careful to include the creature" in his account of God's glory, but "wonders if the emphasis on God's act throughout does not evacuate the creaturely realm of its genuinely finite and creaturely aspects." Barth "seems to do less than full justice to the contingency of action" (38). As noted above, such criticisms have a long history, yet Fout's hesitation indicates how tenuously he has established them. He similarly objects that glory in Barth's view "does not create a creaturely response of love," on the grounds that nowhere in II/1 does Barth argue that "the creature grows in love through the encounter with God's love"—though he also admits that for Barth the "glory of God is not expressed apart from God's love" (45). He observes in a footnote that Barth had discussed the creaturely love of God in I/2 in "The Life of the Children of God," but complains Barth makes "no explicit connection between this section and the glory of God or the glorifying of God" (47). Barth may have missed an opportunity, to be sure, but Fout might also be asking too much: such an objection can be sustained only by minimizing what Barth does say while demanding that Barth say everything about everything at the same time. The absence of an explicit connection to love in Barth's treatment of glory in I/2 minimizes his explicit invocation of the language of the "children of God" in the same context, which alludes backward to his discussion of love in I/2 (above, note 7). Barth's treatment of glory is also conceptually dependent upon Barth's discussion of the being of God who loves in II/1, §28 and on his discussion in §29 of the unity of God's distinct perfections. Similarly, Fout objects that Barth's treatment of honour in II/1 leaves underdeveloped the manner in which God honours creation, which is a softer objection than Fout makes in his introduction (compare 52 with 7). Here again Fout acknowledges Barth's explicit treatment of honour

is "honoured and magnified and respected by God."[28] This revaluation is possible only through our incorporation into God's life by being made children of God through the Holy Spirit. Barth argues that every "appearance—it can be no more than appearance—of dishonour that may still cling to the terms 'command' and obedience' is dispelled" when we consider the "unsurpassable honour done to man when the commanding God who is his Father calls him as His own child not just anywhere or to any great or small achievements and activities, but to Himself." Human freedom consists in being "with this Father as the child of this Father."[29] Paradoxically, such an honour dissolves the obligation to obey: instead, "he may [obey] as the one who has this honour before and from God. To obey is to rejoice in our honour before and from God."[30] As Barth says in his conclusion to the

---

in III/4 and notes that Barth "several times makes connections similar to what I suggest here, namely that God honours the creation through creating and redeeming it." Yet Fout still objects that God's glory is "not the primary theme" of Barth's treatment of honour and that when God's glory does become Barth's primary concern, "God's honouring of creation moves into the background" (53). That Barth would emphasize humanity's honour in a doctrine of creation and God's glory in his doctrine of God seems like no great problem, though, especially since in each context he explicitly affirms the asymmetrical dependence of creaturely honour on God's glory and the way in which God's glory honours creation. Barth writes in IV/2 that "[doxazein] means both to honour, praise, extol and glorify as a creaturely action and also to transfigure as divine. And [doxazesthai] means both the glorification of God by the creature and of the creature by God." Fout suggests this is a concession for Barth, but it is instead the same substantive position Barth had articulated with distinct accents and emphases since I/2 (100). Fout's own vision for a form of human agency that includes questioning God (including his commands) might be the right one; I do not address it here. But his critique of Barth's account of honour is wanting.

28. Ibid. In "Extra Nos—Pro Nobis—In Nobis," which was published in 1962, Barth wrote: "As in general so here in particular, God's omnicausality must not be construed as God's sole causality. The divine change by virtue of which one becomes a Christian is an event of genuine intercourse between God and human beings. As certainly as it originates in God's initiative, so just as certainly human beings are not bypassed in it. Rather, they are taken seriously as independent creatures of God. They are not overrun and overpowered, but placed on their own feet. They are not infantilized, but addressed and treated as adults." His endorsement that humans are treated as adults is an important clarification, given how much he stresses that Christians are to be children of God. See Karl Barth, "Extra Nos—Pro Nobis—In Nobis," *The Thomist: A Speculative Quarterly Review* 50, no. 4 (October 1986): 511.

29. Ibid., 648.

30. Ibid., 650. Locating the divine command in a filial context is not a new theme for Barth by the time he writes III/4. In II/2, Barth writes that the cry 'Abba, Father!' is the "absolutely basic and primal form of the service for which, according to Romans 7:6, we are freed. Obviously, therefore, it is the basic and primal form of the command of God. This is what God's command wants of us—the crying of the child, of the children, who have at last

doctrine of creation, "Our honour is that He, the Word and Son of God, is our Brother, and that we may be His brethren and as such the children of God."[31]

The note of joy that Barth introduces into our hearing of the divine command raises the question of its eudaimonistic character, the second of our aforementioned ways that honour contextualizes it. Barth begins his ethics of limits in III/4 by specifying how the creaturely conditions of human life prepare us for the appropriate recognition of God's command. There is a "specific correlation" between God and the individual, through which God makes the command recognizable. While humanity remains the possession of God, the relationship of command and hearing is characterized by a "reciprocal knowledge" in which God knows the creature and humanity gains a new recognition of our Creator (which was interrupted by sin).[32] As God's creation, humanity is "predisposed and orientated by God as his Creator and Lord to accept His command and become obedient to it."[33] This "predisposition" is not independent of the divine summons, which would entail that humanity has a natural capacity for God. Yet Barth argues that the command of God does not mean the negation of human nature, but rather the "most positive affirmation." The one hearing the command "must recognise his own nature and being in its correspondence to the command of God."[34] In his most succinct formulation, Barth suggests the command of God is the "authentic interpretation in the imperative mood of man's being and nature by its Creator and Lord."[35]

The "authentic interpretation" of humanity's nature in its limits gives the divine command an urgent character that is eschatological in form. Barth had argued in *Dogmatics* III/2 that birth and death draw individuals into a uniquely immediate relationship to God, which means our limited life comes near to being a form of

---

found their father again, have at last been found by him, have at last been freed from all the 'tutors and governors,' at last been freed from the 'schoolmaster,' at last been freed—self-evidently—from the real power of disobedience, at last been freed from the nerve or lever of sin" (II/2, 592). Above, note 7, highlights the way this theme also structures Barth's original conception of gratitude, and how it is rooted in his doctrine of the Holy Spirit. All these themes come together on two magisterial pages at the end of II/2, where Barth suggests that we make use of our "filial right" and fulfill our "filial duty" through the petitions of prayer, in which we correspond to the prayers of the Son who "intercedes with the Father for us in His Spirit." (cf. II/2, 780–1). Fout suggests that Barth's image of a parent telling their child to go to bed as an analogy for understanding how God relates to the world in IV/2, 541–2 is an "oddity" and "uncharacteristic." Yet framing the divine command through the language of parents and children has deep roots in Barth's thought. See Fout, *Fully Alive*, 86.

31. Ibid., 685.
32. Ibid., 565, 566.
33. Ibid., 566.
34. Ibid., 567.
35. Ibid., 568.

prevenient grace. Our limits give life a "staggering" uniqueness and singularity. Christ's assumption of these limits in the Incarnation is humanity's "supreme honour," as it allows us to see our limited life in relationship to the God "who in His eternity is ultimately the same as man is in his time, i.e., once-for-all and therefore single and unique."[36] The offer that God makes to us in this limited time demands a heightened ethical response: what is "offered with such exclusiveness by God is surely worthy of honour, attention and reflection," even if its significance is not immediately obvious.[37] We still need a "special revelation of God" to take our proper place in His world. Yet the limits on our lives mean any individual can "only be a dependent clause in the main sentence" and indicate that the individual is "pointed directly to the grace of divine calling, that he is orientated on the covenant which God has made with man, that he is disposed for participation in the salvation history proceeds from this covenant and which constitutes the fulfillment of the particular decree and Word and work which form the internal basis of creation and the centre and meaning of the whole cosmos and history"[38] There is a "direction, orientation and disposition" in humanity's existence that allows for a "correspondence—no more, but a real correspondence—between the free and gracious calling of God and the existence of man in his strict singularity."[39] Reflecting on how the command bears on the limits of such a singular, unrepeatable life generates an "urgency" that "may rightly be described as eschatological." And because those two limits sum up every other, the "whole of Christian ethics acquires an eschatological tone and character."[40]

The eschatological character of our limits intensifies our life's value in such a way that the grammar of honour becomes necessary to explain life's goodness. Honour takes two forms: the improper honour every human has as God's creatures and the proper honour we have of those who have heard God's commands.[41] Proper honour takes the form of the "service of witness," through which humanity responds to God's special summons. In calling humanity, God tells us He "needs [us] in a definite and concrete respect, that He has a use for [us]."[42] Being a witness is a superfluity to God, but it is a "superfluity of grace."[43] Such a calling is indispensable if human action is to be honourable: all "human action which lacks the character of service is either not yet or no longer honourable."[44] But the primacy of this proper honour does not hollow out our improper honour that every human has, which consists in the distinction the individual has as a person whom God has created. "That man was and is and will be from and in the hand

---

36. Ibid., 571.
37. Ibid., 572.
38. Ibid., 575.
39. Ibid., 576.
40. Ibid., 579.
41. Ibid., 650.
42. Ibid., 657.
43. Ibid.
44. Ibid., 659.

of God, this precisely, no less and no more," Barth writes, "is his honour, the special honour of every man, which he cannot alter, which he cannot diminish nor augment, which he cannot discard nor lose, which cannot be taken from him by others, just as he himself cannot create it or maintain it for himself."[45] Barth's individualism with respect to this improper honour—our "human dignity"—is emphatic: improper honour is not based on membership in the human species, or on membership in any other group or collective, but is founded "directly, personally and exclusively."[46] As Biggar summarizes, it makes the "human creature not just a specimen but an individual."[47] The singularity of God's summons of the individual in the divine command corresponds to the distinction of being given limited time: the improper honour of an individual's unrepeatability is neither "untrue or unreal," but is the "presupposition to which God reaches back" in His summons to service. Creaturely honour is the "form waiting for this content" of the covenant and so should be "taken no less truly and seriously than the other."[48] In that way, proper honour has an eschatological dimension: it is the form our participation in God's glory takes now. As Barth writes, the "new honour is proper as compared with [the improper honour] because it is the meaning and goal envisaged in it, the final and eternal [glory] (*Herrlichkeit*) which has only to be brought of its concealment to be revealed."[49] The Christian lives "as the creature of God" on one side, and the "child of his Father" on the other, and so lives in the "honour (*Ehre*) and glory (*Herrlichkeit*) with which God clothes him."[50]

Honour is not only a baseline category, though, for Barth: it also names humanity's good, our flourishing. The honour of humanity, Barth writes, is the "significance, the worth, the distinction, which he now has in the eyes of God; the value, which is now ascribed to him by the mouth and in the Word of God; the adornment, vesture and crown with which he is now clothed by God."[51] Barth notes that honour has "often been called a 'good,' and even the supreme earthly good of every man." Barth does not reject this description, but rather reasserts the theocentric—and specifically, Christocentric—character of both improper and proper honour. "All honour of man is always God's honour. Nevertheless," Barth goes on, "God allows man to participate in His honour, not in such a way that this participation ceases to be His grace, yet not in such a way that He refuses it to him in His grace."[52] The Incarnation is the ontological foundation

45. Ibid., 652.
46. Ibid., 655.
47. Biggar, *Hastening*, 90.
48. *CD* III/4, 653. Theological ethics must understand the honour of creaturely life and the honour of service as "unmixed in their distinction and yet inseparable in their relationship."
49. Ibid., 652. *KD* 757. Translation revised. Barth only invokes *Herrlichkeit* in explicitly theocentric contexts in his discussion of honour.
50. Ibid., 664; *KD* 770.
51. Ibid., 663.
52. Ibid., 654.

for the general, creaturely honour and the epistemic basis for attributing honour to everyone regardless of their situation, for "the glory of God Himself was the honour of this man nailed in supreme wretchedness to the cross."[53] The Incarnation is also the ontic and epistemic basis for the proper honour of our calling into God's service. The two forms of honour "meet in Jesus Christ, and thus belong inseparably together and are one for all their distinction."[54] This Christological basis for humanity's honour gives it a constancy and durability that are otherwise unavailable. Barth concurs that honour is the "supreme earthly good," insofar as it concerns us with "the man himself, with his soul." Barth recapitulates his account of humanity's constitution, suggesting that this differentiating factor does not "exist in and of and by itself, but by the Spirit, by the living breath of God." As such, it is a more secure basis for humanity's honour than any other characteristic or trait.[55] Against any naturalistic accounts of *eudaimonia* or human flourishing, Barth argues that humanity's honour can be safeguarded only by ensuring that it "does not fall out of the hand of God and pass into the hands of man."[56] At the same time, honour's extrinsic basis as a gift of God means we cannot lose it. As the individual's honour "stands in Jesus Christ," it is "no less truly given him as his own."[57] While humanity can and does sin against our honour, we cannot destroy it: as "the reflection of the [honour] of God falling upon him," our honour "cannot be lost," but "belongs to the *character indelebilis* of his human existence."[58]

---

53. Ibid.
54. Ibid.
55. Ibid., 663.
56. Ibid., 663.

57. Ibid. The converse is also true. As Kathryn Tanner writes, God "makes the acts of creatures God's own without jeopardizing their integrity." Tanner, "Creation," 124.

58. Ibid., 652, translation revised. As noted above (Chapter 6, note 1), there has been a lively debate among Barth's interpreters over how eudaimonistic Barth's account is. Those who do read it as having a eudaimonistic character suggest that it is not overt. Matthew Rose argues for a 'Thomistic' interpretation of Barth's ethics, but suggests that Barth's argument for it is "mostly implicit" and "hesitant." See Rose, *Ethics*, 109 ff. Biggar affirms the presence of the human good in Barth's thought is "covert and incomplete." Biggar rightly reads Barth as arguing the divine command must "correspond to the 'definite structure' of creaturely being." But he argues that this appellation means both that God will not reverse His decision to give humanity that particular good *and* that if it has a "stable, God-given nature, then in principle it is *there* to be known independently of direct reference to God." This final claim does not obviously follow: if it is a feature of human nature to exist in a particular kind of relationship with the Triune God, then it is plausible to think that it is both true that human nature has a fixed and definite good and that the knowledge of that good depends on divine revelation (similar to how Barth argues versus Descartes that humanity only *knows* creation is real through God's revelation). See Biggar, "Ethics," 39. As others have noted, Barth's treatment of the divine command in II/2 underscores its transcendence, but also argues that it includes our salvation—which means the "quite justifiable concern of eudaimonism

8. *Honour, Agency, and Reasons to Procreate*

The eudaimonistic character of Barth's ethics of honour raises a question about the extent to which our honour can be pursued or asserted.[59] In his ethics of life, Barth is explicit that the extrinsic character of our lives as gifts and loans from God requires us to endorse and affirm them out of our gratitude and honour to God. Respect for life requires an affirmation of life: it requires a "resolute will to be [ourselves.]" We do not affirm a general "I" or "self" that is our own possession or that we can know and command on our own terms. Yet because the divine summons comes to each individual *as* an individual, it requires that we take ourselves seriously as those who have been addressed by God. As Barth puts it, the "affirmation of life as self-affirmation is thus at root an act of obedience." It is not an act of "desire or rebellion or a bid for power," but is a "supreme responsibility."[60] Barth regards character as the "outline of the I which each thinks he can have and know of himself." Our self cannot be a direct work or aim of ours, but emerges in response to our reception of God's summons and disclosure to us as individuals: character is the "a work of the grace of God on man." The command to "be what you are" can be made because we are already in that form in the "eyes of the eternal God," and thus can will that form obediently "in perfect humility but also in perfect courage," rather than in a "subjective or egocentric" way.[61]

---

need not be displaced." (*CD* II/2, 652). Does this make Barth a eudaimonist? Barth and Rose's formulation that we should obey God's command "out of regard for" our own well-being is too strong. Herdt is right that, for Barth, we do not cleave to God *for* our own good, at least in the sense that our own good can supply independent reasons for action. (cf. Herdt, "Sleeper's Awake," 163 and above, Chapter 6, note 1). The divine command supplies us reason to act—but that reason is manifold, and includes both the disclosure of God's grace and our good, concurrently, as the disclosure of God's grace *is* our good. The division between acting on the basis of God's command and acting on the basis of our good is thus an artificial one. We might revise Biggar and Rose's contention to mollify Herdt's concern by saying that we act *with* regard for our own good, rather than *out of* regard for our own good.

59. The eudaimonistic character that Barth develops in his treatment of the ethics of the limitations of our nature is a deepening and extension of his broader ethics of life, which had introduced a non-exclusive, egoistic dimension into Barth's ethics—egoistic, though not egocentric or egotistical. As noted above (page 155), in the *Leitsatz* to §55's treatment of respect for life Barth writes that humanity is ordered to "honour his own life and that of every other man as a loan." Ibid., 324. And it is also worth noting here again that Barth plausibly regards these sections of the *Dogmatics* as interdependent, and clarifying: as the command of God is a "living commanding," we must "be prepared to see that it continually discloses new and apparently posing aspects, like successive steps along the same path or ensuing pages of a single book, which certainly limit, supersede and supplement, though they do not, of course, negate those which precede." Ibid., 470.

60. Ibid., 388.

61. Ibid.

At the same time, this required affirmation of our lives must be responsive to our recognition of their goodness in light of God's revelation lest it become the basis for self-love—which Barth strenuously rejects. Barth's polemic against self-love is unsparing: there is no commandment to love oneself and loving one's neighbor puts an end to one's self-love. Love demands an object that is *not* ourselves, which means that our "self-love can never be anything right or holy or acceptable to God."[62] God's own love is paradigmatically not self-seeking. In IV/2, Barth contends that God "does not seek Himself, let alone anything for himself, but simply man, man as he is and as such, man himself." Barth goes on: "In this self-giving to man He is God in all His freedom and glory." Humanity's response to this love similarly consists in his self-giving, which "certainly means there can be no more self-love, no more desiring and seeking the freedom and glory of the self."[63] Barth's "eudaimonism" thus has sharp limits: he objects in IV.3.2 to making "salvation" the goal of our Christian vocation, as it smacks of "the sanctioning and cultivating of an egocentricity which is only too human."[64]

Barth is aware of the impetus to egocentrically seek our own honour, but is realistic about its place in the moral life. Every individual is tacitly aware of the improper honour God has given us in our unrepeatable distinction and, as such, craves more honour and esteem from others. Every individual, when reflecting on the once-for-all character of their life that its limits clarify, sees "that he has something of his own which in his way he has once for all and uniquely in and by virtue of his limitation."[65] An individual "would not be a man" if "he did not recognise that he is already honoured" in this way by God.[66] This tacit recognition of our value and weight stands beneath our aspiration for more honour. While we may fail to remember the theocentric basis of our honour, the individual could not "be a man without in some way affirming and asserting this value of his" and doing so in and for the sake of being noticed by our neighbors.[67] The individual is thus dependent for his validity and value not only "to know it himself but, in confirmation of this knowledge, to see that it is noticeable to others."[68]

---

62. Barth, *CD* I/2, 388.

63. Barth, *CD* IV/2, 750. Note that Barth uses *Herrlichkeit* here, rather than *Ehre* (honour). As with III/4, Barth in IV uses *Herrlichkeit* to name either the glory that God possesses in Himself or the glory into which the church eschatologically participates in, while *Ehre* names God's reputation in salvation history. As such, Barth's criticisms of "self-love" here are not obviously a criticism of the assertion or defense of temporal goods just as such, though they certainly call such a pursuit into question, but a critique of the attempt to deify ourselves by striving to possess what is only God's to give. Cf. *KD* 855.

64. Barth, *CD* IV/3.2, 567.

65. Ibid., 655.

66. Ibid.

67. Ibid., 656.

68. Ibid.

The inner value that we have from God's honouring of us thus seeks an external correspondence and confirmation, which together form our "inner and outer reputation."[69] The ascription and recognition of our worth and significance is our "external honour."[70] Barth concludes that the once-for-all character of our lives, which grounds "his value to himself and in the eyes of others, his reputation, is the honour which is his as the creature of God before God and from God."[71]

While Barth recognizes that our aspiration to make our inner value noticeable to others is inevitable, his theocentric account of honour transforms its basis so that it does not become a sinful, egocentric assertion of the self against the world. Properly speaking, our action is honourable only insofar as it is in service to God. We can seek honour "only in [our] willingness for service."[72] Serving God frees our action from the need for an external, social confirmation of its worth.[73] Even in its creaturely form, though, Barth argues that the honour of humanity can be had with a modesty that keeps us from claiming it as our own possession.[74] The fact that God honours humanity entails that our honourable conduct must happen in thankfulness, humility, and humor—the last of which is "the opposite of all self-admiration and self-praise."[75] The "modesty" that Barth thinks encompasses these three characteristics is not a negation or privation, nor is it a diminution of honour. Barth notes that it "may and must be compatible with a certain healthy pride" (*Stolzes*).[76] The real need is to assert our honour, which paradoxically involves modestly looking away from ourselves as the basis for our own lives and remaining reliant upon God.[77] Such simple, non-anxious enjoyment of our honour is distinct from the assertion that it is our own and the attempt to see it proclaimed as such by others. The arrogance of pride (*Hochmut*) is "an evil to be avoided because it does not make for honour but against it."[78] The theocentric basis of our honour disentangles it from the social forms that it takes shape within and makes our effort to increase our honour self-defeating. The honour of service might take a decidedly bourgeois form and overlap with worldly honour, or it might contradict them (much like the divine command and creaturely goods).[79] The social aspects

---

69. Ibid.
70. Ibid., 658.
71. Ibid., 656.
72. Ibid., 661.
73. Ibid. In such service, our action is "not merely justified in itself; in all its limitation it is clothed with [glory]." That is, it participates in the eschatological glorification that the church enjoys, even if it is currently concealed from view.
74. Ibid., 664.
75. Ibid., 665.
76. Ibid., 666. *KD* 772.
77. Ibid.
78. Ibid.
79. Ibid., 672. "If there is thus no law in virtue of which man's honour before God must be continually and necessarily in contradiction and conflict with what he would like to

of honour are inevitable, but have only a "hypothetical and heuristic significance" for determining the shape of the summons of God.[80] They are to be measured against the Word of God, rather than vice versa. The correspondence between the honour of humanity and any particular society's conception of honour is thus incidental and contingent. Yet there is a sense in which such a social context is also irrelevant for our honour, as "no circumstances and no man can increase or diminish it, can give it to him or take it from him," Barth contends, because "God alone is competent to decide his dignity and worth."[81]

Barth's account of honour is preoccupied with the ethics of seeking and maintaining it: he has considerably less to say about the ethics of ascribing it to others. Yet his contention that God honours the individual in their uniqueness and service invites us to consider a corresponding form of honour among humans, which acknowledges the humility and modesty of the person whose conduct is honourable. Barth argues that the futile pursuit of honour—vainglory—can be pursued vicariously, as when "one man boasts of another to whom he has attached himself, and may thus bask in the reflected glory."[82] Because the Corinthians do not "belong to" Paul or Apollos, their attempt to honour themselves indirectly through them is wrong. Yet Barth's critique is squarely against the attempt to exalt ourselves, whether vicariously or independently, rather than against the concept of honouring each other. There is "for man a real exaltation or honouring," in which it can be said to another "Friend, go up higher." The service which allows

---

regard as his honour from the human and worldly standpoint, there is also no law in virtue of which the two must normally agree." The ethical criterion for deciding whether we have kept ourselves free for God's command in the face of our presuppositions is joy. This joy might need to subsist even in the open form of our "abasement, i.e., of a limitation, diminution, and even annihilation of what he earlier regarded as his honour" (ibid., 672). Barth recapitulates this line of reasoning in IV/2, where he argues that the kingdom of God heralds the "destruction ... of what is generally accepted as honour or fame among men." The ordinary conceptions of what constitutes status or honour undergo a "transvaluation of all values where the grace of God rules" (*CD* IV/2, 548–9). This is the same context where Barth reiterates the kingdom's dissolution of the absoluteness of family (ibid., 550–1). At the same time, Barth argues in his account of the "Dignity of the Cross" that the Christian cannot desire or seek the negation and destruction of human life, for "he sees and honours and loves in life a gift of God" (ibid., 602).While Barth contends that the cross means we must affirm the negation of our lives, and that in being given a cross to bear, the Christian is "honoured by this special fellowship with Jesus Christ" (ibid., 602–3). We are not permitted to seek this suffering, even if we should not strive to avoid it. And the cross is not an end in it, but rather, it indicates the "provisional nature of the Christian existence and sanctification. The crown of life is more than this" (ibid., 613). While Barth is speaking here of "life," the same pattern applies to his conception of honour.

80. Ibid., 669.
81. Ibid., 678.
82. Ibid., 667.

us to have honour, and which takes us to the lowest place, cannot be a "means by which to try secretely to create or ensure [our honour], but only the condition in which he will actually receive it." The publican who prays for mercy is thus the "truly obedient and therefore the truly honourable man."[83] Yet these critiques admit the real possibility of honouring those who have, in fact, been truly obedient and honourable—and even of honouring those who vicariously contribute to another's honourable conduct, provided that they maintain the modesty and humility that appropriate honour requires.

Barth's theocentric account of honour simultaneously intensifies the urgency with which we regard our own lives and dissolves the anxiety that characteristically attends our pursuit of our own well-being. The once-for-all character of our limited life, which Jesus Christ entered into in the Incarnation, means our lives have an irreplaceable weight and dignity that demand our reverence and that generate our concern for our well-being and reputation. Yet because our honour remains strictly in the hands of God, there is nothing we can do to expand or deepen it: we can only confirm the honour that God has shown us by honouring Him with the service of our witness and by asserting our honour with the thankfulness, humility, and humor that indicate it is not our possession. At the same time, the fact that our honour falls upon us as a reflection of God's honour makes it inalienable: Christ's disclosure of the honour God gives to humanity places our honour on a more secure foundation than any other type of distinction could supply. Barth's approach to honour supplies, then, what we might describe as a theocentric, disinterested eudaimonism. It is theocentric in that our supreme earthly happiness and good remain outside of us, in God. It is disinterested, in that the modesty required for the truthful assertion of our honour paradoxically involves a "final and profound unconcern" about the fact that it is our honour being asserted.[84] And it is eudaimonistic in that the divine command that discloses God's honouring of us in Christ responds to aspects of our nature that allow us to recognize it as good for us. While we do not act in Barth's account for the sake of our good, the divine command necessarily includes our good.

The Honour of Procreative Parenthood

Barth's formal treatment of honour offers ways to expand on themes in Barth's ethics of procreation that Barth either leaves tacit or underdeveloped. While Barth's ethics of parenthood and childhood inevitably make use of honour as the pre-eminent moral category, his description of the agency involved in generating human life invokes it as well, in a way that offers a glimpse for how construing reasons to procreate through the lens of honour might go in a Barthian framework. Barth's account of parenthood frames biological bonds as subordinate

---

83. Ibid., 668.
84. Ibid., 679 ff.

to and founded upon the covenantal mission of parents to prepare their children for their encounter with God. But he also argues that procreative relationships endure even in cases where the marriage has dissolved. Parenthood involves the immanent relationship of honouring between the parent and child, and is itself an honourable form of life—that is, parenthood is a form of life that must be respected by third parties once it is established and that imposes obligations on parents which are indissoluble. Barth contends that parenthood must be undertaken with the awareness "both of the honour and also of the duty" involved in fatherhood and motherhood.[85] While parenthood remains a "free and optional gift," it is inalienable in the same way humanity's improper honour is inalienable: fatherhood and motherhood "always confer a *character indelebilis*" and bring about an "indissoluble relationship" to the child now born.[86] This character survives the dissolution of the marital relationship: the honour and obligations of parenthood persist in the "boundary cases" of single parenthood. The unmarried mother is the "recipient of a special gift and a special charge from God, and is not an inferior kind of mother." Nor does the unmarried father escape his obligation to the child: he is "responsible for this event and therefore for the existence of this new person," and he will "remain responsible as long as he lives."[87]

The obligation to honour single parents is not based on their genetic or biological similarity, but rather on their action in generating human life. Crucially, Barth contends that the honour of procreative parenthood "consists in the fact that an individual is permitted to be immediately concerned, not simply as a witness but in action and suffering, in the [astonishing] event by which a new human being comes into the world as the bearer of his own flesh and blood."[88] Parental obligations arise from the agents' respective responsibility for the creation and life of the new individual.[89] Each party should "feel both aspects": one cannot "assume the burden of obligation without feeling joy in the accompanying honour," nor can one "rejoice in the honour without taking to heart the seriousness of the obligation."[90] Yet Barth also introduces an asymmetry between these dimensions

---

85. Ibid., 276.

86. Ibid., 277. The *Grenzfall* here does not refer to the eschatologically oriented disruption of ordinary conventions, but the disorder of family life because of sin. However, both cases carry the same point: the *Grenzfall* is not a rejection of natural obligations, but their confirmation: obligations persist both when the ordinary social conventions of parenthood are voluntarily disrupted for the sake of the kingdom and when those social conventions are disrupted due to disobedience or sin.

87. Ibid.

88. Ibid. The translation is revised in order to avoid conflating what happens in ordinary procreation with the 'miracle' of the birth of Jesus Christ at the Incarnation. The German reads: "Die Ehre besteht darin, daß ein Mensch unmittelbar, als Zeuge nicht nur, sondern tätig und leidend, bei dem erstaunlichen Geschehen dabei sein durfte, wie ein neuer Mensch und dieser als Träger des eigenen Fleisches und Blutes ins Dasein trat."

89. Ibid.

90. Ibid.

along gender lines, suggesting it would be a "proper and effective exchange" if the mother is more conscious of the honour and the father of the obligation.[91]

Situating Barth's description of the peculiar "action and suffering" involved in procreation against the backdrop of Barth's understanding of divine-human action helps clarify the significance of Barth's ascription of honour to procreative parents. As we have seen, Barth is concerned to ground the individual's life and origin exclusively in God. Additionally, he is insistent that procreation neither perpetuates nor fulfills the *imago Dei,* but is the occasion in which God creates a new person in His image. The danger of such an approach is that it empties procreative agency of its significance and undermines human responsibility for the generation of human life. While Barth explicitly avoids reducing procreative decisions to chance or providence, his account of procreation's theological status risks doing precisely that. How procreative parenthood can be the "free and in some sense optional gift of God" while also being a matter of heightened human responsibility is a puzzle.

Barth's construal of honour helps resolve the quandary. For Barth, human action is not *solely* human action. Barth parses the role of parents in generating life very carefully: they are not only witnesses to God's action but are immediately present and involved in the "the [astonishing] event by which a new human being comes into the world." The child shares their "flesh and blood," but this is only a subordinate theme to the fact that God has given parents a role in His action that goes beyond being a witness to it. God's role as the source of the honour of procreative parenthood both relativizes biology *and* strengthens the basis for the honour that we owe to procreative parents. As we have seen throughout Barth's corpus, locating procreative action in a theological context heightens its gravity and importance, rather than diminishes it. It is worth remembering here that procreative sexual activity can be an "offer" from God, just as life in its limits is an "offer" from God"—and, as such, sexual activity needs to be treated with a similar urgency to that which Barth thinks arises when we consider our lives at the moments of birth and death.[92] Yet if procreating is not our act alone, it is genuinely our action: it is also worth remembering that parents can seek a child "which was not offered by God," which means that a life can be generated "of whom it might well be said from the parents' standpoint that they would have been better without it."[93] Barth notably does not say it would have been better overall for the child to not exist. Yet his point underscores the extent to which God honours human action, as He bestows the *imago Dei* on those who only exist through our wrongdoing. The birth of Christ might remove the obligation to procreate—but it heightens the drama and responsibility of doing so.

Even so, Barth conspicuously fails to implement crucial resources from his theology to describe the unique way divine and human agency come together

---

91. Ibid.
92. Ibid., 269, 341.
93. Ibid., 271.

in procreating. Barth suggests the positive decision to procreate must be a "venture of faith."[94] What is only a passing reference in this context is pregnant with possibilities: elsewhere in his corpus such "ventures of faith" happen when we aim at what is outside or beyond human disposal or control [*Unverfügbares*]. The close association between the venture of faith and that which lies beyond our control specifically structures Barth's account of the love that grounds marriage. As marital love has to do with a "divine joining together," it "intends something which only God can know about these two and do for them." That is, such love "aims at something which is not under human control [*Unverfügbares*]." By aiming at divine action, marital love "ventures something which can only be ventured in faith in the divine wisdom and grace"—language that is nearly identical to his description of the decision to procreate.[95] In one of his earliest substantive uses of the concept in *Church Dogmatics*, Barth contends that the "[unavailability] of faith and its object guarantees that divine certainty cannot become human security. But it is this [unavailable] faith and its [unavailable] object which make possible the certain divine knowledge which is at issue in dogmatics."[96] Barth's emphasis on the need for divine action to create an individual in the *imago Dei* and his construal of the child as a gift makes the absence of the term in his ethics of procreation curious.[97] Though no explanation can be decisive, it is plausible that behind the absence lies Barth's concern to regard procreation as an independent sphere from marriage.

---

94. In the positive decision to procreate, the "venture of faith and obedience are required." III/4, 271.

95. Ibid., 218. Such love can only be an "intention, aim and venture," because it aims at *divine* action. *KD* III/4, 245.

96. *CD* I/1, 12–13. While the translators render the term here "intractable," Barth mostly uses it to speak of that which lies beyond or outside human comprehension and control. See *KD* I/1, 11. In IV/1 Barth qualifies the term, such that to speak of that which is "unavailable" is "not by a long way to speak of God." But he also suggests that our lives are "hid with Christ in God" "in a way that we cannot comprehend or control." God Himself is not reducible to those actions or events that are outside our control; but faith in its lived form is a venture which specifically has reference to them (*CD* IV/1, 301, 356).

97. On this reading, procreation is a form of human action that comes very close to Barth's account of action as invocation, the paradigmatic form of which is prayer. As Hunsinger notes, prayer represents the "mysterious concept of ... double agency at its very epitome and height." Hunsinger, *How to Read*, 221. See also A. J. Cocksworth, "Attending to the Sabbath," *International Journal of Systematic Theology* 13, no. 3 (2011): 251–71. As Eberhard Jüngel observes, invocation is the point "where the distinction between divine and human action is experienced most clearly and sharply." While Barth sharply differentiates between divine and human action in procreating, it is distinct from invocation in that Barth's later work seems to grant humanity the 'Lordlike' possibility of procreating an individual whom God would not have otherwise brought into existence. See Eberhard Jüngel, *Theological Essays*, trans. John Webster (London: Bloomsbury T&T Clark, 2014), 162.

The more conspicuous shift from Barth's account of marriage to his treatment of procreation and parenthood is the displacement of love by honour as the pre-eminent moral category. Barth's depiction of marriage as a venture in faith is animated by trying to understand the "specific love which unites a man and woman" beneath the command of God.[98] By contrast, Barth says practically nothing about love between parents and children: parents loving their children is mentioned only once.[99] Again, Barth might be motivated to ensure that procreation remains a distinct realm of moral reasoning. Yet Barth's normative commitments might supply other reasons for the shift. Though Barth's relative silence about love might seem cold-hearted, it tracks Barth's pattern of the immanent love of God's inner life overflowing through the display of His glory. The expanding marital fellowship that has love at its center "overflows," in a sense, when God honours the couple through entrusting them with the care of a child. In that respect, love does not disappear from view entirely—rather, it is the pretext and presupposition for the life of the child. At the same time, the guardrails that Barth puts in place preserve a sharp disanalogy between marital love/procreation on the one side and God's immanent love/glory the other. While marriage is an expanding fellowship, marital love does not proleptically reach out and enfold an individual the way God's election does: as Barth argues in III/1, God's love is not responsive to the "presupposition" of an existing individual as human love is, "but creates the presupposition."[100] Moreover, tying together love and procreation too closely would enshrine the "family" as a discrete unit of theological reflection and concurrently reduce procreating to the "natural" overflow of the prior decision to marry. Barth explicitly rejects the former, and the latter seems to risk allowing procreation to run on a track that is independent of the divine command, which

---

98. Barth, *CD* III/4, 217.

99. Barth uses 'love' (*Liebe*) only four times in the section, a marked contrast from the dominant role it plays in his treatment of marriage. The first two times refer to the love a couple has for each other, which leads them to a sexual encounter that is procreative (*CD* III/4, 241). The third refers to the wife's love for her husband, and the requirement of sacrifice that it entails (276). Barth's single mention of it in the context of parents and children stresses that the "seriousness and effectiveness of [parents'] love will depend [on] whether this witness [to God's position as the child's Advocate and Guardian] is given" (279). Barth never mentions children loving their parents. For the German text, see *KD* III/4, 269, 310, 314.

100. *CD* III/1, 96. In Barth's famous formula, because "the election of God is real, there is such a thing as love and marriage" (*CD* III/1, 318). For Gary Deddo, "Procreation ... is an election of the child in love of soul and body even before it is born" (Deddo, *Theology*, 348). While this seems like a plausible way to understand the relationship between love and glory in God's life, and so marriage and procreation in theological anthropology, I have tried to underscore that it is not *Barth's* way of framing things and in some respects cuts against the grain of aspects of Barth's thought.

would offer few grounds (if any) to resist the ethnonationalist pro-natalism that Barth was so attuned to.

In shifting moral registers to honour, then, Barth simultaneously frames procreation as our immediate presence for God's act of generating life and disentangles procreation from the views that would reify "blood and soil." The procreative bond does not disappear for Barth: it matters that we are present in action and suffering for God's action in creating a human being who shares our "flesh and blood." Procreative bonds are indelible and inalienable. Yet they are not what supplies procreation its value. The honour of procreating comes from God and remains God's, even while it calls forth our responsibility to conform our parenting to God's command for the sake of God's honour. Granting procreative bonds special significance because the individual shares our genetic or biological material would be tantamount to an invidious pride: it would constitute an assertion of our worth that is founded not upon the honour received from God, but upon our own identity.

Second, this account indicates that for Barth procreation and parenthood are overlapping concepts, so that the former includes and leads to the latter and cannot be properly understood without it.[101] Barth's theocentric account of procreation, in which parents can only be ready to procreate until God permits them to be present in "action and suffering" for His act of creating new life, runs parallel to his argument that parents cannot bring about the decisive event in the child's life (their encounter with God) through their own efforts or work. The limits on human agency in procreating thus correspond to the limits on human agency in God's summoning of the child. And they also underscore Barth's contention that the *whence* of human life is answered by God alone. Barth is nothing if not consistent.

---

101. Deddo reads Barth as saying procreation is "an actual participation in God's own act of giving life." He then infers on this basis that the honour ascribed to individuals for their agency in it gives procreation its own "wonder, value and meaning even apart from parenting." He proposes on this basis that procreation is a "reflection of our being created in the image of God," a stance he also attributes to Barth (Deddo, *Theology*, 347). There are problems here. For one, terms like "invocation" or "mutual co-ordination" would be more accurate than "participation" as a description of human agency. There are two actors in procreation, and Barth is concerned to keep them distinct but not separate, together but not confused. Second, Barth worked against associating procreation with the completion of or continuation of the *imago Dei*. Deddo's terms here are unclear: procreation "reflects," is "related to," and "manifests" the *imago Dei*. However we read them, I am skeptical that any of them apply to Barth's account. More pressingly, Deddo borrows the wrong lesson from Barth's use of honour to describe parental procreative agency: his point is not to say that it has a value *independent of* parenthood, but rather that procreation is *itself parental*: the same honour that is bestowed on parents belongs to those who procreate, because the latter is inextricable from the former. Such is the force of Barth's contention that the "two tasks" of parenting belong together and are mutually entailing.

Third, the modesty that Barth thinks is central to our recognition of the honour that God bestows upon us might allow us to extend his account of procreation toward establishing limits on the means that couples pursue to generate life. Though Barth does not explicitly invoke modesty in his treatment of parents and children, his contention that parents ought not assert their status comes very near it: though they are the natural representatives of God for the child, parents are permitted only to bear witness to the "fact that these young lives exist under the hand of God" without any "deliberate intention of adopting and asserting this status and role."[102] In a procreative context, aspiring to the honour of parenthood might generate similar qualifications about pursuing biological children. While a full treatment of the matter lies beyond the scope of this book, Barth's account of the theocentric basis of life, his argument for life's limits, the cheerfulness and alternate forms of fruitfulness he commends to childless couples and the modesty he builds in to honour together could form the basis for distinctions between therapeutic and non-therapeutic interventions into fertility and sharp limits on making human life outside the womb. What does it mean to be "immediately" present, not only as a witness but in "action and suffering," in the inherently mediated processes that artificial reproductive technologies deploy?[103]

Mary and the Reasons to Procreate, Revisited

Barth's description of the honour God gives to humanity opens up intriguing possibilities both for reconceiving his understanding of Mary and for offering couples reasons to procreate that intersect with their good. Barth had stressed the exclusivity of God's agency in his treatment of the Virgin Birth. As he put it there, human generation arises from "willing, achieving, creative, sovereign man" (male), which enabled him to frame Mary's virginity exclusively as a negation of this striving.[104] The Virgin Birth shows that "God does it all Himself," that "God Himself has the initiative."[105] As we saw, Barth's treatment of procreative agency in his later ethics of parents and children still puts a premium on divine action in creating a human life who bears the "flesh and blood" of the originating couple. Yet the honour of procreative parenthood is that the "individual is permitted to be immediately concerned, not simply as a witness but in action and suffering," in this event.[106] Procreative parents must feel this honour (alongside their obligations) and children must honour their parents for their role even when they fail in their duties to conform to God's love.

---

102. *CD* III/4, 278.
103. Barth could argue that some interventions—such as hormonal adjustments to increase the odds of procreating—are not alternate means of creating, but rather of restoring health to individuals.
104. Barth *CD* II/1, 192.
105. Ibid., 182.
106. Barth *CD* III/4, 277.

Barth's later description of procreative agency might allow us to reconstruct his earlier account. The "miracle" of the Virgin Birth clarifies and reveals what is true about every conception and birth, namely that *God does it*. Yet does God do it *alone*? Barth's invocation in III/4 of the "action and suffering" required for procreative agency offers one way of reconceiving Mary's role in the Incarnation on his own terms. Barth is conscious of the asymmetrical burdens on the sexes in procreation, which makes it plausible that he divides the "action and suffering" involved in procreating along gendered lines. Barth's account of how couples should decide to have more children treats it as a paradigmatic case for his account of gender relations, with all its limitations. In deciding whether to procreate or not, "it is the wife who is directly and primarily affected and concerned." Yet while the decision can only be made jointly, as an act of solidarity by the two partners, the male retains the initiative (as in his construal of the Virgin Birth).[107] There may be circumstances, Barth suggests, when "a man cannot believe himself justified" in expecting his wife to have a "cheerful confidence in life." Barth includes both the woman's physical and psychological health as reasons to avoid conception.[108] Male initiative in this realm, then, means "initiative in surrendering his own wishes and shouldering the dangerous burden" of procreating, as there can be no genuine agreement without such sacrifice. The "fact that biologically [the woman] is always in greater danger than he is" in procreating means the wife "must therefore bear the lighter burden, and [the husband] the greater."[109] The "action and suffering" involved in generating life are thus likely divided between the sexes in Barth's framework.

This distinction has important ramifications for understanding the legitimacy of honouring Mary for her procreative work in the Incarnation. Mary is subject to all the same burdens and risks of gestation and labor that Barth names in III/4, which means that God requires her consent in order to embody the eschatologically oriented consort and harmony between male and female that Barth thinks is necessary for an appropriate procreative decision. At the same time, Mary's suffering in gestation and labor entails that she is worthy of honour by her Son and by us. Barth notes that children are "summoned to honour God by honouring their parents" when parents strive to conform to God's action.[110] Barth makes clear that this is true of Christ's relationship to Mary. Even if Christ's honour toward His parents sometimes takes paradoxical forms, Christ's relativization of the parent–child bond deepens and confirms it as well. Moreover, as Christ discloses the content of the divine command, the honour He gives Mary becomes vicariously incumbent upon us. Barth gives us a hint of this socially mediated extension of honour in his

---

107. Ibid., 276.

108. Ibid., 272.

109. Ibid., 276. Barth does not specify what these "burdens" might be for the male. It may be the case that he has psychological burdens in mind. In his evaluation of the options for avoiding childbirth, Barth rejects permanent abstention from intercourse on grounds that it leads to "undesirable psychological repressions which might have fatal consequences for the marital fellowship, which as such includes sexual fellowship" (274).

110. *CD* III/4, 247.

description of single mothers, who have become "the recipient of a special gift and a special charge from God." Barth is cognizant that single mothers are liable to social reproach and stigmas, yet contends that "nothing can take from her the dignity which has been conferred upon her, not only in the face of her child but *in the face of all others*, by the very fact that like any other mother she has given birth to this child at the risk of her own life While others might fail to recognize such an honour, Barth contends that the woman "must not allow this dignity to be removed from her."[111] Similarly, Mary is justified in feeling the honour and dignity of being involved in suffering in the Incarnation—and we are obligated to respect that honour.[112]

Such a path again comes near to Charlotte von Kirschbaum's view, albeit by marshalling very different resources. Von Kirschbaum argues that Mary is given the "greatest mark of distinction that could come woman's way" by being the "first to experience the incarnation of the Son of God in her own body." Yet where Barth argues that the counter-sign of the Virgin Birth undermines male pre-eminence but does not establish a positive female pre-eminence, von Kirschbaum seems to embrace the conclusion. Not only is "man's lordship ... disregarded" in the incarnation, but "woman is accorded pre-eminence in a manner that surpasses every other form of pre-eminence." Such a status is not based on merit, but grace—but is also based on Mary having real agency. Even "from a Protestant point of view," von Kirschbaum writes, Mary "is not simply a piece of earth, a 'lump of clay' ..., but a human being whom God has summoned to perform the most wondrous service that a human being has ever been chosen to do."[113] If the Virgin Birth is not only a way of side-stepping original sin, but is a disclosure of the peace that Christ establishes in the eschaton, then it means not simply a qualification of male pre-eminence but its eradication. Such an inversion is entirely in keeping with Barth's principle that within creation, the last shall be first and the first—last.

Mary is honourable on Barth's account not only for her suffering in giving birth, though, but for the way she modestly declines to seek her own honour. Barth invokes Mary's Christocentrism to justify his own: her attention is "directed away from herself to the Lord."[114] In his substantive treatment of honour, Barth allows that self-abnegation in service of Jesus Christ merits our honour. There is "for man a real exaltation or honouring," he writes, in which one says "Friend, go up higher." Yet this exaltation "definitely applies to him only as the one who has seated

111. Ibid., 277, emphasis mine.
112. Such a reading comports with Dustin Resch's reconstruction of Barth's understanding of Mariology on the basis of Volume IV of *Church Dogmatics*. Resch writes that for Barth, "Mary actively participates with God in the economy of salvation. For both Barth and Rome, this participation is genuine human action that is elicited by grace." For Barth, Mary is "a picture of what Christian existence looks like in response to the grace of God in Jesus Christ as it is evoked by the Holy Spirit." Resch, *Interpretation*, 187, 196. This does not necessarily entail the development of Mariology as an independent stream of theological reflection or liturgical practice.
113. Charlotte von Kirschbaum, *The Question of Woman*, 133.
114. *CD* I/2, 141.

himself in the lowest place…or allows himself to be brought down to them."[115] While Barth points to the publican who prays for mercy as his example, it is hard to avoid echoes of the Magnificat in his formulation: "He hath exalted the humble and meek, and the rich He hath sent empty away." Barth construes Mary as an exemplar of self-abnegating humility—as "little Mary"—which means there are grounds for correspondingly honouring her by saying, "Friend, go up higher." As Mary directs attention away from herself and toward the Lord, we honour God by honouring her in and through God.[116]

Honour's vicariousness has important ramifications for understanding the parent–child relationship and the reasons to procreate. While Barth criticizes seeking honour through others, he leaves its formal vicarious structure untouched—which raises questions about whether the honour God gives parents extends to their children. Consider Barth's treatment of the "curious, incidental remark" by Paul that the children of believers are "not as such impure but holy." On its face, Paul seems to be suggesting that what is true of the parents accrues in some way to the child by virtue of the parent–child relationship. Yet Barth here expands the sanctifying influence that makes children "holy" away from the parent–child relationship *per se*, suggesting that there is an "actual sanctifying power which men can exercise over their neighbors by the simple fact of their existence and presence as Christians."[117] Though Barth steadfastly repudiates the notion that this is an argument for infant baptism, his treatment of the same passage in IV/4 argues that the Christian influence matters even when the other remains a non-Christian. The sanctification Paul speaks of has "a predominately objective sense" that has little to do with conversion, but involves a "constant unsettlement which is salutary even down to the smallest things" for the unbelieving person.[118] The

---

115. *CD* III/4, 668.

116. Resch argues against Risenhuber's similar proposal that Mary has a distinguished position as the "archetype of humanity" on grounds that ascribing this "neglects entirely the Christological center of Barth's thought." On his view, Mary's paradigmatic function depends upon the "*form* of the work of Christ's Spirit upon her." Yet in Barth's account of honour, we see reasons to think that Christocentrism and honouring others are not as incompatible as this formulation implies. See Resch, *Interpretation*, 196 n.114.

117. *CD* III/4, 278. Barth's abstracting move here is very similar to his early attempt, noted above, to disentangle the claim that Christ will turn the hearts of parents and children toward each other from the actual content of parenthood and childhood. There is a hint here in Barth's thought that he reduces the parent–child relationship to one of neighbors, in which the duties and responsibilities of parents are generalized duties (if ecclesiastically grounded) that the parents bear as the most proximate neighbor to the child. In critiquing the use of 'family' in Christian theology, Barth argues that in the New Testament parents and children "are still emphasized … but as persons and for the sake of their personal connexions and duties" (*CD* III/4, 242). Barth's unwillingness to allow personhood to be conditioned by parenthood *or* childhood means that he must construct the latter out of the former—clearly a difficult task.

118. *CD* IV/4, 185.

"Christian life cannot be inherited as blood, gifts, characteristics and inclinations are inherited." Yet Christian children who are "born and brought up in the community of Jesus Christ" enjoy "a very special *praevenire* of the grace of God."[119] As the "presuppositions" to the child's life, God honours the parents who honour Him by extending Christ's to their children in an objective way, even without their conversion.[120] As Barth observes, Paul does not take into account any counter-influence on the part of the non-Christian parent, so "confident was he of the holy power of Jesus Christ and also of the Christian!"[121]

At the same time, this vicarious honour might go the other direction as well, so that the honour that children receive extends to their parents. Where parents are the presupposition to the child, the child is a "figure" of the parents' whole life-history—a visible manifestation of it.[122] In this way, the child's life retrospectively sheds light on the parents': the significance of the presupposition is only known when the child is born and dies. Parenthood becomes "an integral part of [the parents'] existence," yet as an inherently relational trait, its meaning and content are contingent upon the way the child's life goes.[123] In this way, the child embodies the parents' "external honour," their "outer reputation." When the child lives in correspondence to God's commands, the honour the child receives remains extrinsic to the parents, just as its ultimate source remains extrinsic to the child. Their child is the one who lives, not they, so they have no more grounds to claim the child's honour for themselves than the child has for claiming their honour as

---

119. Ibid., 183–4.

120. Barth writes that parents are the "presupposition and starting-point of [the child's] whole life history" (*CD* III/4, 241). Barth argues later that the "presupposition" names the specific context in which the divine command is heard, and without attention to which the divine command cannot be properly heard. The presupposition of one's historical location is not accidental, but is "prepared for [an individual] in wisdom and goodness." But it is *only* a presupposition—a "cradle." An individual must not simply accept the education, social context, spirit of the age, and so on that they are given, but consciously adopt (or question) them as they "represent to him the opportunity which he is given." Humanity is summoned *within* that opportunity by the command of God, which calls humanity to "freedom, reflection and resolution" and a deed that "will transcend the previous form of his situation" (*CD* III/4, 622).

121. *CD* IV/4, 185. One danger of describing parents as the divinely ordained presuppositions to the child is that it might entail Mary's agency precedes and prepares for Christ on its own initiative. Such an implication would entail that she has a natural capacity for God, overturning a core tenet of Barth's dogmatic theology. Yet this implication does not have to follow. Barth's account of parental honour does not mean that parents are *themselves* the source of the light that falls on the child through them: parents bear witness to the fact that the child is immediately derived from God, and in that way extend an "actual sanctifying power" to the child. The same self-abnegating "pointing" that Mary demonstrates lies at the core of parenthood, as well.

122. *CD* III/4, 241.

123. Ibid.

his own. Yet as the child is a figure of their life-history, the quality of the child's life seems to have some bearing on the honour the parents are ascribed, in a way similar to how their honourable action prepares the way for the child.

The vicariousness of honour that Barth permits in the case of parents and children must qualify his rejection of the honour that is given to Mary for her role in the Incarnation. As noted in the previous chapter, Barth argues that the honour we give to God is strictly non-reciprocal: humanity can give "honour only to Him and never, however indirectly, to himself as well."[124] The indirect, vicarious ascription of honour too easily turns it into our self-possession and inclines us to elevate Mary to a plane equal to Christ. Ironically, though, honouring parents vicariously on the basis of their role as God's representatives more effectively underscores Mary's dependence on Christ than denying reciprocity outright. God posits creation as a presupposition for the sake of Christ's Incarnation—and Mary's *fiat* is a response to God's initiative in the Annunciation. Christ's conception by the Spirit and life as a human becomes a figure of Mary's life, as He honours the Father through honouring her. The honour God bestows upon Mary (and Joseph) must be answered by our honouring of the same. Without such an account, Barth's doctrine of creation really does risk dissolving into air.

The honour that children can bring to their parents might tempt us to instrumentalize children, reducing them to projects for parents' self-aggrandizement and satisfaction. Barth's inclusion of modesty gives no quarter to such impulses. The honour of procreative parenthood includes their agency, but is dependent upon the honour God gives them in creating new human life. Because procreative agency is dependent for its fulfillment upon God's blessing in this way, the honour that procreative parents feel, assert, and are given must incorporate modesty and its attendant virtues of gratitude, humility, and humor. Parents cannot assert their own honour through the child, as the Corinthians did with Paul and Apollos, and the honour they enjoy as parents is not founded upon their own egoistic attachment to their "flesh and blood." Parents are only honourable when they recognize and respect the limits God has placed upon their agency in the child's life: they are permitted and commanded to conform to God's life, but can do no more for the child than that. Honouring parents on the basis of their child puts them in the second place, as they are only honourable for the contents of the child's life if they genuinely embodied the modesty that honourable conduct requires. This modesty-constraint, then, keeps honour from being used to justify reducing children to a project of the parents' aspirations for glory or reducing them to an extension of the parents' lives.[125]

---

124. Ibid., 146. Barth reiterates this judgment in IV/2: "It was to safeguard this unity of the person of Jesus Christ as the Son of God and Son of Man (as was necessary against Nestorious) that the title 'mother of God') ... was ascribed to Mary—not to her own honour, but to that of Jesus Christ—at the Council of Ephesus in 431." (IV/2, 71).

125. This is not to untether honour from the causal relation of parents and children, but rather to ensure that the causal relation does not become an independent basis or grounds

The socially mediated and divinely established honour of participating through action and suffering in the miracle and mystery of the formation of human life supplies a theologically animated reason to pursue parenthood through procreating. Barth objects to honour becoming an aspirational category: it is not the sort of good that ought to be self-consciously pursued, even while it is inevitable that humans will seek it. And while Barth contends that we need to assert our honour, it must remain bound by modesty. Such constraints limit how the honour of procreative parenthood might function as a reason to procreate for deliberating parents. If nothing else, Barth's construal of what happens in procreating comes near to recapitulating Barth's account of the "blessing" that animals need to bring their ventures to fruition by placing the gift of human life in God's hands. At the same time, prospective parents are permitted to stand in "readiness" for God's gift of children.[126] "Readiness" for children acknowledges the dual, divine-human agency required for procreating and the quality of sexual intercourse has as an "offer" from God: parents engage in procreative activity for the sake of the limited, unrepeatable opportunity to be a recipient of God's offer of human life and thus bear the honour He bestows upon those to whom He entrusts such a gift. The readiness for children is reasonable, as parenthood is an honourable vocation: honour's unapologetically eudaemonistic dimension indicates that parenthood contributes to the flourishing of those who enjoy it. Yet in standing ready for parenthood through acts that open themselves to God's offer of new life, couples do not regard the honour of procreative parenthood as a claim, right, or assertion of their own value. The pursuit of procreative parenthood must be modest. At bottom, a Barthian defense of procreative parenthood treats it as a manifestation of God's honouring of humanity that happens when humanity stands ready for such an honour through a confidence in life grounded in faith. Together with Barth's contention that our affirmation of life must include our animal impulses unless we hear a divine command to the contrary, a strong presumption on behalf of pro-natalism seems warranted from within his theological framework: those who marry are to stand in readiness to procreate not reluctantly, but gladly, in hopes that the widened sphere of their marital fellowship will come to them through God's invitation to be present in action and suffering at the miracle of His creative activity in the form of a person who bears their own flesh and blood.

---

for honour. To put the point in Barthian terms, the causal relation is only the "external grounds" of honour, while honour is the "inner basis" of the causal relation. Tying honour to causality together in this way helps explain why the sense of honour might dissipate as the causal relations become less clear (such that great-grandparents might be honoured, but distant great-great uncles might not be in the same way).

126. "Marriage as life-partnership implies, of course, an inner readiness for children and therefore for the family to the extent that it is full sexual communion." *CD* III/4, 189.

Conclusion

God has glorified himself in Jesus Christ and answered the ethical question on our behalf. But we have not yet honoured Him in time as our grateful response to His grace. Though Barth contends that time will come to an end, the eschaton is not yet. The time of the church has its own distinct glory, and the eternalization of our lives in God means our action here and now has the highest possible stakes for us. To be a creature means to be "prepared for the place where [God's] honour dwells."[127] God pre-eminently honours humanity in the Incarnation of Jesus Christ, in which God invites and summons us into communion and fellowship with Himself—calling us into the honour of His service, which clarifies and confirms the weight and distinction as creatures who are honoured as such by God.[128] The divine command does not undermine nature, but answers and responds to it, crystallizing its significance so that we are capable of recognizing our nature in the command of God.

The honour that God gives to humanity in Jesus Christ thus illuminates the nature of ordinary procreative activity, even as Barth's account of ordinary procreation allows us to reconstruct his Mariology. The miracle of the Virgin Birth underscores that in every case of new human life, God has acted to bring a new person into the world—even when He did not command the parents to do so. At the same time, humanity participates in ordinary conception and labor through "action and suffering." The honour we give parents for their presence for God's work is emblematic of the honour that creation has as a real and distinct work of God. Honouring Mary because Christ's life is the "figure" of her own does not entail an invidious honouring of ourselves any more than children honouring God by honouring their parents entails an invidious reciprocal endorsement of their own lives. The eccentric account of honour that Barth develops in his doctrine of creation permits its assertion, even as his eccentric account of life in the same volume required that it be "affirmed and willed by man" through a "determination and readiness for action in the direction of its confirmation."[129] In honouring Mary as the presupposition for His life, Christ honours creation not as an independent and autonomous reality, but as the gift of God's grace. Mary's suffering in gestation and labor is not vicariously redemptive, in the sense that we are saved by it: rather, it is a natural sign or indication of God's love in reconciliation and redemption. Where Christ's sacrifice is the prototype of such love, the suffering of childbearing is a type.[130]

---

127. *CD* III/1, 364.
128. *CD* III/4, 649–50.
129. Ibid., 341.
130. There is biblical warrant for understanding birth this way. John 16:21 uses labor and childbirth as analogues for Christ's death and resurrection. But there is also some basis in Barth's thought: he puts the sign of the Virgin Birth on par with the sign of the Empty Tomb, a correlation that is strengthened if Mary's suffering and childbirth are

In a similar manner, the "readiness" for procreation that couples are permitted to have through their "confidence of life" is not equivalent to the readiness for grace that Barth saw as grounding Roman Catholic Mariology.[131] While couples are permitted (and might be exhorted) to stand ready for God's action in honouring them with a child who bears their flesh and blood, this readiness is neither intrinsically grounded nor equivalent to the readiness for God's revelation to them in Jesus Christ. The grace of creation and redemption are the same in this respect, namely, that we cannot bring them about ourselves. The Virgin Birth and ordinary procreation both underscore the limits of human control and agency in generating new life. Yet a readiness for the grace of natural procreation does not entail a natural readiness for the grace of redemption or a natural capacity for God: it only means that it is natural for life to beget more life. In standing ready to do so, humans look to the "blessing" of divine action that we naturally need to bring our works to fruition (as Barth argued in *Dogmatics* III/1). God's "blessing" on fertility is required because of the intrinsic fragility of human procreative action. God honours our vulnerability in the Incarnation, even as prospective parents honour the Incarnation when they modestly stand ready to receive God's offer of a new unrepeatable life.

Our interest in the good of being honoured by God in this way is not freestanding or independent: the honour of God's affirmation of human life falls upon us as a light from above, at the incarnation of Jesus Christ. Our "readiness" for the honour of being present in "action and suffering" for God's action is not a response to the value of "life" as an independent principle, but is animated by a "confidence in life grounded *in faith*," in which we answer the Spirit's secret

---

an anthropological analogue to Christ's death and resurrection. The origins and ends of Christ's life constitute a "single sign," so that the miracle of Christmas and the miracle of the empty tomb belong together. (*CD* I/2, 182–4). In his doctrine of providence (discussed above, Chapter 5), Barth argues that the "spiritual relationship of the creature in the covenant of grace is the dominant pattern or type of what God does when He preserves creation as such in being," and that God maintains the existence of the creature "in a way which is not parallel but corresponds to the significance which it acquires in this covenant" (*CD* III/4, 63, 64–5). My description of procreation here is one attempt to expand on this picture, even if I also frame it as an instance of the love that God shows in the eschaton— which Barth does not.

131. "This is what is meant by Mariology: Mary affirming grace on the basis of grace *loco totius humanitatis*; in this Mary, therefore, the divine *Sophia* dwelling in the world apart from the incarnation of the Logos; this *sophia* in the sense of the creature's openness or readiness for its God." Barth, *CD* I/2, 145.

affirmation of our life with our own "yes." God has honoured humanity in the Incarnation, which means that the honour of God's action in confirming life through procreation is good for everyone, regardless of whether they recognize the proper theological basis on which it rests. Yet as it does rest on that basis, the honour of being present for God's action in such an immediate way provides a strong reason to pursue parenthood by undertaking the definite aim and venture in love of conceiving and giving birth.

CONCLUSION

How confident should we be in life, and so in our reasons to procreate? Barth's theocentric, procreative fideism is grounded in our recognition of the offer God has made to us to know Him in time, an offer that corresponds to the opportunity to be present in "action and suffering" in His creation of a new person who bears His image and our flesh and blood. As we have seen, even though Barth is a divine command theorist, our "animal impulses" deserve a "conditional respect" that gives their use a presumptive validity until we hear a clear command to the contrary from God.[1] This presumption in favor of procreating, though, is neither absolute nor uncritical. On the one side, Barth seems to think there are times when the church's exhortation to reject nihilism and despair about life could take a distinctly pro-natalist form. On the other side, this pro-natalism cannot be reified into an absolute obligation, much less be transformed into the basis for a nationalist project. As I noted at the outset of Chapter 4, Barth's endorsement of Christian hope in the aftermath of the Second World War is hardly triumphalistic: Christians are only enabled to "live a *little more* positively, joyfully, patiently, thankfully and confidently than the reverse."[2]

Barth's pro-natalism is more stable than one which can be philosophically grounded, though. As we saw in Chapter 1, David Heyd recognizes the difficulty of attaining some sort of neutral, non-evaluative standpoint from which we might ground our reasons to procreate and concludes that there is no theoretical difference between procreating and allowing the species to die out. Jeff McMahan's argument indicates that neutrality about procreating leads to a *de facto* anti-natalism and generates puzzles that he thinks so profound that they threaten moral realism. Even those philosophers sympathetic with procreating assume a neutral position toward the practice and embrace a corresponding default presumption against it. While few philosophers dispute that parenthood is a valuable form of life, and so can ground reasons to enter into it, the arguments for why we should do so through procreation nearly all bottom out in convention. As Niko Kolodny observes, the "significance, if any, of biological relationships lies

---

1. Barth, *CD* III/4, 346.
2. Barth, "The Christian Message in Europe Today," 179.

in the significance, if any, of biology to personal identity."[3] But the difficulty of accounting for the value of biology in a parental context proves enormous: regard such bonds as only conventionally important and it becomes a question as to why we should preserve them; inflate their value, and one risks establishing an invidious inequality between birth and adoptive children. Philosophical efforts to frame life as a "gift" underscore the way generating human life lies beyond the reach of our intentions (though not our intentional action). Yet the realities of embryo death also highlight the limitations of those philosophically optimistic accounts, as they call into question the reliability of the judgment that the broad background of "nature" is disposed in our favor after all. The contest of intuitions and ambiguities of "weighing" reasons in moral philosophy is intractable: even David Benatar, that most strident of philosophical pessimists, gets lost amidst the morass of intuitions, helping himself to them when they aid his case and rejecting them when they do not.

By contrast, Barth's "Christian optimism" is secured by Jesus Christ's fundamental "yes" to creation, which entails that creation is a benefit and that its form is adapted to the covenant. The meaning, content, and significance of creation are disclosed by Jesus Christ—which both ensures that creation is real and that it is good. Though the non-neutrality of creation cannot ground a natural theology, Barth does allow that everyone has an inarticulate knowledge of certain moral norms (like the prohibition on murder). Covenant and creation are distinct but united, interdependent but not confused. This account of creation forms the broad theological backdrop against which our assessment of life's theological significance is made: Christian optimism is more stable than philosophical variations precisely because it can take evils more seriously than they can. And Christian optimism is more consistent than philosophical pessimisms, which invariably fail to acknowledge the default affirmation of life that constitutes both individuals' and the species' practical orientations toward the world. As Barth notes, grounding creation in Jesus Christ allows us to "live and die on the basis of this hypothesis."[4]

The covenant's revelation of creation's meaning and content forms a prototype for a pattern of reasoning that Barth employs in his theological anthropology and his treatment of procreation. While the Holy Spirit is the "event of the gift of life," our constitution in time bears secret and silent witness to our life before God.[5] On the one hand, our basic form of humanity as male and female is adapted to the covenant. On the other hand, the "constant" of our limits at birth and death draws us into immediate contact with God and heightens our awareness of our need for His grace. This intensification of human life within its limits means that it is especially worthy of honour (which animates Barth's treatment of the subject at the end of his doctrine of creation), as it indicates that life is not simply a sequence of opportunities but a discrete offer from God. It also structures

---

3. Ibid., 73.
4. Barth, *CD* III/1, 5.
5. *CD* III/2, 359.

Barth's sexual ethics: prospective parents must take seriously the fact that such an offer is made by God in determining whether to use contraception, an offer in which God bestows the honour of being present in "action and suffering" for God's work in creating a new human life who bears the parents' flesh and blood. Barth's theocentric account of creation and parenthood simultaneously relativizes the impulse to base relationships on genealogy and blood and re-establishes them on firmer ground. While parenthood is constituted by the spiritual mission of conforming our action to God's as His representatives to the children, God's action in redemption forms the "original process" that shows that parenthood and procreation belong together.[6]

Barth's decision to treat procreation as an independent realm from marriage is (astonishingly) consistent across his corpus, yet it entails that procreating's theological significance is exclusively limited to its role in creation and providence. As we saw in Chapter 5, Barth's exposition of the first creation narrative frames procreation as a natural sign of hope in God and an indicator of humanity's need for God's blessing to accomplish our aims. But his construal of the second creation account underscores that male and female in marriage are complete in themselves; parenthood forms a distinct and independent sphere of ethical reflection. This latter approach comports with Barth's treatment of procreation in III/4, where marriage is given an eschatological consecration while procreation is treated as a natural (and optional) expansion of marriage. God continues to give humanity "time, space and opportunity" in His providence—but the consummation of Christ and the church puts an end to time, which dissolves the obligation to procreate and ensures procreation remains an exclusively natural phenomenon. Time continues after the advent of Christ, and Barth contends that it has its own distinct glory. Yet procreating is a sign of God's patience, and in an important respect no longer signifies the hope for the eschaton that marks the Christian's existence.

Such an account seems to be animated by Barth's aversion not only to what he takes to be a Roman Catholic pro-natalism, but specifically to Mariology. As I noted in Chapter 7, Barth's account of the Virgin Birth underscores God's action and humanity's passivity and emphasizes the independence of Christ's humanity (via the anhypostatic/enhypostatic union) from what he inherits from Mary. Barth's relativization of procreative bonds in his treatment of humanity's *whence* comports with this picture, as Barth argues that our origins are found exclusively in God through baptism after the advent of the Christ rather than in the *prius* of parents, as in Israel. At the same time, Barth's ethics of parenthood contends that the eschatologically oriented "deliberate orphanhood" reestablishes and confirms the parent–child bond, as it is a paradoxical form of the honour that children owe to parents. The eschatological disclosure of Christ can be understood as a confirmation and clarification of what is true in creation.[7] Similarly, Barth's Christocentric account of Mary offers a way of construing her procreative agency

---

6. Barth, *CD* III/4, 247.

7. Though I did not include it in the main text, this parallels Barth's treatment of miracles as complementary clarifications of nature as I outlined it in Chapter 7, note 126.

as a proleptic response to God's eschatological disclosure in Christ, which would entail that giving birth would have an eschatological confirmation akin to that which Barth thinks marriage has—if we reject Barth's contention that time and the creature's existence come to an end in God's eternal preservation of us, that is.

Even if procreation has an eschatological consecration, its theological meaning is distinct from the reasons particular couples might have to procreate. As we saw in Chapter 6, Barth's defense of "respect for life" requires that we honour the constitution God has given us, which introduces a self-referential dimension to the command of God. Barth's unremittingly theocentric account of life, which points to the Spirit as the basis and grounds for our participation in it, ensures that the honour we owe to our own bodies does not become invidiously egoistic. Instead, the divine command to honour our life collapses any real distinction between egoism and altruism, by enjoining us to see our own life in solidarity with all those who are like us. This inclusion of a eudaimonistic dimension in Barth's divine command ethics becomes more prominent in his treatment of honour, which occupied us in Chapter 8. While the aspiration to expand and protect our honour is inevitable, Barth deflates such anxieties through making honour thoroughgoingly theocentric and correspondingly infusing it with modesty, the virtue that names the gratitude, humility, and humor that mark off a distinctively Christian construal of honour. We must be indifferent to our own honour even when asserting it—yet Barth contends that we *need* to assert our honour, and that doing so is not the invidious pride he elsewhere critiques. Barth's account seems to leave intact the possibility of honouring others (like parents) and permits vicariously honouring third parties for their modesty ("Friend, come up higher!"). Such an account requires a further reconfiguration of Mary in Barth's theology, as it is precisely her self-abnegation in pointing exclusively toward Christ that makes her an honourable figure for us.

The honour that completes life also supplies reasons to procreate—or, rather, to stand in "readiness" to procreate, to *try* to procreate, which is as much as we can do. In Barth's framework, the honour that God gives humanity makes our action a meaningful response to God's disclosure of His glory in time. This honour is especially acute in our procreative agency: God honours procreative parents with the unrepeatable offer to be present for His generation of an irreplaceable life in an act that will signify God's great work of creation to the child. While parents are emphatically not the child's Creator, it is their peculiar honour that their flesh and blood has been adapted to God's service in creating a new human life. The dual agency at work in procreation grounds its peculiar value, rather than the identification of blood or biology that conception and birth establish. As this honour is given by God alone, we can only remain ready for it. Such a readiness involves acknowledging and affirming parenthood's content as the permission and obligation to be God's representatives to the child and be honoured as such by them. And it means acknowledging that the child is a "figure" of parents' lives, which makes the social form of their honour in some sense dependent on the child. In both respects, the honour of parenthood requires modesty: parents must not assert their status as God's representatives to gain leverage over the child or instrumentalize their children to vicariously enhance their own honour. Instead, parents must point away from themselves toward God in the first place, and toward their children in the second. In the Christological context, Mary remains in a secondary place to Christ, even while a real—if derivative—reciprocal glory extends from child to parent.[8] Though prospective parents are not permitted to anxiously grasp after the honour of being present for God's action in creating new life, we are responsible to make ourselves ready to receive it and to not prevent it when God would otherwise give it.

While Barth is clear that creation can never be merely natural, this reconstructed Barth*ian* fideism imbues humanity's procreative powers with a significance they otherwise lack on his account by drawing them more closely into contact with the doctrines of redemption and reconciliation. While Barth contends that birth and death for the individual correspond to God's great actions of creation and consummation, the "action and suffering" involved in bringing life into the world can also serve as a type of Christ's work in creation, redemption, and the resurrection. Childbirth is a blessing from God: it indicates the consummation of creation through the pains and travail of human labor—of Christ in the work of new creation and of the woman in the work of procreation. By aiming at that which is beyond human control, procreative actions tacitly and unwittingly embody a natural correlate to the faith that is disclosed in baptism—a faith that is transformed into hope when procreative agency is frustrated and involuntarily childlessness arises.

Developing this procreative fideism out of Barth's theology risks reinscribing the Roman Catholic natural theology that Barth argued Mariology embodied, not to mention lending support to ethno-nationalist pro-natalisms like those Barth opposed. Regarding the first, if Mary's work in the incarnation does give childbirth an eschatological consecration (and is a complement and clarification of ordinary procreation), it does not follow that her readiness to be present for God's action in Christ indicates a natural theology. Nor does it mean that our readiness for natural procreation entails such a framework, either. While such a view might generate something nearer to a Roman Catholic pro-natalism, it is still compatible with the obligation to procreate being dissolved and the corresponding diminishment of anxiety about our lineage and genealogy. Regarding the second, nothing about the account proffered here entails that the "family" is a discrete object of theological reflection, much less that the ties of genealogy can be reified and extended farther through the "clan" and into a people who would compose a nation. While Barth's repudiation of infant baptism is unpopular even among his admirers, procreative

---

8. The difficulties of understanding how a mother might be secondary in honour, even if prior in time, are familiar ones for Barth, for whom the first Adam is secondary in honour but prior in time. Perhaps the best distillation of this modified Barthian Mariology is from Matthew Bridges' description of Jesus in *Crown Him with Many Crowns*: "Fruit of the mystic Rose, As of that Rose the Stem."

fideism leaves it untouched—and thus preserves it as a bulwark against reducing the church to a natural community like a family.

Instead, procreative fideism describes the theological and anthropological landscape in which Christians make procreative decisions. It offers a thick description of the moral world the church inhabits and so offers a theological basis for the church's exhortation to take seriously the "confidence in life" Christians are called to have in light of Jesus Christ's work reconciling creation and our conformity to it through the Holy Spirit. The theological basis for the church's exhortation to be "confident in life" is still general: open questions remain about how casuistical judgments can be made about the conditions in which such exhortation is necessary and what kinds of technological aids for conceiving and giving birth might be licit. The most one can say from within Barth's divine command framework is that the "readiness" for children establishes a strong skepticism about contraceptive practices (as, in fact, Barth does say). Additionally, the modesty Barth builds into his account of honour, his emphasis on God's action in generating life, and the claim that such a benefit is unavailable to human action could plausibly generate a similar skepticism about artificial reproductive technologies that strive to bring procreative agency within the purview of (positive) human control. These types of derivations, though, involve questions of health and technology that deserve independent consideration. My central aim of unpacking this Barthian procreative fideism is to explore its theological presuppositions and contours to offer some kind of answer to the "weird, distorted question" (in Anscombe's memorable phrase) of why Christians, or anyone else, should have children.

Barth among the Moral Philosophers, Revisited

The truthfulness of procreative fideism is not determined by whether it satisfies moral philosophy's criteria for persuasiveness, but whether it faithfully conforms to the revelation of Jesus Christ as attested to in Scripture. Though Barth maintains his opposition to natural theology throughout his *Church Dogmatics,* at many points he also argues that those outside the faith unwittingly participate in the truth of God's creation as it has been revealed and confirmed in the covenant. Procreative fideism is the antithesis of procreative skepticism—but with a foundation that is secured much more deeply and broadly than the intuitions beneath "procreative optimism." The revelation of Jesus Christ is both the ontic and the epistemic basis for our understanding of creation and human nature, but Barth's affirmation that there is such a thing as human nature supplies grounds for expecting some kind of convergence between the moral judgements we make in light of the Gospel and those we undertake based on direct consideration of the world. To that extent, a theologically grounded pro-natalism calls people to become aware of the ways in which their lives presuppose the goodness of God's creation and their need for Him, wakening them to the Gospel by means of the Gospel.

In that light, it is not surprising that the procreative fideism that I developed through Barth's account resonates at several points with moral philosophy's discussion of the questions of procreation and parenthood. For one, framing procreative agency as a "venture in faith" that aims at what is unavailable to human control clearly recapitulates Chapter 3's discussion of the involuntariness *within* and *of* the procreative process. Jürgen Habermas even uses the same term Barth does (*Unverfügbares*) to name the unavailability of human nature to genetic editing.[9] My discussion of why we can only intend *to try* to procreate helps specify what is otherwise elusive in Barth's account. And there are other moments of convergence. Barth's discussion of life at its limits offers interesting possibilities for dialogue with the role non-existence plays in moral philosophy's discussions of procreative ethics. David Benatar's argument requires comparing a life to its non-existence, which alternately heightens or diminishes our assessment of its value. Barth is acutely aware of the heightened stakes such a comparison seems to generate; yet he also argues the positive value of our life is secured only when we encounter God at our limits, rather than when we compare our lives to non-existence *per se*. Barth's theocentric framework thus escapes evaluating life by balancing the harms and benefits while also avoiding reducing our affirmation of life to the brute assertion that existence is superior to non-existence.[10]

In many respects, procreative fideism inverts the justificatory threshold for procreating that philosophers adopt—yet, ironically, manages to save more ordinary intuitions and practices than philosophical defenses of procreative optimism do. For instance, procreative fideism defends a presumptive affirmation of procreation's licitness on the basis of the honour we owe to our animal capacities, which are apt to and correspond to the covenant. Such a stance avoids the procreative neutrality that philosophical discussions struggle to escape and comports well with the default practice of generating new life. Barth raises the epistemic threshold for what kind of view we should accept by arguing that we need an account of the world we can "live and die on." Yet his default presumption in favor of procreation does not minimize the seriousness or gravity of suffering. If Barth manages to hold both positions together, his account would satisfy ordinary practices and intuitions better than the lowered epistemic threshold that many philosophers adopt to secure their view. Similarly, Barth's argument that the union of procreative and social parenthood is grounded in the "original process" of God's work of redemption offers a more satisfactory and stable explanation for why we keep procreative parents together with their children. Moral philosophy's defenses of the value of procreative bonds almost universally bottom-out in an assertion of their conventionality, which undermines their stability. By correlating them to baptism, Barth gives such bonds a permanence that helps explain why

---

9. See Gerald McKenny, *Biotechnology, Human Nature, and Christian Ethics* (Cambridge: Cambridge University Press, 2018), 33; Habermas, *The Future of Human Nature*, 27.

10. Meilaender's theologically informed argument contends that our gratitude for existence is founded upon the fact that there is something rather than nothing: "Before the sheer wonder of existence we must simply bend the knee." See Meilaender, *Should We Live*, 69.

attempts to revise our ordinary practices of keeping parents and children together are so troubling. Remember Niko Kolodny's judgment that the value we put on procreative bonds is commensurate with the value we place on biology for personal identity. Barth maximizes that value by arguing that humanity's constitution bears secret witness to God's action in the covenant. Procreative fideism has more to say about the origin and content of procreative bonds than the philosophical assertions that procreative parenthood is valuable because of its (vague and underspecified) "biological joys."[11]

At the same time, Barth's view of parenthood escapes the dilemma of establishing invidious inequalities between adopted and procreated children. Procreative parenthood exceeds adoptive parenthood with respect to the transparency of divine action in bringing a child into a marriage, and with respect to the peculiar opportunity it affords parents to be present for God's work in creating a new individual who shares their flesh and blood. In a crucial sense, the child is *not* from their parents on Barth's view, but from God. While the means of entry into the family might be distinct, the adopted and procreated child similarly enter it from the outside, as it were. Biological parenthood might be more transparent in its reference to God's action in creation, but adoptive parenthood brings into focus parents' responsibility to conform their actions to God in order to legitimate the honour children owe them. In that way, it more transparently refers to God's work in reconciliation. Moreover, adoptive parenthood underscores that the "original process" which grounds keeping procreation and parenthood together is the non-biological work of baptism. In that respect, adoption and procreation are distinct ways of entering into a family but equal forms of parenthood. This gives prospective parents distinct reasons to procreate without establishing an invidious hierarchy or inequality that subordinates adoptive children.

At the same time, it is important to underscore that the account of procreative fideism on offer is still underspecified. Its most serious limitation is that it does not name a threshold or criterion of well-being that would make it irresponsible to create an individual. Barth's Christocentric understanding of creation provides a plausible response to theodicy problems and an attractive explanation for why those under conditions of extreme deprivation or suffering still retain human dignity. Yet it also raises the possibility that suffering can never generate a reason against creating, since the covenant and the resurrection mean goodness endures despite sin and sorrow. On Barth's view, humans can reject God's "offer" of a child. We can also go wrong in creating a child through failing to respect the marital union or their health. But Barth says nothing about whether it is licit to intentionally undertake a procreative act when we have reason to think the child's suffering would be considerable. Procreative fideism thus seems to suffer from all the problems any other form of fideism suffers from: it eliminates the possibility of decisive objections and so undermines reason itself. Yet such a limitation is

---

11. In the face of existing obligations to adopt, the possibility of discovering a child shares his mother's mannerisms or nose hardly seems like a weighty reason to procreate.

not necessarily fatal to the account offered here. After all, Barth *does* think there are situations where procreating is imprudent and Christians are permitted to be only a "little more" confident in life than others. Instead, such worries indicate the project's current incompleteness.[12]

The Honour and Joy of Procreating

I conclude, then, by naming one final dimension of procreative fideism—and one final modification to Barth's account. As we saw, Barth specifies procreative parenthood around honour and obligation, both of which are necessary for procreative parents to feel. One cannot "assume the burden of obligation without feeling joy in the accompanying honour," nor can one "rejoice in the honour without taking to heart the seriousness of the obligation."[13] The possibility of rejoicing in such an honour requires setting off such procreative fideism from a Pollyannish optimism that might try to sound similar notes. For Barth, the life that parents have confidence in is not *merely* or even *only* biological life. It is, instead, the "will for joy, delight and happiness." Joy is a moment of temporal arrest, a suspension of time that happens when we attain our goal. Joy happens when life momentarily "gives [an individual] no more trouble but offers itself as a gift."[14] Joy lies beyond human control, as procreating does—but, like procreation, the Christian "should continually hold himself in readiness for joy" rather than leave it to chance. Our readiness for joy means our expectation that "life will reveal itself as God's gift of grace" and that there will be "provisional fulfilments of its meaning and intention as movement."[15] Such an expectation means action: it is ours to "create opportunities for [real joy] in anticipatory joy, but we cannot create or construct or produce or force it by various plans and measures."[16]

Barth's depiction of joy incorporates the critiques he had lodged against eighteenth-century optimism at the end of *Church Dogmatics* III/1. Joy does not mean avoiding the world's harshness, as optimism does, but leads to an "intensification, strengthening, deepening and elevation of the whole awareness of life which is necessarily more than joy."[17] There is no looking away from creation's shadow side here: when bounded by joy, the droughts that invariably afflict humankind "serve to fresh, console and encourage" us.[18] As our little fulfillments of joy here and now are "reflections of the great fulfillment" that has taken place

---

12. One might plausibly turn to his account of health and the ethics of resisting illness that he develops in his treatment of life for resources to expand his reasoning.
13. *CD* III/4, 277.
14. Ibid., 376.
15. Ibid., 376–7.
16. Ibid., 379.
17. Ibid., 382.
18. Ibid.

in Christ's death and resurrection, the true test for our joy is that we "do not evade the shadow of the cross of Jesus Christ and are not unwilling to be genuinely joyful even as we bear the sorrows laid upon us."[19] The "little fulfillments" of joy are real, but provisional and anticipatory: they must be received with gratitude, but only prefigure the joy we have in the "definitive revelation of the fulfilment of life accomplished for us and addressed to us by God."[20] Joy is faith sustained by hope.

Here, then, lies final addition to procreative fideism—and the final modification to Barth's account of procreation. Where childbirth is a figure or type of the resurrection, and so receives the same eschatological consecration as marriage, it becomes for the parents a provisional and anticipatory joy of the great joy they will know in the consummation of Christ and the church. Such joy is distinct from the "biological joys" moral philosophers posited to explain a preference for procreation. Instead, it is tied to the recognition that God's act of giving life corresponds to His action in the resurrection. As the arrival of joy lies beyond human control, so the creation of the child remains primarily and properly the act of God. Whence, then, the modification? Barth acknowledges that procreation still happens that the "joy of parenthood should still have a place."[21] Yet as we saw, his description of God's attitude toward procreation is more tepid: it is "under God's longsuffering and patience, and is due to His mercy, that in these last days [procreation] may still take place." The gap between the human and divine attitudes Barth names is striking, and worth rejecting. If the honour of procreative parents falls upon them from God, so must their joy. Procreation continues after the resurrection because God delights in abundantly blessing creation by extending His unique and unrepeatable offer of life to new humans who share the flesh and blood of their parents. In giving procreation to humanity, God makes visible the eternal *and* endless joy that the church will know when we are united at last with His own abundant life. Those who actively wait in readiness to be honoured thus by God joyfully echo God's own joyful "yes" to creation. On this basis they stand ready for the blessing of new life that only God can bestow.

---

19. Ibid., 383.
20. Ibid., 385.
21. Ibid., 266.

BIBLIOGRAPHY

Adams, Robert. "Must God Create the Best?" *Philosophical Review* 81, no. 3 (1972): 317–32.

Anderson, Matthew Lee. "Anti-Abortionist Action Theory and the Asymmetry between Spontaneous and Induced Abortions." *The Journal of Medicine and Philosophy: A Forum for Bioethics and Philosophy of Medicine* 48, no. 3 (May 16, 2023): 209–24.

Anderson, Matthew Lee. "What the State Owes 'Bastards': A Modest Critique of Modest One-Child Policies." *Journal of Applied Philosophy* 37, no. 3 (July 2020): 393–407.

Anscombe, G. E. M. *Intention*. 2nd ed. Cambridge, MA: Harvard University Press, 2000.

Anscombe, G. E. M. "On Humanae Vitae." In *Faith in a Hard Ground: Essays on Religion, Philosophy, and Ethics*, edited by Mary Geach and Luke Gormally, 192–8. Exeter: Imprint Academic, 2008.

Anscombe, G. E. M. "Why Have Children?" *Proceedings of the American Catholic Philosophical Association* 63 (1989): 48–53.

Archard, David, and Benatar David, eds. *Procreation and Parenthood: The Ethics of Bearing and Rearing Children*. Oxford: Oxford University Press, 2010.

Aung, Salai Hla. *The Doctrine of Creation in the Theology of Barth, Moltmann and Pannenberg: Creation in Theological, Ecological and Philosophical-Scientific Perspektive*. Regensburg: Roderer Verlag, 1998.

Austin, Michael W. *Conceptions of Parenthood: Ethics and the Family*. Ashgate Studies in Applied Ethics. Aldershot: Ashgate, 2007.

Balboa, Jaime Ronaldo. "'Church Dogmatics,' Natural Theology, and the Slippery Slope of 'Geschlecht': A Constructivist-Gay Liberationist Reading of Barth." *Journal of the American Academy of Religion* 66, no. 4 (1998): 771–89.

von Balthasar, Has Urs. *The Theology of Karl Barth*. Translated by Edward T. Oakes. San Francisco: Ignatius, 1992.

Banner, Michael. *The Ethics of Everyday Life: Moral Theology, Social Anthropology, and the Imagination of the Human*. Oxford: Oxford University Press, 2014.

Barth, Karl. *Anselm, Fides Quaerens Intellectum: Anselm's Proof of the Existence of God in the Context of His Theological Scheme*. Pittsburgh Reprint Series 2. Pittsburgh: Pickwick Press, 1985.

Barth, Karl. *Christmas*. Translated by Bernhard Citron. Edinburgh: Oliver and Boyd, 1959.

Barth, Karl. *Church Dogmatics*. Edited by Geoffrey W. Bromiley and Thomas F. Torrance. Translated by Geoffrey W. Bromiley. 2nd ed. Peabody, MA: Hendrickson Publishers, 2010.

Barth, Karl. *Credo: A Presentation of the Chief Problems of Dogmatics with Reference to the Apostles' Creed: Sixteen Lectures Delivered at the University of Utrecht in February and March, 1935*. Translated by J. Strathearn McNab. New York: C. Scribner's Sons, 1936.

Barth, Karl. *Die kirchliche Dogmatik*. Zürich: Theologischer Verlag Zürich, 1980.

Barth, Karl. *Letters 1961–1968*. Edited by Jürgen Fangmeier and Hinrich Stoevesandt. Translated by Geoffrey William Bromiley. Edinburgh: T&T Clark, 1981.

Barth, Karl. "The Christian Message in Europe Today." In *Against the Stream: Shorter Post-War Writings 1946–52,* edited by Ronald Smith, 165–80. London: SCM Press, 1952.

Barth, Karl. *The Faith of the Church: A Commentary on the Apostles' Creed According to Calvin's Catechism.* Translated by Gabriel Vahanian. Zürich: Theologischer Verlag Zürich, 1958.

Barth, Karl. *The Great Promise: Luke 1.* Translated by Hans Freund. New York: Philosophical Library, 1963.

Barth, Karl. *Wolfgang Amadeus Mozart.* Eugene, Or: Wipf and Stock, 2003.

Baylis, Francoise, and Carolyn McLeod, eds. *Family-Making: Contemporary Ethical Challenges.* Issues in Biomedical Ethics. New York: Oxford University Press, 2014.

Benagiano, Giuseppe, Manuela Farris, and Gedis Grudzinskas. "Fate of Fertilized Human Oocytes." *Reproductive BioMedicine Online* 21, no. 6 (2010): 732–41.

Benagiano, Giuseppe, Maurizio Mori, Norman Ford, and Gedis Grudzinskas. "Early Pregnancy Wastage: Ethical Considerations." *Reproductive BioMedicine Online* 22, no. 7 (2011): 692–700.

Benatar, David. *Better Never to Have Been: The Harm of Coming into Existence.* Reprint. Oxford: Oxford University Press, 2009.

Benatar, David. "Every Conceivable Harm: A Further Defence of Anti-Natalism." *South African Journal of Philosophy* 31, no. 1 (2012): 128–64.

Benatar, David. "Still Better Never to Have Been: A Reply to (More of) My Critics." *Journal of Ethics* 17, no. 1–2 (2013): 121–51.

Benatar, David, and David Wasserman. *Debating Procreation: Is It Wrong to Reproduce?* Debating Ethics. Oxford: Oxford University Press, 2015.

Berkouwer, G. C. *The Triumph of Grace in the Theology of Karl Barth.* Grand Rapids: Eerdmans, 1956.

Biggar, Nigel. *Aiming to Kill: The Ethics of Suicide and Euthanasia.* Cleveland: Pilgrim Press, 2004.

Biggar, Nigel. "Barth's Trinitarian Ethic." In *The Cambridge Companion to Karl Barth,* edited by John Webster, 212–27. Cambridge Companions to Religion. Cambridge, UK: Cambridge University Press, 2000.

Biggar, Nigel. "Karl Barth's Ethics Revisited." In *Commanding Grace: Studies in Karl Barth's Ethics,* edited by Daniel Migliore, 26–49. Grand Rapids: Eerdmans, 2010.

Biggar, Nigel. *The Hastening that Waits: Karl Barth's Ethics.* Oxford Studies in Theological Ethics. Oxford: Oxford University Press, 1993.

Bishop, Jeffrey. *The Anticipatory Corpse: Medicine, Power, and the Care of the Dying.* Notre Dame Studies in Medical Ethics. Notre Dame: University of Notre Dame Press, 2011.

Blanchard, Kathryn. "The Gift of Contraception: Calvin, Barth, and a Lost Protestant Conversation." *Journal of the Society of Christian Ethics* 27, no. 1 (2007): 225–49.

Bodley-Dangelo, Faye. *Sexual Difference, Gender, and Agency in Karl Barth's Church Dogmatics.* T&T Clark Explorations in Reformed Theology. London: Bloomsbury T&T Clark, 2021.

Brighouse, Harry, and Adam Swift. *Family Values: The Ethics of Parent–Child Relationships.* Princeton: Princeton University Press, 2014.

Busch, Eberhard. *The Great Passion: An Introduction to Karl Barth's Theology.* Edited by Darrell L. Guder and Judith J. Guder. Translated by Geoffrey W. Bromiley. Grand Rapids: Eerdmans, 2004.

Cassidy, James. *God's Time for Us: Barth's Reconciliation of Eternity and Time in Jesus Christ.* Bellingham: Lexham Press, 2016.

Cocksworth, A. J. "Attending to the Sabbath: An Alternative Direction in Karl Barth's Theology of Prayer." *International Journal of Systematic Theology* 13, no. 3 (2011): 251–71.

Conly, Sarah. *One Child: Do We Have a Right to More?* New York: Oxford University Press, 2016.

Cortez, Marc. *Embodied Souls, Ensouled Bodies: An Exercise in Christological Anthropology and Its Significance for the Mind/Body Debate*. T&T Clark Studies in Systematic Theology. London: T&T Clark, 2011.

Dawson, R. Dale. *The Resurrection in Karl Barth*. Barth Studies. Aldershot, England; Burlington, VT: Ashgate Pub, 2007.

Deddo, Gary W. *Karl Barth's Theology of Relations: Trinitarian, Christological, and Human: Towards an Ethic of the Family*. Eugene, OR: Wipf and Stock, 2015.

DeGrazia, David. *Creation Ethics: Reproduction, Genetics, and Quality of Life*. Oxford: Oxford University Press, 2012.

Di Nucci, Ezio. "Embryo Loss and Double Effect." *Journal of Medical Ethics* 39, no. 8 (2013): 537–40.

Dreyer, Yolanda. "Karl Barth's Male–Female Order as Asymmetrical Theoethics." *HTS Teologiese Studies* 63, no. 4 (2007): 1493–521.

Dugan, Kaitlyn, and Philip Gordon Ziegler, eds. *The Finality of the Gospel: Karl Barth and the Tasks of Eschatology*. Studies in Reformed Theology, vol. 43. Leiden; Boston: Brill, 2022.

Dunstan, Andrew, ed. *Karl Barth's Analogy of Beauty: Its Basis and Implications for Theological Aesthetics*. Barth Studies. Abingdon, Oxon; New York: Routledge, 2022.

Ferracioli, Luara. "Procreative-Parenting, Love's Reasons and the Demands of Morality." *Philosophical Quarterly* 68, no. 270 (2018): 77–97.

Fout, Jason A. *Fully Alive: The Glory of God and the Human Creature in Karl Barth, Hans Urs von Balthasar and Theological Exegesis of Scripture*. Paperback ed. London: Bloomsbury T&T Clark, 2016.

Fiddes, Paul. "Mary in the Theology of Karl Barth." In *Mary in Doctrine and Devotion: Papers of the Liverpool Congress, 1989, of the Ecumenical Society of the Blessed Virgin Mary*, edited by Alberic Stacpoole, 111–26. Collegeville, MN: Liturgical Press, 1990.

Friedrich, Daniel. "A Duty to Adopt?" *Journal of Applied Philosophy* 30, no. 1 (2013): 25–39.

Frykberg, Elizabeth. *Karl Barth's Theological Anthropology: An Analogical Critique Regarding Gender Relations*, vol. 1, no. 3. Studies in Reformed Theology and History. Princeton: Princeton Theological Seminary, 1993.

Gabriel, Andrew. *Barth's Doctrine of Creation: Creation, Nature, Jesus, and the Trinity*. Eugene, OR: Cascade Books, 2014.

George, Robert P., and Christopher Tollefsen. *Embryo: A Defense of Human Life*. 2nd ed. Princeton: Witherspoon Institute, 2011.

Gheaus, Anca. "Biological Parenthood: Gestational, Not Genetic." *Australasian Journal of Philosophy* 96, no. 2 (2017): 225–40.

Gheaus, Anca. "The Right to Parent One's Biological Baby." *Journal of Political Philosophy* 20, no. 4 (2012): 432–55.

Gorringe, Timothy. *Karl Barth: Against Hegemony*. Christian Theology in Context. Oxford; New York: Oxford University Press, 1999.

Green, Christopher C. *Doxological Theology: Karl Barth on Divine Providence, Evil and the Angels*. T&T Clark Studies in Systematic Theology, vol. 13. London; New York: T&T Clark International, 2011.

Habermas, Jürgen. *The Future of Human Nature*. Cambridge, UK: Polity, 2003.

Hannan, Sarah, Samantha Brennan, and Richard Vernon, eds. *Permissible Progeny?: The Morality of Procreation and Parenting*. New York: Oxford University Press, 2015.

Harris, John. *Enhancing Evolution: The Ethical Case for Making Better People*. Princeton: Princeton University Press, 2007.

Harris, John. "Sexual Reproduction Is a Survival Lottery." *Cambridge Quarterly of Healthcare Ethics* 13, no. 1 (2004): 75–90.

Harris, John. "Stem Cells, Sex, and Procreation." *Cambridge Quarterly of Healthcare Ethics* 12, no. 4 (2003): 353–71.

Haslanger, Sally. "Family, Ancestry and Self: What Is the Moral Significance of Biological Ties." *Adoption and Culture* 2, no. 1 (2009).

Haslanger, Sally, and Charlotte Witt, eds. *Adoption Matters: Philosophical and Feminist Essays*. Ithaca, NY: Cornell University Press, 2005.

Herdt, Jennifer. "Sleepers Wake! Eudaimonism, Obligation and the Call to Responsibility." In *The Freedom of a Christian Ethicist: The Future of a Reformation Legacy*, edited by Brian Brock and Michael G. Mawson, 159–73. T&T Clark Theology. London; New York: Bloomsbury T&T Clark, 2016.

Hauerwas, Stanley. *A Community of Character: Toward a Constructive Christian Social Ethic*. Notre Dame: University of Notre Dame Press, 1981.

Hauerwas, Stanley. *Disrupting Time: Sermons, Prayers, and Sundries*. Eugene, OR: Cascade Books, 2004.

Hauerwas, Stanley. "On Honour." In *Reckoning with Barth: Essays in Commemoration of the Centenary of Karl Barth's Birth*, edited by Nigel Biggar, 145–69. London: Mowbray, 1988.

Hauerwas, Stanley. *Suffering Presence*. Notre Dame: University of Notre Dame Press, 1986.

Hauerwas, Stanley. *The Work of Theology*. Grand Rapids: Eerdmans, 2015.

Hauerwas, Stanley. *With the Grain of the Universe: The Church's Witness and Natural Theology*. Grand Rapids: Baker, 2001.

Hauerwas, Stanley, John Berkman, and Michael G. Cartwright. *The Hauerwas Reader*. Durham: Duke University Press, 2001.

Hauerwas, Stanley, Richard Bondi, and David B. Burrell. *Truthfulness and Tragedy: Further Investigations into Christian Ethics*. Notre Dame: University of Notre Dame Press, 1977.

Henry, Martin. "Karl Barth on Creation." *Irish Theological Quarterly* 69, no. 3 (2004): 219–23.

Heyd, David. *Genethics: Moral Issues in the Creation of People*. Berkeley: University of California Press, 1992.

Hielema, Syd. "Searching for 'Disconnected Wires': Karl Barth's Doctrine of Creation Revisited." *Calvin Theological Journal* 30, no. 1 (1995): 75–93.

Hitchcock, Nathan. *How to Read Karl Barth: The Shape of His Theology*. Oxford: Oxford University Press, 1991.

Hitchcock, Nathan. *Karl Barth and the Resurrection of the Flesh: The Loss of the Body in Participatory Eschatology*. Eugene, OR: Pickwick Publications, 2013.

Hitchcock, Nathan. "Karl Barth's Christology: Its Basic Chalcedonian Character." In *The Cambridge Companion to Karl Barth*, edited by John Webster, 127–42. Cambridge Companions to Religion. Cambridge, UK: Cambridge University Press, 2000.

Hitchcock, Nathan. *Reading Barth with Charity: A Hermeneutical Proposal*. Grand Rapids: Baker Academic, 2015.
Hunsinger, George, ed. *For the Sake of the World: Karl Barth and the Future of Ecclesial Theology*. Grand Rapids: Eerdmans, 2004.
Hunsinger, George, and Keith L. Johnson, eds. *The Wiley Blackwell Companion to Karl Barth*. Wiley Blackwell Companions to Religion. Hoboken: Wiley Blackwell, 2020.
Hursthouse, Rosalind. *Beginning Lives*. Oxford: B. Blackwell, 1987.
Irfan, Umair. "'We Need to Talk about the Ethics of Having Children in a Warming World.'" *Vox.Com*, March 11, 2019. https://www.vox.com/2019/3/11/18256166/climate-change-having-kids.
Jarvis, Gavin E. "Early Embryo Mortality in Natural Human Reproduction: What the Data Say." *F1000Research* 5 (2016): 2765.
Jones, Paul Dafydd. *The Humanity of Christ: Christology in Karl Barth's Church Dogmatics*. London: T&T Clark, 2008.
Jones, Paul Dafydd, and Paul T. Nimmo, eds. *The Oxford Handbook of Karl Barth*. 1st ed. Oxford Handbooks. Oxford: Oxford University Press, 2019.
Jüngel, Eberhard. *Theological Essays*. Translated by John Webster. London: Bloomsbury T&T Clark, 2014.
Kass, Leon R. "Ageless Bodies, Happy Souls: Biotechnology and the Pursuit of Perfection." *The New Atlantis* 1 (2003): 9–28.
Kass, Leon R. "Averting One's Eyes, or Facing the Music?: On Dignity in Death." *Hastings Center Studies* 2, no. 2 (1974): 67–80.
Kass, Leon R. *Life, Liberty, and the Defense of Dignity: The Challenge for Bioethics*. San Francisco: Encounter Books, 2002.
Kass, Leon R. *Toward a More Natural Science: Biology and Human Affairs*. New York: Free Press, 1988.
Kelsey, David. "Aquinas and Barth on the Human Body." *The Thomist: A Speculative Quarterly Review* 50, no. 4 (October 1986): 643–89.
Kerr, Fergus. "Cartesianism According to Karl Barth." *New Blackfriars* 77, no. 906 (July 1996): 358–68.
Kim, JinHyok. *The Spirit of God and the Christian Life: Reconstructing Karl Barth's Pneumatology*. Emerging Scholars. Minneapolis: Fortress Press, 2014.
Kolodny, Niko. "Which Relationships Justify Partiality? The Case of Parents and Children." *Philosophy and Public Affairs* 38, no. 1 (2010): 37–75.
Last, Jonathan V. *What to Expect When No One's Expecting: America's Coming Demographic Disaster*. 1st American ed. New York: Encounter Books, 2013.
Lee, Patrick, and Robert P. George. *Body-Self Dualism in Contemporary Ethics and Politics*. Cambridge, UK: Cambridge University Press, 2008.
Leighton, Kimberly. "Being Adopted and Being a Philosopher: Exploring Identity and the 'Desire to Know' Differently." In *Adoption Matters: Philosophical and Feminist Essays*, edited by Sally Haslanger and Charlotte Witt, 146–70. Ithaca, NY: Cornell University Press, 2005.
Levy, Neil and Mianna Lotz. "Reproductive Cloning and a (Kind Of) Genetic Fallacy." *Bioethics*, 19-3 (2005): 232–250.
Long, D. Stephen. *Saving Karl Barth: Hans Urs von Balthasar's Preoccupation*. Minneapolis, MN: Fortress Press, 2014.
Lotz, Mianna. "Procreative Reasons-Relevance: On the Moral Significance of Why We Have Children." *Bioethics* 23, no. 5 (2009): 291–9.
Lotz, Mianna. "Rethinking Procreation: Why It Matters Why We Have Children." *Journal of Applied Philosophy* 28, no. 2 (2011): 105–21.

Louth, Andrew. *Mary and the Mystery of Incarnation*. Oxford: SLG Press, 1977.
Mangina, Joseph L. *Karl Barth on the Christian Life: The Practical Knowledge of God*. Issues in Systematic Theology, vol. 8. New York: P. Lang, 2001.
Mangina, Joseph L. *Karl Barth: Theologian of Christian Witness*. Louisville, KY: Westminster John Knox Press, 2004.
Marsh, Jason. "Procreative Ethics and the Problem of Evil." In *Permissible Progeny?: The Morality of Procreation and Parenting*, edited by Sarah Hannan, Samantha Brennan and Richard Vernon, 65–86. New York: Oxford University Press, 2015.
Marsh, Jason. "Quality of Life Assessments, Cognitive Reliability, and Procreative Responsibility." *Philosophy and Phenomenological Research* 89, no. 2 (2014): 436–66.
Massmann, Alexander. *Citizenship in Heaven and on Earth: Karl Barth's Ethics*. Minneapolis: Fortress Press, 2015.
May, William E. *Catholic Bioethics and the Gift of Human Life*. 3rd ed. Huntington, IN: Our Sunday Visitor, 2013.
McCormack, Bruce. "Grace and Being: The Role of God's Gracious Election in Karl Barth's Theological Ontology." In *The Cambridge Companion to Karl Barth*, edited by John Webster, 92–110. Cambridge Companions to Religion. Cambridge, UK: Cambridge University Press, 2000.
McKenny, Gerald. *Biotechnology, Human Nature, and Christian Ethics*. Oxford: Oxford Univ. Press, 2018.
McKenny, Gerald. "Karl Barth and the Plight of Protestant Ethics." In *The Freedom of a Christian Ethicist: The Future of a Reformation Legacy*, edited by Brian Brock and Michael G. Mawson, 17–37. T&T Clark Theology. London; New York: Bloomsbury T&T Clark, 2016.
McKenny, Gerald. *Karl Barth's Moral Thought*. 1st ed. Oxford Studies in Theological Ethics. Oxford: Oxford University Press, 2021.
McKenny, Gerald. *The Analogy of Grace: Karl Barth's Moral Theology*. Oxford: Oxford University Press, 2013.
McKenny, Gerald. *To Relieve the Human Condition: Bioethics, Technology, and the Body*. Albany: State University of New York Press, 1997.
McMahan, Jeff. "Asymmetries in the Morality of Causing People to Exist." In *Harming Future Persons: Ethics, Genetics and the Nonidentity Problem*, edited by Melinda A. Roberts and David T. Wasserman, 35:49–68. International Library of Ethics, Law, and the New Medicine. Dordrecht: Springer, 2009.
McMahan, Jeff. "Causing People to Exist and Saving People's Lives." *Journal of Ethics* 17, no. 1–2 (2013): 5–35.
McMahan, Jeff. "Genethics: Moral Issues in the Creation of People." *Philosophical Review* 103, no. 3 (1994): 557–9.
McMahan, Jeff. *The Ethics of Killing: Problems at the Margins of Life*. Oxford Ethics Series. New York: Oxford University Press, 2003.
McMaken, W. Travis. *The Sign of the Gospel: Toward an Evangelical Doctrine of Infant Baptism after Karl Barth*. Minneapolis: Fortress Press, 2013.
Meilaender, Gilbert. *Bioethics: A Primer for Christians*. Grand Rapids: Eerdmans, 1996.
Meilaender, Gilbert. *Body, Soul and Bioethics*. Notre Dame: Notre Dame University Press, 1995.
Meilaender, Gilbert. *Not by Nature but by Grace*. Notre Dame: University of Notre Dame Press, 2016.
Meilaender, Gilbert. *Should We Live Forever? The Ethical Ambiguities of Aging*. Grand Rapids: Eerdmans, 2013.

Meilaender, Gilbert. "Time For Love: The Place of Marriage and Children in the Thought of Stanley Hauerwas." *Journal of Religious Ethics* 40, no. 2 (2012): 250–61.
Mele, Alfred R. "Intention, Belief, and Intentional Action." *American Philosophical Quarterly* 26, no. 1 (1989): 19–30.
Mele, Alfred R., and Paul K. Moser. "Intentional Action." *Noûs* 28, no. 1 (1994): 39–68.
Mele, Alfred, and Steven Sverdlik. "Intention, Intentional Action, and Moral Responsibility." *Philosophical Studies* 82, no. 3 (1996): 265–87.
Migliore, Daniel, ed. *Commanding Grace: Studies in Karl Barth's Ethics*. Grand Rapids: Eerdmans, 2010.
Mills, Catherine. *Futures of Reproduction: Bioethics and Biopolitics*. International Library of Ethics, Law, and the New Medicine 49. Dordrecht: Springer, 2011.
Mountbatten-Windsor, Harry. "From the Archive: When the Duke of Sussex Interviewed Dr Jane Goodall about the Future of Sustainability." *British Vogue*, September 2019. https://www.vogue.co.uk/article/prince-harry-jane-goodall-september-2019-issue.
Moschella, Melissa. *To Whom Do Children Belong?: Parental Rights, Civic Education, and Children's Autonomy*. New York: Cambridge University Press, 2016.
Muers, Rachel. "The Personal Is the (Academic) Political: Why Care about the Love Lives of Theologians?," *Scottish Journal of Theology* 73, no. 3 (August 2020): 191–202.
Mumford, James. *Ethics at the Beginning of Life: A Phenomenological Critique*. Oxford Studies in Theological Ethics. Oxford: Oxford University Press, 2013.
Neal, Deonna. *Be Who You Are: Karl Barth's Ethics of Creation*. PhD diss., University of Notre Dame, 2010.
Nelson, Jenae et al., "Transcendent Indebtedness to God: A New Construct in the Psychology of Religion and Spirituality." *Psychology of Religion and Spirituality* 15, no. 1 (2023): 105–17.
Nimmo, Paul T. *Being in Action: The Theological Shape of Barth's Ethical Vision*. London: T&T Clark, 2007.
Nimmo, Paul T. "The Orders of Creation in the Theological Ethics of Karl Barth." *Scottish Journal of Theology* 60, no. 1 (2007): 24–35.
Oakes, Kenneth. *Karl Barth on Theology and Philosophy*. Oxford: Oxford University Press, 2012.
O'Donovan, Oliver. *Begotten or Made?* Oxford: Oxford University Press, 1984.
Overall, Christine. *Why Have Children?: The Ethical Debate*. Basic Bioethics. Cambridge, MA: MIT Press, 2012.
Page, Edgar. "Donation, Surrogacy and Adoption." *Journal of Applied Philosophy* 2, no. 2 (1985): 161–72.
Page, Edgar. "Parental Rights." *Journal of Applied Philosophy* 1, no. 2 (1984): 187–203.
Parfit, Derek. *Reasons and Persons*. Oxford: Oxford University Press, 1992.
Perry, Tim. "'What Is Little Mary Here For?' Barth, Mary, and Election." *Pro Ecclesia* 19, no. 1 (2010): 46–68.
Poulson, Anna Louise. *An Examination of the Ethics of Contraception with Reference to Recent Protestant and Roman Catholic Thought*. PhD diss., King's College, 2006.
Prusak, Bernard G. *Parental Obligations and Bioethics: The Duties of a Creator*. Routledge Annals of Bioethics 14. New York: Routledge, 2013.
Pruss, Alexander R. *One Body: An Essay in Christian Sexual Ethics*. Notre Dame Studies in Ethics and Culture. Notre Dame: University of Notre Dame Press, 2013.
Pruss, Alexander R. "One Body: Responses to Critics." *Roczniki Filozoficzne* 63, no. 3 (2015): 155–75.

Puffer, Matthew. "Taking Exception to the Grenzfall's Reception: Revisiting Karl Barth's Ethics of War." *Modern Theology* 28, no. 3 (2012): 478–502.

Pugh, Jonathan. "Autonomy, Natality and Freedom: A Liberal Re-Examination of Habermas in the Enhancement Debate." *Bioethics* 29, no. 3 (2015): 145–52.

Quine, Maria Sophia. *Population Politics in Twentieth-Century Europe: Fascist Dictatorships and Liberal Democracies*. Historical Connections. London; New York: Routledge, 1996.

Resch, Dustin. *Barth's Interpretation of the Virgin Mary: A Sign of Mystery*. Farnham: Ashgate, 2012.

Rieder, Travis N. "Procreation, Adoption and the Contours of Obligation." *Journal of Applied Philosophy* 32, no. 3 (2015): 293–309.

Rieder, Travis N. *Toward a Small Family Ethic: How Overpopulation and Climate Change Are Affecting the Morality of Procreation*. 1st ed. SpringerBriefs in Public Health Ethics. Cham: Springer International Publishing : Imprint: Springer, 2016.

Roberts, Christopher C. *Creation and Covenant: The Significance of Sexual Difference in the Moral Theology of Marriage*. New York: T&T Clark, 2007.

Rose, Matthew. *Ethics with Barth: God, Metaphysics and Morals*. Barth Studies Series. Farnham: Ashgate, 2010.

Rosner, Jennifer M. *Healing the Schism: Karl Barth, Franz Rosenzweig, and the New Jewish-Christian Encounter*. Studies in Historical and Systematic Theology. Bellingham, WA: Lexham Academic, 2021.

Rothman, Joshua. "'The Case for Not Being Born.'" *New Yorker*, November 27, 2017. https://www.newyorker.com/culture/persons-of-interest/the-case-for-not-being-born.

Rulli, Tina. "Preferring a Genetically-Related Child." *Journal of Moral Philosophy* 13 (2014): 1–30.

Rulli, Tina. "The Ethics of Procreation and Adoption." *Philosophy Compass* 11, no. 6 (2016): 305–15.

Sandel, Michael J. "Procreative Beneficence: Why We Should Select the Best Children." *Bioethics* 15, nos. 5–6 (2001): 413–26.

Sandel, Michael J. *The Case against Perfection: Ethics in the Age of Genetic Engineering*. Cambridge, MA: Belknap Press of Harvard University Press, 2007.

Scanlon, Thomas. *Moral Dimensions: Permissibility, Meaning, Blame*. 1st paperback ed. Cambridge, MA: Belknap, 2010.

Suzanne Selinger. *Charlotte von Kirschbaum and Karl Barth: A Study in Biography and the History of Theology*. The Penn State Series in Lived Religious Experience. University Park: Pennsylvania State University Press, 1998.

Sonderegger, Katherine. "Barth and Feminism." In *The Cambridge Companion to Karl Barth*, edited by John Webster, 258–73. Cambridge Companions to Religion. Cambridge, UK: Cambridge University Press, 2000.

Stacpoole, Alberic, ed. *Mary in Doctrine and Devotion: Papers of the Liverpool Congress, 1989, of the Ecumenical Society of the Blessed Virgin Mary*. Collegeville, MN: Liturgical Press, 1990.

Sumner, Darren O. *Karl Barth and the Incarnation: Christology and the Humility of God*. T&T Clark Studies in Systematic Theology, vol. 27. London New Delhi New York Sydney: Bloomsbury, 2014.

Tanner, Kathryn. "Creation and Providence." In *The Cambridge Companion to Karl Barth*, edited by John Webster, 111–26. Cambridge Companions to Religion. Cambridge, UK: Cambridge University Press, 2000.

Teichmann, Roger. "The Voluntary and the Involuntary: Themes from Anscombe." *American Catholic Philosophical Quarterly* 88, no. 3 (2014): 465–86.

Thompson, John. *The Holy Spirit in the Theology of Karl Barth*. Eugene, OR: Pickwick Publications, 1991.

Tietz, Christiane. "Karl Barth and Charlotte von Kirschbaum." *Theology Today* 74, no. 2 (2017): 86–111.

Tietz, Christiane. *Karl Barth: A Life in Conflict*. New York: Oxford University Press, 2021.

Togman, Richard. *Nationalizing Sex: Fertility, Fear, and Power*. New York: Oxford University Press, 2019.

Tran, Jonathan. "The Otherness of Children as a Hint of an Outside: Michel Foucault, Richard Yates and Karl Barth on Suburban Life." *Theology and Sexuality* 15, no. 2 (2015): 189–209.

Tseng, Shao Kai. *Barth's Ontology of Sin and Grace: Variations on a Theme of Augustine*. Barth Studies. Abingdon, Oxon; New York: Routledge, 2019.

Velleman, J. David. "A Theory of Value." *Ethics* 118, no. 3 (2008): 410–36.

Velleman, J. David. "Family History." *Philosophical Papers* 34, no. 3 (2005): 357–78.

Velleman, J. David. "I. The Identity Problem." *Philosophy and Public Affairs* 36, no. 3 (2008): 221–44.

Velleman, J. David. "II. The Gift of Life." *Philosophy and Public Affairs* 36, no. 3 (2008): 245–66.

Velleman, J. David. "III. Love and Nonexistence." *Philosophy and Public Affairs* 36, no. 3 (2008): 266–88.

Viands, Jamie. *I Will Surely Multiply Your Offspring: An Old Testament Theology of the Blessing of Progeny with Special Attention to the Latter Prophets*. Eugene, OR: Pickwick Publications, 2014.

Viazovski, Yaroslav. *Image and Hope: John Calvin and Karl Barth on Body, Soul, and Life Everlasting*. Princeton Theological Monograph Series. Eugene, OR: Pickwick Publications, 2015.

Wallace, Jay R. *The View from Here: On Affirmation, Attachment, and the Limits of Regret*. New York: Oxford University Press, 2013.

Ward, Graham. "The Erotics of Redemption—After Karl Barth." *Theology and Sexuality* 4, no. 8 (1998): 52–72.

Wasserman, David. "Harms to Future People and Procreative Intentions." In *Harming Future Persons: Ethics, Genetics and the Nonidentity Problem*, edited by Melinda A. Roberts and David T. Wasserman, 35:265–85. International Library of Ethics, Law, and the New Medicine. Dordrecht: Springer, 2009.

Waters, Brent. *Reproductive Technology: Towards a Theology of Procreative Stewardship*. Ethics & Theology. Cleveland: Pilgrim Press, 2001.

Waters, Brent. *The Family in Christian Social and Political Thought*. Oxford Studies in Theological Ethics. Oxford: Oxford University Press, 2007.

Watt, Helen. "Intending Reproduction as One's Primary Aim: Alexander Pruss on 'Trying for a Baby.'" *Roczniki Filozoficzne* 63, no. 3 (2015): 143–54.

Webster, John. *Barth's Ethics of Reconciliation*. Cambridge, UK: Cambridge University Press, 1995.

Webster, John. *Barth's Moral Theology: Human Action in Barth's Thought*. Grand Rapids: Eerdmans, 1998.

Webster, John. *Karl Barth*. 2nd ed. London: Continuum, 2004.

Weinberg, Rivka. "Existence: Who Needs It? The Non-Identity Problem and Merely Possible People." *Bioethics* 27, no. 9 (2013): 471–84.

Weinberg, Rivka. "Is Having Children Always Wrong?" *South African Journal of Philosophy* 31, no. 1 (2012): 26–37.

Weinberg, Rivka. *The Risk of a Lifetime: How, When, and Why Procreation May Be Permissible*. New York: Oxford University Press, 2016.

Werpehowski, William. *Karl Barth and Christian Ethics: Living in Truth*. Barth Studies Series. Farnham: Ashgate, 2014.

Werpehowski, William. "Reading Karl Barth on Children." In *The Child in Christian Thought*, edited by Marcia J. Bunge, 386–405. Grand Rapids: Eerdmans, 2001.

Whiteford, Linda M., and Lois Gonzalez. "Stigma: The Hidden Burden of Infertility." *Social Science and Medicine* 40, no. 1 (1995): 27–36.

Willis, Robert. *The Ethics of Karl Barth*. Leiden: E.J. Brill, 1971.

Witt, Charlotte. "A Critique of the Bionormative Concept of the Family." In *Family-Making: Contemporary Ethical Challenges*, edited by Francoise Baylis and Carolyn McLeod, 49–64. Issues in Biomedical Ethics. New York: Oxford University Press, 2014.

Wittman, Tyler. *God and Creation in the Theology of Thomas Aquinas and Karl Barth*. New York: Cambridge University Press, 2019.

Woollard, Fiona, and Frances Howard-Snyder. "Doing vs. Allowing Harm." Edited by Edward N. Zalta. *The Stanford Encyclopedia of Philosophy* (2016). https://plato.stanford.edu/archives/win2016/entries/doing-allowing/.

Wyatt, Jess. "Does Barth's Understanding of Sexual Difference Conflict with His Theological Anthropology?" *Scottish Journal of Theology* 76, no. 1 (February 2023): 44–55.

Young, Thomas. "Overconsumption and Procreation: Are They Morally Equivalent?" *Journal of Applied Philosophy* 18, no. 2 (2001): 183–92.

Ziegler, Philip G., ed. *Eternal God, Eternal Life: Theological Investigations into the Concept of Immortality*. Paperback ed. London: T&T CLark, 2018.

INDEX

Adam 112–14, 118, 161, 237 n.8
adoptive parenthood 38, 43, 47–51, 75, 240
Anderson, Elizabeth 205 n.18
Anscombe, Elizabeth 1–3, 11, 61, 62 n.42, 75
anti-natalism 24, 29–30, 31 n.69, 56, 76, 132
   categorical 19, 22–5
   counterintuitive 23
   de facto 19, 21, 31–2, 77, 233
   philosophical 104
   presumptive 19, 28
Aquinas, Thomas 146 n.53, 188 n.130
Arendt, Hannah 67, 68 n.67
Aristotle 5
artificial reproductive technologies (ARTs) 3–4, 6, 57, 238
The Asymmetry 17–19, 17 n.2, 22–9, 30, 32–3, 35–6, 38–9, 76, 100, 120–1, 128, 162, 179, 182 n.116, 202 n.7, 218
Aung, Salai Hla 120, 121 n.86
Austin, Michael 40

Banner, Michael 3–4, 8, 14
Barth, Karl 10–15, 10 n.65, 12 n.68, 13, 13 n.69, 76–7, 81 n.19, 82 n.23, 83 n.26, 85, 87 n.53, 88–9, 90 n.65, 92 n.73, 94–5, 100, 102, 105, 107, 114, 128 n.123, 128 n.126, 129–30, 137, 145 n.52, 146 n.53, 152 n.92, 153 n.97, 155 nn.109–10, 158, 163, 167 n.30, 180, 184 n.121, 185, 187–8, 188 n.131, 195 n.152, 199 n.1, 200, 201 n.3, 203 n.8, 205 n.18, 206, 206 n.19, 209, 213 n.59, 214, 214 n.63, 219–24, 225 n.112, 227–8, 230–1, 231 n.130, 233–5, 238, 241–2
   actualism 93 n.74, 145 n.52, 174 n.64, 178 n.92, 195 n.152

agent-perfective eudaimonism 138 n.1
anthropology (*see* theological anthropology)
"The Christian Message in Europe Today" 11 n.64
Christocentrism 172 n.53, 226 n.116
concrete monism 146 n.53
covenantal ontology 144
doctrine of creation (*see* doctrine of creation, Christian)
ethics of honour (*see* honour)
ethics of procreation 14, 81, 81 n.20, 83, 106–7, 134, 136, 154, 156, 177, 217, 220
"Freedom for Life" 82 n.23, 136, 151
"Freedom in Limitation" 82 n.23
Jews and Jewish theology 135 n.163
The Life of the Children of God 202 n.7, 207 n.27
Mariology 14, 105, 161–6, 173, 185–98, 200, 225 n.112, 230, 231 n.131, 235, 237, 237 n.8
temporal existence 123, 123 n.101, 191, 192 n.146, 194
Benatar, David 2, 2 n.6, 19, 22 n.24, 29, 33, 38, 104, 234, 239
   categorical anti-natalism 19, 22–5
   categorical pessimism 25, 29–30
   existence and non-existence 22–4, 22 n.27, 23 n.30
   person-affecting approach 19, 22, 25
Berkouwer, G. C. 89 n.61
Bible 91, 91 n.73, 109
Biggar, Nigel 59 n.30, 81, 137–8 n.1, 187 n.124, 211, 212 n.58, 213 n.58
Bishop, Jeff 61 n.36
Bodley-Dangelo, Faye 120 n.81, 125 n.111, 145 n.52, 172 n.53
Brighouse, Harry 35 n.1, 41
Brunner, Emil 154–5 n.109
Burrell, David B. 9 n.58
Busch, Eberhard 83 n.24, 90

Cassidy, James 93 n.74, 195 n.152
child/childbirth 36, 41, 50, 54, 120, 129–30, 159, 162, 181, 185, 227, 227 n.121, 230 n.130, 237, 242
   children of God 181, 199 n.1, 201, 201 n.3, 202–3 n.7, 203, 207 n.27, 208–9, 208 n.28
   equality and autonomy 70
   genetic inheritance 68–9
   as God's gift 9 n.58, 60, 220
   involuntariness 54, 60–5, 239
   well-being 10, 35, 42
Christian optimism 98, 102, 102 n.131, 103, 234
Christocentrism 108, 172 n.53, 211, 225, 226 n.116, 235, 240
Christology 81, 83, 91–2 n.73, 94, 139, 162–7, 167 n.25, 171, 173, 185, 195 n.152
   anhypostatic/enhypostatic distinction 165–6, 165 n.17, 165 n.20
   Incarnation 92 n.73, 147, 153, 157 n.118, 164, 166, 169–70, 174, 185–6, 200, 210, 212, 228, 230, 232
Christopanism 195 n.152
climate change 2 n.6
confidence in life 13–14, 77–8, 82 n.23, 100, 132, 134–5, 153, 156, 224, 231, 238
   grounded in faith 130, 134, 136–7, 199, 229, 231
   procreative fideism and 10–11
Conly, Sarah 2 n.6
Cortez, Marc 141
creatio ex nihilo 166, 169, 174
Creator–creature relationship 121–2

Deddo, Gary 82 n.23, 133, 158, 178 n.93, 222 n.101
DeGrazia, David 30
Descartes, René 95–6, 98
Di Nucci, Ezio 71–2
divine command 81–2, 87 n.53, 93 n.74, 100, 108, 124, 137, 138 n.1, 144, 151–3, 155 n.110, 156–8, 179, 181, 184, 200, 204–5 n.15, 204 n.13, 207, 208 n.30, 209, 209 n.30, 211, 212–13 n.58, 217, 221, 224, 227 n.120, 229–30, 236, 238

divine freedom 170, 173
divine nature 91–2 n.73, 93 n.74, 172, 201 n.3
doctrine of creation, Christian 11, 13–15, 77, 79, 79 n.7, 81 n.17, 82 n.23, 90, 91 n.72, 108–16, 136, 157–8, 166, 193 n.152, 199–200, 200 n.2, 206–7, 230, 235
   covenant 86, 86 n.39, 90–1, 94–6, 100, 105, 108, 110, 112, 114–15, 145 n.52, 158, 185, 196, 234
   glorification of God 86–9, 87 n.53, 88 n.54, 89 n.58, 200
   natural history 91, 108–9
   nature 91–3, 93 n.74, 95
   non-neutrality 90, 103, 234
   Old and New Testaments 94, 105
   optimism and pessimism (*see* optimism and pessimism)
   philosophy in 81, 81 n.17, 97
   space and time 87, 87 n.53, 122
   Trinitarian Ground of Creation 83–95
   Word of God 81, 109–10
doctrine of reconciliation 81, 201 n.3, 206 n.25, 230, 237
doctrine of redemption 81, 88 n.24, 123, 140 n.20, 146 n.53, 206, 230–1, 237, 239
Donum Vitae (Vatican) 4
double-effect 70–1, 71 n.81

egocentric perspective 44, 46
egoistic concern 43, 48, 51
egoistic dimension 137, 151, 213 n.59
equality (procreative bonds) 49–51
eschatological confirmation
   Abrahamic blessing 176
   Christology for Mariology 163–6
   consecration and 124, 133, 161–2, 193–4, 196, 235–7, 242
   limitation 183 n.116, 184
   parental bonds 182, 182 n.116
   Virgin Birth as sign 166–73
   whence and natural parenthood 173–8
ethno-nationalist pro-natalisms 237
eudaimonism 105 n.139, 137–8 n.1, 207, 209, 212 n.58, 213–14, 213 n.59, 217, 236
existential benefits 26–7, 27 n.47

fatherhood 58, 109, 115–16, 119–20,
    127 n.122, 129 n.132, 175, 179
    n.100, 180–1, 218
Ferracioli, Laura 42–9, 50 n.73
Fiddes, Paul 197, 197 n.160
fideism, procreative 10–15, 77–8, 79 n.7,
    104, 233, 237–42
Finnis, John 152 n.92
Fout, Jason 89 n.57, 199 n.1, 207–8 n.27,
    209 n.30
Freidrich, Daniel 30

Gabriel, Andrew 85 n.34, 102 n.131, 120
genetic kinship/bonds 42, 46, 51–2
genetic resonance 42–3
George, Robert 71 n.84
Gerhardt, Paul 174 n.71
Gheaus, Anca 35 n.1
gift analogy 53–4, 70
    embryo death 70–3
    ethic of willfulness 66
    involuntariness of natural
        reproduction 60–5, 73
    limits of optimism 73–6
    risks 73
    value of our limits 65–70
gratitude 202, 202 n.7, 205 n.16
Gorringe, Timothy 148 n.65
Green, Christopher C. 123 n.101
Grenzfall case 155 n.110, 163, 182,
    182 n.116, 187 n.124, 198, 218 n.86

Häbermas, Jürgen 54, 69 n.75, 239
    therapeutic genetic modifications 69
    value of our limits 65–70
Harris, John 54, 67, 70–2, 71 n.80
Haslanger, Sally 45–6
Hauerwas, Stanley 1 n.3, 2, 7–10, 9 n.58,
    10, 14, 199 n.1
Herdt, Jennifer 138 n.1, 204 n.15, 213 n.58
Heyd, David 18–21, 21 n.19, 21 n.21, 22,
    29, 32, 104, 233
Hielema, Syd 89 n.61
Hitchcock, Nathan 192 n.147, 194–5 n.152
Holy Spirit 84–5, 85 nn.34–5, 87, 87 n.53,
    89, 91 n.72, 139–40, 146 n.53,
    148, 156, 161, 162 n.3, 172–3, 185,
    186 n.124, 192 n.147, 197 n.161,
    201 n.3, 202–3 n.7, 208, 209 n.30,
    234, 238

Spiritus Creator 140 n.20
Spiritus Redemptor 140 n.20
hope 142, 235
honour 89 n.57, 153 n.96, 178–9, 198–9,
    199 n.1, 236, 239–40
    and glory 203 n.8, 214 n.63
    God 94, 198, 200, 204–5, 205 n.15,
        205 n.18, 207–8 n.27, 230, 232
    gratitude and 204, 204 n.13,
        204–5 n.15, 205 n.16, 213
    human life and agency 200–17
    and joy of procreating 241–2
    Mary and reasons to procreate,
        revisited 223–9
    and obligation 241
    of procreative parenthood 217–23
    seeking and maintaining 216
    venture of faith 220–1
human agency 54, 109, 162, 194 n.152,
    200, 208 n.27, 219, 222, 222 n.101
human extinction, badness of 27, 39 n.22
humanity 82 n.23, 85, 92 n.73, 108,
    110–11, 110 n.12, 114, 114 n.37,
    117–19, 122 n.91, 137 n.1, 140–1,
    143–4, 143 n.41, 164, 187 n.129,
    202, 206–7, 215, 237
    basic form of 141 n.27
    divine determination 118, 118 n.67
    God and 119, 119 n.73
    passivity and potentiality 165
    rationality 143–4
    self-reflexive awareness 143, 143 n.41
    soul 140–1
    structural differentiation 119, 128
        n.125, 133
    whence 173–8, 175 n.71, 189, 191, 235
    Word of God 110 n.12, 143, 151–2,
        205 n.16, 211, 216
human life 11, 15, 17 n.2, 20, 22, 24, 33,
    35, 37, 50–1, 57 n.24, 70, 112, 118,
    122, 131–4, 137–8, 140–1, 144, 146
    n.53, 152–4, 156–8, 161–2, 172,
    182–3 n.116, 194, 196, 200–17,
    222–3, 228–31, 234–6
    birth and death 149–50
    gift analogy (*see* gift analogy)
    gladness 74
    honour of 200–17
    as life in time 147–50
    mortality 56, 58

prospects and limits 156–9
respect for life as reason to create 151–6, 236
human nature 57, 59, 82, 88 n.54, 92 n.73, 93 n.74, 117–18, 143, 147, 149, 153, 164–5, 165–6 n.20, 169–70, 169 n.37, 172–3, 178 n.92, 179, 179 n.95, 185, 209, 212 n.58, 238–9
human procreation 18, 30, 111, 132, 159, 170, 177 n.87
humility 66, 153, 201 n.3, 216–17, 226, 228, 236
Hunsinger, George 78, 79 n.7, 93 n.74, 197 n.159, 220
Hursthouse, Rosalind 40, 40 n.23

imago Dei 108, 112–13, 119–22, 131–2, 168, 175, 177, 219–20, 222 n.101
immortality 5, 58–9, 192 n.146, 193 n.152
intuitions 14–15, 17, 22, 24, 26 n.44, 28, 33, 39, 59–60, 65, 73, 75, 77, 99, 104, 106, 234, 238–9
involuntariness of natural reproduction 54, 60–5, 239
  intention 63–4, 63 n.42, 64 n.46
  practical knowledge 63–5
I–Thou relationship 119, 119 n.76, 136

Jarvis, Gavin 71 n.83
Jesus Christ 7, 10–11, 11 n.64, 13–15, 77–80, 84, 84 n.30, 87, 89–90, 92 n.73, 97, 100 n.117, 107 n.2, 122, 134, 147, 149, 164, 164 n.14, 166, 166 n.20, 174, 177, 185, 188, 191 n.146, 193, 199, 201, 203, 206, 212, 217, 225, 230, 234, 238
  covenant 102, 107, 176
  humanity 212, 230
  primacy of 97, 102
  reconciliation 103
  resurrection 126, 177, 191 n.146, 193
  as Son of God 164 n.14, 166 n.20, 228 n.124
  Word of God 158
Johnson, Keith 162 n.5
Jones, Paul Dafyyd 145 n.52, 162 n.5
Joseph 13, 182, 190–1, 190 nn.140–1. *See also* Virgin Mary
Jüngel, Eberhard 177 n.88, 220 n.97

Kant, Immanuel 205, 205 n.18
Kass, Leon 54, 57 n.24, 65, 70–1, 71 n.80, 74, 77, 104
  on giftedness of life 54–60
  IVF 58–60
  lineage and connectedness 55
  natural sociality 56
Kelsey, David 146 n.53
Kim, JinHyok 88 n.54, 89 n.57, 141 n.20, 203 n.8
Kolodny, Niko 42–9, 233, 240

Leibniz 98, 103
Leighton, Kimberly 49
Levy, Neil 41
liberal equality 68
liberal individualism 1, 7–9, 9 n.58
Lindsay, Mark 135 n.163
Long, D. Stephen 162 n.5
Lotz, Mianna 37 n.6, 41
Louth, Andrew 196

Mangina, Joseph 89 n.59, 101 n.128
Marcion 94, 97, 105, 135
Mariology 14, 105, 161, 163, 225 n.112, 230, 231 n.131, 235, 237, 237 n.8
  Christology and 162–3
  independent 164, 166
  primacy of Christology for 163–6
  procreation and 161
marriage and procreation 9 n.58, 12, 55, 108, 113, 115–16, 120, 124–7, 131–2, 131 n.143, 159, 221 n.100, 229 n.126, 240
  eschatological consecration/reconfiguration 115–16, 161–2, 190, 196, 235–6, 242
  new consecration 132–3
  and parenthood 55, 120, 124, 135–6, 218, 221, 235
  prototype for 120–1, 126
  relativization of 125, 190
  theological significance 126
  and Triune life 121
Marsh, Jason 17, 30–1
Mary. *See* Virgin Mary
Massmann, Alexander 93 n.74
May, William 65–6

McKenny, Gerald 14, 58, 80 n.15, 88 n.54, 107 n.2, 145 n.52, 153 n.97, 155 n.110, 182 n.116, 183 n.116, 192 n.147, 204 n.15
McMahan, Jeff 19, 21–2, 21 n.19, 24–9, 26 n.44, 31–3, 233
McMaken, Travis 177 n.88
Meilaender, Gilbert 4–7, 9 n.58, 53, 74, 239 n.10
Michel, Ernst 177 n.89, 189 n.135
Mills, Catherine 53, 69
Moschella, Melissa 42–9, 47 n.64
motherhood 58, 115–16, 116 n.52, 119–20, 127 n.122, 129 n.132, 175, 176 n.81, 190, 218, 237 n.8
Mozart 63, 101–2
Muers, Rachel 12 n.68
Mumford, James 122 n.91

natural theology 14, 78, 98, 103, 120, 138, 142, 145 n.52, 147, 150, 163, 169, 173, 188 n.130, 234, 237–8
Neal, Donna 93 n.74
Nelson, Jenae 205 n.15
neutrality, procreative 18–21, 25, 29–32, 53, 76, 143–4, 233, 239
New Testament 85, 94, 105, 116, 120, 128, 135, 138–9, 139 n.4, 144, 145–6 n.52, 155, 155 n.113, 159, 161, 168 n.34, 175–7, 181, 183, 189–90, 203, 226 n.117
Nimmo, Paul 93 n.74, 162 n.5

Oakes, Kenneth 79, 81 n.17
Ocasio-Cortez, Alexandria 2
O'Donovan, Oliver 6, 13
Old Testament 4, 94, 105, 112, 115–16, 119, 126, 135, 155, 164, 175–7, 180, 184, 189
optimism and pessimism 3, 19–20, 22, 32, 82 n.23, 83, 95–102, 106, 238–9
  creation's goodness 100–2, 100 n.119, 104
  doctrine of creation against 95–102
  ethical/existential criteria 95
  immutability and humanity 96 n.95, 97
  indolence and neutrality 99, 99 n.113
  limits of 73–6
  Lisbon earthquake of 1755 99, 99 n.108
  philosophical 102–3, 234
  Pollyannish 106, 241
  and pro-natalism 75, 134–5
  pure becoming 79, 97, 97 n.100
ordinary procreation 50 n.73, 54, 58–62, 64–5, 68–9, 71–3, 75, 163, 168, 173, 186, 187 n.124, 218 n.88, 230–1

Page, Edgar 40–1, 41 n.31
parent–child partiality 35, 42–3, 42 n.36
parent–child relationship 7, 33, 35, 35 n.1, 37–8, 42 n.36, 44, 46–8, 74, 120, 127 n.120, 135, 178, 181–5, 182 n.116, 200, 224, 226, 226 n.117, 235
parenthood 4, 6–7, 9–10, 9 n.58, 14, 33, 47–8, 50, 50 n.73, 53, 74, 76–7, 107, 124, 135, 158, 163, 173, 178, 200, 232, 235, 240
  biological/biological joys 4, 38–40, 47, 190, 240, 242
  biology and personal identity 42–9
  dilemma of procreative bonds 40–2, 48, 51
  ecclesiastical *whence* and natural 173–8
  honour of 217–23, 228
  independent of 222 n.101
  non-procreative 33, 177
  partial bonds of 35
  presuppositions 227, 227 nn.120–1
  procreation and adoption 35–6, 39, 48–51, 75, 158, 240
  response-independent 43
  sacrifice 49–50, 49 n.72
  self-glorification 200
  Virgin Birth and 158, 173
  weight and dignity of biological 178–85
Parfit, Derek 27, 28 n.53
Perry, Tim 197 n.160
Plato 5, 35
Pollyanna Principle 24–5
Pope Paul VI 157
Poulson, Anna Louise 1 n.3, 131 n.143
procreation 2, 11, 17, 19, 24, 30–1, 33, 37, 39, 42, 49–51, 50 n.73, 105, 107, 115, 156, 161, 193, 242
  appreciation and critique (Barth) 132–6

and biological processes 43, 62, 64, 64 n.48
and child-rearing 6
political questions of 3 n.9
presumptive licitness 29, 75, 155 n.110, 156
and providence 122–4, 126
relational reasons to 36–40
relativization (*see* relativization of procreation)
theological significance 11, 15, 78, 82 n.23, 105, 107, 110, 124, 126–7, 132, 136–7, 144, 159, 161–3, 185, 199–200, 235
value of 3, 7, 14, 17, 32, 53, 75–7, 105, 120, 130, 154, 156, 178, 186, 188, 222, 239
procreative agency 39, 54, 65–7, 70, 73 n.90, 75, 178, 185, 200, 219, 222 n.101, 223–4, 228, 235–9
procreative decision-making 17
procreative liberty 5–7
procreative pessimism. *See* optimism and pessimism
procreative rationality 29–30
pro-lifers 73 n.90
pro-natalism 10, 32, 78 n.5, 105–6, 124, 127, 130, 134, 137, 154, 156, 158, 199, 222, 233, 238
  ethno-nationalist 126 n.113, 222, 237
  Jewish and Roman Catholic 162, 162 n.5
  optimism 75
Protestant moral theology 3–10, 14, 80
providence, doctrine of 92 n.73, 107–8, 110, 122–4, 126, 149, 199, 219, 231 n.130, 235
Prusak, Bernard 41, 47
Pruss, Alex 54, 60–5
Puffer, Matthew 173 n.63
Pugh, Johnathan 69

relativization of procreation 7, 82 n.23, 124–32, 135, 155, 173, 189–90, 235
  eschatological 135
  ethics of marriage 124–7, 131–2, 135
  parents and children, ethics 127–8, 128 n.128, 136
  sexual intercourse 130–1

Resch, Dustin 161, 165 n.20, 166–8, 190 n.141, 225 n.112, 226 n.116
responsibility 43, 50, 66–7, 66 n.61, 73, 127 n.120, 132, 204 n.15
Rieder, Travis 2, 31
Roberts, Christopher 145 n.52
Robertson, John 5–6. *See also* procreative liberty
Roberts, Richard 89 n.61, 147 n.54, 195 n.152
Roman Catholic Mariology 164, 172–3, 178, 196, 196 n.156, 231
Roman Catholic pro-natalism 162, 235, 237
Rosato, Philip 85 n.34, 140–1 n.20, 197 n.161
Rose, Matthew 82 n.23, 137 n.1, 178 n.92, 212–13 n.58
Rulli, Tina 30, 36, 41, 43, 46, 50 n.73, 51 n.75

Sandel, Michael 54, 65–70
Savulescu, Julian 72
Scanlon, Thomas 37
Schopenhauer, Arthur 19, 97, 99, 102–3, 134
Schweitzer, Albert 151
Second World War 10, 83, 233
self-love 214, 214 n.63
Selinger, Suzanne 13 n.69
sex differentiation 144, 145 n.52
skepticism, procreative 3, 18, 29–32, 31 n.69, 39 n.22, 238
socialization process 68–70
social practice of sexual reproduction 65
sola scriptura 94 n.76
solidarity 66–7, 152–4, 170 n.43, 224, 236
spontaneous abortion 54, 71–3, 73 n.90
Sumner, Darren 92 n.73
Swift, Adam 35 n.1, 41

Tanner, Kathryn 212 n.57
theological anthropology 13, 82 n.23, 92 n.73, 107, 116–22, 136, 155, 158, 165 n.17, 166, 168 n.34, 173, 188, 193 n.152, 195 n.152, 204, 221 n.100, 234
  and ethics 105, 161
  and human constitution 138–46

theology 11, 14–15, 76, 78–80, 82 n.23, 85 n.34, 91 n.73, 95, 97 n.100, 105, 107, 107 n.2, 142, 148 n.65, 159, 162 n.5, 165 n.18, 195 n.152, 196, 199, 204 n.13, 236–7
Thompson, John 85, 85 n.34
Tietz, Christiane 12, 12 n.65, 12 n.68, 174 n.71
Tollefsen, Christopher 71 n.83
Tran, Jonathan 132
Triune God 83, 120, 150, 212 n.58
Tseng, Shao Kai 93 n.74

Valentinus 168
Velleman, David 42–9, 53
Virginal Conception 198
Virgin Birth 159, 162–3, 177–8, 180 n.102, 186, 190, 196–7, 223–5, 231, 235
   miracle 187 n.124, 230
   and ordinary procreation 231
   as sign 166–73, 230 n.130
Virgin Mary 13, 82 n.23, 105–6, 159, 161–3, 168–9, 178, 197–8, 200, 236–7
   adaptability for God 170
   economy of salvation 178, 185, 225 n.112
   Elizabeth's "blessing" of 189–90
   fiat mihi 164, 187, 188 n.130, 196, 197 n.160, 228
   honouring 224, 228, 230
   humanity 166, 169
   mother of God 164, 170, 185, 190
   and reasons to procreate, revisited 223–9
   virginity 171–3, 173 n.62, 185, 188, 190, 190 n.140
von Balthasar, Hans Urs 162 n.5, 165 n.18
von Kirschbaum, Charlotte 12–13, 12 n.65, 12 n.68, 13 n.69, 115, 115 n.52, 116 n.52, 126 n.111, 176 n.81, 189, 189 n.136, 225

Ward, Graham 145 n.52
Warnock Report (UK) 4
Wasserman, David 36–9, 37 n.6, 37 nn.10–11
Waters, Brent 5–7
Watt, Helen 63 n.42, 64
Webster, John 107 n.2, 177–8 n.92
Weinberg, Rivka 36–9, 37 nn.6–7, 37 n.11, 38 n.14, 53
well-being 10, 18 n.5, 19, 22, 24–5, 30–1, 33, 37–8, 39 n.22, 40 n.24, 42, 44, 86, 100, 105, 158, 199, 213 n.58, 217, 240
Wendler, David 73 n.90
Werpehowski, William 78 n.5, 162 n.5
Willis, Robert 81 n.18
Wiseman, Rachel 63 n.43
Witt, Charlotte 45, 45 n.54
Wittman, Tyler 87 n.53
Wyatt, Jess 172 n.53

Yoder, John Howard 173 n.63

www.ingramcontent.com/pod-product-compliance
Lightning Source LLC
Chambersburg PA
CBHW051518230426
43668CB00012B/1657